EUROCALL Conference

Gothenburg, Sweden
22-25 August 2012

Proceedings

CALL: Using, Learning, Knowing

Linda Bradley and Sylvie Thouësny (Eds.)

Published by Research-publishing.net
Dublin, Ireland; Voillans, France
info@research-publishing.net

© 2012 by Research-publishing.net
Research-publishing.net is a not-for-profit association

CALL: Using, Learning, Knowing
EUROCALL Conference, Gothenburg, Sweden
22-25 August 2012, Proceedings
Edited by Linda Bradley and Sylvie Thouësny

The moral right of the authors has been asserted

All articles in this book are licensed under a Creative Commons Attribution-Noncommercial-No Derivative Works 3.0 Unported License. You are free to share, copy, distribute and transmit the work under the following conditions:
- Attribution: You must attribute the work in the manner specified by the publisher.
- Noncommercial: You may not use this work for commercial purposes.
- No Derivative Works: You may not alter, transform, or build upon this work.

Research-publishing.net has no responsibility for the persistence or accuracy of URLs for external or third-party Internet websites referred to in this publication, and does not guarantee that any content on such websites is, or will remain, accurate or appropriate. Moreover, Research-publishing.net does not take any responsibility for the content of the pages written by the authors of this book. The authors have recognised that the work described was not published before (except in the form of an abstract or as part of a published lecture, or thesis), or that it is not under consideration for publication elsewhere. While the advice and information in this book are believed to be true and accurate on the date of its going to press, neither the authors, the editors, nor the publisher can accept any legal responsibility for any errors or omissions that may be made. The publisher makes no warranty, expressed or implied, with respect to the material contained herein.

Trademark notice: Product or corporate names may be trademarks or registered trademarks, and are used only for identification and explanation without intent to infringe.

Typeset by Research-publishing.net
Cover design: © Raphaël Savina (raphael@savina.net)
Aquarelle reproduced with kind permission from the illustrator: © Sylvi Vigmo (sylvi.vigmo@ped.gu.se)
Fonts used are licensed under a SIL Open Font License

ISBN13: 978-1-908416-03-2 (paperback)
Print on demand (lulu.com)

British Library Cataloguing-in-Publication Data.
A cataloguing record for this book is available from the British Library.

Bibliothèque Nationale de France - Dépôt légal: décembre 2012.

Preface

For the first time, the annual conference of the European Association for Computer-Assisted Language Learning (EUROCALL) took place in Sweden. The University of Gothenburg was delighted to welcome EUROCALL to Gothenburg on the west coast of Sweden. The conference took place at the Faculty of Education on historic ground on the old fortification walls of Carolus Dux from the 17th century right in the centre of the city.

This year's host comprised the University of Gothenburg in collaboration with Chalmers University of Technology. The local committee members represented three collaborating institutions: *Faculty of Education, the University of Gothenburg*; *Department of Languages and Literatures, the University of Gothenburg*; and *Division for Language and Communication, Chalmers University of Technology*.

Concerning the academic programme, many of the 280 delegates took the opportunity of attending one of the five conference workshops during the Wednesday. The workshops had the following titles: *Tools for CLIL Teachers*, *Language Learning Through Tools for Communication and Collaboration*, *Using and Creating Corpora for Language Teaching and Learning*, *Creating Adaptive Learning Materials with Hot Potatoes Quizzes and the QuizPort and TaskChain Modules for Moodle*, and *User Generated Content*. Also, late Wednesday afternoon there was an Educational Showcase Programme with 14 different showcases.

From Thursday to Saturday, there were 110 presentations. More specifically, 64 of them were 30-minute-presentations and the remaining 46 were 45-minute-presentations. In addition, there were three conference symposia, *Teacher Education SIG Symposium – Pecha Kucha*, *Publishing in CALL Symposium*, and *Telecollaboration: Where We Are and Where We Are Headed*. There were also courseware exhibitions as well as 42 posters distributed in three presentation sessions.

EUROCALL 2012 introduced a poster award competition. Posters presented at the conference were eligible for the EUROCALL new "*Award for best poster*" in two categories: post-graduate, and non-postgraduate. Winners are named on the EUROCALL website and their poster is also published on the site. In addition, the authors received a certificate from EUROCALL, a free online membership for one year, and a voucher.

This year's conference theme was *CALL: using, learning, knowing*. The conference sought to establish the current state of the art, how using technologies shape what and how we learn, and what we consider we know from research and development within CALL. These three dimensions are in a continuous flux and interplay as an upward spiral, contributing together to create a dynamic learning experience for the student. The presentations were delivered on the following sub-themes:

- Theoretical perspectives in CALL
- Hybrid spaces
- Emergent technologies
- Social media and networking
- Perspectives on corpora
- Interdisciplinarity and interculturality
- Multimodality
- The 21st century learner
- New practices - new contexts
- Assessment and feedback
- Less widely taught languages
- Mobile learning
- Virtual learning environments
- Computer-Mediated-Communication
- Virtual worlds
- Courseware design
- Managing multimedia environments
- Distance and collaborative learning
- New pedagogical developments

The conference hosted two excellent keynote speakers, Paige D. Ware and Roger Säljö, who gave insightful presentations which have been archived in EUROCALL's member area (http://www.eurocall-languages.org/login/).

EUROCALL 2012 continued the tradition of extending the conference experience to the virtual community. The keynote speeches were streamed live via the Virtual Strand. The VS also had a blog with delegates commenting on the parallel sessions they were attending, as well as plenty of tweets via EUROCALL's own Twitter account.

Authors of all accepted presentations (papers, posters, educational showcases) were able to send a 1500-word text (not including abstract and bibliography) for publication in the proceedings. All in all, 59 papers are included in these proceedings.

Finally, thank you to those presenters who submitted their paper, and last but by no means least, to all the presenters and delegates for making EUROCALL 2012 the success it was.

Linda Bradley and Sylvie Thouësny,
in charge of the proceedings for EUROCALL 2012

Conference Committees

The 2012 EUROCALL Conference on *CALL: Using, Learning, Knowing* was organised by the University of Gothenburg in Sweden.

Programme Committee

Programme chairs
- Françoise Blin, *Dublin City University, Ireland*
- Ana Gimeno Sanz, *Universidad Politécnica de Valencia, Spain*

Committee members
- Christine Appel, *Universitat Oberta de Catalunya, Spain*
- David Barr, *University of Ulster, UK*
- Françoise Blin, *Dublin City University, Ireland*
- Alex Boulton, *Université 2, Nancy, France*
- Claire Bradin Siskin, *Excelsior College, US*
- Angela Chambers, *University of Limerick, Ireland*
- Thierry Chanier, *Université de Clermont-Ferrand, France*
- Jozef Colpaert, *University of Antwerp, Belgium*
- John Gillespie, *University of Ulster, UK*
- Muriel Grosbois, *Université de Paris 4, France*
- Nicolas Guichon, *Université de Lyon 2, France*
- Sarah Guth, *Università degli studi di Padova, Italy*
- Regine Hampel, *The Open University, UK*
- Mirjam Hauck, *The Open University, UK*
- Trude Heift, *Simon Fraser University, Canada*
- Francesca Helm, *Università degli studi di Padova, Italy*
- Phil Hubbard, *Stanford University, USA*
- Marie-Noëlle Lamy, *The Open University, UK*
- Mike Levy, *University of Queensland, Australia*
- Peter Liddell, *University of Victoria, Canada*
- Dominique Macaire, *Université de Nancy, France*
- Vera Menezes, *Universidade Federal de Minas Gerais, Brazil*
- Detmar Meurers, *University of Tübingen, Germany*
- Gary Motteram, *University of Manchester, UK*
- Liam Murray, *University of Limerick, Ireland*
- Robert O'Dowd, *University of Leon, Spain*
- Sue K Otto, *University of Iowa, USA*
- Salomi Papadima Sophocleous, *Cyprus University of Technology, Cyprus*
- Hans Paulussen, *University of Leuven, Belgium*

- Pascual Pérez-Paredes, *University of Murcia, Spain*
- Randall Sadler, *University of Illinois at Urbana-Champaign, USA*
- Mathias Schulze, *University of Waterloo, Canada*
- Lesley Shield, *Freelance CALL Consultant, UK*
- Oranna Speicher, *University of Nottingham, UK*
- Glenn Stockwell, *Waseda University, Japan*
- Peppi Taalas, *University of Jyvaskyla, Finland*
- Maija Tammelin, *Aalto University School of Economics, Finland*
- June Thompson, *Editor, ReCALL*
- Cornelia Tschichold, *Swansea University, UK*

Local Organising Committee
- Becky Bergman, *University of Gothenburg, Sweden*
- Rhonwen Bowen, *University of Gothenburg, Sweden*
- Linda Bradley, *Chalmers University of Technology, Gothenburg, Sweden*
- Sylvi Vigmo, *University of Gothenburg, Sweden*

EUROCALL Executive Committee 2011/2012

President and vice-president
- Françoise Blin, Presisent, *Dublin City University, Ireland*
- Peppi Taalas, Vice-President, *University of Jyväskylä, Finland*

Elected officers
- Nicholas Guichon, *University of Lyon 2, France*
- Mirjam Hauk, *Open University, UK*
- Francesca Helm, *University of Padova, Italy*
- Oranna Speicher, *University of Nottingham, UK*

Appointed officers
- John Gillespie, Treasurer, *University of Ulster, Coleraine, Northern Ireland*
- Toni Patton, Secretary, *University of Ulster, Coleraine, Northern Ireland*

Co-opted officers
- Sylvi Vigmo, *The University of Gothenburg, Sweden*
- Kent Andersen, *Syddansk Erhvervsskole, Denmark*

Table of Contents

iii   Preface

v   Conference Committees

Matthew Absalom
1   Teachers and Technology: Comparing University and School Languages Educators' Perceptions of Technology and Their Own IT Literacy

Christopher Allen & David Richardson
5   Exploring Digital Literacy in Student-Teacher ICT Projects

Ali Alshahrani & Scott Windeatt
10   Using an e-Portfolio System to Improve the Academic Writing Performance of ESL Students

Christine Appel, Jackie Robbins, Joaquim Moré, & Tony Mullen
15   Task and Tool Interface Design for L2 Speaking Interaction Online

Anke Berns, Manuel Palomo-Duarte, & David Camacho Fernández
20   Designing Interactive and Collaborative Learning Tasks in a 3-D Virtual Environment

Kate Borthwick & Alison Dickens
26   One Size Doesn't Fit All: Contrasting Approaches to Building Communities of OER Users Amongst the Language Teaching Community

David L. Brooks
32   New Music Technologies: Platforms for Language Growth Through Content

Giovanna Carloni
37   Online CLIL Scaffolding at University Level: Building Learners' Academic Language and Content-Specific Vocabulary Across Disciplines Through Online Learning

Mei-Mei Chang & Mei-Chen Lin
43   Integrating Cognitive-Motivational Strategies Into Multimedia-Based English Instruction for Low-Achievers

Table of Contents

Frieda Charalabopoulou, Maria Gavrilidou, Sofie Johansson Kokkinakis, & Elena Volodina
49 Building Corpus-Informed Word Lists for L2 Vocabulary Learning in Nine Languages

Tatiana Codreanu & Christelle Combe Celik
54 A Plurisemiotic Study of Multimodal Interactive Teaching Through Videoconferencing

Julian Coppens, Mercedes Rico, & J. Enrique Agudo
59 Blogs: Learning Through Using and Reusing Authentic Materials

Maria de Lurdes Correia Martins, Gillian Moreira, & António Moreira
64 Web 2.0 and Authentic Foreign Language Learning at Higher Education Level

Anna De Marco & Paola Leone
70 Computer Mediated Conversation for Mutual Learning: Acknowledgement and Agreement/Assessment Signals in Italian as L2

Géraldine Fauville, Annika Lantz-Andersson, & Roger Säljö
76 International Student Carbon Footprint Challenge – Social Media as a Content and Language Integrated Learning Environment

Jonás Fouz González
81 Can Apple's iPhone Help to Improve English Pronunciation Autonomously? State of the App

Christine Fredriksson
88 About Collaboration, Interaction, and the Negotiation of Meaning in Synchronous Written Chats in L2-German

Eri Fukuda, Hironobu Okazaki, & Shinichi Hashimoto
93 Enhancing Metacognitive Awareness on First and Second Language Reading and Writing Mediated by Social Networking Websites

Marie Garnier
99 Automatic Correction of Adverb Placement Errors for CALL

Mayumi Hamada
104 A Facebook Project for Japanese University Students: Does It Really Enhance Student Interaction, Learner Autonomy, and English Abilities?

Zöe Handley
111   Investigating the Use of Interactive Whiteboards During the Pre-Task Phase of Speaking Tasks in the Secondary English Classroom

Laura M. Hartwell & Marie-Paule Jacques
117   A Corpus-Informed Text Reconstruction Resource for Learning About the Language of Scientific Abstracts

Francesca Helm, Sarah Guth, & Robert O'Dowd
124   Telecollaboration: Where Are We Now?

Maki Hirotani, Kazumi Matsumoto, & Atsushi Fukada
129   Longitudinal Study on Fluency Among Novice Learners of Japanese

Chi-yin Hong
134   How English Learners Manage Face Threats in MSN Conversations

Nor Fadzlinda Ishak & Paul Seedhouse
139   Interactive Digital Kitchen: The impact on Language learning

Yasushige Ishikawa, Mutsumi Kondo, Reiko Akahane-Yamada, Craig Smith, Hiroshi Hatakeda, & Norihisa Wada
144   Selected Can-Do Statements and Learning Materials for ATR CALL BRIX: Helping University Students in Japan Improve Their TOEIC Scores

Kristi Jauregi & Silvia Canto
151   Impact of Native-Nonnative Speaker Interaction Through Video Communication and Second Life on Students' Intercultural Communicative Competence

Jonny Laing, Khaled El Ebyary, & Scott Windeatt
156   How Learners Use Automated Computer-Based Feedback to Produce Revised Drafts of Essays

Annika Lantz-Andersson, Sylvi Vigmo, & Rhonwen Bowen
161   Students' Framing of Language Learning Practices in Social Networking Sites

Christine Leahy
167   Learner Behaviour in a Collaborative Task-Based CALL Activity

Huifen Lin
172　Effects of Multimedia Vocabulary Annotations on Vocabulary Learning and Text Comprehension in ESP Classrooms

Huifen Lin
177　The Effectiveness of Computer-Mediated Communication on SLA: A Meta-Analysis and Research Synthesis

Mathieu Loiseau & Katerina Zourou
182　Paradoxes of Social Networking in a Structured Web 2.0 Language Learning Community

Zhihong Lu, Fuan Wen, & Ping Li
187　Individualized Teaching and Autonomous Learning: Developing EFL Learners' CLA in a Web-Based Language Skills Training System

Paul A. Lyddon
192　A Diagnostic Approach to Improving the Pedagogical Effectiveness of Tutorial CALL Materials

Maria-Luisa Malerba
198　L2 Learners' Informal Online Interactions in Social Network Communities

Antonio Martínez, Ana Sevilla, Ana Gimeno, & José Macario de Siqueira
204　Feedback: A Key Component in the Design, Development and Validation Stages of Online English/FL Materials

Jaber Ali Maslamani, Scott Windeatt, Patrick Olivier, Phil Heslop, Ahmed Kharrufa, John Shearer, & Madeline Balaam.
211　Collaborative Strategic Reading on Multi-Touch and Multi-User Digital Tabletop Displays

Terumi Miyazoe & Terry Anderson
217　Visualizing Blogs: The "to-do-or-not-to do dilemma" in EAP Writing Online

Hiroyuki Obari & Stephen Lambacher
223　Improving the English Proficiency of Native Japanese Via Digital Storytelling, Blogs, and e-Mobile Technologies

Hironobu Okazaki, Shinichi Hashimoto, Eri Fukuda, Haruhiko Nitta, & Kazuhiko Kido
228 Development of an e-Learning Program for Extensive Reading

Therese Örnberg Berglund
234 Corrective Feedback and Noticing in Text-Based Second Language Interaction

Martine Pellerin
240 Mobile Technologies Put Language Learning into Young Second Language Learners' Hands

Maria Dolores Ramírez-Verdugo
245 From Research to Development on Virtual Language, Content and Intercultural Learning Across European Schools

Mercedes Rico, Paula Ferreira, Eva M. Domínguez, & Julian Coppens
250 Get Networked and Spy Your Languages

Jan-Mikael Rybicki & Juhana Nieminen
254 KungFu Writing, a New Cloud-Based Feedback Tool

Mahnaz Saeidi & Mahsa Yusefi
259 The Effect of Computer-Assisted Language Learning on Reading Comprehension in an Iranian EFL Context

Takeshi Sato & Akio Suzuki
264 From a Gloss to a Learning Tool: Does Visual Aids Enhance Better Sentence Comprehension?

Flora Sisti
269 Online Scientific Language Teaching and Web 2.0

Sylvana Sofkova Hashemi & Leona Johansson Bunting
274 Text and Language Practices in One-to-one Environments in a Swedish Primary School

Pia Sundqvist & Liss Kerstin Sylvén
280 Computer-Assisted L2 English Language-Related Activities Among Swedish 10-Year-Olds

Table of Contents

Sylvie Thouësny
286 Scoring Rubrics and Google Scripts: A Means to Smoothly Provide Language Learners with Fast Corrective Feedback and Grades

Cornelia Tschichold
292 What's Wrong with Welsh Adjectives?

Eva Maria Unterrainer
296 Mobile Learning in Foreign Language Learning: Podcasts and Lexicon Acquisition in the Elementary Instruction of Italian

Jane Vinther
302 Mobile Learning and High-Profiling Language Education

Elena Volodina & Lars Borin
307 Developing an Open-Source Web-Based Exercise Generator for Swedish

Julie Watson & Steven White
314 Designing and Delivering an e-Presessional Course in EAP for the 21st First Century International Student

Shona Whyte, Gary Beauchamp, & Emily Hillier
320 Perceptions of the IWB for Second Language Teaching and Learning: the iTILT Project

327 Author Index

UNIVERSITY OF
GOTHENBURG

Teachers and Technology: Comparing University and School Languages Educators' Perceptions of Technology and Their Own IT Literacy

Matthew Absalom*

School of Languages & Linguistics, The University of Melbourne, Parkville, Australia

Abstract. Educators at all levels of education are increasingly required to adopt information technology (IT) and integrate it into their teaching practice. Some researchers have found that this goal is "neither value neutral or universally understood" (Jamieson-Proctor, Burnett, Finger, & Watson, 2006, p. 511). In this paper, I discuss an ongoing study of the perceptions of three groups of language educators relating to the use of IT in their teaching practice and of their own IT literacy collected via responses to a short questionnaire. The three cohorts are distinct: the first is a cross-section of school teachers of diverse languages and experience; the second is a group of school teachers of different languages but who have identified as "leaders" (previously discussed in Absalom, 2011). These two school-based groups are compared with language teachers in higher education. The analysis of questionnaire responses will explore perceptions of information and communication technology (ICT) in relation to factors such as gender, age, teaching context and disciplinary identity. The paper will explore the implications of the study, including those relating to professional learning needs.

Keywords: university language programs, teacher perceptions, ICT integration, language education.

1. Introduction

Like other educational institutions, universities are enthusiastically embracing technology in all spheres of their activity: from learning and teaching, to research design and information management, to staff and student systems and cornering market share. While there is clearly a desire for such integration or mainstreaming of ICT at the policy level, there remains a clear disconnect between policy and practice. With talk of Web 3.0 ever more frequent (Agarwal, 2009), many language educators

---

* Contact author: mabsalom@unimelb.edu.au

seem to be late adopters of Web 2.0 technologies, some even wrestling with Web 1.0 systems (Teo, 2009). Sang, Valcke, van Braak, Tondeur, and Zhu (2011) and Park and Son (2009) describe the explicit relationship between teachers' perception of ICT and their adoption of it in teaching and learning contexts. This paper builds on previous research exploring the perceptions of two groups of language educators (Absalom, 2011). In that preliminary study, I found that the older the teacher, the stronger the perception that students outstripped her ICT knowledge and/or competency (Absalom, 2011, p. 623). While 75% of respondents in the previous study indicated that they used computers a lot in their everyday life, this did not translate to high levels of integration in teaching and learning (Absalom, 2011, p. 622). In this paper, I will revisit the data from the previous study as well as adding new data from Australian university language educators to explore the relationships between perceptions of ICT and ICT competency and use in life and teaching practice. I will also explore the barriers to integration of ICT in language programs at university level.

2. Method

2.1. Data collection

The current study uses an online survey instrument to interrogate university language educators' perceptions and uses of ICT and technology. The survey was developed using SurveyMonkey and, after appropriate human ethics clearance, an invitation email was sent to language academics in language programs around Australia as shown in Table 1. It was decided to concentrate on academic staff in modern foreign language programs. The invitation also encouraged academic staff to invite their sessionally employed colleagues to respond to the survey. At the time of writing, 46 respondents had completed the online survey.

Table 1.

State/Territory	Number of institutions	Number of academics	Languages
New South Wales	Six	130	Arabic, Chinese, Croatian, French, German, Greek, Hebrew, Indonesian, Italian, Japanese, Korean, Polish, Russian, Spanish
Victoria	Six	144	Arabic, Chinese, French, German, Greek, Hindi, Indonesian, Italian, Japanese, Korean, Russian, Spanish, Swedish, Ukranian
Tasmania	One	29	Chinese, French, German, Indonesian, Japanese
Western Australia	Four	30	Chinese, French, German, Greek, Indonesian, Italian, Japanese
South Australia	Three	37	Chinese, French, German, Greek, Italian, Japanese, Spanish
Queensland	Seven	108	Chinese, French, German, Indonesian, Italian, Japanese, Korean, Spanish
Australian Capital Territory	Three	41	Arabic, Chinese, French, German, Hindi/Urdu, Indonesian, Italian, Japanese, Korean, Persian, Spanish, Thai, Vietnamese
Northern Territory	One	5	Chinese, Greek, Indonesian

2.2. The data

The survey instrument asks a series of demographic questions relating to age, work situation, length of employment in a university, etc. It then interrogates respondents' use of ICT and technology in work and life situations as well as exploring the types of technologies utilised and any barriers to integration in teaching and learning. Finally, respondents are asked to rate their agreement with 31 statements that answer the question "What do you think of computers and ICT?".

3. Discussion

An initial analysis of the data reveals that around 85% of respondents are over 36 years of age and a full 50% of respondents over 50 years of age. In terms of gender, 41% were male and 59% female, with the majority of responses from Victoria so far (37%), followed by NSW (24%). Respondents were mostly in continuing positions (82%) with 18% of respondents in casual or sessional employment. Given the age demographic, it is perhaps not surprising that 26% of respondents have been working in universities for over 20 years, with well over half (63%) having had careers of more than 10 years. In terms of level of appointment, most respondents (65%) are in lecturer or senior lecturer positions.

All respondents use computers and ICT in their teaching: 72% a lot, 18% a little. Notably, when asked about computer and ICT use in non-teaching related work activities those declaring "a lot" increased to 96%. This type of use, termed 'supportive use of ICT' by Sang et al. (2011), is a useful predictor of "classroom use of ICT" (Sang et al., 2011, pp. 167-168). Similarly, high levels of ICT and technology use are indicated in everyday life, with 91% indicating this occurs a lot. 85% of respondents rate their ICT competency as "fairly good" with 11% indicating they have novice level capacity and 4% stating they are 'experts'. Ironically, the expert users indicated that they only use ICT and computers a little in their teaching and learning context. The importance of using computers and ICT in teaching was rated as high by 83% of respondents and as low by the remainder.

Respondents describe a range of uses of technology in their teaching and learning with a large prevalance of Web 1.0 style presentational approaches such as deployment of course content using learning management systems like BlackBoard or Moodle, creation of PowerPoint versions of lecture notes balanced with instances of the integration of Web 2.0 approaches using tools such as wikis. Respondents detail the use of multimedia objects (video, audio, etc.) and online assessments as other important uses of technology.

In terms of barriers to the integration of technology into teaching and learning of languages, the most recurrent factor indicated was time. This has been found to be one of the key limiting factors in other studies (e.g., Park & Son, 2009, p. 97). Other challenges include institutional barriers; ever changing applications, interfaces, etc.;

slow bandwidth; outdated software or learning management systems; and lack of training.

4. Conclusions

At the time of writing, a full analysis of the data from the current project, as well as a reanalysis of the data from the previous study, is still to occur. Given the preliminary findings discussed above, however, we can tentatively trace a relationship between teachers' general use of ICT and computers and a willingness to integrate this into their teaching practice. While university teachers seem to represent a reasonably well-equipped cohort of ICT users, factors limiting the application of technology to teaching and learning of languages continue to be those that have been identified for many years: institutional support (in the form of training and up to date hardware and software) and time. This has implications for how academia is conceived and for professional learning for academics who are increasingly asked by their employers to embrace technology.

References

Absalom, M. (2011). What Do Languages Teachers Think of Technology and Their Own IT Literacy? In S. Barton et al. (Eds.), *Proceedings of Global Learn Asia Pacific 2011* (pp. 620-626). AACE.

Agarwal, A. (2009). *Web 3.0 Concepts Explained in Plain English* [presentation]. Retrieved from http://www.labnol.org/internet/web-3-concepts-explained/8908/

Jamieson-Proctor, R. M., Burnett, P. C., Finger, G., & Watson, G. (2006). ICT integration and teachers' confidence in using ICT for teaching and learning in Queensland state schools. *Australasian Journal of Educational Technology, 22*(4), 511-530. Retrieved from http://www.ascilite.org.au/ajet/ajet22/jamieson-proctor.html

Park, C. N., & Son, J.-B. (2009). Implementing computer-assisted language learning in the EFL classroom: Teachers' perceptions and perspectives. *International Journal of Pedagogies and Learning, 5*(2), 80-101.

Sang, G., Valcke, M., van Braak, J., Tondeur, J., & Zhu, C. (2011). Predicting ICT integration into classroom teaching in Chinese primary schools: Exploring the complex interplay of teacher-related variables. *Journal of Computer Assisted Learning, 27*(2), 160-172. doi: 10.1111/j.1365-2729.2010.00383.x

Teo, T. (2009). Modelling technology acceptance in education: A study of pre-service teachers. *Computers & Education, 52*(2), 302-312. doi: 10.1016/j.compedu.2008.08.006

UNIVERSITY OF
GOTHENBURG

Exploring Digital Literacy in Student-Teacher ICT Projects

Christopher Allen[*] and David Richardson

School of Language and Literature, Linnaeus University, Kalmar, Sweden

Abstract. This paper reports on the evaluation of student teacher information and communications technology (ICT) projects in English language didactics in accordance with recently proposed frameworks of digital literacy in both language-teaching and wider working and educational contexts (Dudeney, Hockly, & Pegrum, forthcoming; Hockly, 2012; Pegrum, 2011). The challenge for teachers, regardless of what stage they are at in their careers, is to be able to operationalize in Hockly's (2012) terms the notion of digital literacy in the foreign language classroom while at the same time incorporating these concerns into a task-based framework in which communication is balanced with a focus on linguistic form. Students in their second term of studies in language didactics were given the task of creating an ICT-based project in English, encorporating both internet and classroom-based inquiry activities aimed at either lower or upper secondary levels in the Swedish school system. The project brief given to the student teachers more specifically addressed their ability to plan and organize a set of learning activities around an extended webquest in addition to demonstrating the procedural usage of a wide range of ICT tools such as wikis, blogs, podcasts, etc. in English language teaching (ELT). The four areas of language-, information-, connection-, and re-design-based digital literacies, as proposed by Pegrum (2011), form the basis for the evaluation of the projects.

Keywords: digital literacy, language teacher training, ICT.

1. Introduction

This paper examines a group of English student teachers' perceptions of digital literacy through the design and implementation of ICT-based project work as part of their coursework assessment during Spring 2012 at a university in southern Sweden.

In the decade which has passed since Prensky's (2001) distinction between 'digital natives' and 'digital immigrants', attention has increasingly been focused on the educational prerequisites of a generation of young people born into a world of computers

---

[*] Contact author: christopher.allen@lnu.se

and mobile telephony. With this in mind, there is a widespread acknowledgement that we need to address the challenges of responding to an increasingly digitalized and globalized world. The notion of digital competence is but one of a number of evolving professional competencies as exemplified by the PISA framework put forward by the OECD* in the context of a commitment to lifelong learning. This paper draws extensively on the four part sub-division of digital literacies as put forward by Hockly (2012):

- Language-based literacies;
- Information-based literacies;
- Connection-based literacies;
- (Re-) design-based literacies.

In Eshet-Alkalai and Chajut's (2009) terms, *Language-based literacies* encompass photo-visual skills and include not only 'traditional' reading and writing transferred to the graphical display environment but also knowledge of the 'new' online genres such as blogs, wikis, tweets, etc (Belshaw, 2011). In contrast to language-based literacies, *information-based literacies* include the ability to make sense of digital information such as using search engines such as *Google*, tagging digital resources, etc. In recent years, the rising importance of social media and networking has been recognised in the third of the groups outlined above, that of *connection-based literacies.*

The final area of digital literacy in Hockly's (2012) framework is that of *(re)-design-based literacies*. The example given here is the 'repackaging' and 'recasting' of existing digital content, such as film clips from *YouTube* in video and audio content production, and a sensitivity to potential intellectual property freedoms and creative commons considerations as a consequence of this editing process.

2. Method

As part of the course assessment of the language teaching methodology module (9 ECTS credits), student teachers were given the task of planning an extended teaching project making extensive use of online / ICT tools and resources for their intended teaching level (i.e., secondary or upper secondary level) in English in the Swedish state school system. This included a theoretical and historical overview of CALL based on Levy (1997), underpinning more recent surveys of ICT in English and modern language teaching (Dudeney & Hockly, 2008). Digital literacy as a concept was introduced in the form of a *PowerPoint* presentation within a general focus on ICT.

---

* OECD (2005). The OECD Program Definition and Selection of Competencies. The definition and selection of key competencies. Executive summary. 30. June, 2005. Retrieved from http://www.oecd.org/dataoecd/47/61/35070367.pdf

3. Results and discussion

3.1. General

The nine projects reviewed were all heavily focused around geographical themes such as planning international travel itineraries as an overarching task / extended webquest. Activities mainly centred around the planning, feasibility, evaluation and budgeting of excursions abroad, typically in groups of 4-6 pupils, based on the structured retrieval of information available online. Specific aspects of digital literacy taken up in the projects will now be described and illustrated below, based on the four part sub-division of digital literacy described by Hockly (2012).

3.2. Language-based literacy

A number of projects made references to specific online writing genres, with a particular focus on blogs and wikis. The emphasis here was on productive skills in producing these online genres based on the information retrieved as a result of the search in response to the webquest task. A number of student teachers seemed to take for granted, however, that pupils would automatically recognize these genres as well as being able to assemble the retrieved information into the form of a text. One project on travel to South America recognized the need to provide mediating questions as a 'scaffold' in socio-cultural terms in the writing process.

While many pupils are no doubt aware of *Wikipedia* as an information source, it is not automatically the case that they are familiar with the type of collaborative writing activities involved in constructing a wiki. Online collaborative writing activities need a more careful and explicit set of instructions and considerations of group dynamics on the part of the teacher, although these were largely absent from the project outlines submitted.

3.3. Information-based literacy

The most important aspect of digital literacy as explored in the projects was information-based literacy. All projects involved some sort of internet-based / digital search of available information as a task to be fulfilled. Student teachers were very much influenced by the notion of webquests (Dodge, 1997) and a number of examples were loosely based on webquest project outlines[*] retrieved from online webquest repositories. Student projects were characterized by a lack of selected hyperlinks to guide pupils in the achievement of the task outcome. Teacher selection, 'filtration' and management of the potential information overload was an important aspect of information-based literacy often overlooked in the projects. Little consideration was given to assisting pupils in developing their skills to critically evaluate the trustworthiness of information sources.

---

[*] See http://www.webquest.org or http://www.questgarden.org

3.4. Connection-based literacies

Surprisingly, for a group of teachers representing a generation supposedly immersed in social networking, this aspect of digital literacy received little attention in the projects. Only one project, the planning of a round-the-world itinerary, actually mentioned *Facebook* as a means of sharing or disseminating ideas and information.

As with other aspects of the projects, little attention was given to how this sharing might take place in practice, such as the choice of the *Facebook* group administrator, what aspects of information should be shared, size of pupil groups involved, etc. Another project saw *Facebook* as a negative aspect of the classroom, a potential distraction for other more focused classroom activities. None of the projects reviewed mentioned mobile learning.

A number of projects did, however, bring up the possibility of using podcasting, which is another way of disseminating information via a node. In the light of a planned school visit to Auschwitz, one student teacher discussed the use of podcasting by groups of students working with a podcasting tool such as *GarageBand* or *Podomatic*.

There was little discussion however of the extent to which podcasting could involve scripting, recasting and drafting of linguistic / news information for a wider broadcast audience. The teacher's role portrayed here seems to be more consistent with that of a technician rather than language expert.

Information-dissemination via video conferencing is another important facet of connection-based literacy. However, only one project referred to video conferencing, using the *Adobe Connect* tool. This was surprising given the fact that *Adobe Connect* had been extensively used as a sociolinguistics study module forming part of the student teachers' degree programme.

3.5. (Re-) design-based literacy

This was a very much underdeveloped area of digital literacy in the student teacher project work. The reworking of digital video material using widely available software such as *Movie Maker* for Windows or *iMovie* for Mac and sound files using *Audacity* comes into this category but was not given an extensive focus during the 'hands-on' ICT workshop. Student teachers did not appear to have considered the possibilities involved in the editing and repackaging of existing digital material for educational purposes, as a complement to podcasting for example.

4. Conclusions

From this limited pilot study it would appear that the notion of digital literacy among the English student teachers was firmly equated with information search and retrieval in the form of extended webquests along with the consumption and production of blogs and wikis as online genres. Projects however need to contain a much more detailed prior specification and structuring of hyperlinks to avoid pupil information overload and digression from the task. Similarly, online writing activities require greater familiarity with the linguistic and textual aspects of online genres, as well as more detailed instructions to facilitate their implementation and management as learning activities to supplement classroom tasks.

Connection-based literacy involving social media was an underexplored area of digital literacy, presumably because student teachers see social media sites either as part of their leisure identities rather than their professional practice as language teachers. Future teacher training courses in the ICT area should also strive to emphasize the connecting possibilities afforded by *Facebook* and *Twitter* while counteracting their potentially distractive influence in the classroom. Future explorations of digital literacy in terms of language teacher training could also focus on the use of digital video and audio software to permit reworking of existing digital materials.

Acknowledgements. We would like to thank the Department of Language and Literature, Linnaeus University for support in attending the EUROCALL conference, Gothenburg 22-25 August 2012.

References

Belshaw, D. (2011). *What is digital literacy? A pragmatic investigation.* Unpublished Ed.D thesis. Durham University. Retrieved from http://neverendingthesis.com

Dodge, B. (1997). Some thoughts about WebQuests [Weblog]. Retrieved from http://webquest.sdsu.edu/about_webquests.html

Dudeney, G., & Hockly, N. (2008). *How to teach English with Technology.* Harlow: Pearson Longman.

Dudeney, G., Hockly, N., & Pegrum, M. (forthcoming). *Digital Literacies* Harlow: Pearson Longman.

Eshet-Alkalai, Y., & Chajut, E. (2009). Changes over time in digital literacy. *CyberPsychology & Behavior, 12*(6), 713-715.

Hockly, N. (2012). Digital Literacies. *ELT Journal, 66*(1), 108-112. doi: 10.1093/elt/ccr077

Levy, M. (1997). *Computer-Assisted Language Learning: Context and Conceptualization.* Oxford: Oxford University Press.

Pegrum, M. (2011). Modified, multiplied and (re-)mixed: social media and digital literacies. In M. Thomas (Ed), *Digital Education: Opportunities for Social Collaboration.* New York: Palgrave Macmillan.

Prensky, M. (2001). 'Digital natives, digital immigrants' [Weblog]. Retrieved from www.marcprensky.com

UNIVERSITY OF GOTHENBURG

Using an e-Portfolio System to Improve the Academic Writing Performance of ESL Students

Ali Alshahrani[a]* and Scott Windeatt[b]

a. Department of English, King Khalid University, Bisha, Saudi Arabia
b. School of Education, Communication & Language Sciences, Newcastle University, Newcastle upon Tyne, UK

Abstract. Many intensive English language programmes that English second language (ESL) students enrol in adopt a process approach to writing, interpreting writing as a cognitive process that is highly private or individualistic (Atkinson, 2003), where writers use specific cognitive phases, such as pre-writing, drafting, and revising, to generate their text. However, Lefkowitz (2009) claimed that the interpretation of the process approach is often superficial, focusing on improving grammatical accuracy, rather than on the generation, formation and revision of ideas. To tackle the problems of providing appropriate, regular feedback within a "socially and culturally situated" approach to writing, and to tackle the issues of motivation, attitude and confidence among ESL writers, which difficulties with writing are likely to engender, an e-portfolio system was used to support students on an ESL writing course as they worked through the key phases of the writing process. The system provided a framework within which they could write to and receive feedback from each other, as well as from the teacher. 46 ESL students from an English Centre were divided into a conventional group and an e-portfolio group. They submitted a series of essays over a number of weeks on which they received both peer and teacher feedback. Data were gathered using an online questionnaire, samples of writing, online tracking and interviews. The post-intervention test results indicated no significant improvement among the control group's motivational constructs and performance in writing, but significant differences were found in the experimental group's writing performance and in the students' perceived value with regard to writing, writing self-efficacy and writing process approach self-consistency. These findings suggest that e-portfolio software, by facilitating both writing, and the provision of regular peer and teacher feedback on writing, has the potential to encourage a significant improvement in ESL students' writing self-belief and writing performance.

Keywords: writing process approach, ESL writing self-beliefs, writing self-efficacy, process-writing self-consistency, e-portfolio, writing motivational constructs.

---

* Contact author: alalshhrani@kku.edu.sa

In L. Bradley & S. Thouësny (Eds.), *CALL: Using, Learning, Knowing, EUROCALL Conference, Gothenburg, Sweden, 22-25 August 2012, Proceedings* (pp. 10-14). © Research-publishing.net Dublin 2012

1. Introduction

In producing a written text, skilled writers generally begin with a pre-writing activity and then cycle through stages of drafting and revising until they arrive at a final, acceptable, version of their text. This view of writing as a highly private or individualistic cognitive process (Atkinson, 2003) forms the core of a process approach to teaching writing, which many English as a Second Language programmes claim to use in their writing courses. In practice, however, these courses often focus on linguistic (grammatical) products rather than on the process of writing, i.e., the generation and elaboration of ideas (Leifkowitz, 2009).

In addition, it has increasingly been recognized that writing is a socially and culturally situated activity (Hyland & Hyland, 2006), with the focus on writing for an audience. A writing course therefore needs to provide support to learners while they work through the various stages of planning, drafting, and revising a text for a specified audience. Such support can most usefully be given in the form of appropriate, regular feedback, while also taking account of the need to encourage and maintain learners' confidence and motivation. This paper discusses an attempt to achieve those goals through the use of an electronic portfolio system (Taskstream e-portfolio).

This "21st century personal learning environment" (Barrett & Garrett, 2009; Hill, Song, & West, 2009) allows the learners' control of the learning process in more social and authentic contexts and served as a learning tool to support students on an ESL writing course as they worked through the key phases of the writing process. The system allowed learners to write for an audience (each other) and to give feedback to, and receive feedback from, both their intended audience, and their teacher, with the aim of helping them develop a consistent approach to their writing practice (self-consistency), encouraging a positive view of the value and importance of writing (self-belief), and fostering a realistic appraisal of their strengths and weaknesses as writers (self-judgement).

2. Method

2.1. Research questions

The aim of the study was to investigate the effect of using a web-based e-portfolio system in an ESL learners' writing course on the learners' self-motivational constructs (self-consistency, self-belief and self-judgement). The specific research questions were:
- Does utilizing a web-based learning platform encourage a change in ESL learners' writing self-beliefs?
- Does utilizing a web-based learning platform encourage a change in ESL students' writing self-efficacy?
- Does utilizing a web-based learning platform encourage ESL students to consistently apply a process approach to writing?

2.2. Research design

The study adopts a combined inductive-deductive research approach to answer the research questions. This combination enables the researcher both to test the suitability of the existing theories for the participants of the study and to validate, modify or even reject the existing theories, or put forward new theories based on the collected data. Therefore, a multimodal methodology which values both empirical (quantitative) and hermeneutic (qualitative) inquiries is used. This integration of methods adds breadth, richness, and depth to our understanding (Denzin & Lincoln, 2005) of both explanations of phenomenon and social change (axiology). These methods include a survey questionnaire, log files of accessed data, writing samples, and in-depth interviewing.

2.3. Participants and data collection

46 ESL students were recruited from an English language centre and divided into a conventional group and an experimental (e-portfolio) group, with a pre-test showing no significant differences between the participants in the two groups. They submitted a series of essays over a number of weeks on which they received both peer and teacher feedback. Data were gathered using an online questionnaire, samples of writing, online tracking and interviews.

3. Results

The first research question investigated changes in the students' beliefs about the perceived value of writing, their writing self-concepts and anxiety about writing. The analysis of the data collected from self-report questionnaires and interview sessions in the second and final weeks of the study, as well as the online tracking, revealed improvements in the perceived value of writing and writing self-concept beliefs among the experimental group of ESL students. No significant differences were found between the two groups in levels of writing anxiety.

The second research question examined the impact of using the TaskStream e-portfolio on the ESL students' beliefs about the self-efficacy of their writing in terms of the skills of content, organization, word choice and conventions. The analysis of the mixed source data indicated significant differences between the groups in their beliefs about their writing skills. Students in the e-portfolio group were more confident than those in the conventional group in their ability to judge their global and local skills as reflected in their writing products at the end of the study. This difference in levels of confidence in favor of the TaskStream group was of both statistical and practical significance, taking into account effect size (Vaske, Gliner, & Morgan, 2002).

The third question explored changes in the ESL students' self-consistency in using the writing process approach following the use of the TaskStream e-portfolio. The findings showed significant changes in the beliefs of the e-portfolio students concerning the consistent use of strategies appropriate to the writing process approach.

4. Discussion and conclusions

Based on these results, the implications of this research concern three issues: learners, instructors and institutions.

4.1. Learners
- E-portfolios provide a means for students to control their learning by setting their own learning goals and the time line within which these goals are to be achieved;
- E-portfolios provide a means for students to present and develop their identity in a social context and to engage with a wider environment through interaction with their teachers, peers, and external reviewers and evaluators, who provide feedback on their learning;
- E-portfolios record learners' academic development and their strengths and weaknesses with regards to academic knowledge and skills development. This promotes their metacognitive skills, including monitoring and evaluation of their progress;
- E-portfolios allow learners to share, interrelate, collaborate and scaffold each other while learning. This helps them construct meaning from information, develop their understanding of it, and then subsequently transform this understanding into knowledge.

4.2. Instructors
- E-portfolios enable instructors to view, track, and evaluate learners' progress from a single web-based portfolio;
- E-portfolios give instructors detailed insight into each learner's learning experience, beliefs, personal goals, and learning strategies, so as to gain a holistic picture of their development;
- This information permits instructors to gain better understanding of the students' motivational constructs. This can help in identifying appropriate instruction and in selecting e-portfolio assignments, so as to enhance deeper learning and increase the effectiveness of their teaching.

4.3. Institutions
- In the development of practice with e-portfolios, faculties and administrators must have agreed upon goals, intentions, and implementation strategies to enrich learning opportunities;
- E-portfolios should focus on a limited set of aims and skills that are appropriate for each level of the language programme since the use of e-portfolios will probably increase the length of time required to cover the curriculum;

- The use of e-portfolios involves long-term processes that necessitate their gradual implementation into English programmes from the first level, allowing learners to gain experience and confidence in using this technology;
- E-portfolios should be easy to use so as to enable faculties to adapt features to their curricula, train their students to use those features, and help them develop methods of reflection that can enhance their learning experiences;
- E-portfolios enable English language programme administrators to monitor their students' learning processes and evaluate their progress in order to design remedial courses to suit students' needs.

References

Atkinson, D. (2003). Writing and culture in the post-process era. *Journal of Second Language Writing, 12*(1), 49-63.

Barrett, H. C., & Garrett, N. (2009). Online personal learning environments: structuring electronic portfolios for lifelong and life-wide learning. *On the Horizon, 17*(2), 142-152.

Denzin, N. K., & Lincoln, Y. S. (2005). *The SAGE handbook of qualitative research.* London: Sage Publications Ltd.

Hill, J. R., Song, L., & West, R. E. (2009). Social Learning Theory and Web-Based Learning Environments: A Review of Research and Discussion of Implications. *American Journal of Distance Education, 23*(2), 88-103. doi: 10.1080/08923640902857713

Hyland, K., & Hyland, F. (2006). *Feedback in second language writing: contexts and issues.* New York: Cambridge University Press.

Lefkowitz, N. (2009). Colloquium: the future of foreign language writing. *The 2009 Symposium on second language writing* (pp. 22-23). Tempe, AZ.

Vaske, J. J., Gliner, J. A., & Morgan, G. A. (2002). Communicating judgments about practical significance: Effect size, confidence intervals and odds ratios. *Human Dimension of Wildlife, 7*(4), 287-300. doi: 10.1080/10871200214752

UNIVERSITY OF
GOTHENBURG

Task and Tool Interface Design for L2 Speaking Interaction Online

Christine Appel[a]*, Jackie Robbins[a], Joaquim Moré[a], and Tony Mullen[b]

a. Universitat Oberta de Catalunya, MediaTIC - Roc Boronat, Barcelona,Spain
b. Tsuda College 2-1-1 Tsudamachi; Kodairashi Tokyo, Japan

Abstract. Learners and teachers of a foreign language in online and blended learning environments are being offered more opportunities for speaking practice from technological developments. However, in order to maximise these learning opportunities, appropriate task-based materials are required which promote and direct student to student interaction in order to counter learners' possible reluctance to use new language structures in their target language (TL). This paper presents the provisional findings of a case study in which three groups of English as a foreign language (EFL) students worked synchronously (in Skype) in pairs with spot-the-difference pictures presented to them using three different formats: standard HTML format, the Tandem tool (a content management application which distributes the materials in real-time), and a variation of the Tandem tool interface which incorporates confirmation buttons aimed at providing a scaffold to the interactions. In order to contextualise the results from the three groups of learners, a group of native English speakers also carried out the tasks. Differences in the interactions were identified, particularly between the HTML format materials and the Tandem materials, mostly due to the fact that students were able to access both students' materials prior to the synchronous interaction, enabling them to prepare for the interactions in various ways, and in some cases, to script their conversations. Other differences were found in terms of the turn-taking, time spent on tasks, and the language used to complete the tasks.

Keywords: synchronous interaction, negotiation of meaning, videoconferencing systems.

1. Introduction

Providing contents for computer-mediated communication (CMC) in an L2 language learning context is a complex issue, particularly if communication is synchronous and oral. Pioneering telecollaborative projects have led the way in experimenting with new applications for CMC with the purpose of putting learners in contact with native

---

* Contact author: mappel@uoc.edu

speakers of each others' TL. These experiences provide evidence of the complexity of finding suitable contents to ensure a successful and sustainable collaboration (Mullen, Appel, & Shanklin, 2008; O'Dowd & Ritter, 2006). Online spoken conversation amongst language learners does not always flow easily: feelings of awkwardness, shyness about their L2 performance and nervousness about being able to understand their interlocutor are some of the issues students report. From a language learning point of view, conversations which are not guided or structured within a task format generally show high levels of avoidance with learners opting to speak about familiar topics they already feel comfortable with and not attempting complex structures beyond their level of interlanguage. Another source of complaint amongst students engaged in telecollaborative projects is not knowing what to talk about if left without enough guidance from their teachers. However, the positive effects of contact and collaboration with native speakers have also been reported, making the pursue for appropriate contents and formats a worthwhile endeavour.

In the context of face-to-face language teaching, lack of sufficient speaking practice often limits the progress learners of a foreign language can make and is a concern for teachers designing foreign language teaching programmes. Scarce contact teaching hours and high student numbers in the classroom may lead to insufficient qualitative opportunities for speaking interaction and the level of teacher feedback possible on interaction. In a distance learning setting, oral production and in particular speaking interaction have often been neglected in the past because of the technological limitations. This has changed with recent technological developments in the areas of VoIP (Voice over IP) and videoconferencing systems which facilitate online voice communication. Speaking interaction is now possible in online environments enriching both distance education programmes as well as face-to-face teaching, which is making increasing use of blended formats. It is at this point that attention should be turned to the lessons learnt from telecollaborative projects in relation to tool affordances and task design for activities involving CMC amongst learners, in this case, of the same TL.

In order to encourage students to use and experiment with new language forms, engage in negotiation of meaning and language use that can lead to learning, it is necessary to design tasks that challenge students and force them to use the language for a real communicative purpose, within a meaningful context working towards the production of a required outcome. Most of these tasks require learners to have access to different materials which will prompt a spontaneous conversation revolving around a negotiation while working together towards a joint outcome (Pica, Kanagy, & Falodun, 1993). We present a study which looks at the design of an application for managing contents distributed to learners while they are communicating synchronously online. This application, Tandem, building on the work initiated by Mullen et al. (2008) has been developed within the framework of the project SpeakApps, a European project funded with support from the Lifelong Learning Programme of the European Commission.

We focus on the design of the interface and look into how elements of the interface can guide the conversation and act as a scaffold influencing the use learners make of their L2 in order to complete the task.

2. Method

The students who participated in this study were enrolled in an English as a foreign language online course at the Open University of Catalonia (UOC), an entirely online distance university based in Barcelona, Spain. Students belonged to the same EFL subject of level B2.1 in the Common European Framework of Reference for Languages (CEFR), a compulsory subject for their college degree. Their ages ranged between 26 and 55 and they were all native speakers of Spanish.

Three groups of these B2.1 students were selected to participate in the study carrying out an activity based on pictures and a number of variations of spot-the-difference and ranking tasks. For this study, students worked in pairs, communicated using Skype in order to carry out a number of speaking interaction tasks and made recordings of the conversations which were submitted to their teachers as part of the course requirements. In addition, a group of native English speakers also carried out the tasks so that patterns of interaction and language used during the tasks could be compared with those identified in the three groups of learners.

In one of the groups, students accessed the materials on a standard HTML format (38 students), the second group used the Tandem tool which distributes the materials in real-time (22 students) and the third group used a variation of the Tandem tool interface with confirmation buttons providing a scaffold to the conversation (22 students). The standard HTML format materials allow students to see their own materials as well as the task partner's materials beforehand. This format had already been used for the course for six semesters before this study took place and teachers have reported over the years that most students prepare for the task and even script parts of the conversation. The Tandem tool only distributes materials if both students are connected at the same time, which means students will never have seen the materials before connecting with their task partners online, with the purpose of prompting more spontaneous and natural conversation.

Data was gathered from a post-questionnaire which was sent to students in all three groups, the recordings of student performance, teacher interviews and entries made to support blogs. In this paper we report on the results of the post-questionnaires, teacher interviews and the analysis of the recordings of the first two of four tasks carried out: a spot-the-difference activity based on a picture related to the topic "Travelling" corresponding to a unit students had been working on prior to the oral task, and a discussion activity based on the same image used for the first task. Vocabulary, grammar, reading and listening activities have taken place as preparation before the oral task.

3. Discussion

Findings show that there is a clear difference between student performance using the HTML format materials and student performance using the Tandem tool, showing a startling difference in the naturalness and spontaneous use of L2. This was an expected result since we had evidence that students were looking at the materials and preparing beforehand, and the survey results confirmed this with over 60% of the students reporting they had done so. Students also reported being more nervous when working with the Tandem tool than with the HTML format materials. This is also an expected result since the HTML format allows the students to prepare beforehand whereas the Tandem tool requires a certain degree of improvisation and spontaneity which put additional pressure on students.

In relation to the difference between the interfaces in the Tandem tool with confirmation buttons for each identified difference, preliminary findings point to the fact that these buttons are helping students structure the conversation and spend more time on the task. These results are based on auditions of the recordings and measurements of time duration of the tasks.

In addition, we are currently undertaking an analysis of turn-taking in order to identify emerging patterns of tackling the task which determine different uses of L2.

4. Conclusions

The focus of the study is not on identifying which format is best, but rather on examining what skills, learning strategies and types of language are used for each format in order to inform decisions related to the inclusion of these tasks at different points of the course syllabus, or even considering whether these tasks are more appropriate for different levels of proficiency. From the results described above, it emerges that students engage in very different activities depending on the technology employed. With the use of HTML, preparation becomes a central activity in which students invest time and effort and during this process, they revise, consolidate previously seen language structures and vocabulary and even look up new forms. However, the actual speaking activity becomes a rehearsed and somehow unnatural conversation, particularly if, as on some occasions, students are reading the exercise from a previously prepared script, leading to students' focussing on the pronunciation of individual words instead of listening and responding to each other. This in turn has a negative impact on students' oral production in terms of various aspects of pronunciation such as intonation and the use of thought groups, fundamental for intelligibility. In most cases, what was originally designed as a speaking interaction activity becomes an alternation of oral production samples. Students who use the Tandem tool are closer to resembling natural interaction, often with shorter turns and a more natural use of transition relevant places

References

Mullen, T., Appel, C., & Shanklin, T. (2008). Chapter VI: Skype-Based Tandem Language Learning and Web 2.0. In M. Thomas (Ed.), *Handbook of Research on Language Acquisition Technologies: Web 2.0* (pp. 101-118). Hershey, Pa: IGI Global.

O'Dowd, R., & Ritter, M. (2006). Understanding and working with 'Failed Communication' in Telecollaborative Exchanges. *CALICO, 23*(3), 623-642.

Pica, T., Kanagy, R., & Falodun, J. (1993). Choosing and using communication tasks for second language research and instruction. In G. Crookes & S. Gass (Eds.), *Tasks and second language learning* (pp. 9-34). Clevedon, UK: Multilingual Matters.

UNIVERSITY OF
GOTHENBURG

Designing Interactive and Collaborative Learning Tasks in a 3-D Virtual Environment

Anke Berns[a]*, Manuel Palomo-Duarte[b], and David Camacho Fernández[c]

a. Department of Modern Languages, Universidad de Cádiz, Spain
b. Computer Science Department, Escuela Politécnica Superior, Universidad de Cádiz, Spain
c. Computer Science Department, Escuela Politécnica Superior, Universidad Autónoma de Madrid, Spain

Abstract. The aim of our study is to explore several possibilities to use virtual worlds (VWs) and game-applications with learners of the A1 level (CEFR) of German as a foreign language. Our interest focuses especially on designing those learning tools which increase firstly, learner motivation towards online-learning and secondly, enhance autonomous learning through a highly interactive environment. Interaction is here seen as a multidirectional process, in which learners are asked to interact with different virtual environments as well as other learners in order to resolve a variety of tasks successfully. By interacting and collaborating in different tasks' performance, students are encouraged to learn from each other, in order to foster and widen their individual knowledge. For our research study we have designed a VW-platform, called VirtUAM (Virtual Worlds at Universidad Autónoma de Madrid). This platform permits us to store and record a huge amount of data related to users' behaviour and in world interactions. Furthermore the platform has been employed to build several virtual spaces, which implement different game levels. The virtual spaces themselves are used to give students basic training in different language skills (listening, reading and writing) related to German as a foreign language. In order to obtain data regarding the game's impact on student learning, we designed a general questionnaire, which was only filled out after the game and which aimed at getting personal feedback from the participants.

Keywords: OpenSim, virtual game-like applications, task-based learning, motivation, foreign language acquisition, collaborative learning.

1. Introduction

The following paper aims at analysing the possibilities and benefits of integrating new technologies such as virtual worlds and game-like applications in the foreign

---

* Contact author: anke.berns@uca.es

In L. Bradley & S. Thouësny (Eds.), *CALL: Using, Learning, Knowing, EUROCALL Conference, Gothenburg, Sweden, 22-25 August 2012, Proceedings* (pp. 20-25). © Research-publishing.net Dublin 2012

language acquisition process. In this sense, our interests specifically focus on the use of VWs combined with videogame-like features, in order to motivate students towards autonomous learning through online tools (Berns, González-Pardo, & Camacho Fernández, 2011a).

In recent years, many universities have started integrating in their *blended teaching* the use of Virtual Learning Environments (VLEs) (Gannon-Leary & Turnock, 2007; Garrison & Kanuka, 2004), such as Moodle, WebCT, etc. or VWs such as Second Life, Active World or OpenSim, which all offer a broad range of possibilities that enhance autonomous learning. Nevertheless, based on our own teaching experience, we believe that neither traditional VLEs nor VWs are able to motivate our students towards autonomous learning. According to a recent survey we did with our students, we can outline that the most frequent demands, for a motivating and successful online learning environment, are referred to those which offer: diversity in assessment, course flexibility in terms of time and space, tasks which provide opportunities for real and versatile interaction (learner-learner, learner-instructor, learner-content) as well as constant feedback on individual task performance.

Taking into consideration the aforementioned aspects, the following research study mainly focuses on the exploration of those online tools which reinforce real interaction, encourage learners to participate actively in their learning process, provide students with regular feedback on their task performance and, last but not least, fulfil the necessary criteria to be integrated into a Learning Management System (LMS). It was at this point of reflection that we started analyzing the possibility of combining VWs and videogame-like applications. The reason why we were interested in combining both is that VWs are often very interesting tools from the teacher's point of view but they are not necessarily that interesting from the student's point of view. Unlike VWs, videogames usually offer great potential to increase students' motivation and learning (Chang & Chou, 2008; Gee, 2007; Lunce, 2006; Malone, 1981a, 1981b; Prensky, 2001). This enhanced motivation can be explained by the fact that videogames are highly entertaining because they are task-based, enhance collaboration and competition by focusing on the achievement of a set of goals, provide immediate feedback to players on failure or success, stimulate willingness to explore, experiment and take risks in problem solving, are challenging because they support different levels of difficulty, and are highly immersive because objects and environments are usually created in 3-D.

The above mentioned features are not only the main components of a booming videogame industry, but also support some of the key-principles of foreign language teaching (Berns, González-Pardo, & Camacho Fernández, 2011b; Dörnyei & Ushioda, 2011; Ellis, 2003; Krashen, 2003; Lightbown & Spada, 2006). Such principles include the need to: motivate learners through meaningful and learner-focused topics; provide learners with comprehensible input through context-based learning; provide learners with opportunities for real and meaningful interaction through task-based and goal-oriented activities as well as cooperative learning; underline the role of failure in successful language acquisition; encourage learners to experiment and take risks while communicating in the target language.

2. Method

2.1. OpenSim and VirtUAM

As we have shown in previous work (Berns et al., 2011a, 2011b) there are however, still other aspects which sometimes make videogames less appropriate or even inadequate. Drawbacks may occur because videogames are usually not embedded in a LMS or online platform which both store data on players' actions and behaviour during the game. Consequently, it is extremely difficult for teachers to track learner development and task performance and it is almost impossible to give students the support they need in order to succeed in further learning (Torrente, Moreno-Ger, Martínez-Ortiz, & Fernandez-Manjo, 2009). In order to design a game-like application and to measure its impact on students' language acquisition and motivation, we designed our own virtual platform called VirtUAM (Rico, Martínez, Alamán, Camacho, & Pulido, 2011). The VirtUAM-platform permits us to build our own VLE with an almost unlimited number of objects to interact with. Furthermore, the platform can be accessed only by registered users, which avoids the access of external users who might interfere negatively in our students' task performance (Berns et al., 2011a, 2011b).

2.1.1. Game design and structure

Taking into consideration students' motivation when involved in highly interactive tasks, we selected one of the key-topics from the curriculum planned within the A1 level (CEFR). This topic was related to different shopping tasks to be performed in a virtual city. The game we designed for this purpose was called *The city-game* and aims at the training of specific shopping products, some basic communication strategies as well as some selected grammar structures. In part all had been practised previously in face-to-face teaching and were now being fostered and widened through *The city-game*.

The following table provides a brief overview of the main game structure and its different levels. As Table 1 shows, the game is based on seven rooms (also called levels) which, apart from room one (level 0), all aim to train the learners' listening, reading or writing skills. During the game students have to move through different rooms with their avatar (students' 3-D virtual representation). In each room they face a new language task. The game itself is built on the bottom-up principle, focusing firstly on providing students with the necessary language input (levels 1, 2 and 3), secondly on the opportunity to train newly introduced learning contents (levels 4 and 5) and thirdly, on the performance of the final task (level 6). The final task is based on a collaborative task (or role-play), which requires students to do shopping in an electrical store. Whilst one student takes the part of a customer, another is encharged to perform a shop assistant. Additionally, each player gets a different tool: the client gets several shopping lists, which are displayed on his personal monitor, the shop assistant gets a shopping trolley and the task to gather the shopping products the client asks him to buy. With the additional integration of a score-system and a time-limit we aimed not only to give students real-time feedback on their performance while playing the game, but also to increase their motivation (Berns et al., 2011a, 2011b).

Table 1. Description of *The city-game* structure and levels

Sessions	Rooms	Skills	Goal	Dynamic	Time
1,2	Level 0 Meeting point	reading & writing	attend to students questions	student-instructor	5-8 min.
	Level 1 Training-room	listening	activate & widen previous knowledge	individual training	20-30 min.
3,4	Level 2 Quiz-room	writing	practise writing	small groups/ competition	20-25 min.
	Level 3 Amusement-Arcade	listening, reading, & grammar	practise grammar structures & foster vocabulary	individual/ competiton	20- 25 min.
6,7	Level 4 Cafeteria	reading & writing	practise communication strategies	interaction with different bots	20-30 min.
	Level 5 Clothes-Shop	reading & writing	practise communication strategies	interaction with one bot	20-30 min.
8	Level 6 Electrical Store	reading & writing	check/ consolidate reading & writing	collaborative task (role-play)	25-35 min.

3. Discussion

3.1. Empirical evaluation

During the present case study one language instructor was on hand to answer queries from the players. Furthermore one external observer analysed the data registered by the VirtUAM-platform. The target group consisted of about 30 Spanish university students learning German as a foreign language (A 1). During the different sessions students were connected from home and invited to use the text chat by communicating solely in the target language.

To measure *The city-game's* impact on student language acquisition and motivation we designed a general questionnaire, which had to be completed by the players at the end of the game. The results from the survey can be summarized as follows: 92% of the enrolled students comment that their motivation towards autonomous learning through VLEs increases significantly when learning contents are embedded in a game-based environment. In addition to this 95% of the students confirm that language acquisition becomes easier, when learning is task-based and enhances interaction with others; 88% emphasize that learning becomes even more entertaining than in other VLEs. Moreover, 91% of the students stress their remarkable improvements in terms of vocabulary, 76% with regard to their grammar and 86% with regard to their writing skills. According to the questionnaire, as well as the information retrieved from the database, many learners practised their writing not solely during the explicit writing activities within the game (levels 2, 4, 5 and 6) but also by using the text-chat to make small talk with other players. The analysis of the questionnaire shows that the game environment reduces, in most of the learners, the feeling of anxiety: 38% of the learners feel more relaxed than in a face-to-face teaching scenario, while 68% feel more comfortable than in other VLEs. In our opinion this can be explained by the fact that students do not feel the same anxiety, in terms of evaluation, as they might do in face-to-face teaching or traditional VLEs. Unlike the former, games are perceived by students as activities related to fun and entertainment rather than to evaluation by the teacher (Berns et al., 2011b).

4. Conclusion

In view of the aforementioned results from the questionnaire, the pre- and posttests as well as the data retrieved from our VirtUAM-database, some final conclusions can be drawn: virtual game-like applications increase students' motivation towards autonomous learning, as they provide real-time feedback and help players succeed in the different game activities and in turn enhance the language skills which are targeted. Game features such as competition and collaboration with others motivate students to be more active and encourage them to challenge themselves in order to outperform other players. Virtual game-like applications offer a lot of possibilities to create immersive environments providing numerous opportunities for versatile interaction and thus for practising the target language with other learners. In this sense we believe that virtual-gamelike applications can be considered a very useful online tool to increase learner autonomy. The latter is seen here not only as an individual but as a social process in which a group of learners will collectively take responsibility for and control of their learning (Blin, 2004).

Acknowledgements. This work has been partially funded by the Consejería de Innovación under the project "Actuaciones Avaladas para la Mejora Docente 2011/12" (AAA_53: El empleo de videojuegos para el apoyo al aprendizaje de lenguas extranjeras aplicado al alemán) as well as by the Spanish Ministry of Science and Innovation under the project ABANT (TIN2010-19872/TSI). We would also like to thank the game developer team Francisco Rodríguez (UAM) and Raúl Goméz (UCA).

References

Berns, A., González-Pardo, A., & Camacho Fernández, D. (2011a). D*esigning videogames for foreign language learning*. Milan: Simonelli Editore.

Berns, A., González-Pardo, A., & Camacho Fernández, D. (2011b). Implementing the use of virtual worlds in the teaching of foreign languages (level A1). In *Proceedings of Learning a Language in Virtual Worlds: A Review of Innovation and ICT in Language Teaching Methodology. 2011. Warsaw* (pp.33-40). Warsaw Academy of Computer Science.

Blin, F. (2004). CALL and the development of learner autonomy: Towards an activity-theoretical perspective. *ReCALL*, *16*(2), 377-395. doi:10.1017/S0958344004000928

Chang, W.-Ch., & Chou, Y.M. (2008). Introductory C Programming Language Learning with Game-Based Digital Learning. *ICWL*, 221-231.

Dörnyei, Z., & Ushioda, E. (2011). *Teaching and researching motivation* (2nd ed.). Harlow: Longman.

Ellis, R. (2003). *Task-based Language Learning and Teaching*. Oxford: Oxford University Press.

Gannon-Leary, P., & Turnock, C. (2007)*. How a Virtual Learning Environment such as Northumbria's eLP can enhance student learning*. Newcastle: Northumbria University.

Garrison, D. R., & Kanuka, H. (2004). Blended learning: Uncovering its transformative potential in higher education. *The Internet and Higher Education*, *7*(2), 95-105. doi:10.1016/j.iheduc.2004.02.001

Gee, J.P. (2007). *Good Video Games and Good Learning*. New York: Peter Lang.

Krashen, S.D. (2003). *Explorations in Language Acquisition and Use*. Portsmouth, NH: Heinemann.

Lightbown, P. M., & Spada, N. (2006). *How languages are learned*. Oxford: University Press.

Lunce, L. (2006). Simulations: Bringing the benefits of situated learning to the traditional classroom. *Journal of Applied Educational Technology*, *3*(1), 37-45. Retrieved from http://www.eduquery.com/jaet/JAET3-1_Lunce.pdf

Malone, T. (1981a). Towards a Theory of Intrinsically Motivating Instruction. *Cognitive Science*, *5*(4), 333-369.

Malone, T. (1981b). What makes computer games fun? *Byte*, *6*(12), 258-276.

Prensky, M. (2001). *Digital game-based learning.* New York: McGraw-Hill.

Rico, M., Martínez, G., Alamán, X., Camacho, D., & Pulido, E. (2011). Improving the Programming Experience of High School Students by Means of Virtual Worlds. *International Journal of Engineering Education*, *27*(1), 52-60.

Torrente, J., Moreno-Ger, P., Martínez-Ortiz, I., & Fernandez-Manjon, B. (2009). Integration and Deployment of Educational Games in e-Learning Environments: The Learning Object Model Meets Educational Gaming. *Educational Technology & Society*, *12*(4), 359-371. Retrieved from http://www.ifets.info/journals/12_4/30.pdf

UNIVERSITY OF
GOTHENBURG

One Size Doesn't Fit All: Contrasting Approaches to Building Communities of OER Users Amongst the Language Teaching Community

Kate Borthwick* and Alison Dickens

University of Southampton, Southampton, UK

Abstract. The LLAS Centre for Languages, Linguistics and Area Studies, at the University of Southampton, UK, has led a number of projects aimed at creating and building communities of sharers and users of open educational resources (OERs). We have worked with very different groups within the language teaching community to raise awareness about OERs, encourage practical engagement with OERs, and foster good practice in the use and re-use of open content. All of our projects sustain continuing community activity. We have found that a 'one size fits all' approach is often offered by institutions to those wishing to engage with open practice, but that it is unlikely to be as effective as a more direct, personalised approach. Through an analysis of the needs and challenges of different groups of language teachers we have worked with, we will show that a flexible approach, which takes into consideration existing practice and indicates how OERs relate to this, ensures a greater chance of OER uptake and use, and increases the likelihood of open practice sustaining in the longer term.

Keywords: open educational resources, language teaching, professional development, technology.

1. Introduction

The LLAS Centre for Languages, Linguistics and Area Studies**, at the University of Southampton, UK, has led a number of projects aimed at creating and building communities of creators and users of open educational resources. Projects such as JISC*** – funded HumBox (Dickens et al, 2010) and Community Café (Borthwick & Dickens, 2011) have worked with very different groups within the language

---

* Contact author: k.borthwick@soton.ac.uk

** A research and enterprise group which promotes the study and teaching of languages, www.llas.ac.uk

*** UK funding body, the Joint Information Systems Committee, www.jisc.ac.uk

---

In L. Bradley & S. Thouësny (Eds.), *CALL: Using, Learning, Knowing, EUROCALL Conference, Gothenburg, Sweden, 22-25 August 2012, Proceedings* (pp. 26-31). © Research-publishing.net Dublin 2012

teaching community to raise awareness about open educational resources, encourage practical engagement with OERs, and foster good practice in the use and re-use of open content. Activity within these communities of open practice continues beyond the life of the projects which created them and LLAS is now working with a new group of language teachers, within the higher education sector, on the FAVOR (JISC) project. We are applying the knowledge and experience gained on previous projects to this new community group within the Languages discipline areas. Our experience indicates that the most effective method to encourage actual sharing and resource re-use is to use direct and personalised approaches which take into consideration existing practice, understand where OERs may meet a need, and weave OERs into the web of everyday professional activity.

2. Background

OERs are "teaching, learning, and research resources that reside in the public domain or have been released under an intellectual property license that permits their free use or re-purposing by others" (Atkins, Brown, & Hammond, 2007, p. 4). In recent years, the UK government has devoted large amounts of funding, via the JISC (2012), to encouraging the publication of open educational resources by the academic community in the UK, and to exploring issues around the publication, creation and re-use of OERs. Nonetheless, the 'adoption of open practice in UK higher education remains patchy,' (Darby, 2012) and Comas-Quinn, Beaven, Pleines, Pulker, and Delos Arcos (2011) note that interest has increasingly begun to shift from the resources themselves (and the desire to simply put large amounts of open content on the web), to the communities that form around open repositories of content. However, they point out that 'issues that enable or inhibit the use, reuse and remix of OERs' by members of these communities are still emerging areas of research.

Our work with different groups of language educators sits within this context. We have found that while OERs are effective in increasing the pool of high quality resources available to all teachers and promoting individual work, there is a danger that individual users can be lost and alienated by a generic approach (for example the demand to share through institutional or national repositories, such as Jorum[*]) and do not feel 'buy-in' to sharing websites or even to the concept of sharing their resources. This is because they do not see this kind of activity as relevant to them or their professional practice. Our experience confirms the idea that while academics and teachers understand that OER sharing is of benefit in a general way to the whole education sector, many struggle to see how these benefits relate to their day-to-day teaching.

---

[*] www.jorum.ac.uk

3. Method

3.1. The HumBox project
The first of LLAS's two recent OER-related projects worked with language content specialists in higher education. The HumBox project ran from 2009-2010 and it sought to engage eleven higher education humanities practitioners in publishing their work as OERs. Language tutors from five universities participated in the project using the HumBox* website to publish their resources.

3.1.1. The challenge
The challenge for the HumBox project was to get humanities practitioners to share their existing teaching resources as open content. We found at the outset that amongst the project group there was a general inclination to share materials but that this usually happened informally and on a local basis. There was also a wide range of digital materials already in existence amongst their files ready for sharing online. It was also acknowledged that sharing content openly across humanities disciplines was desirable – particularly for language teaching, where there is a great need for adaptable, authentic and suitable materials on a range of topics. In addition, it was felt that excellence in teaching is often unrewarded and unrecognised, but that engaging with open practice may offer a way to showcase good work. This idea had particular resonance with language tutors, who are often on teaching-only contracts and are not engaged in research. Despite these positive attitudes towards sharing materials, there was a reticence to engage with online open practice and practitioners voiced concerns about quality, copyright, abuse of their materials and the time required to engage with OERs.

3.1.2. Our approach
Our approach was a practical one: we intended users to explore their concerns with open practice *while* actually doing it. We created a neutral online environment (the HumBox) which was initially closed to anyone outside the project, and this allowed practitioners to experiment straight away with publishing different resources and to discuss issues associated with quality and copyright in a collective way. This enabled participants to work through their concerns with the advice and support of the project group, and to focus on their teaching and their discipline rather than institutional differences or imperatives. This approach encouraged the general collegiate feeling of professional trust that exists between fellow practitioners to be extended to the online, open HumBox group.

We also engaged the project team in processes that were familiar to them: publishing work for others to view, offering work for peer review, and reflection on their pedagogical practice. All of these activities are part of everyday academic life

---
* www.humbox.ac.uk

and the project simply gave them a new twist by putting them 'out in the open.' This meant that rather than engaging with a totally new process in their professional lives, project participants were revising their understanding of existing processes – but in a new context.

At the close of the project, the HumBox had become open and all resources were available for others' to download and adapt. The community that had been seeded by the project had grown from 20 to 200 (registered users), and it continues to expand (Borthwick, 2012).

3.2. The Community Café project
The Community Café project ran from 2010-2011 and was a collaboration between the University of Southampton, Southampton City Council and Manchester Metropolitan University. Its aim was to create, publish online and share a collection of open access digital resources for community-based language teachers in the Southampton area.

3.2.1. The challenge
Community-based language teachers face different challenges from their colleagues in the higher education sector. They often teach 'out-of-hours,' in informal situations, and are reliant on creating their own materials due to a scarcity of relevant, up-to-date resources. They often work in isolation and do not have the opportunity to meet with other tutors to share ideas and practice, and there are only occasional opportunities for professional development. This was a group that could clearly benefit from sharing resources and ideas in an open way and they were willing – indeed, hungry to do so; however, they lacked the practical and pedagogical skills, training and equipment necessary to engage with open practice.

3.2.2. Our approach
Once again, our approach was a practical one. We held informal café-style meetings which enabled tutors to share practice and ideas across cultural and linguistic groups, and we complemented these sessions with training in the use of technology to create materials, and good practice for OER-sharing. The project ultimately became less about creating a bank of resources and more about using open practice as a vehicle to reflect on and enhance pedagogical practice. Tutors report an ongoing impact on their teaching as a result of work on the project.

3.3. The FAVOR project
FAVOR (Finding a Voice through Open Resources) runs until October 2012. It is working with hourly-paid language tutors across five different institutions to publish existing materials as OERs and create new OERs to support language learning in the UK. The challenge for such tutors is to receive recognition for the important role they

play in the academic life of their institutions, and so our approach in this case, is to highlight institutional affiliations as well as community identity (as language tutors).

4. Discussion

The benefits of engaging with OERs are, on the surface, similar for each group: increasing the pool of resources available; showcasing excellent teaching work; raising the profiles of creators, and enhancing professional practice, but each group has required a different approach in order to begin to realise these benefits.

For higher education language tutors, the principle obstacles to engaging with open practice were conceptual, e.g., fears around copyright and IPR or anxiety over peer reviews; but for community-based tutors, they were practical – e.g., how to create online materials or how to write effective metadata. The new group of FAVOR tutors are finding it more satisfying to realise benefits of open practice through a reconnection with their individual institutions alongside community sharing. The use of a flexible, web 2.0-style community-oriented website has been used for all projects and this also greatly assisted in seeding the online community in each case.

5. Conclusions

Our experience indicates that the nature and concerns of particular groups need to be taken into consideration and addressed directly, in order to best encourage the organic growth of a group of OER sharers and users. We have found that when this method is adopted, OERs have a greater chance of uptake and use. A 'one size fits all' approach to encouraging engagement with open practice does not convey the benefits to individuals of doing so, or how OERs can be contextualised within professional practice.

We have found that being part of an identified community provides reassurance in grappling with issues around open practice; however, the motivations of OER users need further research. The FAVOR project will report its findings later in the year and we hope it will contribute to a greater understanding of how and why OER communities grow and sustain themselves.

References

Atkins, D., Brown, J. S., & Hammond, A. L. (2007). *A Review of the Open Educational Resources (OER) Movement: Achievements, Challenges, and New Opportunities*. Report for the William and Flora Hewlett Foundation. Retrieved from http://www.hewlett.org/programs/education-program/open-educational-resources

Borthwick, K., & Dickens, A. (2011). *The Community Cafe project: final report*. JISC. Retrieved from http://eprints.soton.ac.uk/192825

Borthwick, K. (2012). What HumBox did next: real stories of OERs in action from users of a teaching and learning repository for the humanities. *In Proceedings of OpenCourseWare Consortium Global 2012: Celebrating 10 Years of OpenCourseWare*. Cambridge, MA.

Comas-Quinn, A., Beaven, T., Pleines, C,. Pulker, H., & Delos Arcos, B. (2011). Languages Open Resources Online (LORO) – Fostering a culture of collaboration and sharing. *The EuroCALL review*, *18*, 2-14. Retrieved from http://www.eurocall-languages.org/review/18/index.html#loro

Darby, J. (2012). Engaging institutions: changing the OER culture in your institution. *A presentation given at OER in Languages, 1st June, 2012*, University of Central Lancashire, UK.

Dickens, A., Borthwick, K., Richardson, S., Lavender, L., Mossley, D., Gawthrope, J., & Lucas, B. (2010). *HumBox final report*. JISC. Retrieved from http://eprints.soton.ac.uk/192913

JISC. (2012). *Open Educational Resources Programme*. Retrieved from http://www.jisc.ac.uk/oer

UNIVERSITY OF
GOTHENBURG

New Music Technologies: Platforms for Language Growth Through Content

David L. Brooks*

Kitasato University, Minami-ku,Sagamihara, Japan

Abstract. This educational showcase highlights some of the musical applications and devices that run them for adding music-related content and instructional activities to the foreign language (FL) classroom. Actual instructional uses for these mobile information and communications technology (ICT) devices such as the iPod, iPad, and iPhone, and music apps are introduced, and guidelines for what to consider in making program decisions for adopting such technology are given. Features of a classroom environment that supports language growth, creative self-expression, and increased intercultural competence are special considerations.

Keywords: content-based instruction, music apps, music technology, content and language integration, CLIL.

1. Introduction

Music is a form of universal expression and communication that offers an emotionally satisfying, intellectually stimulating, and culturally uplifting vehicle for learning language. Music is individual and global, while ranging from seriously philosophical to outrageously fun. No doubt, it is also an important part of the lives of foreign language students. Yet, those who take a foreign language at university, especially a required course, may be disappointed to find the same tired approach to language teaching that has exhausted them with myriads of grammar rules and vocabulary words to memorize, and with content divorced from their own daily realities. However, when the essential elements of that foreign culture, i.e., the way people think, what they do, what they eat, and what they listen to – their music – are made available to the learners as objects to explore, they can become enthusiastic about learning the language through life and physical interaction with the other culture.

The advent of content-based language units and courses into foreign language curricula is a welcomed development. Music is a special form of human communication

---

* Contact author: mha00357@nifty.com

In L. Bradley & S. Thouësny (Eds.), *CALL: Using, Learning, Knowing, EUROCALL Conference, Gothenburg, Sweden, 22-25 August 2012, Proceedings* (pp. 32-36). © Research-publishing.net Dublin 2012

that has now become even more ubiquitous, a more accessible form of self-expression and social identity, and a more interactive mode of intercultural communication, thanks to innovations in technology. As a content area for learning a foreign language, music is an art form, a personal avocation, and a common cultural element. It affords teachers the opportunity for interdisciplinary thematic approaches that are historical, anthropological, literary in viewpoint, and that apply the principles of musicology and musicianship to the language learning experience, while also being intrinsically motivating. The myriad of forms of musical expression open up possibilities for exploration of music's interrelationship to language with its traditions of narrative, poetic, and theatrical genres, and for delving into a deeper examination of intercultural values. It is not necessary to be a musician or music teacher to take advantage of music's attraction and its power to elicit emotional and intellectual engagement. The emergence of new mobile communication devices and interactive media technologies have expanded the classroom's boundaries beyond the walls of the school building, permeating into students' lives well beyond the classroom, where music occupies a large space.

2. Methodology

By showcasing several of the major music knowledge, performance, and composition apps that are available for mobile ICT devices such as the iPod, iPad, and iPhone, the presenter demonstrated how adding music-related content to the FL classroom can be accomplished through instructional activities and project-based tasks. The music apps and related websites that were introduced are mainly available for free. They comprise six different categories: 1) media integration tools, such as VoiceThread, SoundCloud, and Animoto 2) music composition and creation apps, studio.M, Garageband, iRig Midi Adaptor, 3) recording apps, such as Hokusai, and Overdub, 4) instrument apps, e.g. Zampona, 4) musical content apps, such as World Music, and 5) audio sources, such as NPR Music and PRX apps. Basic guidelines for making program decisions when adopting such technology were shared. The characteristics of an instructional environment, which supports music content and creation for language growth, include acceptance of diversity, allowances for creative self-expression, and increased awareness of intercultural competence. In addition, provisions for successful integration of music content and skills into the language curriculum development were addressed.

3. Instructional focus

The rapid emergence of new mobile communication devices and interactive media technologies has expanded the classroom's boundaries beyond the walls of the school building, permeating into students' lives well beyond the classroom. Addressing instruction that supports language growth, and creative self-expression is a special consideration. A major focus is on ascertaining the factors conducive to developing intercultural competence via music-related content through the use of computer tools, and computer mediated communication technology, as well as the voice, body and instruments.

Developing cognitive skills and fostering academic growth are important facets of the content-based foreign language course in music. While learning strategy instruction is primarily focused on language, it is also the responsibility of all teachers of any students and especially at the college level to teach learners to use their minds. Language teachers in content-based courses can teach EFL students to think critically, to reason logically, to employ fluency, creativity and flexibility in their mental processes, to establish habits of mind that help them infer the main ideas, draw conclusions, and summarize effectively.

Clearly there is strong overlap with these goals and learning strategy instruction. Yet there should be definite plans for teaching these skills through directed instruction, modeling, think-aloud activities (verbalizing one's own thinking process), and cognitive organizational techniques, such as mind mapping, semantic threads, brainstorming, graphic organizers, recognition of discourse markers and patterns of logical discourse. Recognizing and validating cross-cultural differences in situated cognition (Oxford, 1990, p. x), the notion that the development of knowledge is defined, framed and influenced by the cultural context of the learners and the nature of the learning and its meaning within that culture, is vitally important. Moreover, helping students learn about and appreciate how other people of the world think through understanding their music, its values and forms of expression is an admirable and achievable undertaking for a content-focused, strategy-based, intercultural course in world music.

Promoting a global perspective and building intercultural competency is particularly feasible in a content-based course in world music. The intercultural dimensions almost inherent in such a course provide avenues for teaching students about diversity and can open doors to cross-cultural understanding. The nature of the content affords students to look for similarities or universalizabilities among humans through their musical cultures and then to develop an appreciation for diversity by looking at the reasons for the differences. Such instructional activities can take the form of world music discovery tours via the Internet, Prezi poster presentations, songwriting and musical compositions in the Orff style, and other music-based projects. The essence of the goals for promoting an intercultural perspective should include: 1) Developing respect in our students for the cultures and values of other ethnic groups as well as an increased understanding of their own; 2) Helping students appreciate human similarities as well as differences; 3) Providing opportunities for students to experience people's different ethnicities and an exposure to the diversity of world cultures in positive and supportive ways; 4) Demonstrating active efforts to understand and redress issues of intolerance, inequality, prejudice, and social inequities; 5) Nurturing in students the ability to contemplate environmental and social problems, assess different perspectives on moral issues, and to seek compassionate and just solutions (Meyers, 1993, p. 103).

4. Discussion and conclusions

Some actual instructional uses for these mobile ICT devices were illustrated with guidelines for what to consider in making program decisions for adopting such emerging and still rapidly evolving technology. In addition, provisions for successful curriculum development and making instructional accommodations for the accompanying new technological competencies in the face of such rapid development of globally available mobile learning technology tools were addressed; in particular a framework for assisting ICT resource managers, training specialists and educational administrators in making commitments to and in implementing new mobile media was included.

Content-based instruction, especially with a cross-disciplinary field such as ethnomusicology, affords the opportunity to simultaneously teach for content mastery, to support language acquisition, to enhance application of language learning strategies, to foster cognitive growth, and to build a global perspective while increasing competency in intercultural communication. Enthusiasm and commitment are vital and determining forces in learning; therefore, it behooves us all to teach something we truly enjoy and to reap the rewards of attempting the challenge of significant learning in our classrooms.

Teaching resources

World music textbooks

Broughton. S. (2000). *World Music: 100 Essential CDs – The Rough Guide.* Penguin Books. Useful reference on influence and trends of ethnic music on world music of today; includes discography. Related CD collections are available separately.

Lieberman, J. L. (1998). *Planet Musician: The World Music Sourcebook for Musicians*. New York: Hal Leonard. Includes CD featuring practice material and technical exercises.

Reck, D. (1997). *Music of the Whole Earth.* Da Capo Press.

Walther, T. (1981). *Make Mine Music!* Little, Brown & Company. Description of the families of musical instruments and plans for making a variety of simple ones.

Wilson, C. (Ed.) (1996). *The Kingfisher Young People's Book of Music*. New York: Kingfisher Publications. Short articles and abundant visual images; written for children; covers all types of music; more appropriate for reference than textbook.

YouTube offers a wide assortment of vocal and instrumental music from various countries.

Audio Recordings

Smithsonian Folkways World Music Collection – CD anthology of 28 sample provides an excellent resource for class or independent student listening. Find them at your favorite music store or go to http://www.folkways.si.edu

The Rough Guide Series (World Music Network) – CD collections on specific geographic areas, highlights traditional and current world music stars http://www.worldmusic.net

Internet and iPad Resources

Indiana University Music Resources for Ethnomusicology http://www.music.indiana.edu/music_resources/ethnic.html

iPhone or iPad apps: World Music, GarageBand, studio.M, Componendo, various instruments

Worldwide Music Podcasts – access to playable samples of all kinds of music (or purchase) http://www.mondomix.com, http://www.pbsfm.org.au/world

References

Meyers, M. (1993). *Teaching to diversity: Teaching and learning in the multi-ethnic classroom.* Toronto: Irwin Publishing.

Oxford, R. (1990). *Language learning strategies: What every teacher should know.* Boston: Heinle & Heinle.

UNIVERSITY OF GOTHENBURG

Online CLIL Scaffolding at University Level: Building Learners' Academic Language and Content-Specific Vocabulary Across Disciplines Through Online Learning

Giovanna Carloni[*]

University of Urbino "Carlo Bo", Urbino, Italy

Abstract. Over the last two years, the University of Urbino, Italy, has been implementing Content and Language Integrated Learning (CLIL) courses in English across all disciplines. This study focuses on the online self-study CLIL scaffolding designed to help students involve in an Internationalization Project to build academic language and content-specific vocabulary autonomously. Within a CLIL counterbalanced instructional framework, which integrates content-based and form-focused instruction as advocated by Lyster (2007), learners' awareness and acquisition of English academic language and subject-specific terminology have been promoted by means of online course-tailored activities delivered through self-access materials. The profile of the 21st century digital-age university learner has had a deep impact on the instructional design of the online CLIL learning environment implemented. Noticeably, the online self-study materials have been created using corpus- and web-based tools aimed to cater to CLIL learners' cognitive, subject-specific, and language needs. Activities have been set up to engage learners in active learning and to trigger students' self-directed learning processes effectively. Online out-of-class academic and content language scaffolding, informed by sound foreign language acquisition research and pedagogy, have been enhanced.

Keywords: CLIL, technology-enhanced learning, corpus-based tools, autonomous learning.

1. Introduction

The University of Urbino, Italy, has been implementing an Internationalization Project since the 2010-2011 academic year. The project aims to foster multilingualism and student mobility in higher education. To achieve these objectives, Content and

---

[*] Contact author: giovanna.carloni@uniurb.it

Language Integrated Learning (CLIL) courses have been taught in English across all departments in the last two academic years.

2. Theoretical framework

2.1. The CLIL approach

The CLIL approach entails teaching subject-specific content through a foreign language: "Content and Language Integrated Learning (CLIL) is a dual-focused educational approach in which an additional language is used for the learning and teaching of both content and language. That is, in the teaching and learning process, there is a focus not only on content, and not only on language" (Coyle, Hood, & Marsh, 2010, p. 1). In particular, the CLIL approach features four main components: "content (subject matter), communication (language learning and using), cognition (learning and thinking processes) and culture (developing intercultural understanding and global citizenship)" (Coyle et al., 2010, p. 41).

As advocated by Lyster (2007), to scaffold learners' content knowledge and foreign language acquisition, the CLIL counterbalanced instructional framework integrating content-based and form-focused instruction in both proactive and reactive forms (pp. 134-135) has been implemented in this University of Urbino-based project: "Content-based instructional options include: (a) techniques that teachers employ to make subject matter comprehensible to second language learners; (b) opportunities for students to use the second language to mediate content learning during academic tasks; (c) negotiation replete with questions and feedback employed by teachers to scaffold verbal exchanges with students in ways that ensure their participation and appropriation of the targeted content. [...] Form-focused instruction refers to 'any pedagogical effort which is used to draw the learners' attention to language form either implicitly or explicitly" (Spada, 1997, p. 73 cited in Lyster, 2007, pp. 43-134). Specifically, a CLIL blended learning model combining technology-enhanced activities and face-to-face classroom instruction has been developed. To this purpose, a password-protected *CLILlearning* website accessible also from mobile devices has been created with *Weebly*, a free website builder. The online learning objects have been devised to foster students' awareness and development of academic language and content-specific vocabulary, which are likely not to be the focus of face-to-face classroom practices. Noticeably, one of the main objectives of CLIL instruction is to promote the acquisition of "content-obligatory language [which] includes technical vocabulary and other domain specific expressions" (Lyster, 2007, p. 28). Likewise, the development of academic language is pivotal in CLIL settings where students consistently engage with academic discourse.

In the online CLIL learning environment, proactive form-focused instruction in terms of academic language and subject-specific vocabulary has been implemented: "Proactive form-focused instruction involves pre-planned instruction designed to enable students to notice and to use target language features that might otherwise not be used or even noticed in classroom discourse" (Lyster, 2007, pp. 44-45). Online academic and content language learning has been designed mainly in a self-study mode. Autonomy is a core tenet in CLIL instruction. Marsh, Mehisto, Wolff, and Frigols Martín (2010) advocate "Learner autonomy and agency – Deciding on and managing one's own learning" (p. 34). Active, strategic and self-directed learning has been enhanced in the customized online CLIL learning environment in keeping with Pedagogy 2.0: "The challenge for educators is to enable self-direction, knowledge building, and learner control by providing options and choice while still supplying the necessary structure and scaffolding" (McLoughlin & Lee, 2008, p. 17).

3. Online academic language and subject-specific vocabulary learning

Within a counterbalanced instructional framework, students are introduced to the Academic Word List (AWL) devised by Averil Coxhead through a tutorial uploaded on the CLIL website: "The AWL [...] offers a 'fingerprint' of written academic vocabulary, the common core items which make it different from other types of writing. Most fruitfully, focusing on AWL in vocabulary teaching and learning offers the possibility of increasing comprehension of academic text far more rapidly and efficiently than through just enlarging one's general vocabulary" (O'Keeffe, McCarthy, & Carter, 2007, pp. 198-199). To enhance learners' awareness of the instructional value of subject-specific terminology, word clouds displaying the most common content words and clusters featured in students' English course reading materials are embedded in the CLIL website. The statistically-based data used to create word clouds are retrieved through *AntConc*, free concordancer software program.

To meet students' needs effectively, online tools and activities are tailored to learners' CLIL course materials. To enable students to identify the academic and content-specific vocabulary targeted in their CLIL lessons autonomously, corpus- and web-based tools are introduced through tutorials uploaded on the CLIL website. Learners can use the *Vocabulary Profiler* (VP), free online software, to analyze English academic texts. The VP runs the General Service List and AWL. Moreover, the VP produces an off-list featuring mainly content-specific words. To retrieve the vocabulary profile of the assigned English reading materials, students can paste the targeted texts into the box provided. The data retrieved show the percentage of the words belonging to the three lists. Through a color-coded system, learners can visually access the distribution of the vocabulary belonging to the three lists across the texts processed. To further promote learners' awareness about academic and content-specific language in a self-directed learning perspective, *Word and Phrase – Academic*, implemented by the *Corpus of Contemporary American English*, is introduced. Students can paste English academic texts into the box provided and select the subject-specific content of the targeted texts. The texts processed display academic and content-specific words through a color-coded system; learners can thus visualize the vocabulary items belonging to the two lists. Furthermore, learners can click on any color-coded academic and content-specific word to retrieve concordances and thus identify collocations. To analyze English study materials, learners can also paste their English reading materials in *WordSift* to obtain word clouds displaying the fifty most frequent vocabulary items featured in the texts. Academic words can be highlighted; the process is supported by Coxhead's AWL. Learners can also have Social Studies, Language Arts, Science, and Math words highlighted.

Gap-fill academic and discipline-specific language-focused exercises are made available on the website. Free AWL Highlighter software of Nottingham University is used to identify and boldface the academic words featured in English course reading materials. The frequency level of academic words[*] that best suits students' competence in English is selected. The HTML text generated features all the targeted academic words in bold. Interactive gap-fill exercises are then created with *Learnclick,* online software. English assigned readings are pasted into the box provided. The academic words identified with AWL Highlighter software are manually selected. Drop-down or drag-and-drop answer choices are generated. The HTML gap-fill exercises thereby created are embedded in the website. Learners can check their answers and decide to have the solutions displayed. Moreover, through the concordancer and corpus-based tools mentioned thus far, subject-specific vocabulary items are identified in English reading materials. The corpus-retrieved data are used to create course-tailored interactive *Learnclick*-generated gap-fill exercises zeroing in on content language; the exercises are embedded in the website.

Learners can also study key discipline-specific words through technology-enhanced activities created with *Word Dynamo*, a free web-based tool for creating matching activities and flashcards where content vocabulary items and their definitions can be accessed in the written and audio mode. Embedded in the website, *Word Dynamo*-generated exercises work as pre-listening activities. Noticeably, English content-specific reading materials are made available through podcasts that students can download and listen to on the move. While listening, text- and image-based multiple-choice activities are created with *Quipper*, a free online quiz app which allows learners to carry out activities on the go with mobile devices. Students can save their place in a quiz and review quizzes they have already taken. Furthermore, course-tailored interactive crosswords focusing on subject-specific concepts are created with *ProProfs*, a free web-based tool, and embedded in the website. Crosswords are devised to be used as post-listening activities.

---

[*] "the Academic Word List [...] is divided into 10 sublists in order of frequency" http://www.nottingham.ac.uk/~alzsh3/acvocab/wordlists.htm

Tasks requiring learners to create cooperatively in English and share course-tailored content-specific end-user generated knowledge are provided. To this purpose *EduGlogster*, a free online collaborative platform for creating interactive multimedia-rich posters, is used. As Pedagogy 2.0 holds: "Students are capable of creating and generating ideas, concepts, and knowledge, and it is arguable that the ultimate goal of learning in the knowledge age is to enable this form of creativity and productivity" (McLoughlin & Lee, 2008, p. 17). Students are provided with feedback on the written and video output by English language specialists. Learners are also required to produce and embed in interactive glogs podcasts in English created with *SoundCloud*, a free web-based and mobile audio-recording tool. English native-speaker experts provide learners with private feedback on their English oral output inserting comments in specific points along the *SoundCloud*-generated audio track waveform. When students play the track, comments pop up. Learners can reply to comments if they so desire. Reactive form-focused instruction, that is "corrective feedback […] draw[ing] learners' attention to language features in relatively unplanned and spontaneous ways" (Lyster, 2007, p. 47), is thus enhanced even though not in real time; corrective feedback is pivotal in vocabulary acquisition: "a reactive approach is ideal for pushing students in their lexical choices" (Lyster, 2007, p. 47).

4. Conclusions

The online course-tailored scaffolding provided to CLIL learners has been implemented within a metacognitive framework. Students are encouraged to take responsibility for their own learning process. Moreover, learners can decide when and how to use the resources provided. Personalized learning is enhanced. Overall, students are enabled to engage effectively in academic and discipline-specific vocabulary learning through online self-directed study.

References

Coyle, D., Hood, P., & Marsh, D. (2010). *CLIL Content and Language Integrated Learning*. Cambridge: CUP.

Lyster, R. (2007). *Learning and Teaching Languages through Content. A Counterbalanced Approach*. Amsterdam: John Benjamins Publishing House.

Marsh, D., Mehisto, P., Wolff, D., & Frigols Martín, M. J. (2010). *European Framework for CLIL Teacher Education*. Retrieved from http://clil-cd.ecml.at/EuropeanFrameworkforCLILTeacherEducation/tabid/2254/language/en-GB/Default.aspx

McLoughlin, C., & Lee, M. J. W. (2008). The Three P's of Pedagogy for the Networked Society: Personalization, Participation and Productivity. *International Journal of Teaching and Learning in Higher Education, 20*(1), 10-27. Retrieved from http://www.isetl.org/ijtlhe/pdf/IJTLHE395.pdf

O'Keeffe, A., McCarthy, M., & Carter, R. A. (2007). *From Corpus to Classroom*. Cambridge: Cambridge University Press.

Spada, N. (1997). Form-Focussed Instruction and Second Language Acquisition: A Review of Classroom and Laboratory Research. *Language Teaching, 30*(2), 73-87. doi:10.1017/S0261444800012799

Websites

Academic Word List: http://www.victoria.ac.nz/lals/resources/academicwordlist
AntConc: http://www.antlab.sci.waseda.ac.jp/software.html
AWL Highlighter: http://www.nottingham.ac.uk/~alzsh3/acvocab/awlhighlighter.htm
CLILlearning website: http://clillearning.weebly.com
EduGlogster: http://www.eduglogster.com
Corpus of Contemporary American English: http://corpus.byu.edu/coca
Learnclick: http://www.learnclick.com
ProProfs: http://www.proprofs.com/games/crossword
Quipper: http://www.quipper.com
SoundCloud: http://www.soundcloud.com
Vocabulary Profiler: http://conc.lextutor.ca/vp
Weebly: http://www.weebly.com
Word Dynamo: http://dynamo.dictionary.com
Word and Phrase – Academic: http://www.wordandphrase.info/academic
WordSift: http://www.wordsift.com

UNIVERSITY OF GOTHENBURG

Integrating Cognitive-Motivational Strategies Into Multimedia-Based English Instruction for Low-Achievers

Mei-Mei Chang* and Mei-Chen Lin

Department of Modern Languages, National Pingtung University of Science and Technology, Taiwan

Abstract. This study investigated whether integrating cognive-motivational strategies into multimedia-based English instruction could improve low-achievers' academic performance in grammar comprehension and reading comprehension. Forty-four students participated in this study for five weeks. They were all in the same class and under the same instruction and classified as high achievers and low achievers based on their English proficiency test scores. An interactive multimedia environment constructed with the integration of cognitive-motivational CALL model (CMMCALL) was developed according to language learning theories and the findings from the literature review. The effect of the CMMCALL on learners was examined after the experiment by comparing the learning outcome between pre-test and post-test. Comprehension tests and questionnaires were used to investigate students' learning performance and their perceptions of the CMMCALL. The results showed that the CMMCALL was able to benefit low-achievers and to increase their success of language learning, and the difference between pre-test and post-test was significantly different ($p < .05$). Their viewpoints and suggestions about using the CMMCALL program were positive and encouraging.

Keywords: cognitive-motivational strategies, multimedia-based English instruction, low-achievers, CALL.

1. Introduction

Keller (1979) believed that external conditions could be successfully constructed to facilitate and increase learner motivation. Keller (1987) integrated several learning theories and developed the ARCS (Attention, Relevance, Confidence, and Satisfaction) model, which has drawn much attention in the area of instructional design due to its systematic approach to influencing learner motivation by including the external condition within instruction (Chang & Lehman, 2002).

---

* Contact author: mmchang@mail.npust.edu.tw

Multimedia and Internet technology have become popular distribution channels for information delivery (Mayer, 2005). Students were more motivated and liked working with the computer-based instruction when learning from a multimedia program (e.g., Chang & Lehman, 2002; Puerto, Dominguez, Vaca, & Sanchez, 2010). Learning programs, instructionally designed to help learners become self-directive, active and exploratory, are key issues for educators (Chang & Lehman, 2002).

Strategy application could be a powerful approach to foster learners' learning (Dole, Duffy, Roehler, & Pearson, 1991). The use of strategies help students develop the ability to become aware of their own knowledge construction process, which facilitates cognitive growth and leads to better learning achievement (Chang, 2005). The strategy instruction should be direct and explicit, giving conditional metacognitive knowledge about when and how to use a strategy (Pressley, Snyder, & Cariglia-Bull, 1987).

To date, some of the studies regarding strategy application focus on investigating what kinds of strategies students tend to use in learning (e.g., Chang, 2005), while some focus on applying instructional strategies to instruction (e.g., Chang, 2005). Few studies applying the integration of cognitive-motivational model in multimedia assisted language learning for low-achievers have been reported.

This study examined the effect of the cognitive-motivational multimedia CALL on grammar learning. Two research questions guided this study:
- Did low-achievers benefit from the cognitive-motivational multimedia CALL on grammar learning?
- What are low-achievers' perceptions of the cognitive-motivational multimedia CALL?

2. Method

A cognitive-motivational multimedia CALL (CMMCALL) platform which consists of elements including attention, relevance (motivational aspect) and selecting and integrating (cognitive aspect) guided the instructional materials design. To validate the content and the embedded strategies, five English majors and five English non-English majors were invited to try the instructional materials. Feedback from the students was used as the reference for editing and revising the instructional materials.

2.1. Experimental design

This is a quasi-experimental study. The treatment was the use of the CMMCALL and the dependent variables were the scores of grammar tests and reading comprehension tests. The experimental design of this study is shown in Table 1.

Table 1. Quasi-experimental research design

Week 1	Week 2 – week 6	Week 7
O_1 (pre-test)	X (CMMCALL practice)	O_2 (post-test)

2.2. Subjects and setting
Forty-four students aged 19 to 20 participated in this study for five weeks. They were all in the same class and under the same instruction and classified as high achievers and low achievers based on their English proficiency test score.

2.3. Instruments
The instruments used in this study include an English proficiency test, a CMMCALL program, a content-based academic performance test, and a self-reported questionnaire to investigate students' perception of CMMCALL and the attitude towards using CMMCALL. These instruments are described as follows.

2.3.1. The cognitive-motivational multimedia CALL
The interactive cognitive-motivational multimedia CALL provides a learning environment that allows students to choose the learning time and control the pace and the sequencing of instructional events. The course is content-based in nature and Figure 1 shows a sample page of the CMMCALL.

Figure 1. A screenshot of the CMMCALL program

2.3.2. English proficiency test
The General English Proficiency Test (GEPT) with 50 multiple choices questions was used to verify students' English proficiency level. Based on the results of the test, students were classified as either high achievers or low achievers.

2.3.3. *Academic performance tests*

Content-based comprehension tests including grammar-based sentence patterns, practice questions and reading comprehension questions, were used to evaluate students' learning achievement before and after the use of CMMCALL.

2.3.4. *Questionnaires*

The attitude survey was designed by the researchers in order to examine students' attitudes and opinions of the CMMCALL. The questionnaire contained open-ended questions to encourage students to talk about the afterthoughts of using CMMCALL.

2.4. Procedures

At the beginning of the semester, students in a freshman English class were recruited as the subjects in this study. All the students learned from the same instructor and under the same instruction when learning from CMMCALL. Figure 2 shows the procedure of the study.

Figure 2. Flowchart of research procedure

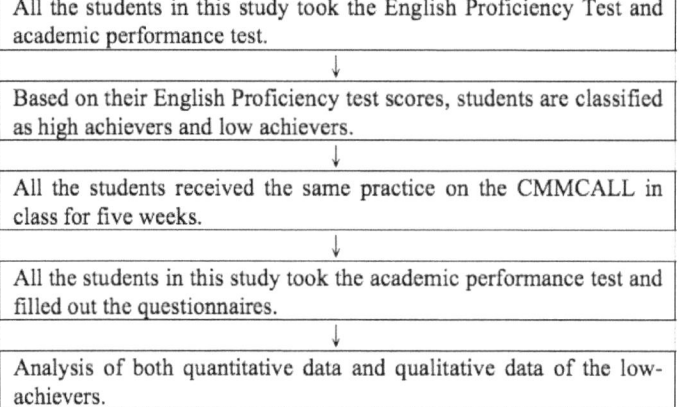

3. Data analysis and results

3.1. Students' scores of academic performance tests

A t-test was used to compare students' academic performance before and after the use of the CMMCALL. Table 2 shows the results of the academic performance for low achievers before and after the experiment. The mean score of the academic performance test 1(the pre-test) was significantly different from the mean score of the academic performance test 2 (the post-test). The mean score of the post-test was significantly higher than the mean score of the pre-test ($p = .003$).

Table 2. t-test for scores of academic performance test between pre-test and post-test for low achievers

	n	M	SD	t	p.
pre-test	11	55.09	8.69	3.845*	.003
post-test	11	65.09	10.17		

3.2. Low-achievers' perception of the CMMCALL program

In terms of low-achievers' perception of the CMMCALL program, 89.5% of the students affirmed the effectiveness of the program; most students (81%) indicated that they found the integration part helped them have clearer concepts of grammar and became more familiar with the sentence patterns and grammar use. Among three different tenses, 89.4% of the students claimed that after learning from this program, they understood better about present tense and were able to put it into practice. More than 77% of the students indicated that they recognized the past tense better and 72% of the students claimed that the program helped them better comprehend future tense. Data from open-ended questions were sorted into three categories: benefits, limitations and suggestions.

4. Discussion and conclusions

The study has yielded both quantitative and qualitative data in support of using the CMMCALL program. Based on the quantitative data, the difference between the pre-test score mean and post-test score mean in terms of the academic performance tests for the low-achievers was statistically significant. The results indicated that the CMMCALL program benefited lower-achievers' learning performance and coincided with previous research which reported that strategy application could be a powerful approach to foster learners' learning (Dole et al., 1991). With the use of strategies, students are able to develop the ability to become aware of their own knowledge construction process, which according to Chang (2005), facilitates cognitive growth and leads to better learning achievement.

In terms of the qualitative data, the positive findings resulting from the questionnaire also provide a promising perspective of the CMMCALL program in language instruction. As Mayer (2005) noted, multimedia and Internet technology have become a popular distribution channel for information delivery. Students were more motivated and liked working with the computer-based instruction when learning from a multimedia program (e.g., Chang & Lehman, 2002; Puerto et al, 2010). Learners' positive responses suggest that the CMMCALL program is a useful tool for language teachers to be applied in language classes.

References

Chang, M. M. (2005). Applying self-regulated learning strategies in a web-based instruction- An investigation of motivation perception. *Computer Assisted Language Learning, 18*(3), 217-230.

Chang, M. M., & Lehman, J. D. (2002). Learning foreign language through an interactive multimedia program: An experimental study on the effects of the relevance component of the ARCS model. *The CALICO Journal, 20*(1), 81-89.

Dole, J. A., Duffy, G. G., Roehler, L. R., & Pearson, P. D. (1991). Moving from the old to the new: research on reading comprehension instruction. *Review of Educational Research, 61*(2), 239-264.

Keller, J. M. (1979). Motivation and instructional design: A theoretical perspective. *Journal of Instructional Development, 2*(4), 26-34.

Keller, J. M. (1987). Development and use of the ARCS model of instructional design. *Journal of Instructional Development, 10*(3), 2-10.

Mayer, R. E. (2005). *The Cambridge Handbook of Multimedia Learning.* New York: Cambridge University Press.

Pressley, M., Snyder, B. L., & Cariglia-Bull, T. (1987). How can good strategy use be taught to children? Evaluation of six alternative approaches. In S. Cormier & J. Hagman (Eds.), *Transfer of learning: Contemporary research and applications* (pp. 81-120). Orlando, FL: Academic Press.

Puerto, G. D., Dominguez, E. M., Vaca, J. M., & Sanchez, H. (2010). Language multimedia blended courses as motivation-enhancers for immigrant students. *Selected paper of Motivation and Beyond, Fourteenth International CALL Conference Proceedings* (pp. 66-69).

UNIVERSITY OF GOTHENBURG

Building Corpus-Informed Word Lists for L2 Vocabulary Learning in Nine Languages

Frieda Charalabopoulou[a]*, Maria Gavrilidou[a], Sofie Johansson Kokkinakis[b], and Elena Volodina[b]

a. ILSP/"Athena" R.C., Artemidos and Epidavrou, Maroussi-Athens, Greece
b. Språkbanken, Institutionen för svenska språket, Göteborgs universitet, Göteborg, Sweden

Abstract. Lexical competence constitutes a crucial aspect in L2 learning, since building a rich repository of words is considered indispensable for successful communication. CALL practitioners have experimented with various kinds of computer-mediated glosses to facilitate L2 vocabulary building in the context of incidental vocabulary learning. Intentional learning, on the other hand, is generally underestimated, since it is considered out of fashion and not in line with the communicative L2 learning paradigm. Yet, work is still being done in this area and a substantial body of research indicates that the usefulness of incidental vocabulary learning does not exclude the use of dedicated vocabulary study and that by using aids explicitly geared to building vocabularies (such as word lists and word cards), L2 learners exhibit good retention rates and faster learning gains. Intentional vocabulary study should, therefore, have its place in the instructional and learning context. Regardless of the approach, incidental or intentional, the crucial question with respect to vocabulary teaching/learning remains: which and how many words should we teach/learn at different language levels? An attempt to answer the above question was made within the framework of the EU-funded project titled "KELLY" (**Ke**ywords for **L**anguage **L**earning for **Y**oung and Adults Alike) presented here. The project aimed at building corpus-informed vocabulary lists for L2 learners ranging from A1 to C2 levels for nine languages: Arabic, Chinese, English, Greek, Italian, Norwegian, Polish, Russian and Swedish.

Keywords: intentional vocabulary learning, corpora, CEFR, corpus-informed word lists, digital cards.

1. Introduction

According to Nation (2001), language comprehension and production is heavily dependent on vocabulary size, with 3,000 word families being a crucial threshold. A

---

* Contact author: frieda@ilsp.athena-innovation.gr

systematic and principled approach in order to build and expand the L2 learners' mental lexicon, therefore, results in better L2 learning. Given that vocabulary knowledge constitutes an integral part of general proficiency in L2 and a prerequisite for successful communication, the question is how it should best be taught and learned.

Intentional vocabulary learning (involving focused activities aiming directly at learning lexical items, such as using word cards and vocabulary lists) is often considered out of fashion and dismissed in the context of the communicative approach in L2 teaching and learning. Contextualised and incidental vocabulary learning, on the other hand, where learning vocabulary is considered a by-product of other L2 activities not primarily focusing on the systematic learning of words, seems to fit perfectly within the communicative framework.

While vocabulary learning from context seems to be favoured, a number of studies show that such learning has its drawbacks: it may require learners to engage in large amounts of reading and listening and may be more demanding and slow; it requires exposure to words through reading, listening and speaking, which, however, should be combined with a systematic study of lexical items, collocations etc. In addition, if the L2 learner has limited exposure to L2 outside the classroom, word-focused activities should complement vocabulary learning in context (Hulstijn, 2001; Laufer, 2003; Nation, 2001). On the other hand, considerable amounts of research (Ma & Kelly, 2006; Nation & Waring, 1997; Read, 2000) indicate that intentional vocabulary learning realised by using word lists and cards could be beneficial and should therefore have its place in the instructional/ learning context.

Regardless of the approach, the crucial question is: which and how many words should we teach/learn at different language levels? The aim of the KELLY project was to address the above questions and generate corpus-informed word lists for L2 learners in 9 languages: Arabic, Chinese, English, Greek, Italian, Norwegian, Polish, Russian and Swedish. The overall procedure adopted to carry out the above task is described in the following section.

2. Method

The main goal of the KELLY project was to identify for all nine languages the words that exhibit the highest frequency rates but at the same time are the most useful for L2 learners. The procedure for preparing the word lists comprised the following steps.

2.1. Corpus identification and corpus enhancement

The objective of the endeavour dictated the specifications for the corpus selection: it should contain general, everyday language and it should be large with a variety of texts, so that it would not be biased towards any particular text type or topic and would not miss basic vocabulary. Moreover, all corpora should be 'comparable' in all languages, so that all the lists would represent the same kind of language.

The main advantage of a web corpus is that it provides large bulks of data of general language in a variety of topics and genres and can be created for any language using various methods (see for example Sharoff, 2006). These methods result in corpora that serve the purpose of KELLY better than the BNC-type corpora, which typically have large components of newspapers and fiction, while the predominant language features are past tense verbs, third person pronouns and other prototypical written language features. Web corpora are more personal, action-based and future-oriented, and they include more prototypical spoken language features (e.g., present and future tense verbs, first and second person pronouns, etc.). According to Ferraresi, Zanchetta, Baroni, and Bernardini (2008), there is a better match between Common European Framework of Reference for Languages (CEFR) can-do statements (Council of Europe, 2001) and web corpora compared to BNC-type corpora. Taking into consideration all the above and in combination with the educational needs of our target group (L2 learners), in the KELLY project we opted for building word lists based on frequency from web corpora of general everyday language and comprising of different texts, thus not skewing the project by topic-specific texts.

Yet, a purely corpus-informed approach to build word lists addressing L2 learners may have certain shortcomings, including: the most frequent words may simply not be enough. Some words may not exhibit high frequency rates, yet they may be necessary and useful in the context of L2 learning. Therefore, the additional requirement for the KELLY lists was that they should include the most useful words according to the learner's L2 level and, furthermore, these should be in alignment with the CEFR-specific domain vocabulary. In order to meet this additional requirement, available educational resources (i.e., course books, dictionaries, already available vocabulary lists) were also consulted to enhance the original corpus-informed lists. After this enhancement process, the monolingual (M1) frequency lists were built for all 9 languages.

2.2. Building the bilingual word lists and the KELLY database

Each of the nine M1 lists were then translated into the eight other languages, thus rendering 72 translation lists. This process was followed by a cross-language list comparison and the next step involved handling "back translations" (i.e., words used by translators when translating into a language and not appearing in the monolingual lists of this language) in order to decide which of these should be added to the bilingual lists and which should be deleted or demoted. The emerging lists were translated to all other languages, hence resulting in the final 72 bilingual lists with each translation pair accompanied by word class, frequency, translator notes, etc. These words were ranked according to their frequency range and were equally distributed to the six CEFR-based proficiency levels resulting in approximately 1,500 words per proficiency level after merging two translated lists with each other (for instance Swedish-Greek and Greek-Swedish). The content of the final bilingual list is hosted by the KELLY database (available at http://kelly.sketchengine.co.uk), which contains

74,258 lemmas and 423,848 mappings, hence rendering it an interesting resource that may be deployed and exploited for both research and educational purposes.

3. Discussion

The KELLY project constitutes an experiment in employing automatic solutions for L2 learning. Based on the emerging word lists, the end-product of this endeavour comprises an on-line educational service for vocabulary (self-directed) study in nine languages in the form of bilingual digital cards addressing all language proficiency levels (A1-C2). The cards are divided into subject categories/domains, thus enabling the users to tailor their vocabulary studies to individualised communicative needs and goals. Within KELLY, innovative work has been carried out with respect to the following:

- Innovative methodology for building frequency-based vocabulary lists from web corpora in nine languages;
- Creation of a vocabulary-building tool, which may be employed either for self-study purposes or as supplementary material for enhancing vocabulary skills in the context of guided instruction;
- Development of word lists and digital cards for less widely taught and learned languages and "unusual" language pairs (e.g., Greek-Norwegian, Polish-Italian, Swedish-Arabic etc.), available at http://www.keewords.com/en/;
- Addressing a wide spectrum of L2 learners (i.e., youngsters (-16) and adults, from beginners to advanced, guided and self-directed in L2 learning) and learner types;
- Ranking words according to the Common European Framework and organised to CEFR-based thematic domains.

Apart from the advantages and innovations, the work carried out within the KELLY project has raised a number of issues which need to be addressed in the future. From a language pedagogy perspective, the crucial questions are: how efficient are corpus-informed word lists as pedagogical tools for L2 learning? Is employing purely lexico-statistical approaches to define vocabulary syllabuses for L2 learners a good enough approach? In other words, can we rely merely on technology and purely on objective strategies when it comes to the selection of relevant vocabulary for L2 learners? Even more so, when do word lists need to cover the CEFR-related thematic domains and topics?

4. Conclusions

In this paper we presented the KELLY project and its outcomes as an example of work carried out in order to develop corpus-derived word lists for nine languages that may be used and exploited within the L2 teaching and learning framework as vocabulary-building tools.

The pedagogical potentials of the lists and the digital cards mainly involve their use directly as a learning tool that may be deployed for vocabulary (self-)study as well as indirectly, e.g., for analysis of lexical complexity of L2 texts. As far as their pedagogical effectiveness is concerned, this needs to be validated by the end-users, i.e., actual L2 learners, in order to overcome existing shortcomings and provide a really useful reference tool for vocabulary learning. Evaluation and validation embraces issues such as content from an L2 learning perspective, its relation to the CEFR scale, coverage of the KELLY lists compared to different corpora and/or L2 course books based on CEFR, etc. One interesting aspect that also needs to be investigated is to what extent the KELLY lists could be considered as key resources and potential candidates for official vocabularies, especially with regard to those languages which lack such valuable resources.

References

Council of Europe. (2001). *Common European Framework of Reference for Languages: Learning, Teaching and Assessment.* Cambridge: Cambridge University.

Ferraresi, A., Zanchetta, E., Baroni, M., & Bernardini, S. (2008). Introducing and evaluating ukWaC, a very large web-derived corpus of English. In S. Evert, A. Kilgarriff, & S. Sharoff (Eds.), *Proc. 4th Web as Corpus Workshop (WAC-4) – Can we beat Google?* (pp. 47-54). Marrakech, Morocco.

Hulstijn, J. (2001). Intentional and incidental second language vocabulary learning: a reappraisal of elaboration, rehearsal, and automaticity. In P. Robinson (Ed.), *Cognition and second language instruction* (pp. 258–286). Cambridge, UK: Cambridge University Press.

Laufer, B. (2003). Vocabulary acquisition in a second language: do learners really acquire most vocabulary by reading? Some empirical evidence. *Canadian Modern Language Review, 59*(4), 567-587.

Ma, Q., & Kelly, P. (2006). Computer-Assisted Vocabulary Learning: Design and Evaluation. *Computer-Assisted Language Learning, 19*(1), 15-45. doi: 10.1080/09588220600803998

Nation, P., & Waring, R. (1997). Vocabulary Size, Text Coverage and Word Lists. In N. Schmitt, & M. McCarthy (Eds.), *Vocabulary: Description, Acquisition and Pedagogy* (pp. 6-19). Cambridge University Press.

Nation, P. (2001). *Learning vocabulary in another language.* Cambridge, UK: Cambridge University Press.

Read, J. (2000). *Assessing Vocabulary.* Cambridge, UK: Cambridge University Press.

Sharoff, S. (2006). Creating general-purpose corpora using automated search engine queries. In M. Baroni, & S. Bernardini (Eds.), *WaCky! Working papers on the Web as Corpus* (pp. 63-98). Bologna: Gedit.

UNIVERSITY OF GOTHENBURG

A Plurisemiotic Study of Multimodal Interactive Teaching Through Videoconferencing

Tatiana Codreanu[a*] and Christelle Combe Celik[b]

a. ICAR Research Laboratoty, École Normale Supérieure, Lyon, France
b. LIDILEM, University Stendhal, Grenoble, France

Abstract. The aim of the study is to describe and analyze webcam pedagogical communication between a French Foreign Language tutor and two students during seven online classes. It tries to answer the following question: how does the tutor in a multimodal learning environment change her semio-discursive behavior from the first to the last session? We analyze the tutor's discourse and gestures and the tools that support her communication. Our hypothesis is that the tutor should improve her semio-discursive competencies intuitively, taking into account her interlocutors and the affordance of different interaction tools. We will emphasize the pedagogical, socio-affective and multimodal competencies of the tutor.

Keywords: computer-mediated discourse analysis, desktop videoconferencing, interaction analysis, multimodality, online tutoring.

1. Introduction

The potential for computer-supported learning in educational contexts has opened up the possibilities for students to interact with tutors outside the classroom. Previous research highlighted the potential of the webcam for language instruction (Develotte, Guichon, & Vincent, 2010). The project is based on a desktop videoconferencing platform (DVC), *VISU,* designed for delivering online courses. *VISU* combines videoconferencing features in addition to writing and interaction tools.

The aim of the study is to describe and analyze pedagogical communication by means of webcam between one French foreign language tutor and two students during seven online classes. It addresses the following question: how does the tutor in a multimodal learning environment change her semio-discursive behavior from the first to the last session? We analyze the tutor's discourse and gestures and the tools that support her communication.

---

* Contact authors: tatiawa@gmail.com and christellecelik@hotmail.com

In L. Bradley & S. Thouësny (Eds.), *CALL: Using, Learning, Knowing, EUROCALL Conference, Gothenburg, Sweden, 22-25 August 2012, Proceedings* (pp. 54-58). © Research-publishing.net Dublin 2012

Our hypothesis is that tutors should improve their semio-discursive skills intuitively, taking into account the learners and the affordance (Hutchby, 2001) of different interaction tools. The paper presents the study based on an empirical method of collecting ecological data. We combine both computer mediated communication analysis and plurisemiotic analysis. The qualitative data analysis method is based on the description of online conversation (Develotte, Kern, & Lamy, 2011) in addition to interaction analysis (Kerbrat-Orecchioni, 2005) and plurisemiotic analysis (Cosnier, 2008).

A total of eleven tutors (8 trainees and 3 experienced teachers) and twenty-two UC Berkeley BA students (5th semester of learning French) participated in this experience, from where this current study is derived. Seventy sessions of instruction were documented. For the purpose of this research we have chosen a corpus of study which describes the multimodal pedagogical communication between one online trainee teacher (second year student of the Master of Arts in Teaching French as a foreign language at the university Lumière-Lyon 2, France) and two students of French as a foreign language from UC Berkeley, during the 2010 academic year.

2. Method

2.1. Methodological framework

A corpus of study is proposed to describe the tutoring practices on multimodal synchronous computer mediated communication.

The qualitative data analysis method is based on (1) computer-mediated discourse analysis (Herring, 2004) in addition to recent French research on discourse and interaction analysis (Cosnier, 2008; Kerbrat-Orecchioni, 2005), (2) the degree of the tutor's involvement through the webcam (Develotte, Guichon, & Vincent, 2010), and (3) the study of the framing which refers to the interactants position in the field of view of the webcam (Codreanu & Combe Celik, in press a, in press b). We conducted our analysis based on Cosnier's (2008) concept of "totext" described as a complex phenomenon of communication including symbols, coordinators, co-verbal and extra-communicative gestures. We studied two key concepts, the polyfocality and multimodality in the DVC environment. We discuss the qualitative findings of the research in order to highlight whether the tutor adjusts her behavior when interacting with the two students using the different tools via webcam over the seven online sessions.

2.1.1. Participants
Teachers: the teacher sample for this study consisted of 1 trainee teacher ($N = 1$ female). Before the interactions commenced the trainee tutor claimed that she was comfortable using VISU.

Students: the student sample consisted of 2 UC Berkeley BA students ($N = 2$ females, 5th semester of learning French) working in a pair.

2.1.2. Procedure

Participation was voluntary. The trainee teacher received 20 hours of training on how to use *VISU* in Lyon before the online interactions commenced.

She participated, along with the other trainee teachers, on the design of the online tasks which were based on UC Berkeley's curriculum. The instructional information was entered into the platform two days before the interactions started. The online sessions took place from January to March every Tuesday at 6 PM CET/ 9 AM PST.

2.1.3. Corpus of study

The main corpus consists of a total of 7 sessions of instruction. We studied the tutoring practices and the use of different communication tools for a total of 4 hours, 5 minutes and 39 seconds of online interaction. Our analysis of the data, collected through the ecological method, is descriptive. Moreover, a semi-directed interview was held with the tutor and the two learners. This added another 1 hour and 25 minutes of interviews to our corpus of study.

2.1.4. Data analysis

We focused on multimodal interaction and the polyfocality of attention while taking into account the socio-affective, pedagogical and multimedia competencies of online tutoring as defined by Guichon (2009):

- *The competency of socio-affective regulation refers to the capacity to establish a relationship with a learner or a group of learners* (p. 169).
- *The competency of pedagogical regulation […] consists of proposing clear and concise instructions, providing positive and negative feedback and deploying an array of strategies to facilitate second-language learning* (p. 169).
- *The competency of multimedia regulation relates to the interfacing role of the online tutor who has to learn to use the communication tools (forums, blogs, videoconferencing facilities, etc.) that are the most appropriate to the learning scenarios, and to manage the ensuing interactions with the most adequate modalities* (p. 170).

We studied the following aspects:

- **Pedagogical instruction.** We focused on the mediated oral analysis (Codreanu & Develotte, 2012) and the following two aspects: *the instructional script* (the written form of the instruction entered on *VISU*) and *the oral instruction* (verbal instructions close to the original text) following a script. We studied the variations in oral instruction, hesitation marks, self-talk and intrusions in the tutor's speech, the prosody, the transitions between the tasks and the feedback given to learners.
- **Multimodal analysis.** We studied the framing, the degree of use of the webcam, the spatial context, the disturbances and the use of the written tools (chat, tutor's personal notes, multimedia links).

- **Socio-affective analysis.** We studied the opening and ending speech acts (greetings and leave-taking), empathic exchanges, encouragement marks and humor.

3. Results

The mediated discourse analysis shows that the trainee tutor used a form of oral instruction similar to the instructional script during the seven sessions of pedagogical instruction. Her discourse displays intrusive overlaps in speech, self-talk and intrusions which are likely to contribute to the learner's miscomprehension. The prosody analysis shows marks of direct command and the quick pronunciation of spontaneous French speech. There are no transitions between the tasks during the seven sessions. The closing sequence is longer than the opening exchanges and follows a ritual almost identical to the following: long congratulations with intensifiers, an extended prosody, greetings for the week to come, thanks and goodbyes (with or without gesture).

The webcam's potential is less integrated into the trainee-teachers pedagogical practices. The analysis shows a shifting close-up framing for six out of seven sessions. The tutor moves restlessly in her chair while delivering the pedagogical instruction, while talking to students or reading the lesson plan. When interviewed about her use of the webcam the tutor acknowledged that she was often focused on her own image. During the seven sessions, the degree of use of the webcam is 2 or 3 (we noted an involuntary degree 4 during a centred close-up framing). It was observed that the chat is used to write words already pronounced either by the tutor or the learners and not to communicate new vocabulary. We noted the following ritual: the tutor sends multimedia links (on average 4 per activity within less than one minute), asks a question and starts writing personal notes on student's grammatical and phonetic errors (in average 4-5 per activity). We also observed that the tutor decreases use of the chat tool and increases use of the marker tool (used to take a personal note). However, at the end of the session she only gives a single phonetic correction.

The tutor shares her knowledge of American society. Her ethos is relaxed and casual from the beginning of the session. She shows empathy in regard to students' life and work. Prosody and lexicon used are characteristic of young people. We did not notice any marks of humour.

4. Discussion

In DVC, oral discourse, intonation and knowing how to effectively use the webcam are part of the tutoring ethos. Also, mimogestuality and framing are important in influencing the image that tutors want to give of themselves to students. The study shows that the teacher has an intuitive approach to online tutoring. Her teaching is not based on any pre-determined pedagogical rule. It shows the ethos of a young woman who is still a student, developing an ethos similar to that of the American students by marks of generational empathy.

5. Conclusions

It appears that in order to effectively use the various tools offered in *VISU*, tutors require training. As the study highlights, the trainee tutor did not perceive the full potential of the webcam. Overall, as acknowledged by the teacher herself, she was focused on her own image. As a result, this could have impacted the pedagogical interactions between her and the students. Awareness of one's image and its potential to communicate more effectively is one of the essential abilities tutors should display in order to maximize the learners experience through DVC.

Acknowledgements. We would like to thank Pr. Dr. Christine Develotte and Rahul Dhakal Timilsina for helping review this paper.

References

Codreanu, T., & Combe Celik, C. (in press a). La médiation de l'interaction pédagogique sur une plateforme vidéographique synchrone. *ALSIC*.

Codreanu, T., & Combe Celik, C. (in press b). Effects of webcams on multimodal interactive learning. *RECALL*.

Codreanu, T., & Develotte, C. (2012). How do tutors deliver instruction in the desktop videoconferencing environment? Tutoring practice analysis: Trainee tutors and experienced teachers. *Procedia-Social and Behavorial Sciences, 34*, 45-48. doi: 10.1016/j.sbspro.2012.02.010

Cosnier, J. (2008). Les gestes du dialogue. In P. Cabin & J.-F. Dortier (Eds.), *La communication, état des savoirs* (pp. 119-128). Auxerre: Editions Sciences Humaines.

Develotte, C., Guichon, N., & Vincent, C. (2010). The use of the webcam for teaching a foreign language in a desktop videoconferencing environment. *ReCALL, 22*(3), 293-312. doi: 10.1017/S0958344010000170

Develotte, C., Kern, R., & Lamy, M.-N. (2011). *Décrire la conversation en ligne*. Lyon: ENS Editions.

Guichon, N. (2009). Training future language teachers to develop online tutors' competence through reflective analysis. *ReCALL, 21*(2), 166-185. doi: 10.1017/S0958344009000214

Herring, S.-C. (2004). Computer-Mediated Discourse Analysis: An Approach to Researching Online Behavior. In S.-A. Barab, R. Kling, & J.-H. Gray (Eds.), *Designing for Virtual Communities in the Service of Learning* (pp. 338-376). New York: Cambridge University Press.

Hutchby, I. (2001). *Conversation and technology: from the telephone to the Internet*. Cambridge: Polity.

Kerbrat-Orecchioni, C. (2005). *Le discours en interaction*. Paris: Armand Colin.

UNIVERSITY OF GOTHENBURG

Blogs: Learning Through Using and Reusing Authentic Materials

Julian Coppens*, Mercedes Rico, and J. Enrique Agudo

University of Extremdaura, Santa Teresa de Jornet, Mérida, Spain

Abstract. Language learning and acquisition requires exposure to a language whether in a formal or informal learning environment as well as opportunities to produce the target language in a meaningful context. Therefore, it is unsurprising that the development of tools and web-based applications that allow written, audio, visual, and audio-visual material to be produced and shared – Web 2.0 – have been embraced by language teachers and learners. Authentic materials, those derived from the culture of the target language rather than specially produced for language learners, can not only be easily adapted to language learning using these new tools, they are potentially more relevant to learners because they increase opportunities for the creation of meaningful contexts for language learning. The objective of this paper is to assess the authenticity of English language learning materials shared by bloggers on blogs aimed specifically at English language learners or teachers. To reach this objective, the blog ranking site Technorati was used to select the most popular blogs for English language learners and teachers and each blog was analysed according to the authenticity of the cultural material used for language learning. The analysis reveals that more than 80% of the material posted on English as a foreign or second language (EFL/ESL) blogs is authentic material reused for language learning. The results show Web 2.0 technologies to be conducive towards providing contemporary authentic material for language learning – the technology itself encourages the use of authentic materials.

Keywords: blogs, web 2.0, EFL, ESL, authentic materials.

1. Introduction

Learning a language requires meaningful learning experiences facilitated by opportunities to interact with and produce language – written, audio, visual, and audio-visual – that involve communication and whether these opportunities occur in a formal learning environment or not. Exposure to a language forms an integral part of the acquisition process (Krashen, 1985).

---

* Contact author: julianc@unex.es

In L. Bradley & S. Thouësny (Eds.), *CALL: Using, Learning, Knowing*, EUROCALL Conference, Gothenburg, Sweden, 22-25 August 2012, Proceedings (pp. 59-63). © Research-publishing.net Dublin 2012

Therefore, the development of tools and web-based applications that enable written, audio, visual, and audio-visual material to be produced and shared have been embraced by language teachers and learners. Whilst these developments have increased the variety and quantity of material available for language learning, quality is also an aspect that needs to be considered. Authentic materials – those derived from the culture of the target language rather than specially produced for language learners – increase the relevance of the learning experience by reusing texts taken directly from the target culture. Web 2.0 technologies increase opportunities for bringing authentic materials into formal language learning environments by allowing material to be collected, reused and shared amongst language teachers and learners (Downs, 2009).

The objective of this paper is to assess the authenticity of English language learning materials shared by bloggers on blogs aimed specifically at English language learners or teachers in order to draw some conclusions concerning the extent to which their potential to increase the use of more authentic learning materials has been developed.

2. Method

In order to evaluate the cultural content of language learning blogs, the criteria for choosing to include a particular blog needs to be established. The popularity of a blog measures the influence its contents have over a particular audience. There are essentially two measures of this: popularity through citations, as well as popularity through affiliation, i.e., blogroll (Technorati, 2010).

While it takes time for a blog to become popular through blogrolls, permalinks can boost popularity more quickly, and are perhaps more indicative of popularity and authority than blogrolls, since they denote that people are actually reading the blog's content and deem it valuable or noteworthy. Technorati (technology + literati) is a blog search engine that ranks blogs based on the number of incoming links, blogroll members, frequency of postings and comments, among other indicators, and uses these to measure a site's standing and influence in the blogosphere, a rating known as Technorati Authority. A site's authority may rapidly rise and fall depending on what the blogosphere is discussing at the moment, and how often a site produces content being referenced by other sites (Technorati, 2010). The sites were selected by cross-referencing the top sites based on Technorati Authority returned by tag searches for English language teaching. All sites rated with a Technorati Authority greater than 1 were evaluated. Of the more than 200 blogs with posts tagged as EFL/ESL only 17 had a Technorati authority rating greater than 1. These 17 blogs form the basis of this study.

The blogs were evaluated according to the authenticity materials (Nation, 2007) provided for language learners or as resources for language learning. One of the most promising aspects of Web 2.0 is the way it can connect learners to each other and to authentic English language culture as opposed to material developed specifically for EFL learners. The criteria used to evaluate the content of the most popular EFL blogs aim to reflect on authenticity: the use of real, authentic material such as an article from a real newspaper rather than an article written for EFL learners to look as though it came from a newspaper.

3. Discussion

3.1. Content

Many cultural genres are represented in the blogs: movies, television and music, current affairs and news, as well as traditional English lessons broadcast by video or podcast. One blog is dedicated to the teaching of grammar through movie clips; several others adapt current news and activities for teaching English. Many use songs for teaching activities. Several cover information and communication technology (ICT), both hardware and software, for the teaching of second languages including news and advice for using ICTs and Web 2.0 for teaching English. Dialogues are also used in a wide range of contexts, especially in the podcasts and videos. Some are dialogues adapted to the class, but many are authentic dialogues recorded in real life situations.

The enormous variety of content available on the most popular EFL blogs provides a diverse, contemporary view of not English speaking cultures but many other cultures around the world. Some blogs use material in English to teach learners about other cultures, such as the Istanbul based blogger[*] who developed a lesson on the environment and the Amazon to teach English to primary school children, or language learning blogs based on Native American cultures.

3.2. Cultural diversity

The image of the English-speaking culture is modern and diverse, and all the blogs use contemporary culture to teach English. However, in terms of cultures, the cultures represented tend to be caucasian and western – occasionally African-American culture appears, but only as shown in hip-hop music or television and film rather than authentic materials relating to everyday life – with one important exception. One of the most popular blogs in second language teaching is entirely devoted to the history of American Indians and includes material and activities related to all major tribes of Native Americans in the United States.

However, the nature of the medium encourages diversity. Blogs allow multimedia use, reader participation and are free and easy to set up and therefore can reflect the diversity of the community they serve more easily than other types of old media such as textbooks, magazines and journals.

---

[*] Burcu Akyol: http://burcuakyol.com and http://tedistanbul5thgraders2009.edublogs.org

3.3. Authenticity: the amount of original material used

A high percentage, over 80%, of the teaching materials and lessons on blogs use authentic materials. This is not surprising. The nature of the environment and how Technorati measures blog popularity means that the blogs that have more frequent entries and more inbound links are rated more highly. This means that blogs that use relevant, contemporary materials are rated more highly by blog search engines and therefore receive more traffic which in turn further increases their rating. Authenticity is structurally encouraged in the medium and the search engines that serve it. Blogs provide direct access to authentic contemporary cultural artefacts taken from the language being learnt. This is theoretically predictable given the nature of the medium and this brief investigation shows it to be reflected in reality.

4. Conclusions

A blog is a chronological log, so it is an effective way for English teachers to share ideas, materials and experiences between themselves and their students, which are current and relevant. It allows the use of various types of media such as image, video, audio, text, as well as user interactivity in all of these different media. This means a blog can provide material, discussion and advice concerning all four skills necessary for second language acquisition: speaking, listening, reading, and writing. This, together with the absence of intermediaries such as editors and publishers means that English learners can experience direct contact with contemporary English-speaking cultures in a way appropriate to their language ability while still enjoying access to authentic materials. This increases the opportunities for English teachers to enhance learning and motivate students.

The blogs analysed are also all excellent examples of a crucial aspect of teaching: sharing good practice. This is an essential aspect of continuing professional development. Previously, the ideas and experiences of teachers could be shared only amongst colleagues; blogs enable ideas and experience to be shared with any teacher or student with access to the internet anywhere in the world. The blogs analysed here harness the immense creativity of ordinary EFL teachers and make it available cheaply and easily for the entire profession.

Finally, this study has shown that blogs represent culture for English teachers and learners in a way that is as rich in its diversity of material as it is in the ways it is presented. It allows easy access to cultures that for many English teachers and learners are obscure or underrepresented in other types of media. The blogs use contemporary culture as the bloggers themselves encounter it, and given the participatory nature of blogs, this puts teachers and learners in control, rather than publishers and editors.

The results show an inherent bias within Web 2.0 technologies towards providing contemporary authentic material for language learning – the technology itself encourages its use – and help to explain the ubiquitous use of these technologies in language learning communities.

References

Downs, S. (2009). *Blogs in Education* [Weblog]. Retrieved from http://halfanhour.blogspot.com/2009/04/blogs-in-education.html

Krashen, S. (1985). *The input hypothesis: issues and implications*. London: Longman.

Nation, P. (2007). The Four Strands. *Innovation in Language Learning and Teaching, 1*(1), 2-13. doi: 10.2167/illt039.0

Technorati. (2010). *What is Technorati Authority* [Weblog]. Retrieved from http://technorati.com/what-is-technorati-authority

UNIVERSITY OF GOTHENBURG

Web 2.0 and Authentic Foreign Language Learning at Higher Education Level

Maria de Lurdes Correia Martins[a]*, Gillian Moreira[b], and António Moreira[b]

a. Polytechnic Institute of Viseu, Viseu, Portugal
b. University of Aveiro, Campus Universitário de Santiago, Aveiro, Portugal

Abstract. Web 2.0 has afforded a number of opportunities for foreign language learning due to its open, participatory and social nature. A crucial aspect is authenticity – both situational and interactional – since students become involved in meaningful tasks, interacting in the target language with an authentic audience. In this paper we will reflect upon the potential of Web 2.0 tools, namely social networks, wikis and podcasts in enhancing foreign language learning opportunities at higher education level under the Bologna process. An action research project was carried out with undergraduate tourism students from Portugal. During two semesters, interactional tasks using Web 2.0 applications and involving the construction of collaborative outputs were designed and implemented, with the main goal of promoting and developing interactive communication skills in English amongst students with low levels of motivation and prior learning. Data was collected at different stages of the project aided by different data collection tools, namely questionnaires, focus group interviews, individual interviews, written reflections and corpus analyses, and a combination of quantitative and qualitative approaches was used. Results point towards impacts on students' language awareness, which has contributed to the creation of opportunities for language self-development, enhancing autonomous learning. In addition, it increased motivation for language learning by providing more opportunities for authentic input, social interaction and collaboration through the target language. Finally, the development of meta-competences such as metacognition and meta-learning can be highlighted.

Keywords: authenticity, collaborative learning, English as a foreign language, web 2.0.

1. Introduction

Web 2.0's open, participatory and social nature has given dialogue a prominent place in the knowledge building process. The construction of meaningful learning will greatly

---

* Contact author: lurdesmartins@estv.ipv.pt

depend on learners' capacity to engage in the creation and maintenance of dialogic processes. However, the primacy of dialogue in learning does not directly emerge from the spread of Web 2.0. Dialogue, according to Ravenscroft (2011), is "coevolving with these technologies, which arguably provide social opportunities that are more open, and are used more often, than was previously possible with the traditional methods of communication, dialogue, and discourse" (p. 142). Associated with dialogue, we have the concepts of dialectic and dialogic, which have been suggested as a structural pedagogy for the twenty-first century (Dalsgaard, 2009; Ravenscroft, Wegerif, & Hartley, 2007). Hence, we consider dialectic and dialogic as two relevant dimensions that focus on complementary aspects of the role of dialogue in the learning process. While dialectic emphasises cognitive and epistemic dimensions, dialogic gives primacy to emotional and interpersonal dimensions. The interrelation of the two dimensions in the learning process is emphasised by Ravenscroft et al. (2007): "The desire to reason to progress towards a rational synthesis does not have to override the need to understand others, and likewise, the desire to understand others does not have to override the often pragmatic need to reach a rational consensus that links to purposeful action in a context" (p. 46).

The integration of these principles in the structuring, planning and execution of communicative tasks is both complex and challenging. First of all, the process begins with a multiplicity of definitions and views of 'task'. Regarding this, Ollivier and Puren (2011), as a result of a critical analysis of different perspectives, listed and summarised the most relevant characteristics of a task:
- Focus should be on meaning and the mobilisation of language skills should come naturally when attempting to solve the task;
- The completion of a task leads to an accurate outcome;
- A task is not, generally, exclusively linguistic;
- Resolution of a task involves social interaction;
- Task execution is affected by certain constraints and limitations;
- Solving tasks involves the deployment of cognitive processes and different skills;
- Tasks involve different steps or sub-tasks;
- Tasks should privilege authenticity.

Authenticity is also emphasised by Nunan (2004), who distinguishes between real world, target tasks and pedagogical tasks. The Common European Framework of Reference for Languages (CEFRL) also alludes to real-life, target or rehearsal tasks conceived as "tasks [...] chosen on the basis of learners' needs outside the classroom, whether in the personal and public domains, or related to more specific occupational or educational needs" (Council of Europe, 2001, p. 157). Ellis (2003) goes deeper in this matter and refers to two types of authenticity: situational and interactional. Situational authenticity is related to real world activities, while interactional authenticity demands that learners' communicative reaction or response is genuine, similar to the real world. In our view, Web 2.0 has promoted new opportunities for foreign language classes, allowing the implementation of tasks that involve both types of authenticity. These capabilities are highlighted by Mangenot and Louveau (2006), who add on the concepts of similarity and likelihood. In addition, Ollivier and Puren (2011) present a diagram that emphasises the role of interaction and co-action in performing a task, stressing the role of Web 2.0 as a privileged space for the assessment of co-action.

2. Method

The methodological approach adopted for this study consisted of an action research project (see Figure 1, adapted from Stringer, 2007) over two semesters, in the English II and English III course units from the degree course in Tourism at the School of Technology and Management, Polytechnic Institute of Viseu. Stemming from the core theme of each course unit and intended learning outcomes, interactional tasks using Web 2.0 tools and involving the construction of collaborative outputs were designed and implemented.

Figure 1. Action research project outline

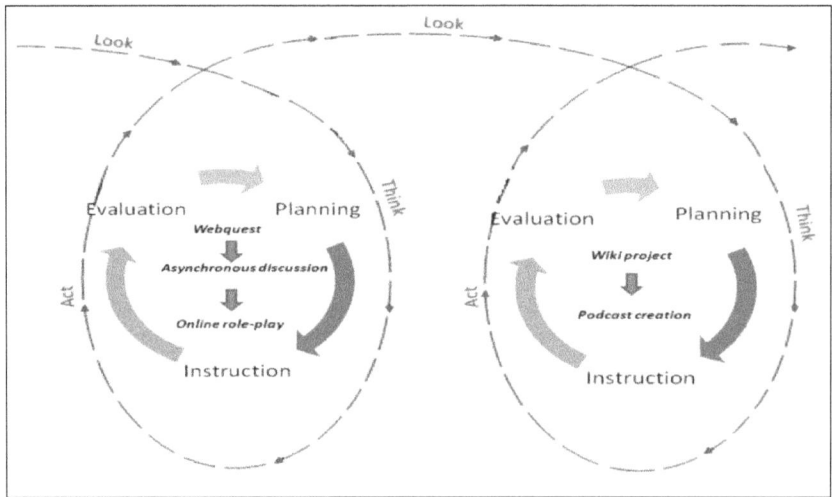

The planning of tasks took into account data analyses from a preliminary demographics questionnaire, more precisely students' low familiarity with Web 2.0 tools, as well as the fact that most of them never had the opportunity to use them in educational settings. The learning outcomes set for the different activities were defined according to the Common European Framework of Reference for Languages, level B2 (comprehension and production) and level B1 (interaction).

3. Findings

Data analysis points to a markedly positive impact of Web 2.0 tools on the implementation of interactional tasks in English language learning in higher education. Table 1 summarises the most relevant findings of each task implemented.

Table 1. Most relevant findings

Task	Main strengths	Main difficulties
Webquest "Discover London"	Increased motivation; Vocabulary acquisition; Opportunities for the development of communicative competence in English; Contact with meaningful tourism-related information.	Understanding the information displayed on some websites.
Asynchronous Discussions	Vocabulary learning; Writing skills; Information sharing; Metacognition skills.	Collaborative work; Written comprehension; Fear of exposure.
Online role-play: planning a school trip to London	Writing skills; Vocabulary learning; Increased opportunities to use English; Cultural awareness.	Collaborative work; Selection of accurate information.
Wiki project: Visit Viseu	A positive attitude toward online group collaboration; Integrity of contributions; Fulfilment of agreed-upon roles; Constructive additions and revisions to improve the project outcomes.	Most information sources were only available in Portuguese; Portuguese – English translation using Google Translate (mistranslation problems); Linguistic performance correlated with a lack of strategic competence in using available tools.
Podcast creation: Viseu attractions you mustn't miss!	Accurate information and succinct concepts are presented; Students' assessment of the final output is positive; Students' perceptions are influenced by their metalinguistic awareness.	Delivery is hesitant, and choppy, giving the impression of reading; Enunciation, expression, and rhythm are sometimes distracting.

4. Discussion

The use of authentic materials proved to be very positive, since students were confronted with authentic language, which, most of the time, is different from the one that commonly appears in textbooks where the practice is confined by the language structures and vocabulary defined for a given level of proficiency and, therefore, decontextualised from their speakers, values and cultural norms. It also allowed respecting students' idiosyncrasies and learning styles, given that activities combined face-to-face with e-learning. Another aspect that should be highlighted is the promotion of autonomy in conducting research in English language and the promotion of strategic competence, since students frequently used online translation tools and online dictionaries. The creation of the learning community "English for Tourism" in Grouply social network was the driving force of the collaborative work developed over the two semesters. In order to play an active role in the asynchronous discussions, students needed to understand and select relevant information to later write a comment sustained at specific facts. This way, it was possible to promote eclectic learning, combining reception and interaction activities.

Students recognised Web 2.0 potential in learning English, emphasising the acquisition of vocabulary and the development of writing skills. This was mainly due to increased opportunities to communicate in English outside the physical walls of the classroom. Also, the sharing of ideas among participants contributed to the production of more complete outcomes and it also promoted an increased metalinguistic awareness.

Regarding interactional authenticity, there was a concern with the sociolinguistic appropriateness of their written productions, particularly the use of a formal style in the task related to the creation of the wiki "Visit Viseu". Collaborative work was transverse to the different activities and constituted a strength and an obstacle to the proposed activities. This difficulty in working collaboratively as a class can be explained by the innovative character of the tasks implemented. It is common practice for students to complete work in pairs or small groups, but not so when the group is constituted by all the students in the class.

5. Conclusions

This study represents an innovative and very positive contribution for applied linguistics studies, legitimising Web 2.0 applications as an exceptional strategy in meeting the goals raised by the Bologna process, allowing us to highlight the following aspects:
- Web 2.0, for enhanced English language learners among undergraduates, has allowed an active involvement of students in solving authentic tasks, combining both situational and interactional authenticity, and articulating different linguistic activities defined by the CEFRL, thus contributing to the development of a plurilingual and pluricultural competence;
- Students who participated in both action research cycles developed capabilities to manage their own learning process, making decisions about contents and materials (what), strategies (how), time / pace (when) and space (where);
- The dialectical, dialogical and actional approaches used promoted a deeper student involvement in interactive processes through the use of diverse strategies, hence promoting the development of skills leading to improvements in English language teaching and learning in higher education;
- There was a correlation between linguistic performance and the strategic use of available tools, namely the use of cognitive and metacognitive strategies by some learners, allowing them to plan and monitor their learning process, and become aware of the strategies used to solve the proposed tasks and, ultimately, their language learning strategies.

References

Council of Europe. (2001). *Common European Framework of Reference for Languages: Learning, Teaching and Assessment*. Cambridge: Cambridge University Press.

Dalsgaard, C. (2009). From transmission to dialogue: Personalised and social knowledge media. *MedieKultur, 25*(46), 18-33. Retrieved from http://ojs.statsbiblioteket.dk/index.php/mediekultur/article/download/1333/1486

Ellis, R. (2003). *Task-based language learning and teaching*. Oxford: Oxford University Press.

Mangenot, F., & Louveau, E. (2006). *Internet et la classe de langue*. Paris: CLE International.

Nunan, D. (2004). *Task-Based Language Learning*. Cambridge: Cambridge University Press.

Ollivier, C., & Puren, L. (2011). *Le web 2.0 en la classe de langue.* Paris: Editions Maison des Langues.

Ravenscroft, A. (2011). Dialogue and connectivism: A new approach to understanding and promoting dialogue-rich networked learning. *The International Review Of Research In Open And Distance Learning, 12*(3), 139-160. Retrieved from http://www.irrodl.org/index.php/irrodl/article/view/934

Ravenscroft, A., Wegerif, R. B., & Hartley, J. R. (2007). Reclaiming thinking: Dialectic, dialogic and learning in the digital age. In J. Underwood & J. Dockrell (Eds.), *Learning through Digital Technologies* (pp. 39-57). Leicester : British Psychological Society.

Stringer, E. (2007). *Action Research*. London: Sage.

UNIVERSITY OF
GOTHENBURG

Computer Mediated Conversation for Mutual Learning: Acknowledgement and Agreement/Assessment Signals in Italian as L2

Anna De Marco[a*] and Paola Leone[b**]

a. University of Calabria, Via P. Bucci, Arcavacata, Rende, Italy
b. University of Salento, P.zza A. Rizzo 1, Lecce, Italy

Abstract. The current study aims to investigate form, composition, distribution of acknowledgement and agreement/assessment signals in upper intermediate/advanced Italian as L2 speakers. Data are video-transcribed computer mediated conversations for mutual language learning (Teletandem) during which two female volunteer university students (L1: English and German) talk with a native speaker (NS) female interlocutor (L1: Italian) for developing L2 language proficiency. For each pair, data have been collected during two different meetings: meeting 1 comprises free discussion for mutual introductions; meeting 2 is a discussion on a topic chosen by the Italian non- native speaker. The analysis shows that L2 subjects employ a great variety of (1) acknowledgement and agreement listener responses, (2) both lexical and non-lexical units whose functions, positions and frequency are affected by the level of involvement in the discourse, and (3) acquaintance of the two speakers and by the type of task. Particularly in the second meeting, when a topic is discussed, non-native speakers (NNSs) use more lexical units than in the first meeting, thus highlighting the relevance of situational variables over the discourse structure.

Keywords: teletandem, discourse markers, agreement signals, acknowledgment signals, listener responses.

1. Introduction

The current study focuses on the use of two types of listener responses (LR) in L2: acknowledgement particles, which are used to show either attention or discourse

---

* Contact author: demarco.anna@gmail.com

** The paper is the result of the joint work of the two authors. Particularly, De Marco is responsible for sections 2 and 6, and Leone for sections 1, 3, and 4. Section 5 has been written by both authors.

In L. Bradley & S. Thouësny (Eds.), *CALL: Using, Learning, Knowing, EUROCALL Conference, Gothenburg, Sweden, 22-25 August 2012, Proceedings* (pp. 70-75). © Research-publishing.net Dublin 2012

perception (e.g., Eng: *hm, huh*; in Italian: *sì, mhm*; Yngve, 1970) and reactive expressions (Clancy, Thompson, Suzuki, & Tao, 1996), named as well agreement/ assessment signals (e.g., Eng.: *oh really/really*, It.: *bene, ok*) by which the listener wants to align to what has been previously said, also showing surprise (e.g., Eng.: *yeah, wow, gosh*). Listener responses are discourse markers (DM) produced by the listener in order to mark transition points, link two discourse units, and give relevance to different discourse levels (e.g., interpersonal, cognitive; Bazzanella et al., 2007a, 2007b; Bazzanella & Borreguero Zuloaga, 2011; Louwerse & Mitchell, 2003). DM, hence LR, are characterized by:

- Syntactic independence, i.e., if they are erased the sentence structure does not change;
- Multifunctionality both at paradigmatic (i.e., the same token can have different functions in different contexts, in relation to the linguistic co-text in which it occurs) and at syntagmatic levels (i.e., it is not always easy to assign to a unit just one function among the following: metatextual, interactional and cognitive);
- Possibility to combine in different ways (e.g., It: *ah sì bene allora*).

Teletandem conversations are a form of computer mediated "conversation for learning" (Kasper, 2004), during which speakers talk via chat and videocalls having a "dual-focus" in mind (Apfelbaum, 1993; Bange, 1992): the language used for communication (e.g., the discourse includes turns for recast, for meaning negotiation) and the topics under discussion (e.g., there are appraisal/agreement sequences). During Teletandem conversations a communication strategy is code-switching which is employed for facilitating content exchange and for being more effective in communication (Anderson & Banelli, 2005; Leone, 2009).

2. Acknowledgement/reception and agreement/assessment signals in L2

Studies on different L1 speakers' discourse have shed light on how syntactic, prosodic and pragmatic resources are used to negotiate social practices (Couper-Kuhlen & Ford, 2004; Schegloff, 2007) and speech acts. Less extensive and systematic work has been dedicated to how L2 speakers employ DM to organize and expand their turn.

Concerning listener responses, several studies (Xudong, 2008) have investigated criteria for identifying and classifying DM: for instance, the possibility of "claiming or not claiming the floor", their acoustic, lexical and non-lexical form and the sequential context of occurrence (Cerrato, 2007).

Research shows that across languages these conversational strategies are used differently: Japanese NSs use backchannels (BC), for example, more frequently than English NSs, whereas the latter use them more frequently than Mandarin NSs. Chinese speakers rarely use minimal responses during conversation with German NSs (Xudong, 2008). Conversely, German speakers use BC frequently during conversation with Chinese interlocutors.

Differences among speakers have been related to where listener responses are located. Researchers refer to the 'Transitional Relevance Places' (TRP, Sacks, Schlegoff, & Jefferson, 1974) and distinguish among points of transition from one speaker to another or during another's speaker turn (Xudong, 2008).

The analysis of functions, type and position of different DM in Swedish learners of Italian as a foreign language (Bardel, 2004) have shown that most frequent non-lexical DM (e.g., *eh, hm, mhm*) are produced either at the beginning of the turn or for keeping the turn, thus showing difficulties in discourse planning. Furthermore, non-lexical units are employed to request clarification and to show attention. Form, frequency and function of DM have been investigated in Croatian L1 Italian learners (Nigoević & Sučić, 2011). The research, based on data collected during interviews, shows that advanced learners of Italian as L2 use different DM such as fillers, mitigating devices, agreement/assessment and turn taking signals. Non-lexical DM are more frequent in less advanced interlanguage, whereas lexical forms appear in advanced L2 speakers.

3. Research questions

The study aims to highlight the use of acknowledgement and agreement/assessment signals (e.g., Xu, 2009), in upper intermediate/advanced Italian as L2 speakers, particularly:
- Form and composition of the short utterance, i.e., is it a lexical or a non-lexical unit? Does the unit appear in discourse together with other turn components? (Schegloff, 2007);
- Distribution and function in the conversational sequence, e.g., are signals employed for acknowledgement or for assessment? Do they overlap primary speakers' turns? Do they occur at or near transition space and determine movements to new positions?

4. Data

Subjects were 2 female volunteer university students forming 2 Teletandem pairs who talked via computers using instant messaging and VoIP software (i.e., Skype). Each pair was composed of one Italian NS (ITL1) and one English NS (ENGL1) (PAIR1) and one German NS (GERL1) (PAIR2). Their language proficiency in L2 ranged from upper intermediate to advanced.

Data are based on 3 hours conversation (1 hour and 30 minutes for each pair). The first 30 minutes are part of a 1 hour session during which participants talked fifty-fifty in their L1 and L2 for knowing each other (M1). The subsequent 1 hour conversation was recorded after a few days; ENGL1 and GERL1 chose the conversation topic (M2).

5. Data analysis and discussion

Data analysis highlighted forms that satisfied the functions of acknowledgment and assessment.

PAIR1M1, ENGL1 (Table 1) employs a variety of LR for acknowledgement/ reception and agreement/assessment signals that are often more than one single unit. Most of the agreement signals are lexical forms like *sì, bene, esatto*, which are also used as a acknowledgement/reception function. For this latter function the mentioned lexical forms combine with *bene, benissimo* and non-lexical forms such as *ah*.

In PAIR1M2, the level of involvement in topic discussion and task characteristics such as topic choice seem to affect the frequency and the overlapping position of listener responses. A greater variation of lexical (*sì ho capito, ah sì eh allora, sì bene, sicuro sì, vero*) and non-lexical forms (e.g., *ahh, oooh, wow, a:h, ah ah*) is also an interesting interactional strategy. *Sì* seems to carry a greater variety of pragmatic meaning than other forms, i.e., it also signals that the speaker wants to go on talking or that she has nothing more to add to the topic.

Table 1. Acknowledgement and agreement/assessment signals in Italian as L2 (B2; C1) in a corpus of Teletandem conversations.

	Acknowledgement signals	Agreement/Assessment signals
PAIR1ENGL1- M1	sì, molto bene, sì è chiaro, benissimo, ah bene, ah bene sì + laugh	mm, sì, mm bene, sì esatto, sì sì, sì, sì sì no, no sì no,
PAIR1ENGL1- M2	sì allora e:hm yeah, sì ma, sì allora, ah ok, sì esatto, [sì ho capito], [sì chiaro], ah sì eh allora, ah ah sì, ah sì ahh bene	sì, sì, esatto esatto, ah è molto bene sì, sì chiaro, [sì] ah sì + laugh, ah sì sì molto be[ne], sì a:h, ahh vero wow, oooh, sicuro sì a:h
PAIR2GER1- M1	ahah, ah, ehm, sì, ah ok, sì ah ja, ok	sì + laugh ah ok sì + repetition ah sì ah ja sarebbe bello +laugh uhm uhm bello,
PAIRGERL1- M2	ah, sì, uhuh sì, ok sì, sì sì, sì + concept/form repetition, form repetition + ja, (ah) ja+ form repetition	è vero, sì certo, uh sì, sì ok, (eeeh) sì + repetition, ah ok sì +repetition

In PAIR2M1 (Table 1) between the two types of LR under discussion the majority are acknowledgement signals in the form of non-lexical units.

In PAIR2M2 the number of acknowledgements and assessments is more balanced. As for PAIR1ENGL1M1 *sì* is a largely used lexical signal for acknowledgement and assessment. When it occurs in sequences of focus on form (e.g., a recast by the NS), it seems to have the function of reception signal (not always followed by a repetition), conversely in sequences of focus on meaning, it has the function of agreement. But formally in both contexts, it combines with other discourse parts in the same way (i.e., *sì* + content/repetition).

Both L2 speakers switch code also when they use DM, combining lexical units in L1 and in L2 during their L2 talk (e.g., *ah sì ah ja*).

In some sequences the functions of acknowledgement and assessment overlap. Listener responses rarely overlap primary speakers' turn; particularly, they occur at transition space and in some sequences they open a new turn, thus determining movements in the position from listener to speaker.

6. Concluding remarks

The analysis shows that even learners with intermediate competence in L2 employ a great variety of acknowledgement and agreement LR, both lexical and non-lexical whose functions, position and frequency are affected by the level of involvement/acquaintance of the two speakers and by the type of task. Therefore:
- It is advisable to plan Teletandem sessions including different typology of tasks since each of them presents various discourse structures at interactional and transactional levels (see also Leone, forthcoming);
- Research on interlanguage pragmatics and on the use of DM cannot be based on one typology of discourse (e.g., interview);
- Pragmatic competence (particularly the use of DM) should be evaluated considering more than one typology of conversation.

References

Anderson, L., & Banelli, D. (2005). La commutazione di codice negli incontri Tandem. In G. Banti, A. Marra, & E. Vineis (Eds.), *Atti del 4° Congresso di Studi dell'Associazione Italiana di Linguistica Applicata* (pp. 89-110). Perugia: Guerra Editore.

Apfelbaum, B. (1993). *Erzählen im Tandem. Sprachlernaktivitäten und die Konstruktion eines Diskursmusters in der Fremdsprache (Zielsprachen: Französisch und Deutsch)*. Tübingen: Narr.

Bange, P. (1992). A propos de la communication et de l'apprendissage de L2 (notamment dans ses formes institutionnelles). *Aile*, 1, 53-85. Retreived from http://aile.revues.org/pdf/4875

Bardel, C. (2004). La pragmatica in italiano L2: l'uso dei segnali discorsivi. In F. Albano Leoni, F. Cutugno, M. Pettorino, & R. Savy (Eds.), *Il Parlato Italiano. Atti del Convegno Nazionale (Napoli, 13-15 febbraio 2003)*. Napoli: D'Auria.

Bazzanella, C., Garcea, A., Bosco, C., Gili Fivela, B., Miecznikowski, J., & Tini Brunozzi, F. (2007a). Italian *allora*, French *alors*: functions, convergences, and divergences. *Catalan Journal of Linguistics*, special issue, M. J. Cuenca (Ed.), *Contrastive Perspectives on Discourse Markers* (pp. 9-30), Universitat Autònoma de Barcelona. Servei de Publicacions, Bellaterra.

Bazzanella, C., Bosco, C., Gili Fivela, B., Miecznikowski, J., & Tini Brunozzi, F. (2007b). Segnali discorsivi e tipi di interazione. In C. Bosisio, B. Cambiaghi, E. Piemontese, & F. Santulli (Eds.), *Aspetti linguistici della comunicazione pubblica e istituzionale. Atti del VII Congresso della Associazione italiana di Linguistica Applicata (AItLA)* (pp. 239-265), Perugia: Guerra Editore.

Bazzanella, C., & Borreguero Zuloaga, M. (2011). Allora e entonces: problemi teorici e dati empirici. *Oslo Studies in Language,* 3(1), 7-45.

Cerrato, L. (2007). *Investigating Communicative Feedback Phenomena across Languages and Modalities.* (Unpublished doctoral dissertation). University of Stockholm, Sweden. Retrieved from http://www2.gslt.hum.gu.se/dissertations/thesis_final2_070412.pdf

Clancy, P. M., Thompson, S.A., Suzuki, R., & Tao, H. (1996). The conversational use of reactive tokens in English, Japanese, and Mandarin. *Journal of Pragmatics, 26,* 355-87.

Couper-Kuhlen, E., & Ford, C.E. (2004). *Sound Patterns in Interaction.* John Benjamins Publishing Company.

Kasper, G. (2004). Participant orientations in German Conversation-for-Learning. *The Modern Language Journal,* 88(4), 551-567.

Leone, P. (2009). Processi negoziali nel corso di scambi comunicativi mediati dal computer. In C. Consani, C. Furiassi, F. Guazzelli, & C. Perta (Eds.), *Oralità/scrittura. In memoria di G. R. Cardona. Atti del IX Congresso Internazionale dell'Associazione Italiana di Linguistica Applicata (AItLA)* (pp. 389-412). Perugia: Guerra Edizioni.

Leone, P. (forthcoming). Content domain and language competence in computer-mediated conversation for learning. *Apples - Journal of Applied Language Studies.*

Louwerse, M. M., & Mitchell, H. H. (2003). Towards a taxonomy of a set of discourse markers in dialog: a theoretical and computational linguistic account. *Discourse Processes, 35,* 199-239.

Nigoević, M., & Sučić, P. (2011). Competenza pragmatica in italiano L2: l'uso dei segnali discorsivi da parte degli apprendenti croati. *Italiano LinguaDue,* 3(2), 94-114. Retrieved from http://riviste.unimi.it/index.php/promoitals/article/view/1917/2170

Sacks, H., Schegloff, E. A., & Jefferson, G. (1974). A simplest systematics for the organization of turn-taking for conversation. *Language,* 50(4), 696-735. Retrieved from http://www.jstor.org/stable/412243

Schegloff, E. A. (2007). *Sequence organization in interaction,* Cambridge: Cambridge University Press.

Xu, J. (2009). *Displaying overt recipiency: Reactive tokens in Mandarin task-oriented conversation.* (Unpublished doctoral dissertation). University of Nottingham, UK. Retrieved from http://etheses.nottingham.ac.uk/1006/1/Thesisphd-2009Final-Xujun.pdf

Xudong, D. (2008). The Use of Listener Responses in Mandarin Chinese and Australian English Conversations. *Pragmatics,* 18(2), 303-328.

Yngve, V. (1970). On getting a word in edgewise. *Papers from the Sixth Regional Meeting of the Chicago Linguistic Society,* 567-577.

UNIVERSITY OF GOTHENBURG

International Student Carbon Footprint Challenge – Social Media as a Content and Language Integrated Learning Environment

Géraldine Fauville[a]*, Annika Lantz-Andersson[b], and Roger Säljö[b]

a. Department of Biological and Environmental Sciences, University of Gothenburg, Fiskebäckskil, Sweden
b. Department of Education, Communication and Learning, University of Gothenburg, Gothenburg, Sweden

Abstract. Environmental education (EE) is now clearly specified in educational standards in many parts of the world, and at the same time the view of language learning is moving towards a content and language integrated learning (CLIL) strategy, to make English lessons more relevant and attractive for students (Eurydice, 2006). In this respect, environmental and English instruction can be merged to benefit both purposes and to offer learning experiences that go beyond the school walls. Einztein, the social learning network for the education community, collaborates with the environmental project Inquiry-to-Insight (http://i2i.stanford.edu/) inviting high school students around the world to participate in the International Student Carbon Footprint Challenge (ISCFC), challenging students to learn about the environmental impact of their lifestyle choices on their carbon footprints. In the ISCFC, students use an online carbon footprint calculator to measure the amount of CO_2 (carbon dioxide) released by their everyday choices (food, transportation, etc). Teachers then share student data with other classrooms around the globe and use Einztein to engage students in several environmental discussions online using English as the lingua franca. Students use Einztein to reflect upon their own carbon footprint, envision global and local solutions and share knowledge about environmental issues. For this study we focused on a specific discussion and investigated the discourse structure of students from six different countries (USA, Croatia, Switzerland, Iceland, Greece and Bulgaria) reflecting upon their very own CO_2 emissions. Preliminary results indicate that the students' presumptions about their own impact are crucial and whether they are English natives or not is not as important when it comes to developing an understanding of their own responsibilities regarding carbon footprint. Thus, in relation to a motivating content, the students' English is productive and sufficient enough for communication and collaboration.

Keywords: CLIL, environmental education, international collaboration, English language learning, social media.

---

* Contact author: geraldine.fauville@loven.gu.se

1. Introduction

Environmental education (EE) is highly important in contemporary schooling and has for quite some years been clearly specified in educational standards in most European countries (UNESCO, 1975). For example, issues concerning the carbon dioxide in the atmosphere that now requires immediate reduction, have to be managed both locally and globally. Questions about environmental awareness, for example the impact of an individual's everyday choices regarding travel, food, and lifestyle, is however not everyday knowledge for young people, but rather complex from a knowledge point of view, and require insights into many fields. EE requires critical and action-oriented practices focusing on relevant and practical problems, and such questions are not only interdisciplinary in their nature but also cause undeniable concern for people worldwide. The global aspect of EE thus makes it outermost suitable to deal with in school settings by integrating the content with language learning. The view of language learning in content and language integrated learning with a focus on the subject that is taught through the medium of a second language has also attracted much attention in Europe and other parts of the world in the last decade (Eurydice, 2006). As argued by David Marsh (2008), who coined the acronym of CLIL in 1996, "[t]his approach can be viewed as being neither language learning, nor subject learning, but rather an amalgam of both" (p. 233). This perspective together with the massive development within digital media has resulted in a situation where communication is managed in a variety of new manners that has impact on students' language learning. Already in 2002, Marsh stated that "the recent availability and use of new technologies, in particular, has had a considerable impact on learner attitudes" (Marsh, 2002, p. 10). Today this is truer than ever with ubiquitous possibilities for people to interact in a variety of social media through smartphones, computers, iPads, etc. Social media also imply challenges for educational practices where communication and the easy access to vast sources of information complement, but also sometimes challenge, traditional media, such as, for example, textbooks. Interacting in different social media contexts can be seen as new arenas in which young people use and develop other language skills and competencies relevant to language learning (see e.g., Blattner & Lomica, 2012; Bonderup-Dohn, 2009). From a more traditional perspective, these competencies are not easily defined within the frames of what is usually acknowledged and assessed in school (Thorne, 2009). Thus, we have the multidisciplinary subject environmental education with a goal to globally educate young people in sustainability. We have goals of language learning to involve students in developing communicative skills by using the language for meaningful purposes and we have communicative conditions that are dramatically changing due to the enormous expansion of various kinds of social media. In line with the arguments above, the basis of this research is tripartite; environmental education, English language learning, and social learning network context.

In this study, we explore how high school students from 6 countries learn about EE in a social learning network called Einztein using English as a lingua franca. The study is part of the environmental project Inquiry-to-Insight inviting high school students around the world to participate in the International Student Carbon Footprint Challenge, challenging students to learn about the environmental impact of their own lifestyle choices on their carbon footprints. For this study, we focused on a specific discussion and investigated the discourse structure of students from the countries USA, Croatia, Switzerland, Iceland, Greece and Bulgaria reflecting on their own CO_2 emissions using English to discuss and communicate online.

2. Method

The analysis, as described above, is based on students' asynchronous postings using English in the social learning network Einztein.com. In this study, the high school students discuss their results from the I2I Carbon Footprint Challenge Calculator, which is a calculator for measuring personal carbon dioxide emissions. This calculator is very particular since it takes into account the location of the students and provides an average emission of the country selected, giving the students a way to situate their emission as higher or lower than their country's average. Moreover, when the students answer a question about their habits in the calculator, they immediately observe how this behaviour impacts their emission, making the link between behaviour and emission immediate. In the social learning network Einztein, their postings are gathered around specific discussion links in relation to the subject and their carbon footprint in general. They are also organised into sessions. Every second month a new session starts and all the students involved start posting at the same time in order to maximise the interaction.

There are two ways to participate in the discussions. Students can submit posts, which are direct replies to the main topic, or they can reply to another student by writing comments. This study focuses on a session from November 2012 with 28 posts from students in the six countries. The empirical material is analysed in relation to the integrated content and the students' language use.

3. Result and discussion

In a comparison between the posts written by native English speakers and non-native English speakers, the result implies that the fact that most students are non-native speakers does not hinder the reflection or diminish the level of meaning making. In analysing the language use in relation to the content, the results imply common structures in students' discourse with six different phases or elements: (i) Expectation: students talk about their expectations for their own emission compared to the national average, (ii) Results: students communicate their own emission and compare it to the national average after calculation, (iii) Reflection: students make sense of their own carbon footprint in the light of the knowledge acquired by the calculator, (iv) New resolution: students reflect upon the change they are willing/able (or not) to make to decrease their footprint, (v) Share knowledge: students share pieces of environmental information or give advice to the ISCFC community, and finally (vi) Global dimension: students step back and see the issue globally, involving all of us rather than just their personal behaviours.

If we compare the number of words by posts, the average for US students is 182 while for the non-native English speaker it is 156. There is no significant difference between both groups, $F(1, 26) = 46$, $p = .50$. If we compare the number of phases present in each post, the average for US students is 4.28 while the average is 3.71 for non-native English speakers. There is no significant difference between both groups, $F(1, 26) = 2.31$, $p < .14$.

Our results indicate that the shared space in the social learning network in relation to motivating content implies that the students' language is productive and sufficient enough for communication and collaboration. This space could be described as an *affinity space* (Gee, 2004). Deriving from Lave & Wenger's (1991) concept of communities of practice, Gee's (2004) concept of *affinity space* is defined as a "place or set of places where people can affiliate with others based primarily on shared activities, interests, and goals, not shared race, class, culture, ethnicity, or gender" (p. 73). Affinity spaces are thus spaces where people meet for a certain purpose to pursue a common endeavour or goal, which does not necessarily mean that they share or belong to a community of practice. We would argue that the concept of affinity spaces explains how communication in social media opens up possibilities of considering affordances while discussing and learning about specific content and using language, which in this environment, do not separate language competences into discrete skills. Recognising the interaction as affinity spaces implies that the content of the discussion is in focus, i.e., the students' presumptions about their own impact is crucial and whether they are English natives or not is not as important when it comes to developing an understanding of their own responsibilities regarding carbon footprints.

4. Conclusions

The basis of EE can be regarded as a challenge to the traditional schooling system based on the acquisition of factual knowledge brought to the classroom by the teacher in order to solve a problem with an already existing, single and correct solution. Accompanied by the CLIL approach, which "includes the learning of the target language as a subject in parallel to it being used as a vehicle for content learning" (Coyle, 2007, p. 552), the use of social media could be fruitful. The interlinked goals and the settings where language itself and the communication become meaningful for the students have, thus, in this study, shown to support both the content and the language learning.

Acknowledgements. This work is funded by the Knut and Alice Wallenberg foundation and has been carried out at the Linnaeus Centre for Research on Learning, Interaction and Mediated Communication in Contemporary Society (LinCS), and within The University of Gothenburg Learning and Media Technology Studio (LETStudio).

References

Blattner. G., & Lomicka, L. (2012). Facebook-ing and the Social Generation: A New Era of Language Learning. *Alsic, 15*(1). doi: 10.4000/alsic.2413

Bonderup-Dohn, N. (2009). Web 2.0: Inherent tensions and evident challenges for education. *Computer-Supported Collaborative Learning, 4*(3), 343-363. doi: 10.1007/s11412-009-9066-8

Coyle, D. (2007). Content and Language Integrated Learning: Towards a Connected Research Agenda for CLIL Pedagogies. *International Journal of Bilingual Education and Bilingualism, 10*(5), 543-562.

Eurydice. (2006). *Content and Language Integrated Learning (CLIL) at School in Europe*. Eurydice European Unit. Retrieved from http://www.eurydice.org

Gee, J. P. (2004). *Situated Language and Learning: A critique of traditional schooling*. New York: Routledge.

Lave, J., & Wenger, E. (1991). *Situated learning: legitimate peripheral participation*. Cambridge, MA: Cambridge University Press.

Marsh, D. (Ed.). (2002). *CLIL/EMILE - The European dimension: Actions, trends and foresight potential public services contract DG EAC*. European Commission.

Marsh, D. (2008). Language awareness and CLIL. In J. Cenoz & N. H. Hornberger (Eds.), *Encyclopedia of Language and Education* (pp. 233-246). New York: Springer Science+Business Media LLC.

Thorne, S. (2009). 'Community', semiotic flows, and mediated contribution to activity. *Language Teaching, 42*(1), 81-94. doi: 10.1017/S0261444808005429

United Nations of Education Scientific and Cultural Organisation (UNESCO). (1975). *The International Workshop on Environmental Education Final Report, Belgrade, Yugoslavia*. Paris: UNESCO/UNEP.

UNIVERSITY OF GOTHENBURG

Can Apple's iPhone Help to Improve English Pronunciation Autonomously? State of the App

Jonás Fouz González[*]

Departamento de Filología Inglesa, Universidad de Murcia, Campus de la Merced, 30001, Murcia, Spain[**]

Abstract. This paper is part of a larger project that examines some of the best-selling iPhone apps designed to learn English pronunciation. Informed by the literature on pronunciation teaching/acquisition, Computer Assisted Pronunciation Teaching (CAPT), Computer Assisted Language Learning (CALL) and Mobile-learning (M-learning), it provides a critical evaluation of the strengths and limitations of iPhone apps designed to improve the user's English pronunciation autonomously. The language learning potential of the apps is weighed up, appraising the aspects of pronunciation addressed by each app (individual phonemes, stress, intonation, et cetera). The paper concludes that iPhone apps have a great potential to practise and improve certain aspects of English pronunciation, such as sound discrimination, the learning of English phonemes, or the pronunciation of individual words, and it explores prospective improvement of existing apps in the future. The paper identifies feedback as one of the main limitations of current apps, while acknowledging that these limitations could be overcome relatively easily with existent technology. It also shows directions for future development of iPhone apps for pronunciation teaching so far neglected, such as the teaching of suprasegmental features or communicative practice.

Keywords: English pronunciation, m-learning, language learning, computer assisted language learning, computer assisted pronunciation teaching, mobile phone applications.

1. Introduction

Pronunciation is one of the most challenging aspects of language to master for language learners, given that it entails not only mental capacities but also psycho-motor and perceptual abilities (MacCarthy, 1978, p. 2; Witt & Young, 1997, p. 1).

Because pronunciation is such a demanding competence, and since it is often compromised in the classroom due to time constraints, technologies seem to be the

---

[*] Contact author: j.fouzgonzalez@um.es

[**] Refer to Rafael Monroy or Jose A.Mompeán.

In L. Bradley & S. Thouësny (Eds.), *CALL: Using, Learning, Knowing, EUROCALL Conference, Gothenburg, Sweden, 22-25 August 2012, Proceedings* (pp. 81-87). © Research-publishing.net Dublin 2012

ideal support for pronunciation teaching. CAPT enhances presentation styles and makes materials more 'psychologically accessible' (Pennington, 1996, p. 1), it provides private, stress-free environments which allow unlimited tries and different types of output with different voices and models (Godwin-Jones, 2009, p. 5), as well as the possibility to access virtually unlimited input and to address individual problems (Busà, 2008, p. 165; Neri, Cucchiarini, Strik, & Boves, 2002, p. 1), or the provision of immediate feedback without needing the physical proximity of a teacher (Erben, Ban, & Castañeda, 2009, p. 74).

Today's smart phones are a sort of Swiss-army-knife that proffer countless possibilities, ranging from reading emails to tracking a run via GPS. Thus, why not use them to learn English pronunciation? I have focused on Apple's *iPhone* because it is the one with the widest range of apps devised to tech pronunciation.

2. State of the app

What makes smart phones so versatile is the number of 'apps' at their disposal which add new functions to the phone. However, there seems to be a shortage of apps dealing with English pronunciation. As Colpaert (2004) points out, in the history of CALL, hype has only been achieved when amateurs, not trained professionals, have been able to develop their own applications.

Apps devoted to teaching pronunciation can be divided in two groups: those devised to learn some aspect of pronunciation and those that function as reference tools.

2.1. Reference apps
Some of these apps allow users to look up the pronunciation of a number of words and sentences and hear them pronounced, such as **Pronounce English AZ**, **HowJsay**, **English as it is broken** or **FORVO**; while others, like **iPron**, include a phonemic chart with the symbols and their pronunciation. Some even allow users to record their own pronunciation. Nevertheless, they do not incorporate any activities or practice, nor do users receive feedback on their performance.

2.2. Pronunciation training apps
These apps teach some aspects of English pronunciation and usually provide a range of activities to practice. The six apps analysed here pursue different goals. Besides fostering sound discrimination, **English File Pronunciation, Phonetic Focus** and **Sounds** teach the sounds of English with their phonemic symbols, possible spellings and pronunciations, while **Pronunciation Power** and **Enunciation** focus on articulation, and **Clear Speech** deals with discrimination of final sounds, word stress and syllable awareness.

The first three apps introduce the symbols with interactive sound charts which demonstrate their pronunciation in different positions (therefore showing their possible distributions too), and in *EFP*, also in sentences. *EFP* only has two activities, one for sound discrimination and another one to check users' knowledge of the symbols (Figure 1). Just like *CS* and *Sounds*, it keeps a record of users' scores so that they can concentrate on areas they may need to reinforce.

Figure 1.

PF is the app with the widest variety of activities and presentation styles. It includes four tools to learn the sounds and eight activities to practise, such as sound discrimination exercises, tasks aimed at finding missing phonemes, reading transcriptions aloud, or spotting mistakes in phonemic transcriptions (Figure 2). However, the questions always appear in the same order.

Figure 2.

Sounds incorporates three types of activities (Figure 3): *read* (users read phonemic transcriptions and write their orthographic forms), *write* (users read words and transcribe them phonemically), and *listen* (users listen to words and transcribe them phonemically). It is the app that allows for more user control. Users can select: the model of English (British or American), the particular phonemes they want to practise with, the number of questions, and even choose between three minutes or three lives to complete the game. Moreover, it is the only app that offers the option of buying more packages with extra words and sentences.

Figure 3.

Enunciation and ***Pronunciation Power*** have a different goal; they concentrate on production and illustrate how to articulate English sounds through videos and animations (Figure 4). Moreover, they include recordings of a range of words with the sounds in different positions. ***Enunciation*** also contains the sounds in sentences and it allows users to record their voice. However, even though their aim is to help learners to pronounce the sounds, they do not incorporate any means by which users can truly 'practise' what they produce, nor do they provide any feedback on their performance.

Pronunciation Power, while not targeting phonemes as such, does make use of phonemic symbols. ***Enunciation***, on the other hand, illustrates the pronunciation of /iː/ under the label of "long E", or /eː/ as "A-2", for instance, mixing orthographic spelling with phonemic symbols (Figure 4 on the right). As Pennington (1994) recommends, approaches that encourage equivalence through orthographic or simplified phonemic representations of the L2 sounds should be avoided, since they invite interference with L1 sounds. Reading "long-E" will not mean the same to a Spanish speaker than to an English speaker, for example.

Finally, ***Clear Speech*** is the only app which addresses suprasegmental features. It incorporates two sections devoted to practising sound discrimination of final sounds, one for word stress, and another one for syllable awareness (Figure 5).

Figure 4.

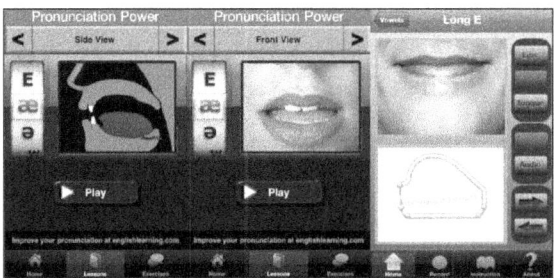

As for the activities dealing with final sounds, ***ball toss*** is a sound discrimination game in which users are presented two minimal pairs below a pin and they have to 'aim for the pin' they hear; and ***stop or flow*** works on the distinction between continuing and stopping sounds, illustrating this contrast with the metaphor of a tap which either closes with stopping sounds, or opens with continuing sounds (as articulators will when producing these).

The two activities that address suprasegmental features are: ***basketball*** and ***push the blob***. ***Basketball*** is devoted to helping users distinguish the number of syllables in words and sentences. Users listen to words and sentences and they have to 'bounce' a ball as many times as syllables they hear, which also helps users understand issues such as vowel reduction, linking and other connected speech phenomena. In ***Push the blob*** users have to recognise the stressed syllables and to 'push the blob through a hole that matches the correct stress pattern'.

Figure 5.

As for the model of English they enforce, apps like ***EFP*** or ***Sounds*** offer users the possibility to choose between British or American English, ***PF*** focuses on British English and the rest on American English. With regard to the type of feedback offered, it is usually a tick or a cross indicating whether the answer is correct or not. The correct answer is shown and sometimes a sound is also played. In the case of *PF,* some activities encourage users to read phonemic transcriptions aloud and hear the correct pronunciation afterwards, thus offering a different type of correction; however, none of the apps measure whether users actually 'pronounce' correctly.

One final issue that is paramount in this type of courseware is that the order of questions is not the same every time users access the app, since otherwise users could memorise the correct answer. Although *CS, EFP,* and *Sounds* do change the order of questions every time users enter the app, the correct response is always the same.

3. Suggestions for future app development

Despite the enormous potential that some of these apps show in order to help users 'understand' English sounds and phonemes – a pre-requisite and the first step towards self-evaluation and autonomous learning –, more attention should be devoted to suprasegmental features and their functions. Apps could include dialogues illustrating issues such as sentence stress or intonation, or video-quizzes to test a speaker's attitude. Furthermore, apps aimed at production should provide some type of feedback. Apps like *Dragon Dictation* could be improved and exploited to this end. This app works with speech recognition software which transcribes everything users say; thus, dialogues could be created where users speak to their phones and see their feedback written. If the machine understands them, the transcription will show what users say, otherwise, users should easily be able to spot what the problem was based on the transcription (e.g., *Can you pass me the Ben, please?* -instead of 'pen'). Users should *always* know why they have made the mistake and, if possible, be given suggestions for improvement (see Levis, 2007; Neri et al., 2002). SIRI, *iPhone's* virtual assistant, which also uses speech recognition, could be similarly exploited for communicative practice.

Additionally, activities could make use of authentic materials in order to check that users really understand what they learn; for instance, they could incorporate a function by which users listened to podcasts and had to look for certain sounds or pronunciation features (elisions, assimilations, etc.).

To conclude, simple explanations illustrating differences between the phonological system of English and that of the users' L1 might be useful, preferably reinforced with sound discrimination practice. Many users will assume that an English /t/ will be the same as a /t/ sound in their L1, or that intonation patterns convey the same information in both languages, when this is not necessarily the case.

Acknowledgements. I would like to thank Cambridge English Online Ltd., Cambridge University Press, English Computerized Learning Inc., Kevin Litton, Macmillan Publishers Ltd. and Oxford University Press for giving me permission to include screenshots of their apps in this paper.

References

Busà, M. G. (2008). New perspectives in teaching pronunciation. In A. Baldry, M. Pavesi, C. T. Torsello, & C. Taylor (Eds.), *From DIDACTAS to ECOLINGUA. An ongoing research project on translation and corpus linguistics* (pp. 165-82). Trieste: Università degli Studi di Trieste.

Colpaert, J. (2004). From courseware to coursewear? *Computer Assisted Language Learning, 17*(3-4), 261-266. doi: 10.1080/0958822042000319575

Erben, T., Ban, R., & Castañeda, M. (2009). *Teaching English Language Learners through Technology.* New York: Routledge.

Godwin-Jones, R. (2009). Emerging technologies speech tools and technologies. *Language Learning & Technology, 13*(3), 4-11.

Levis, J. (2007). Computer technology in teaching and researching pronunciation. *Annual Review of Applied Linguistics, 27*, 184-202. doi: 10.1017/S0267190508070098

MacCarthy, P. (1978). *The Teaching of Pronunciation.* Cambridge: Cambridge University Press.

Neri, A., Cucchiarini, C., Strik, H., & Boves, L. (2002). The pedagogy-technology interface in Computer-Assisted Pronunciation Training. *Computer-Assisted Language Learning, 15*(5), 441-467. doi: 10.1076/call.15.5.441.13473

Pennington, M. C. (1994). Recent Research in L2 Phonology: Implications for Practice. In J. Morley (Ed.), *Pronunciation Pedagogy and Theory: New Views, New Directions* (pp. 94-108). Alexandria, Va: TESOL Publications.

Pennington, M. C. (1996). The power of the computer in language education. In M.C. Pennington (Ed.), *The Power of CALL* (pp. 1-14). Houston, TX: Athelstan.

Witt, S. M., & Young, S. (1997). Computer-assisted pronunciation teaching based on automatic speech recognition. In *Proceedings of the International Conference on Language Teaching, Language Technology* (pp. 25-35). Groningen, Netherlands.

iPhone apps*

Clear Speech From the Start. (Version 1.01) [iPhone app]. Cambridge University Press. (2011).
English As It Is Broken. (Version 1.1) [iPhone app]. Singapore Press Holdings. (2010).
English File Pronunciation. (Version 1.1) [iPhone app]. Oxford University Press. (2012).
Enunciation. (Version 2.1). [iPhone app]. Kevin Litton. (2011).
Forvo English Pronunciations. (Version 1.1) [iPhone app]. Forvo Media SL. (2011).
Howjsay Pronunciation Dictionary. (Version 4.2) [iPhone app]. Consilium Software. (2009).
iPron. (Version 1.0) [iPhone app]. SoundsEnglish (2009).
Phonetic Focus. (Version 1.3) [iPhone app]. Cambridge English Online Ltd. (2010).
Pronounce English A-Z. (Version 1.2) [iPhone app]. Ahmet CEPNI. (2011).
Pronunciation Power. (Version 1.0.0) [iPhone app]. English Computerized Learning Inc. (2010).
Sounds: The pronunciation App. (Version 2.0.1) [iPhone app]. Macmillan Publishers Ltd. (2011).

---

* Retrieved from http://itunes.apple.com

UNIVERSITY OF
GOTHENBURG

About Collaboration, Interaction, and the Negotiation of Meaning in Synchronous Written Chats in L2-German

Christine Fredriksson*

Högskolan Dalarna/Dalarna University, Falun, Sweden

Abstract. In this paper I will show the preliminary findings from my study of the discourse in synchronous written chats performed by students who study modern German literature within their first term of German studies. The focus of the study is on learning strategies and discourse strategies and how the Swedish learners make use of them when chatting with students at the same level of proficiency (peer groups) and in groups with students who are native speakers of German/or Swedish speakers at a high level of L2-proficiency. The data was collected from four chat-sessions within the period of September 2011 to January 2012. Based on socio-cultural and cognitive SLA-theory, the study has its focus on the relationship between interaction and the possibilities for language learning in mixed groups and peer groups of L2-German learners. The main questions are: In which constellation, native speaker/non-native speaker vs. peer-groups, do L2 German students meet the best opportunities for producing meaningful and rich output? When and to what extent do they find opportunities for self-repair, using direct or indirect feedback from their collocutors as an expression for meta-linguistic consciousness of the students? Which strategies do they use to keep the communication going and to learn special features of the language?

Keywords: learning strategies, discourse, group dynamics, lexical variety, syntactical complexity.

1. Introduction

This paper is an introduction to an on-going research project on the interaction and communication in synchronous written chats and their influence on learning German as a foreign language in an academic literature course. The project started in September 2011 and is expected to be finished in August 2014. In this first part the focus is on the learners' participation in different formations and the instances of conscious attention to form or meaning (self-monitoring, corrective feedback, and repair) in the output. The

---

* Contact author: cfr@du.se

next step is to examine the discourse strategies and learner strategies to find out how the subjects create their discourse and how they pick up new L2-knowledge through the negotiation of meaning.

From a socio-cultural view (see Vygotsky, 1978), a learner benefits from the interaction with a more competent speaker because the latter puts him/her forward in the learning process. In a conversation with a native speaker on the other hand, a learner always has an inferior position because he/she lacks the linguistic knowledge to produce adequate utterances in the L2. Ellis (2008) suggests that this will lead to less learner participation, and also restrict the learner to a limited range of speech acts.

The collaboration and the social practice within an interconnected community is seen by researchers such as Goodyear, Banks, Hodgson, and McConnell (2004) as a positive factor for learning because of the special affordances (see Gibson, 1979) the learner meets in this context. As Crystal (2001) has pointed out, synchronous written chats can be placed on both sides of the speech and writing divide because on the one hand they have certain elements in common with oral face-to-face-conversation, and on the other hand, with written language. Because of the written language in chats the learners have the opportunity to go back to items that have been discussed before. They can use this information in their own production and thereby pay attention to language items (see Warschauer & Kern, 2000). This, from a language processing view, is important for acquiring new skills. What a learner pays attention to highly depends on social context and the situation in which the interaction is taking place and this will have influence on the learning outcome (see Fredriksson, 2006).

Although we can see an increasing interest in computer-mediated communication for language learning (CMCL), there is still little knowledge about how it works for a learner of an L2 (see Lamy & Hampel, 2007). First, the intention of this study is therefore to find out how the learners´ interactions and language productions are influenced by the constellation of speakers in a chat, and secondly, which opportunities for language learning they offer to the learner.

2. Method

2.1. Data-collection

The data has been collected in four chat-sessions from 30 students of a literary course within their first term of academic German studies. The students have different language backgrounds and different levels of language proficiency in German: 8 subjects are native speakers of German and are living in Sweden (L1G), 14 subjects are Swedish students who have been exposed to L2-German for a short time (L1S) (they have a level comparable to A2/B1 in the Common European Framework of Reference for Languages), and 8 subjects are Swedish students who have lived in a German speaking country for a long time and have almost native speaker competence

(L2G). The students usually meet in Adobe Connect every fortnight to orally discuss specific questions concerning the literature they have read. For the purposes of this study, they performed four discussions in MSN/Adobe Connect by chatting in groups of mainly three, but sometimes also two or four participants. The constellation of learners, competent and native speakers varied in each chat. The students prepared the questions in advance. This gave them not only the opportunity for pre-planning the language they used but also the possibility to use the ready-made answers and paste them directly in their chat. This has to be taken into account for the analysis of when the learners' focus is on the task.

The groups:
- A: L1S/L1S/L1S, equal L1, homogenous group (9 L1S-subjects);
- B: L1S/L1S/L1G, unequal L1, unequal competence (4 L1S-subjects);
- C: L1S/L1S/L2G, equal L1, unequal competence (14 L1S-subjects);
- D: L1S/L1G/L1G, native speaker dominance (5 L1S-subjects);
- E: L1S/L1G/L2G, learner dominance (4 L1S-subjects);
- F: L1S/L2G/L2G, competent speaker dominance (2 L1S-subjects).

2.2. Data analysis

Based on a model which has been developed by Henrici (1995) to analyse the relationship between the interaction and L2-acquistition in traditional oral language discourse, I used a modified model to analyse the discourse in written chats. Following Henrici's (1995) model, I used a combination of conversation analysis and discourse analysis to find out how the more or less competent speakers of L2-German and native speakers of German organized the discourse (strategies for discourse management and discourse repair) in different constellations and which opportunities they created for language learning. I used quantitative and qualitative analysis methods to describe the discourse in terms of the L1S-students':

Participation in the different chat-groups:
- Rate of turns per chat;
- Rate of sentences, complex sentences per answer
  (subordinated and coordinated clauses);
- Rate of words per answer/chat;
- Strategies of discourse management/discourse repair: introduction and change of topics, questions for clarification, other corrections and self-repair.

Learning strategies:
- Cognitive strategies: self-monitoring as an expression of the learners' attention to form or meaning, imitation and reproduction of words or structures;
- Socio-affective strategies: expressions for cooperation (e.g., smileys).

3. Discussion

3.1. Participation
The results from the quantitative analysis indicate that the average rate of the L1S-learners' turns is higher in groups of three learners (A: 33%) or two learners and one competent speaker of L2 German (C: 32%). In groups of L1S-learners and one or two native speakers, the average rate is lower: 28% for B and 26% for D. Interestingly, there is not much difference between the homogenous L1S-learner groups (A) or groups with one native speaker and one competent L2 German speaker (E: 30%). This indicates that the presence of a native speaker seems to be less relevant for the learners' participation when they and a competent speaker share the same background and are in the majority. It is important to mention that these results are based on cross-sectional data from L1S-learners in the different formations and that the comparison is of limited value because of the various sizes of the compared groups. There is also a significant individual variation between the learners due to certain factors, e.g., the participants' interest in the book, in the task or in the other participants.

3.2. Language complexity
The analysis of the frequency of words and sentences in the learners' answers show that the presence of one or two native speakers (B or D) seem to have a positive influence on the learners' language production. They produce more words (29% or 36% of their answers contain 11 to 30 words) and more sentences (30% or 38% of their answers contain 2 to 4 sentences), compared with homogenous learner groups (23% for both categories). The rate of empty answers (6%) or answers without sentences (42%) is highest in homogenous learner groups. In formations with two native speakers (D), the learners also use more complex sentences (39.9% have subordinate or coordinate clauses) and with a higher accuracy rate (74% compared to 65.3% in homogenous L1S-groups).

3.3. Monitoring and repair
The first results of the study indicate that there is very little monitoring in the Swedish students' discourse and when it occurs the learners will not get feedback in a way that helps to develop L2-knowledge. Wrong hypotheses about grammatical rules are seldom corrected.

3.4. Formulas
I have found that the learners often rely on language items which they may have learned as formulas, especially when they are chatting in unequal constellations. These formulas can be characterized as units containing phrases like *ich mag 'I like'*, *ja* + lexical word (wirklich, Drama, klar) or partly analyzed features like *kann/muss* + uninflected V2 (muss sein, kann sein). This helps them to keep the discourse going.

4. Conclusions

To summarize my preliminary findings, on the one hand, the common language background in homogenous L1S-learner groups (A) or groups with one competent speaker of the L2 (C) seem to enhance the learners' participation. On the other hand, the presence of a native speaker appears to push the learners to produce more words and complex sentences. Both aspects have to be taken into consideration when forming collaborative groups in chats. Although the learners will not participate as much in unequal formations, they probably will use the language more creatively and with greater correctness. This may in the end further the acquisition of the L2. There are still many questions left, as they require more detailed analysis of the material. Conclusions from this preliminary study are:
- Instructions on how to construct the interaction in order to facilitate the learners' participation seem to be important;
- The little amount of conscious monitoring indicates that learning cannot be based on this strategy;
- Further attention has to be spent on learners' strategies, on formulaic speech and creative language use.

References

Crystal, D. (2001). *Language and the Internet*. Cambridge: Cambridge University Press.

Ellis, R. (2008). *The Study of Second Language Acquisition* (2nd ed.). Oxford: Oxford University Press.

Fredriksson, C. (2006). *Erwerbsphasen, Entwicklungssequenzen und Erwerbsreihenfolge. Zum Erwerb der deutschen Verbalmorphologie durch schwedische Schülerinnen und Schüler.* Uppsala: Acta Universitatis Upsaliensis.

Gibson, J. J. (1979). *The Ecological Approach to Visual Perceptions.* Bostob, MA: Houghton Mifflin.

Goodyear, P., Banks, S., Hodgson, V., & McConnell, D. (2004). Research on Networked Learning: An Owerview. In P. Goodyear, S. Banks, V. Hodgson, & D. McConnell (Eds.), *Advances in Research on Networked Learning* (pp. 1-9). Boston, MA: Kluwer.

Henrici, G. (1995). *Spracherwerb durch Interaktion? Eine Einführung in die fremdsprachenerwerbsspezifische Diskursanalyse*. Hohengehren: Schneider Verlag.

Lamy, M., & Hampel, R. (2007). *Online Communication in Language Learning and Teaching.* Palgrave: Macmillan.

Vygotsky, L. S. (1978). *Mind in Society: The Development of Higher Psychological Processes.* Cambridge, MA: Harvard University Press.

Warschauer, M, & Kern, R. (Eds.). (2000). *Network-based Language Teaching: Concepts and Practice.* Cambridge: Cambridge University Press.

UNIVERSITY OF GOTHENBURG

Enhancing Metacognitive Awareness on First and Second Language Reading and Writing Mediated by Social Networking Websites

Eri Fukuda[a]*, Hironobu Okazaki[b], and Shinichi Hashimoto[a]

a. Soka University, Hachioji-shi, Tokyo, Japan
b. Akita Prefectural University,Tsuchiya, Yurihonjo-shi, Akita, Japan

Abstract. The purpose of this research is to study how second language (L2) learners' metacognitive knowledge on first and second language reading and writing would differ according to L2 language proficiency levels. Extending the study conducted by Carrell (1991) and Victori (1999), this research draws on interview data collected from Japanese learners of English. The interview data indicated that some effective L1 metacognitive knowledge could transfer across languages as L2 language proficiency improves; however, it appears that most learners tend to focus on language rather than content in L2 tasks. The study further explores the possibility of online reading together with sharing summaries on a social networking website to improve learners' perception of literacy skills.

Keywords:EFL reading, EFL writing, transferability, metacognitive knowledge, social networking website.

1. Introduction

Influenced by first language (L1) research on reading-writing relationships, recent English language education has highlighted the connection between these two literacy skills. The assumption underlying this trend is that cognitive knowledge is shared by domains of reading and writing (Fitzgerald & Shanahan, 2000). This shared cognitive domain was also hypothesized to function as a basic competence from which literacy skills stem regardless of language in the interdependence hypothesis as advocated by Cummins (1994).

In the field of L2 reading research, Clarke (1980) introduced the short circuit hypothesis, which argued that the transfer of reading skills from first to second language can be restricted by limited L2 language proficiency, which has not reached

---

* Contact author: efukuda@soka.ac.jp

the threshold level where the transfer begins to occur. Regarding this intervention of language proficiency, Alderson (1984) asked whether poor L2 reading skills were due to poor L1 reading skills or due to low L2 language proficiency. Carrell (1991) examined this issue and found both L1 reading skills and language proficiency were critical elements to predict L2 reading skills.

In contrast, L2 writing research on the transferability of the skills across languages has remained inconclusive. Nevertheless, according to Grabe (2001), the transferability of L2 writing skills is also determined by the L2 threshold level. The author pointed out that this notion of the L2 threshold level was versatile in L2 writing as well. Moreover, theoretically, the transferability of writing skills could be supported by Flower and Hayes's (1981) cognitive process theory of writing when combined with the interdependence hypothesis (Cummins, 1994). The authors described the process of writing in terms of the cognitive functions, and this skill could be shared across different languages if Cummins's (1994) hypothesis was valid. The result of Edelsky's (1982) research empirically supported Cummins; whereas, Carson, Carrell, Silberstein, Kroll, and Kuehn (1990) revealed that the interlingual transfer of writing skills is more difficult compared to that of reading. In order to further understand the L1 and L2 reading and writing relationships, Japanese learners of English were surveyed in this study.

2. Method

2.1. Participants

In the current study, semi-structured interviews were conducted within a cross-sectional design. The data were collected from two private universities which are located in Tokyo and Okayama. The participants were 11 Japanese undergraduate students including four elementary, two intermediate, and five advanced level learners. They were purposefully selected based on their Test of English for International Communication (TOEIC) scores.

2.1.1. Procedure

A questionnaire inquiring metacognitive knowledge on reading was adapted from Hashiguchi (2002), which was a Japanese translation of a questionnaire devised by Carrell (1989), and this questionnaire was altered to interview questions. Because the purpose of this study was to investigate the L1 and L2 reading strategies employed by the students, not to assess the degree to which the participants were able to manipulate the strategies, the questions were asked as open-ended questions except the statements on confidence describing the proficient reading behaviors. Furthermore, in order to inquire into metacognitive knowledge on L1 and L2 writing, the present study modified the interview questions developed by Victori (1999). The interviews were recorded with the consent of the respondents and transcribed.

3. Discussion

The interview data showed that the respondents at elementary level had barely acquired effective reading and writing strategies in L1 or L2. On the other hand, the intermediate and advanced level learners had obtained some effective metacognitive knowledge on both reading and writing in L1, but most of them seemed to be unable to transfer these strategies to L2 tasks. Therefore, as Clarke (1980) noted, the threshold level is not as definitive as can be determined by the standardized test.

In Carrell's (1989) study, proficient readers utilized the global reading strategies focusing on content while poor readers depended on the local reading strategies focusing on linguistic information. Also, the author found that the higher L2 language proficiency was, the higher the level of the strategies employed. The present study followed this result; however, even though the level of strategies used by the advanced level group was higher compared to the lower L2 proficiency level groups, most participants reported that they would switch from the global to local strategies when they read in L2. This could be explained by the strong influence of Japan's English education at secondary level, which primarily focuses on grammar instruction and translation. Because the main goal of the education is often to pass university entrance exams, assumingly, learners were trained to use local strategies in order to precisely answer exam questions but were less likely to develop global strategies concurrently.

In regard to writing, Victori (1999) found that the proficient writers were more aware of their writing problems, and their knowledge of the requirements of writing tasks was broader and more accurate. Also, the effective writers responded that they would plan before writing and revise the content even after completing the essay. Compared to this observation, the intermediate and advanced level participants of the current study seemed to have developed some effective writing metacognitive knowledge in L1, but not in L2. The interview data showed the metacognitive awareness on text organization and the perception of a proficient piece of writing were the only knowledge shared across languages.

Moreover, metacognitive knowledge relating to causes to stop writing and revising process were contrastive across languages. The learners reported that they would stop to think what to write next, which is the process presented in Flower and Hayes (1981) while they would stop writing in order to examine language use in L2 writing. The respondents also indicated that they would review the content when they revise in L1, which is a proficient writing habit (Krashen, 1984), but they would fall into the confusion of editing and revising in L2 composition. These results might also be because of Japan's English education. As is often the case with Japanese undergraduate students (Okabe, 2004), all the respondents revealed they had never received writing instruction in L2, nor had they been assigned to write an essay or report in English. Therefore, they were provided with few opportunities to focus on global message in composing or revising.

Comparing different L2 language proficiency level groups, for the elementary level respondents, limited L1 linguistic knowledge in addition to limited L2 linguistic knowledge and the lack of experience in writing instruction seemed to have contributed to poor metacognitive knowledge on both skills in both languages. According to Krashen's (1984) theory, although the author only described L1 writers, these learners could be categorized as *remedial writers* in L1 and L2, who lack language input and writing instruction in either language. Therefore, these learners had not acquired the language, neither in L1 nor L2, to express their abstract ideas nor the metacognitive knowledge on structure to convey their thoughts in accordance with the conventions of academic writing. On the other hand, the intermediate and advanced learners could be categorized as *blocked writers* in L1, who have received input but not writing instruction, and as remedial writers in L2.

Therefore, writing instruction is necessary for any English proficiency level learners in order for them to effectively communicate their thoughts. In addition, for lower proficiency level students, input in both L1 and L2 should be offered through reading as they need the language to verbalize their abstract concepts into language; whereas, input in L2 might suffice in order for higher proficiency level students to improve their L2 reading and writing skills and metacognitive knowledge. Although instructors tend to focus on students' L2 language proficiency, it might be necessary to be aware that students' L1 language proficiency could also account for their lower success in L2 learning.

4. Conclusions

As a means to implement the activities to expose learners to input in both L1 and L2, the Internet would be a useful tool in reading and writing instruction. The present paper suggests assigning students to read news articles in L1 and L2 online on the same topic and to write summaries in L1 as Mason and Krashen (1997) found that summary writing in L1 improved students' reading and writing skills. Furthermore, sharing summaries and articles through a social networking website might reinforce instruction. Although finding articles written in students' L1 might be difficult for instructors who speak another language than that of students, the Internet allows students to look for articles themselves, and the instructor could easily see what articles students are reading if they are posted on the social networking website. Moreover, reading the articles on the same topic might help students to compare text organization, and this exposure to actual texts could provide more concrete examples which enrich what they learn in the classroom.

The interview data suggested that the participants were inclined to be preoccupied with bottom-up information when reading English texts; thus, their effective L1 reading strategies should be highlighted. In addition, as Carson et al. (1990) noted that the writing instructor should not assume the automatic transfer of L1 to L2 writing skills, students need opportunities to recognize their L1 and L2 writing strategies to compare the similarities and differences of their metacognitive knowledge. In order to accomplish that, cognitive load in L2 reading needs to be lowered. Through reading both L1 and L2 texts, the L1 text might serve as a springboard for comprehension of L2 text and induce metacognitive awareness to evolve. The researchers of the present study have implemented these activities, and validity of this approach should be explored in the future research.

Acknowledgements. The authors would like to thank all colleagues and participants who contributed to this research.

References

Alderson, J. C. (1984). Reading in a foreign language: A reading problem or a language problem? In J. C. Alderson, & A. H. Urquhart (Eds.), *Reading in a foreign language* (pp. 1-24). London: Longman.

Carrell, L. P. (1989). Metacognitive awareness and second language reading. *The Modern Language Journal, 73*(2), 121-134.

Carrell, L. P. (1991). Second language reading: Reading ability or language proficiency? *Applied Linguistics, 12*(2), 159-179.

Carson, J. E., Carrell, P. L., Silberstein, S., Kroll, B., & Kuehn, P. (1990). Reading-writing relationships in first and second language. *TESOL Quarterly, 24*(2), 245-266.

Clarke, M. A. (1980). The Short Circuit Hypothesis of ESL reading: Or when language competence interferes with reading performance. *The Modern Language Journal, 64*(2), 203-209.

Cummins, J. (1994). Primary language instruction and the education of language minority students. In C. F. Leyba (Ed.), *Schooling and language minority students* (2nd ed.) (pp. 3-46). Los Angeles: Legal Books Distributing.

Edelsky, C. (1982). Writing in a bilingual program: The relation of L1 and L2 texts. *TESOL Quarterly, 16*(2), 211-228.

Fitzgerald, J., & Shanahan, T. (2000). Reading and writing relations and their development. *Education Psychologist, 35*(1), 39-50.

Flower, L., & Hayes, J. R. (1981). A cognitive process theory of writing. *National Council of Teachers of English, 32*(4), 365-387.

Grabe, W. (2001). Reading-writing relations: Theoretical perspectives and instructional practices. In D. Belcher, & A. Hirvela (Eds.), *Linking literacies: Perspectives on L2 reading-writing connections* (pp. 15-47). Ann Arbor: The University of Michigan Press.

Hashiguchi, M. (2002). Awareness of reading strategies and reading proficiency in EFL. *Kanoya taiiku daigaku gakujutsu kenkyuu kiyou, [Proceedings of the National Institute of Fitness and Sports in Kanoya], 27,* 29-41.

Krashen, S. (1984). *Writing: Research, theory and applications.* Oxford: Pergamon Institute of English.

Mason, B., & Krashen, S. (1997). Extensive reading in English as a foreign language. *System, 25*(1), 91-102.

Okabe, J. (2004). The nature of L2 writing by Japanese learners of English. In V. Makarova, & T. Rodgers (Eds.), *English language teaching: The case of Japan* (pp. 181-201). Munich: Lincom Europa.

Victori, M. (1999). An analysis of writing knowledge in EFL composing: A case study of two effective and two less effective writers. *System, 27*(4), 537-555. doi:10.1016/S0346-251X(99)00049-4

UNIVERSITY OF
GOTHENBURG

Automatic Correction of Adverb Placement Errors for CALL

Marie Garnier*

Equipe Cultures Anglo-Saxonnes, Université Toulouse Le Mirail, Toulouse, France
Institut de Recherche en Informatique de Toulouse, Université Paul Sabatier, Toulouse, France

Abstract. According to recent studies, there is a persistence of adverb placement errors in the written productions of francophone learners and users of English at an intermediate to advanced level. In this paper, we present strategies for the automatic detection and correction of errors in the placement of manner adverbs, using linguistic-based natural language processing (NLP) techniques in the <TextCoop> platform. Feedback messages are generated as a complement to corrections. We use grammatical information as well as the results of grammaticality judgement tests performed by native English speakers in order to predict correct positions for manner adverbs used as verb phrase (VP) modifiers or clause adjuncts. Detection and correction strategies are based on detection patterns and rewriting rules. The system has a precision of 87.23%, and a recall of 79.61% on a corpus of learner productions and emails. We discuss these results and present the limits of the system. Finally, we introduce the protocol used for the generation of feedback messages.

Keywords: adverb placement, grammar checking, error patterns, corrective feedback.

1. Background

The canonical positions of adverbs in English, especially when used as modifiers in the verb phrase or adjuncts in the clause, overlap only partially with the canonical positions of adverbs in French. Such partial overlap may give rise to syntactic transfer in francophone learners and users of English. According to Osborne (2008), there is indeed a persistence of adverb placement errors in the productions of English learners at the post-intermediate level, especially among those whose native languages accept Verb-Adverb-Object structures, like French. These conclusions are confirmed by the analysis of errors in our corpus, which is composed of 100,000 words of texts written by users of English with L1 French, and includes scientific productions, emails and learner productions at B2-C1 level from the *International Corpus of Learner English*

---

* Contact author: garnier@irit.fr

In L. Bradley & S. Thouësny (Eds.), *CALL: Using, Learning, Knowing*, EUROCALL Conference, Gothenburg, Sweden, 22-25 August 2012, Proceedings (pp. 99-103). © Research-publishing.net Dublin 2012

v. 2 (Granger, Dagneaux, Meunier, & Paquot, 2009). Adverb placement errors are the fourth most frequent error type in our corpus. Errors concerning the placement of manner adverbs in modifier or adjunct function account for 40% of adverb placement errors. A survey of existing grammar checkers for English revealed that adverb placement is one of the blind spots of such systems, whether created for commercial or research purposes.

The aim of the research presented in this paper is to design strategies for the automatic detection and correction of adverb placement errors produced by francophone learners and users of English at an intermediate to advanced level (i.e., *CEFRL** levels B2-C1). We focus on manner adverbs used as modifiers in the verb phrase or adjuncts in the clause. Adverb placement errors are automatically detected and corrected using linguistic-based NLP techniques in the framework of <TextCoop> (Saint-Dizier, 2011), a logic-based platform for language processing implemented in Prolog.

2. Correcting adverb placement errors using linguistic-based techniques

2.1. Predicting correct adverb placement

In a previous article (Garnier, 2012), we highlighted the fact that adverb placement was governed by a variety of factors, including the meaning and scope of the adverb and the syntactic structure of the VP or clause. There is a lack of precise and synthetic rules about adverb placement, by the own admission of the authors of authoritative works on grammar or adverbs (Guimier, 1988; Huddleston & Pullum, 2002; Quirk, Greenbaum, Leech, & Svartvik, 1985).

As a way to gain more insight into adverb placement in specific configurations, we asked three native English speakers to complete a grammaticality judgment test comprising 56 sentences organized in 13 sets illustrating a range of different possible positions for a manner adverb. English speakers were asked to decide whether the position of a manner adverb in a sentence seemed correct, grammatically correct but unnatural, or incorrect. They were also asked to identify the best position among the 3 to 5 propositions. Semantic variation in the adverb and the sentences was kept to a minimum. Complete agreement between the three English speakers was reached in only 36 % of cases; however, there was agreement as to the best position for the adverb in 69 % of cases.

2.2. Implementation of detection and correction strategies

The system is based on detection patterns and rewriting rules written in Prolog. We designed 22 detection patterns, each of which is associated with 1 to 3 different rewriting rules to enable the system to issue several propositions when there is more

---

* Common European Framework of Reference for Languages

than one possible correction. Table 1 presents a schematized example of a pattern and its associated rewriting rules.

Table 1. Schematized representation of a pattern and rewriting rules

Error	*Carefully she opened the window.
Detection pattern	ADV NP1 (AUX) (AUX) VLEX (PREP) NP2
Rewriting rules	1. Adv / [comma] / NP1 / (Aux) / (Aux) / Vlex / (Prep) / NP2 2. NP1 / (Aux) / (Aux) / Adv / Vlex / (Prep) / NP2 3. NP1 / (Aux) / (Aux) / Vlex / (Prep) / NP2 / Adv
Corrected sentence	1. Carefully, she opened the window. 2. She carefully opened the window. 3. She opened the window carefully.

Each pattern is designed to describe as many syntactic configurations as possible, such as the presence of auxiliaries and prepositions, or the use of adverbs in non-finite sentences. Specific patterns have also been created in order to accommodate for modifications that influence adverb placement, such as modifications of the main adverb with very, too, and more (e.g., *She carefully opened the window* vs. **She more carefully opened the window*), and the presence of a long noun phrase (NP) after the lexical verb (e.g., *She carefully opened the window that she had repaired the day before* vs. **She opened the window that she had repaired the day before carefully*). As can be seen from the example given in Table 1, the system also deals with errors linked to an unnatural use of punctuation.

3. Evaluation

3.1. Results of testing

The system was first evaluated on an 80,000-word corpus of well-formed English composed of British and American online newspaper articles, British and American blog posts, and scientific publications from English native speakers. The rate of false positives was inferior to 4%, with most false positives being due to terms belonging to several grammatical categories (e.g., *purchase*, n. vs *purchase*, v.), which is a frequent issue when dealing with the English language. When such false positives are not taken into account, the rate falls to 1.5%.

Next, the system was evaluated on a modified 10,000-word corpus of English learner productions and emails written by English users. One of the challenges of researching new methods for automatic grammar checking is the lack of usable learner/user productions with the appropriate proportion of errors to make evaluation both significant and manageable (Foster & Andersen, 2009). In order to overcome this problem, we asked a francophone English user to introduce manner adverbs in existing English learner productions, producing correct and incorrect sentences.

For the first correction proposed, the system has a precision of 87.23% and a recall of 79.61%. When a second correction is proposed, the precision for this proposition is only of 70.15% (recall is irrelevant in this case).

The patterns and rewriting rules that deal with default configurations (i.e., adverb without modification by another adverb, in a finite sentence with an object NP of less than 5 words) are used in 83% of all cases. Among "default" patterns, the pattern dealing with Verb-Adverb-Object errors is used in 48% of all cases.

3.2. Limits of the system

A study of the causes for non-detection, incorrect propositions or false positives shows that the system is still limited by the number of syntactic configurations that it can recognize. Embedded clauses and verb phrases with more than one complement are common issues that can be solved by the extension of the number of configurations described in the patterns. Reducing false positives and incorrect propositions that result from homonymy and semantic incompatibility (e.g., *They are convinced of their righteousness blindly*) is a much more challenging task that requires a specific in-depth study.

Since patterns rely on the description of segments of text, the system is also limited by the fact that the sentences it processes need to be mostly grammatical. However, this is a minor problem when dealing with intermediate to advanced francophone learner/ user productions. In addition, patterns use syntactic categories (e.g., adverb, verb, preposition) instead of actual words, which allows for a margin of errors in the input text, such as number or subject-verb agreement, ungrammatical choice of auxiliary, or ungrammatical passive and aspectual constructions.

4. Feedback messages

The grammar-checking strategies presented in this paper are designed to be part of a CALL system enabling intermediate to advanced learners and users of English to benefit from grammatical information about their errors. Previous studies on the use of corrective feedback in CALL have shown that meta-linguistic feedback combined with highlighting have positive effects on uptake and learning (Heift, 2004; Heift & Schulze, 2007). We have designed a protocol for creating feedback messages that integrates these feedback types. It is based on a study of the feedback offered by existing grammar checkers and includes the five following steps (Garnier, 2011):
- **Error marking:** error is highlighted;
- **Error diagnosis:** possible mention of error type, description of the erroneous segment, information as to the nature and/or causes of the error;
- **Meta-linguistic feedback:** exposition of the relevant grammar/style rules;
- **Remediation:** instructions enabling the user to successfully correct the segment;
- **Illustrations:** examples of the correct use the grammar/style rules in question.

This protocol is portable to other error types. Feedback messages are written in the user's native language, i.e., French, and can be adapted to the profile of the user. For example, learners receive the entire feedback message without the correction from the system in order to elicit self-correction, while users wishing to have more information about the different possibilities for correction can limit the feedback to steps 1 and 2. The implementation and evaluation of this step in the project is ongoing.

5. Conclusion

This paper has highlighted the various aspects that make correcting adverb placement errors both relevant and difficult. We have shown that the use of linguistic methods for automatic detection and correction relying on detection patterns and rewriting rules can yield satisfactory results at an intermediate stage, providing that the model used for patterns and rules is based on a synthesis of sound linguistic information. A protocol for the generation of corrective feedback messages has also been proposed, and awaits implementation and testing. Further research will look into the application of the same methods to the correction of errors linked to the use of nouns in modifier functions in noun phrases.

References

Foster, J., & Andersen, O. (2009). GenERRate: generating errors for use in grammatical error detection. *Proceedings of the NAACL Workshop on Innovative Use of NLP for Building Educational Applications.* Boulder, Colorado. Retrieved from http://www.computing.dcu.ie/~jfoster/resources/genERRate.html

Garnier, M. (2011). Explanation and corrective feedback in grammar checking systems. *Proceedings of the 6th International ExACt workshop at IJCAI'11* (pp. 81-90).

Garnier, M. (2012). Automatically correcting adverb placement errors in the writings of French users of English. *Procedia – Social and Behavioral Sciences, 34*, 59-63. doi: 10.1016/j.sbspro.2012.02.013

Granger, S., Dagneaux, E., Meunier, F., & Paquot, M. (Eds). (2009). *International Corpus of Learner English* v.2. Louvain La Neuve: Presses Universitaires de Louvain.

Guimier, C. (1988). *Syntaxe de l'adverbe anglais*. Lille: Presses Universitaires de Lille.

Heift, T. (2004). Corrective feedback and learner uptake in CALL. *ReCALL, 16*(2), 416-431.

Heift, T, & Schulze, M. (2007). *Errors and Intelligence in Computer-Assisted Language Learning: Parsers and Pedagogues.* New York: Routledge.

Huddleston, R., & Pullum, G. K. (2002). Adjectives and Adverbs. In R. Huddleston & G. K. Pullum (Eds), *The Cambridge Grammar of the English Language.* Cambridge: Cambridge University Press.

Osborne, J. (2008). Adverb placement in post-intermediate learner English: a contrastive study of learner corpora. In G. Gilquin, S. Papp, & M. B. Díez-Bedmar (Eds), *Linking up Contrastive Linguistics and Interlanguage Research* (pp. 127-146). Londres: Rodopi.

Quirk, R., Greenbaum, S., Leech, G., & Svartvik, J. (1985). *A Comprehensive Grammar of the English Language*. London: Pearson Longman.

Saint-Dizier, P. (2011). <TextCoop>, un analyseur de discours basé sur des grammaires logiques. *Proceedings of TALN'11*. Montpellier, France.

UNIVERSITY OF
GOTHENBURG

A Facebook Project for Japanese University Students: Does It Really Enhance Student Interaction, Learner Autonomy, and English Abilities?

Mayumi Hamada*

University of Marketing and Distribution Sciences, Nishi-ku, Kobe, Japan

Abstract. Facebook is the most popular social network service (SNS) in the world and a great platform for a link to the world. It can also be used effectively for language learning in EFL environments. However, that is not the case in Japan. The number of Facebook users accounts for less than 6 % of the population. This is partly because the most popular SNS in Japan is MIXI, which is available only in the Japanese language. This study examined the potential of Facebook for Japanese university students to develop their English skills as well as student interaction and learner autonomy. It describes how to introduce and integrate Facebook into a freshmen English course in a Japanese university. The survey conducted at the beginning of the semester revealed that only 15% of the students had a Facebook account. In order to habituate the students to using Facebook and improve their English skills, a writing task on Facebook was assigned every week. The results of the project, based on the feedback from the students and two surveys conducted at the beginning and the end of the semester, will be presented. I will also discuss how Facebook can facilitate not only the language learning of students, but also the interaction between the students, and access to the outer world.

Keywords: social network, Facebook, learner autonomy, writing.

1. Introduction

Facebook is the most popular social network service in the world. Since Facebook launched its service in Japan in 2008, it has been growing rapidly. The company announced this March that the number of Japanese Facebook users has doubled since last September and exceeded 10 million (Nihon, 2012). As a platform for a link to the world, Facebook has great potential for language learning in EFL environments.

---

* Contact author: richmommayumi2002@gmail.com

In L. Bradley & S. Thouësny (Eds.), *CALL: Using, Learning, Knowing, EUROCALL Conference, Gothenburg, Sweden, 22-25 August 2012, Proceedings* (pp. 104-110). © Research-publishing.net Dublin 2012

By integrating Facebook activities into English lessons, the purpose of this study is to investigate how Facebook can help students to improve their English, and whether it can facilitate student interaction and self-motivation for learning English.

The Facebook project is an ongoing one-year research. In the first semester, the main goals were to introduce Facebook to the students, teach them how to use Facebook, and help them to make a habit of writing regularly in English. In the second semester, the students are being given an opportunity to exchange opinions with American university students on Facebook so that they can expand their views about the outer world. This research will investigate the following three questions:

- Does the Facebook project encourage student interaction?
- Does the Facebook project enhance learner autonomy for studying English?
- Does the Facebook project help to develop the students' English skills?

This paper will report on the first part of the study, Facebook project (1), which was conducted in the fall semester of 2011.

2. Methodology

The Facebook project (1) was conducted at University of Marketing and Distribution Sciences in Japan in the fall semester of 2011. The participants were 13 freshmen in the special English course who took three English classes a week. The project was conducted as a homework assignment in the "general English" class.

The students' English level was quite basic, with an average TOEIC* score of around 360. At the beginning of the semester, the first questionnaire was conducted to obtain information about the students' usage of Facebook. It was found that only three out of 13 students had a Facebook account. Subsequently, an orientation session was provided by the teacher and the students were instructed how to set up an account and use Facebook. A closed group was formed on Facebook so that only the members were able to get access to the group.

The teacher provided one topic every week as a homework assignment, and all the students wrote about the same topic in 4-6 lines. The Facebook project (1) lasted throughout the semester and the students wrote about 12 topics. The project was included in their grade.

As for correcting mistakes, the teacher solicited one grammatically incorrect sentence from each student's comment and made an "error correction" worksheet every week. At the beginning of each lesson the students were instructed to correct the mistakes in about 10 minutes. Afterwards, the teacher provided correct answers as well as explanations.

---

* Test of English for international communication

3. Result

In order to collect the students' feedback and investigate the students' views, a post-study questionnaire was administered at the end of the semester.

The first three questions were in the format of a five-level Likert scale: 1. Strongly disagree; 2. Disagree; 3. Neither agree nor disagree; 4. Agree; 5. Strongly agree.

In response to Question 1 (Figure 1), 61.5% of the students either strongly agreed or agreed, with the average of 3.7. It should be noted that a few students showed unfavorable responses to the project. The reason may be that they are not generally fond of any computer-assisted learning.

In the case of Question 2 (Figure 2), 85% of the students either strongly agreed or agreed. The average was 4.2, indicating that most of the students believed that writing a comment in English regularly was very helpful to their English study, and they actually felt their English ability improved.

In response to Question 3 (Figure 3), the average was 4.2. 77% of the students stated that the error correction was beneficial, suggesting that most students appreciated the fact that their mistakes were pointed out and corrected directly by the teacher.

Figure 1. Question 1

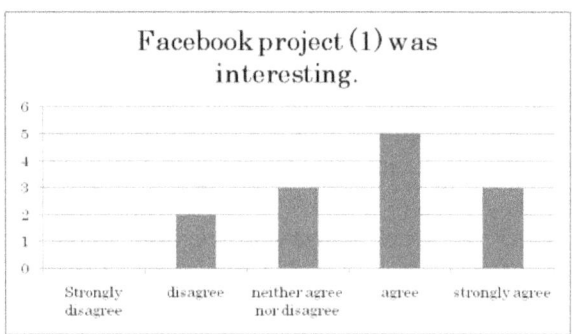

Figure 2. Question 2

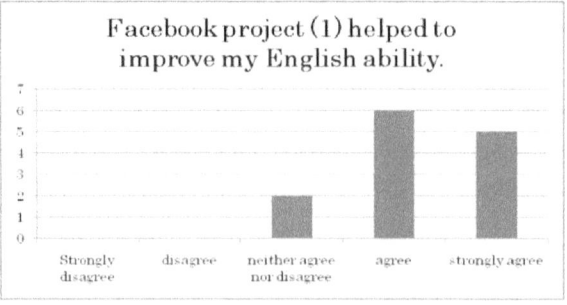

Figure 3. Question 3

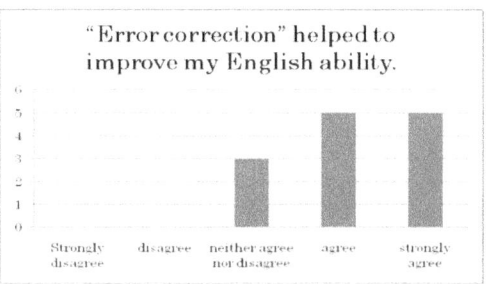

Concerning the number of times they log on to Facebook to perform an action not related to the assignment (Figure 4), five students stated "every day" while two students stated, "hardly ever". Again, it seems that the students are divided into two groups: one in favor of using Facebook, the other not. To Question 5 (Figure 5), the students were allowed to choose more than one answer. It was found that two main purposes were "communication with friends" and "getting information". As regards Question 6 (Figure 6), only four students answered yes. However, the other nine students answered that they want to make foreign friends. This suggests that although the students are interested in making foreign friends on Facebook, most of them are not motivated enough to take action voluntarily.

In addition to the data above, the students were asked to comment freely on the Facebook project (1), and they provided the following feedback:
- I can get a lot of information from abroad;
- I gradually got used to writing in English. It was fun to read the classmates' comments, too;
- I had a lot of chances to make English sentences;
- I made foreign friends;
- I had a chance to communicate with people in different age groups;
- I was happy to receive requests from friends and acquaintances;
- I got in the habit of looking up words in a dictionary and learning new expressions;
- It was fun to look into communities and get information about foreign people;
- I was happy that I got more chances to write in English on Facebook than before. I also communicated with more people on Facebook and enjoyed chatting in English;
- It was good for me to think about how to write what I want to say in English;
- I can catch up on foreign friends' updated information easily;
- I can get information about my favorite foreign artists;
- English is becoming more and more fun for me;
- The topics for writing were interesting;
- It was too bad that I couldn't interact with foreign people on Facebook;

- I think it may be a good idea to upload comments in English outside the closed group;
- It is difficult to make foreign friends.

Figure 4. Question 4

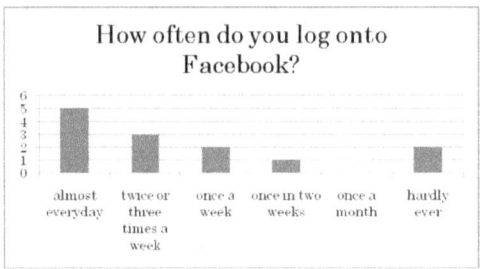

Figure 5. Question 5

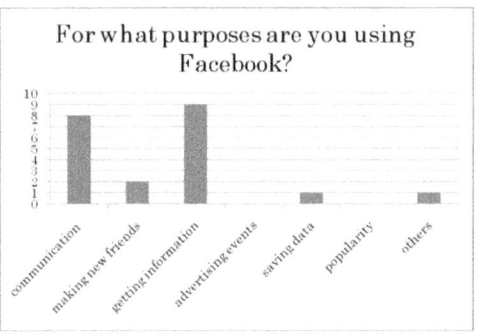

Figure 6. Question 6

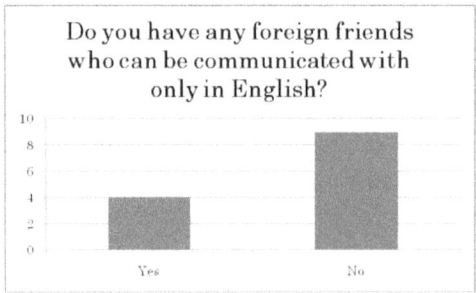

4. Discussion

The goals of the first semester were to familiarize the students with Facebook and help them to make a habit of writing regularly in English. It appears that the goals were successfully accomplished in that the students uploaded comments in English every week and their overall reaction to Facebook was positive.

As for research question one, it was observed that the students commented on the classmates' posts actively. The survey also showed that one of the main purposes of using Facebook is to communicate with friends. As described in the feedback, it seemed fun for the students to read classmates' comments and interact with each other.

Concerning research question two, there was an interesting finding in the feedback. It was found that in addition to the weekly writing assignment, some students voluntarily used Facebook in order to make English-speaking friends or get information that was available only in English. This type of activity will certainly enhance learner autonomy and help the students to become independent, motivated learners of English. However, it should be also noted that most students were still reluctant to make foreign friends on their own. As Schalow (2011) pointed out, Japanese students may be "inhibited learners" who are rather passive without taking voluntary actions. The students may need further support to increase opportunities for interacting with foreign people on Facebook.

In the context of answering research question three, it was found that most students felt that the project helped them to improve their English ability. Based on the feedback in the open-ended question, several students commented that the opportunity to write their own opinions helped them to get used to writing in English as well as learn new expressions and vocabulary. Furthermore, a few students stated that they enjoyed chatting or getting information in English, which indicates that their activities can help them to improve their reading, speaking, and listening skills as well.

5. Conclusion

This paper has presented the results of the first part of the Facebook project to investigate the potential of Facebook for enhancing English study and learner autonomy. It was found that the students' overall reaction to Facebook was positive and they became accustomed to writing English comments on Facebook. It was also indicated that the project could help to develop the students' English ability and facilitate learner autonomy to some extent. More longitudinal research is needed, however, to further investigate how much Facebook can stimulate the students' self-motivation for English learning and improve their English ability. It is expected that further analysis and discussion will be possible when the second part of the research is done and the data is collected.

Acknowledgements. I am grateful to my colleagues Seijiro Sumi and Thomas Schalow for their constructive comments.

References

Nihon no Facebook riyosha 1000 mannincho [The number of Japanese Facebook users exceeded 10million]. (2012, March 22). *Nihon Keizai Shimbun* (p. 15).

Schalow, T. (2011). Building an online learning community in Japan: The challenge of distributed learning in a social network. In S. M. Thang, K, Pramela, F. F.Wong, L. K. Lin, M. Jamilah, & M. Marlyna (Eds.), *Language and Cultural Diversity* (pp. 89-105). Serdang: Universiti Putra Malaysia Press.

UNIVERSITY OF GOTHENBURG

Investigating the Use of Interactive Whiteboards During the Pre-Task Phase of Speaking Tasks in the Secondary English Classroom

Zöe Handley*

Department of Education, University of York, Heslington, York, UK

Abstract. Working within a task-based approach to the teaching of speaking, two interactive whiteboard-based pre-task activities focusing on different phases of the speech production process (Levelt, 1989) were developed and compared with an activity based on the speaking activities currently offered in English as a foreign language course books. The first activity, *Dialogue Expansion*, was based on expansion drills/back-chaining (Larsen-Freeman & Anderson, 2011) and intended to focus on articulation. The second, *Dialogue Reconstruction*, was based on total text reconstruction activities, e.g., *Storyboard* (Levy, 1997), and intended to focus on formulation. The comparison focused on their impact on the quality (fluency and accuracy) of students' oral productions in follow-up dialogue activities. Three classes of 12-13 year old Spanish learners of English participated in the study which had a within-participants design. The independent variable was the pre-task activities. The dependent variables were the (1) fluency, and (2) accuracy of the language produced during follow-up dialogue tasks. The activities developed in this study had a differential impact on both fluency and accuracy, with the Dialogue Expansion activities promoting accuracy and the Dialogue Reconstruction activities promoting fluency. This evidence corroborates previous research which suggests that the focus of pre-task activities has an impact on the quality of language that students produce during the task cycle and demonstrates that teacher-fronted interactive whiteboard activities can play a role in a task-based approach to language teaching.

Keywords: interactive whiteboard, speaking, task-based language learning, English, secondary.

1. Introduction

It is estimated that one in six classrooms Worldwide are now equipped with an interactive whiteboard (IWB; Matthews-Aydinli & Elaziz, 2010). A recent systematic review of

---

* Contact author: zoe.handley@york.ac.uk

In L. Bradley & S. Thouësny (Eds.), *CALL: Using, Learning, Knowing, EUROCALL Conference, Gothenburg, Sweden, 22-25 August 2012, Proceedings* (pp. 111-116). © Research-publishing.net Dublin 2012

empirical research on the use of new technologies in primary and secondary English as a Foreign Language (EFL) classes, however, found few studies investigating IWBs (Macaro, Handley, & Walter, 2012). Moreover, none of these studies are grounded in second language acquisition theory and research or best practice in language learning and teaching.

Spain is one of the countries currently investing in IWBs (Alvarez, 2011). At the same time, an oral component has been added to the English tests which form part of Spanish university entrance examinations (Alastrué & Pérez-Llantada, 2010; Payne, 2009). Working within this context, the study reported here investigates the possibility of developing theoretically-grounded IWB activities to support the development of speaking skills.

2. Pre-task speaking activities for IWBs

The activities developed in this project were based on a task-based approach to language teaching and Levelt's (1989) model of speech production. Task-based language teaching (TBLT; Ellis, 2003) was adopted because, unlike the approach commonly adopted in EFL course books which involve students writing and then performing a dialogue, it has the potential to engage students in the full range of processes involved in speaking, namely conceptualization, formulation and articulation (Levelt, 1989).

Building on research which suggests that IWBs are well-suited to teacher-fronted presentations (Higgins, Beauchamp, & Miller, 2007), IWB activities were developed for use during the pre-task phase of task-based lessons (Harmer, 2001). Following research by Sangarun (2001) which found that the focus of pre-task activities (language, content or both) had an impact on the quality of students' productions during speaking tasks, these activities were designed to focus on the different processes involved in speaking (see Levelt, 1989). The activities which were developed, namely *Dialogue Expansion* and *Dialogue Reconstruction*, and the control activity, *Dialogue Completion*, are described below.

2.1. Dialogue completion

Dialogue Completion activities (henceforth Completion activities) are similar to the speaking activities that are currently offered in students' course books. In the first part of these activities, students listen to a dialogue and answer a question related to it. They are then presented a transcript of the dialogue and are asked to check their answer against it. In the second part, students write their own dialogue based on an outline comprising just the content words and then perform the dialogue with a partner.

2.2. Dialogue expansion

Dialogue Expansion activities (henceforth Expansion activities) focus on articulation. The first part of these activities is the same as that of the Completion activities.

The second part implements expansion drills or back-chaining (Larsen-Freeman & Anderson, 2011) and students are asked to repeat the utterance, or constituent thereof, highlighted in bold on the screen, after their teacher.

2.3. Dialogue reconstruction

Dialogue Reconstruction activities (henceforth Reconstruction activities) focus on formulation. The first part of these activities is similar to that of the Completion and Expansion activities. However, students are not presented a transcript of the dialogue against which to check their answer. They are presented the dialogue transcript in the form of a total text reconstruction activity like *Storyboard* (Levy, 1997).

3. An investigation of IWB-based pre-speaking activities

Following previous research on TBLT, the main research question which guided this research was:
- Does the quality (fluency and accuracy) of the language that students produce during *Dialogue Restoration* activities depend on the way in which the language required to complete the task has been presented in pre-task activities?

3.1. Method

A convenience sample which comprised three first grade secondary school classes of Spanish EFL students from two schools in Madrid was used in this study. One class (Class A) was recruited from a private school in the suburbs and the two other classes (Class B and Class C) were recruited from a publicly funded but privately managed school in the city centre. The classes differed in English language proficiency, with Class A having the highest level of proficiency and Class C the lowest according to the cloze task and vocabulary test administered at the start of the study (see Table 1 below).

Table 1. Results of vocabulary test and cloze task for each class

		Class A	Class B	Class C
Vocabulary test	M	28.25	27.09	22.21
	SD	1.14	2.04	2.93
Cloze task	M	38.57	29.22	16.33
	SD	4.31	6.95	3.92

The independent variable was the pre-task activities. The dependent variables were the fluency (pruned syllables per minute, i.e., repetitions and reformulations were omitted from the syllable count; Ellis, 2009), and accuracy (percentage of error-free clauses; *ibid.*) of the language produced during the tasks. Language proficiency was investigated as a covariate through the administration of a vocabulary test and a cloze task.

The students participated in seven twenty-minute sessions. In the first session the proficiency tests were administered. In the remaining sessions, the students participated in an IWB pre-speaking activity followed by a Dialogue Restoration activity (henceforth Restoration activity) based on the same topic. The Restoration activities were based on the approach described by Brooks (1964); students were provided with the outline of a similar dialogue to the one they had listened to in the IWB pre-speaking activity comprising just the content words and asked to record themselves performing the complete dialogue with a partner. The order of presentation of the activities was counterbalanced across classes to mitigate any potential order effects.

4. Results

The fluency and accuracy data were each submitted to a one-way independent ANCOVA with task as a between-participants factor* and scores on the vocabulary test and the cloze task as covariates.

These analyses suggested that scores on the cloze task were significantly related to the fluency of students' oral productions in the follow-up Restoration activities ($F(1, 92) = 5.148$, $p < .001$, $r = .43$) and that there was a significant effect of pre-task IWB activity after controlling for performance on the cloze task ($F(2, 92) = 3.298$, $p = .002$, partial $\eta^2 = .13$). Planned contrasts found that students produced significantly more syllables per second following the Reconstruction activities ($M = 2.65$) than following the Completion activities ($M = 2.29$; $t(92) = 2.849$, $p = .005$, $r = .38$), but no differences in fluency between the Expansion ($M = 2.20$) and Completion activities ($t(92) = -.533$, $p = .596$, $r = .06$).

The analyses also suggested that the scores on the cloze task were significantly related to the accuracy of the students' production in the Restoration activities ($F(1, 92) = 31.248$, $p < .001$, $r = .50$) and that there was a significant effect of pre-task IWB activity after controlling for performance on the cloze task ($F(2, 92) = 151.318$, $p = .001$, partial $\eta^2 = .77$). Planned contrasts found that the accuracy of students' productions was significantly higher following an Expansion activity ($M = 84.50$) than following a Completion activity ($M = 70.47$; $t(92) = 4.181$, $p < .001$, $r = .40$), which in turn was significantly higher than following a Reconstruction activity ($M = 27.57$; $t(92) = -12.320$, $p < .001$, $r = .79$).

5. Discussion

These results suggest that focusing on different phases of the speech production process has a differential impact on both fluency and accuracy. Specifically, focusing

---

* The students did not work with the same partner in every session.

on formulation, as in the Reconstruction activities, promotes fluency and focusing on articulation, as in the Expansion activities, promotes accuracy.

The beneficial impact of Reconstruction activities on fluency might be explained by the fact that focusing on formulation frees up resources for later processes and articulation (Ellis, 2003). The absence of a beneficial effect of Expansion activities on fluency, on the other hand, is surprising given their focus on articulation which promotes the use of formulaic language. It might be explained by hesitations between prefabricated phrases. An analysis of patterns of hesitation is required to explore this possibility.

The beneficial effect of Expansion activities on accuracy might be explained by the fact that focusing on accuracy promotes the use of formulaic language, while the decrease in accuracy observed following the Reconstruction activities might be explained by the fact that focusing on formulation promotes complexity and the trade-off between accuracy and complexity observed in previous research (Ellis, 2003).

6. Conclusion

Two IWB-based pre-task activities focusing on different phases of the speech production process were developed and compared with the speaking activities currently offered in EFL course books. This comparison which focused on the quality of students' oral productions in follow-up dialogue Restoration activities in terms of fluency and accuracy supports the findings of previous research which suggests that that the focus of pre-task activities has an impact on the quality of language that students produce during the task cycle and demonstrates that teacher-fronted IWB activities can play a role in TBLT.

Acknowledgements. I would like to thank my co-investigators in the Department of Education at the University of Oxford, Prof. Ernesto Macaro and Dr. Catherine Walter, our funder Oxford University Press and the teachers and students who participated in the study.

References

Alastrué, R. P., & Pérez-Llantada, C. (2010). A longitudinal attitude survey of English oral skills: Classroom, curriculum, learning and pedagogy implications. *Revista de Humanidades, 16*, 309-326.

Alvarez, P. (2011). Más de 280. 000 alumnos frente a una pizarra digital. *El País.* 14/02/11. Retrieved from http://elpais.com/diario/2011/02/14/educacion/1297638002_850215.html

Brooks, N. (1964). *Language and Language Learning: Theory and Practice* (2nd ed.) New York: Holt.

Ellis, R. (2003). *Task-based language learning and teaching*. Oxford: Oxford University Press.

Ellis, R. (2009). The Differential Effects of Three Types of Task Planning on the Fluency, Complexity, and Accuracy in L2 Oral Production. *Applied Linguistics, 30*(4), 474-509. doi: 10.1093/applin/amp042

Harmer, J. (2001). *The practice of English language teaching.* Harlow, Essex: Longman.

Higgins, S., Beauchamp, G., & Miller, D. (2007). Reviewing the literature on interactive whiteboards. *Learning, Media and Technology, 32*(3), 213-225.

Larsen-Freeman, D., & Anderson, M. (2011). *Techniques and principles in language teaching.* Oxford: Oxford University Press.

Levelt, M. J. W. (1989). *Speaking from intention to articulation.* Cambridge, Massachusetts: MIT Press.

Levy, M. (1997). *Computer-assisted language learning: Context and conceptualisation.* Oxford: Clarendon Press.

Macaro, E., Handley, Z., & Walter, C. (2012). A systematic review of CALL in English as a second or foreign language: Focus on primary and secondary education. *Language Teaching, 45*(1), 1-43. doi:10.1017/S0261444811000395

Matthews-Aydinli, J., & Elaziz, F. (2010). Turkish students' and teachers' attitudes toward the use of interactive whiteboards in EFL classrooms. *Computer Assisted Language Learning, 23*(3), 235-252. doi: 10.1080/09588221003776781

Payne, C. (2009). Schools of thought. *English Teaching Professional, 63*(July), 4-5.

Sangarun, J. (2001). *The effects of pre-task planning on foreign language performance.* Unpublished doctoral thesis, University of Toronto, Canada.

UNIVERSITY OF GOTHENBURG

A Corpus-Informed Text Reconstruction Resource for Learning About the Language of Scientific Abstracts

Laura M. Hartwell[a]* and Marie-Paule Jacques[b]

a. Grenoble 1 - LIDILEM, UJF, Valence, France
b. Grenoble 1 - LIDILEM and IUFM, Grenoble, France

Abstract. Both reading and writing abstracts require specific language skills and conceptual capacities, which may challenge advanced learners. This paper draws explicitly upon the *Emergence* and *Scientext* research projects which focused on the lexis of scientific texts in French and English. The teaching objective of the project described here was to create a collection of text reconstruction tasks targeting the patterns of English that are uncommon in French. These tasks are to be integrated within the platform *Enigma Plus* (http://elang.ujf-grenoble.fr/enigma/). The current project is the conception of a new module based on data-driven materials collected from Scientext, a corpus of medical and biology abstracts in English (http://scientext.msh-alpes.fr/scientext-site-en/spip.php?article9). This paper discusses the task focusing on the word *hypothesis,* the first of a dozen tasks based on authentic examples and designed to help learners of English as a foreign language to better read and write science abstracts. The results revealed several similarities and contrasts with the French findings. These results were integrated into the text reconstruction task. Findings of user practices reported in previous studies were taken into account to optimize completion of the task by the widest range of user practices and errors.

Keywords: corpora, abstracts, on-line text reconstruction, English for specific purposes, English as a foreign language.

1. Introduction

The reading and writing of abstracts requires specific language and conceptual capacities that may challenge even language skills of advanced learners. These ubiquitous, dense, and brief texts are a key element of written academic discourse as they serve to publicly announce one's work thereby enabling other researchers to identify it among the thousands of other published articles. Scientific abstracts contain

---

* Contact author: hartwell@ujf-grenoble.fr

rhetorical and structural aspects which can be identified through a cluster of linguistic features (Cremmins, 1982; Pho, 2008; Swales & Feak, 2004).

An efficient comprehension of abstracts is essential to productive research by learners of English as a foreign language. In this context, descriptive grammar analyses are essential to language teaching (Oakey, 2002) and especially within contexts of language learning for specific purposes (Gledhill, 2000, 2011; Hartwell, 2011). Citing previous studies, McEnery and Wilson (1996) highlight the substantial differences between language use as empirically revealed through corpora study and the descriptions found in textbooks that may misleadingly offer less common language choices to the detriment of learning more frequent ones. Frequency is a condition for both *collocation*, referring to words that are frequently found together and lexico-grammatical patterns which Hunston and Francis (2000) define as "all of the words and structures which are regularly associated with the word and which contribute to its meaning" (p. 37).

This paper draws explicitly upon the *Emergence* and *Scientext* research projects which focused on the lexis of scientific texts in French and English (Cavalla & Grossmann, 2005; Tutin, 2010). One objective of the previous and current research is to identify collocations or patterns in French and English in order to help foreign language learning. The translation of a collocation does not necessarily employ the same structure as found in the original language. Tutin (2010) offers the example of *émettre une hypothèse* (emit a hypothesis), which can be translated by the English verb *hypothesize*, although no such verb exists in French (p. 136).

The teaching objective of the project described here is to create a collection of text reconstruction tasks targeting the patterns of English that are uncommon in French. These tasks are to be integrated within the platform *Enigma Plus,* which was initially designed to accompany the textbook *Minimum Competence in Scientific English* (Blattes, Jans, & Upjohn, 2003). The platform includes short unauthentic recordings accompanied by synchronized visual supports. After the presentation, a skeleton of the text is automatically displayed on the screen including the first two letters of each word to be identified. If the user types a correct word it appears throughout the skeleton, if not, the user is encouraged to enter a new word or listen to the text. This platform is an adaptation of John Higgins's Storyboard, which emanated from his program Rebuild, inspired by Tim John's Textbag in the early 1980s (Davies, 2007). This paper discusses the task focusing on the word *hypothesis,* the first of a dozen tasks based on authentic examples and designed to help learners of English as a foreign language to better read and write science abstracts.

2. Method

This section begins with a brief description of previous studies of the use of the French word *hypothèse.* Then, a comparison with English is formed by consulting the Scientext corpus. Scientext is a collection of academic works in both French and

English (Falaise, Tutin, & Kraif, 2011; Tutin, Grossmann, Falaise, & Kraif, 2009). The peer-reviewed articles in English, collected by the LiCorn team at the Université de Bretagne-Sud, were originally published by the editor BioMed Central and comprise sixty-two subthemes from the fields of biology and medicine. The corpus of abstracts counts 787,276 words from 3,381 research articles. From the results in both languages, exemplars of expressions were drawn to write a 300-word text for the text reconstruction task.

2.1. Corpus-based analysis of the French word 'hypothesis'

Tutin (2010) consulted the *Cultural Identities in Academic Prose* corpus (KIAP) for the productive relations of the French noun *hypothèse* (pp. 99-100). The most frequent collocation is as the subject of the copula verb *être* (to be), with 1,255 tokens. By order of frequency, the verb *être* was followed by six attributes (*autre* "other", *different* "different", *même,* "same"…) each with 78 to 195 tokens. After the nouns *travail* (work) and *capital* (capital) linked by *de* (of), is a second verb *faire* (to make) with 48 tokens.

Cavalla and Grossmann (2005) took a complementary approach by examining the lexical verbs found in collocation of the noun *hypothèse*. Their study confirms that the first lexical verb to be collocated with *hypothèse* is the French *faire* (to make). Furthermore, they separate the verbs into four categories: propose, elaborate, verify, and argue.

For the present study, these categories have been regrouped into two sets: propose or elaborate and verify or argue (Appendix 1). There are 182 tokens in the first category; the eleven entries include the verb *faire* (make), but also *avancer* (to advance) and *émettre* (to emit). There are fewer tokens (104) but more variety in the second category, in which *tester* (to test), *confirmer* (to confirm), and *défendre* (to defend) head the list of 20 verbs.

2.2. Scientext analysis of the English lemma 'hypothesize'

The Scientext English corpus of abstracts was consulted for the lemma *hypothesis*. A total of 163 occurrences were detected. Thirty-four subheadings found within the abstracts were removed as well as one occurrence inserted within parentheses, leaving 128 tokens (Appendix 2). The results revealed several contrasts with the French findings. The verb *hypothesize* was found 73 times, most often conjugated in the past tense. Contrary to the French results, there were few tokens (14) and a variety of lexical verbs (9) within the category "propose or elaborate".

Within the category "verify and argue", there were a similar amount of tokens (88), verb variety (21) and use of the verb *test* in both languages. In English as in French, *hypothesis* was also the agent of several actions, including *involve, consider, focus on, imply, predict.* There were relatively few occurrences of the lemma *be* compared to the French. Furthermore, the adjectives *different* (2), *other* (1), *first* (2), *same* (0) were rarer, however the expression *working hypothesis* (5) mirrored the use in French (c.f. Tutin, 2010). *Hypothesis* was also found in ten prepositional phrases and within four compound nouns (e.g., *hypothesis tests*), a grammatical construction not found in French.

3. Results

Drawing upon the comparison of the corpora results, eight complete sentences containing frequent uses of the lemma *hypothesize* were chosen as exemplars. Since the verb *hypothesize* is not found in French, it was put forth in the incipit and in the title *To hypothesize or not to hypothesize*. Research has shown that the first part of the reconstruction activity receives more attention from users (Hartwell, 2010a). The next section highlights the notion of research data as the sentence subject and contains the frequent collocation "supports" (Appendix 3). The third paragraph introduces the transparent lemma "test", which was the most frequent lexical verbal collocation of *hypothesis* in English. The last section focuses on the common expression containing a preposition (*are consistent with the hypothesis*), before finishing with the notion of contradiction (Figure 1).

Figure 1. Slide of text before user begins reconstruction

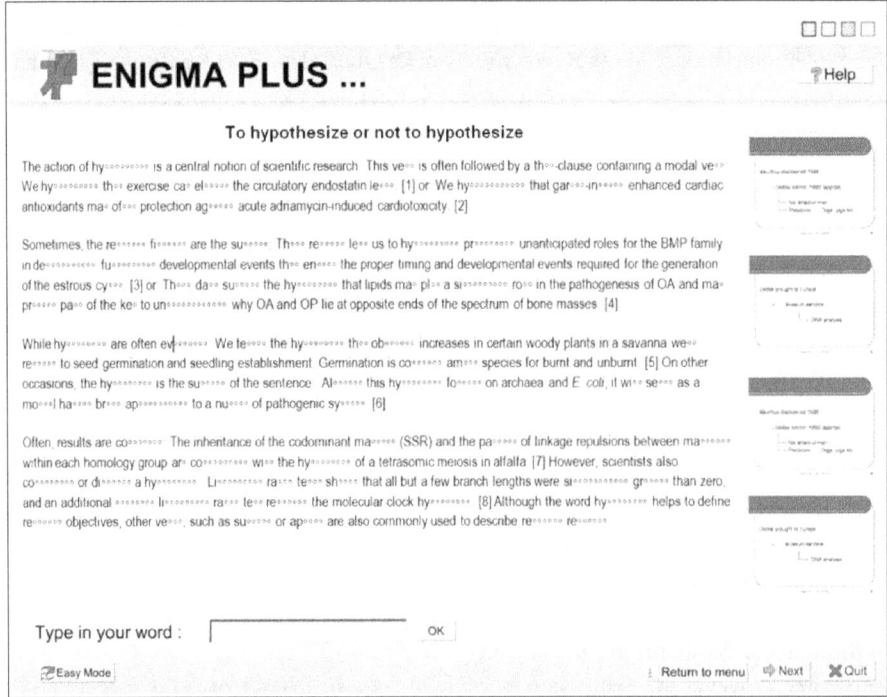

Previous studies have shown that two-thirds (65.5%) of the users will enter 100 entries or more, but only 22.5% will enter more than 150 entries (Hartwell, 2010b). This task includes 92 missing words, which represents 68 different words as several are repeated. The user only enters each individual word once; hence *hypothesis* will appear eight times when entered the first time by the user. These quantities were calculated to optimize completion of the task given a range of user practices and error as noted by the previous studies.

4. Discussion

This task is the first of a dozen to be created for the platform *Enigma Plus*. The lemma *hypothesize* was chosen as previous studies had evaluated the French use of this term within scientific discourse, in which it is most frequently collocated with the verb *faire* (make). However, among the 542 verbs found within the English abstracts of Scientext, the 50 most frequently occurring verbs constituted approximately ninety percent of all the verbs, but *make* was only 38th on the list and was not found to collocate with *hypothesis,* thereby confirming non-transparent differences across the two languages. This task targets discourse features that are unfamiliar to French speakers as they do not mirror practices of the first language.

Within the list of most frequent verbs related to describing the processes of scientific research, we find *show, compare, suggest, report, determine, examine,* and *appear* (Hartwell, forthcoming). For this reason, the reconstruction text ends with a note about two of these more common verbs: *suggest* and *appear.* This comment is also intended to encourage users to complete further reconstruction tasks.

Acknowledgements. The comparative research aspects of this study were financed by the Grenoble 1 Pôle SHS. The on-line computer assisted language learning aspects were funded by Pedagotice of Grenoble 1 and PRES of the Universities of Grenoble.

References

Blattes, S., Jans, V., & Upjohn, J. (2003). *Minimum Competence in Scientific English – Supplementary Materials.* Les Ulis : EDP Sciences. Retrieved from http://grenoble-sciences.ujf-grenoble.fr/papebooks/upjohn/unit9_1

Cavalla, C., & Grossmann, F. (2005). Caractéristiques sémantiques de quelques « Noms scientifiques » dans l'article de recherche en français. *Akademisk Prosa, 3,* 47-59.

Cremmins, E. T. (1982). *The Art of Abstracting.* Philadelphia: ISI Press.

Davies, G. (2007). *Total Cloze Text Reconstruction Programs: A Brief History.* Retrieved from http://www.ict4lt.org/en/FWTHistory.doc

Falaise, A., Tutin, A., & Kraif, O. (2011). Exploitation d'un corpus arboré pour non spécialistes par des requêtes guidées et des requêtes sémantiques. *Proceedings from TALN, Montpellier 2011*. Retrieved from http://pro.aiakide.net/publis/2011TALNPaper-Falaise-Tutin-Kraif.pdf

Gledhill, C. J. (2000). *Collocations in Science Writing*. Tübingen: Gunter Narr Verlag.

Gledhill, C. J. (2011). The 'Lexicogrammar' Approach to Analysing Phraseology and Collocation in ESP Texts. *La Revue du GERAS, 59*, 5-23.

Hartwell, L. (2010a). Impact of software design on on-line text reconstruction. *SYSTEM: An International Journal of Educational Technology and Applied Linguistics, 38*(3), 370-378. doi: 10.1016/j.system.2010.06.009

Hartwell, L. (2010b). Pratiques de reconstruction de texte en autoformation. *Les Cahiers de l'APLIUT, 29*(2), 81-96.

Hartwell, L. (2011). Learning On-Line about Modality in Written and Oral English. *Proceedings from ICT for Language Learning*. Florence, Italy, 2011.

Hartwell, L. (forthcoming). Corpus-informed descriptions: English verbs and their collocates in science abstracts. *Études en didactique des langues*.

Hunston, S., & Francis, G. (2000). *Pattern Grammar: A Corpus-driven Approach to the Lexical Grammar of English*. Amsterdam: John Benjamins Publishing Company.

McEnery, T., & Wilson, A. (1996). *Corpus Linguistics*. Edinburgh: Edinburgh University Press.

Pho, P. D. (2008). Research Article Abstracts in Applied Linguistics and Educational Technology. *Discourse Studies, 10*(2), 231-250.

Oakey, D. (2002). Formulaic Language in English Academic Writing: A Corpus-based study of the formal and functional variation of a lexical phrase in different academic disciplines. In R. Reppen, S. M. Fitzmaurice, & D. Biber (Eds.), *Using Corpora to Explore Linguistic Variation* (pp. 111-129). Amsterdam: John Benjamins Publishing Company.

Swales, J. M., & Feak, C. B. (2004). *Academic writing for graduate students: Essential tasks and skills* (2nd ed.). Ann Arbor: University of Michigan Press.

Tutin, A. (2010). *Sens et combinatoire lexicale : de la langue au discours* (Unpublished Dossier en vue de l'habilitation à dirigier de la recherche). Grenoble: Université de Stendhal.

Tutin, A., Grossmann, F., Falaise, A., & Kraif, O. (2009). Autour du projet Scientext: étude des marques linguistiques du positionnement de l'auteur dans les écrits scientifiques. *Linguistique de Corpus*. Retrieved from http://w3.u-grenoble3.fr/lidilem/labo/file/Lorient_vfinale.pdf

Appendix 1. Lexical verbs collocated with *hypothèse*

Action in relation to the hypothesis	Lexical verbs (number of tokens)
Propose / elaborate (182 tokens)	Faire (113), avancer (17), émettre (16), poser (9) formuler (9), proposer (6), effectuer (4), présenter (4), introduire (2), énoncer (1), former (1)
Verify / argue (104 tokens)	Tester (35), confirmer (12), défendre (9), valider (6), vérifier (6), justifier (4), renforcer (4), infirmer (3), corroborer (3), discuter (3), étayer (3), examiner (3), mettre à l'épreuve (3), conforter (2), privilégier (2), soutenir (2), appuyer (1), légitimer (1), opposer (1), récuser (1)

Appendix 2. Collocates of *hypothesis*

Action in relation to the hypothesis	Verbs (number of tokens) or head noun (number of tokens)
To hypothesize (73 tokens)	hypothesized (35), hypothesize (19), is/are hypothesized (8), has/have been hypothesized (6), have hypothesized (1), hypothesizing (1), may hypothesize (1), was hypothesized (1), hypothesized (1 – part participle as modifier)
Propose / elaborate (14 tokens)	lead to (3), present (3), discuss (2), propose (2), address (1), prompt (1), pursue (1), offer (1), illustrates (1)
Verify /argue (88 tokens)	Test (40), support (21 – including "gave support to"), confirm (2), involve (2), strengthen (2), affected by (1), appears to depend on (1), base on (1), consider (1), contradict (1), disprove (1), evaluate (1), examine (2), explore (1), focus on has (1), imply (1), investigate (1), predict (1), prove (1), reject (2), use (2)
To be (12 tokens)	was (5), is (4), if the ... is true (3),
Other (10 tokens)	consistent with the (5), in agreement with (1), under the [noun phrase] hypothesis (1), in the hypothesis that (1), in accord with (1), compatible with the (1)
Modifier within a compound noun (4 tokens)	Tests (1), generating study (1), testing (1), null-hypothesis behavior (1)

Appendix 3. Reconstruction text

To hypothesize or not to hypothesize

The action of hypothesing is a central notion of scientific research. This verb is often followed by a that-clause containing a modal verb: **We hypothesize that exercise can elevate the circulatory endostatin level.** [1] or: **We hypothesized that garlic-induced enhanced cardiac antioxidants may offer protection against acute adriamycin-induced cardiotoxicity.** [2]

Sometimes, the research findings are the subject: **These results lead us to hypothesize previously unanticipated roles for the BMP family in determining fundamental developmental events that ensure the proper timing and developmental events required for the generation of the estrous cycle.** [3] or: **These data support the hypothesis that lipids may play a significant role in the pathogenesis of OA and may provide part of the key to understanding why OA and OP lie at opposite ends of the spectrum of bone masses.** [4]

On other occasions, the hypothesis is the subject of the sentence: **Although this hypothesis focuses on archaea and *E. coli*, it will serve as a model having broad applicability to a number of pathogenic systems.** [5] When being evaluated, it often becomes a direct object: **We tested the hypothesis that observed increases in certain woody plants in a savanna were related to seed germination and seedling establishment.** [6]

Results may confirm a hypothesis: **The inheritance of the codominant markers (SSR) and the pattern of linkage repulsions between markers within each homology group are consistent with the hypothesis of a tetrasomic meiosis in alfalfa.** [7] However, scientists also contradict or disprove a hypothesis: **Likelihood ratio tests showed that all but a few branch lengths were significantly greater than zero, and an additional likelihood ratio test rejected the molecular clock hypothesis.** [8] Although the word hypothesis helps to define research objectives, other verbs, such as suggest or appear are also commonly used to describe research results.

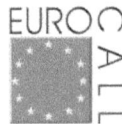

UNIVERSITY OF GOTHENBURG

Telecollaboration: Where Are We Now?

Francesca Helm[a*], Sarah Guth[a], and Robert O'Dowd[b]

a. Università degli Studi di Padova, Italy
b. Universidad de Leon, Spain

Abstract. This paper presents the results of a European-wide survey regarding the practice of foreign language telecollaboration or Online Intercultural Exchange (OIE) in higher education. The survey was carried out as part of a European project, INTENT (Integrating Telecollaborative Networks into Foreign Language Higher Education) which was awarded funding by the European Commission's Lifelong Learning programme primarily to achieve more effective integration of telecollaboration in university institutions. Findings reveal the current 'state-of-the-art' of telecollaboration in Europe: an educational practice which is highly valued by educators and students who have experience with it, but also a time-consuming activity which is difficult to organize and receives limited institutional recognition or support. Recommendations are made on the basis of these findings as to how telecollaboration can be supported and more fully integrated into higher education.

Keywords: telecollaboration, CMC, intercultural exchange, internationalization, project.

1. Introduction

Foreign language telecollaboration or online intercultural exchange engages groups of foreign language learners in virtual intercultural interaction and exchange with partner classes in geographically distant locations (Dooly, 2008; Guth & Helm, 2010; O'Dowd, 2007). In primary and secondary education, telecollaboration projects have been supported by major networks and virtual platforms such as ePals (www.epals.com), the European Union's Etwinning platform (www.etwinning.net) and the global network iEarn (www.iearn.org). In higher education however, it has received little support on an institutional level or on a European level.

This paper reports on a survey carried out as part of a European project, INTENT (www.intent-project.eu) which was awarded funding by the European Commission's Lifelong Learning programme primarily in order to achieve more effective integration

---

* Contact author: francesca.helm@unipd.it

of telecollaboration in university institutions. The first phase of the project consisted of a survey of European educators and students on telecollaboration in order to establish the current state of telecollaboration in Europe.

2. Method

The aim of the survey was to identify the characteristics of telecollaborative practices currently undertaken by European university educators and to explore the barriers which practitioners encounter when organizing online intercultural exchanges (Guth, Helm, & O'Dowd, 2012). The project team also sought the views and opinions of European students with different OIE experiences, with regard to the impact that participating in online exchange has had on them. Three versions of the survey were developed: one for educators with experience in OIE, another for those who have not yet had experience in OIE and a final survey for students with experience in OIE. The survey was translated into French, German and Italian. Complete responses were obtained from 210 university educators in 23 different European countries and 131 students with experience in telecollaboration.

In the second part of the study, the project team also collected various case studies of universities, partnerships and telecollaborative networks which would provide a representative, qualitative picture of the type of online intercultural exchanges which are being carried out around Europe and which have achieved a certain level of integration in their institutions' study programmes. The case studies involved exchanges taking place between universities in Ireland and Germany, Italy and the UK, Sweden and the USA, and Latvia and France, among others. The collection also included an example of a telecollaborative network of various exchange partners working together as well as the description of an Italian university which had staff involved in multiple projects.

3. Discussion

The survey and case study findings confirmed much of what the team already believed to be the case regarding telecollaboration in higher education, but also revealed interesting new information. The findings, which are summarised in this section, have important implications for higher education institutions and policy makers.

The majority of exchanges (63%) reported involved the use of English as a foreign language. However, a considerable number of teachers of French, German and Spanish also responded as well as teachers of less commonly taught languages such as Italian, Chinese, Finnish, Greek, Turkish, Hungarian, Dutch, Polish, Portuguese, Catalan and Rumanian. Bilingual exchanges were the most common type, with over 50% of respondents indicating experience in this type of exchange while a third indicated monolingual exchanges such as those between teacher trainees of, say,

Spanish, with learners of Spanish as a foreign language. A fifth of respondents had implemented exchanges using a lingua franca such as English among predominantly non-native speakers of English.

Most OIEs currently involve classes from European universities collaborating with partner classes in US universities. There are currently few exchanges between universities in European countries and there are also few connecting Europe to Latin America, Africa, the MiddleEast and Asia.

It was also interesting to note that foreign language educators rarely find telecollaborative partners through institutional partnerships such as those established under the Erasmus programme. Instead, most establish exchanges with colleagues from their own academic networks or from contacts made at conferences. Furthermore, whilst OIEs are strongly believed to have the potential of supporting physical mobility by engaging learners with students in their future host institution before departure, and also by supporting learners during their period abroad, the research team found very few examples of such exchanges currently being carried out.

OIEs are generally carried out by highly motivated educators who believe strongly in the outcomes of these exchanges. They have often had experience in OIEs as part of their training and may also have a research interest in OIE. Educators who have had experience in OIE are likely to repeat the experience, since the majority of respondents with experience in OIE had been involved in more than one telecollaborative exchange. Although the majority of experienced telecollaborators reported that OIEs were time-consuming (83%) and difficult to organize (54%), and that often collaborating with partner teachers was challenging (55%), the vast majority (93%) agreed that carrying out OIEs in their classes had been a positive experience.

Whilst telecollaborative exchanges are recognized by some universities as valuable activities for internationalization and for the development of student mobility, few institutions are aware of the extra time and workload such projects require and are either unwilling or unable to provide adequate support to staff who want to organize such exchanges. In fact, educators with experience in telecollaboration indicated lack of time and the difficulty of organizing online exchanges as the main factors they believed were hindering the adoption of OIE by other educators, as well as the lack of institutional recognition and support.

Telecollaboration seems to have different levels of integration in study programmes, and it is not always assessed. Most practitioners who do assess students focus on the intercultural and communicative learning outcomes of their exchanges. Although participation in OIEs does not always bring students academic credit, the impact of OIEs seems to be educationally significant. Many students reported that participating in a telecollaborative exchange led them to become more open to others, accepting and understanding of differences and to realise that their own points of view were not necessarily "the best or only ones". Many also reported establishing long term friendships with their telecollaboration peers, keeping in touch once exchanges were over and some even visiting one another. OIEs are often an incentive for students to engage in mobility. Telecollaboration not only benefits students' learning but can also contribute to educators' academic careers, for example, by establishing connections to new academic networks and enabling them to engage in staff mobility visits with other universities.

The most frequently used tools in OIEs in Europe are email and virtual learning environments. However, there is also a considerably high use of audio/video conferencing which until recently was not so widely available. The main difficulty reported in using audio/video conferencing was organization due to the difficulties in working with partners in very different time zones. Social networking tools and Web 2.0 technologies, however, are also being used, and their use is likely to increase.

Data from the case studies also helped to identify factors which can help practitioners to integrate telecollaborative projects more seamlessly into their institutions and classes. First of all, the support of department heads is vital for the successful integration of exchanges. Their support ensures that exchanges continue even when particular staff members change institutions. Also, by maintaining the same exchange partners over long periods, telecollaborative exchanges are more likely to become integrated into an institution's activities. Signing an exchange agreement or memorandum of understanding can provide partners with a sense of security when planning exchanges and drawing up course guides for the coming academic year. Finally, although we found different levels of integration of OIEs in institutions, ensuring that students will receive credit for participating in OIEs undoubtedly helps both institutions and students give more importance to the experience.

4. Conclusions

The survey and case study findings clearly reveal the positive impact of OIEs both for educators and students, and at the same time the barriers which need to be overcome in order to facilitate the integration of OIE in higher education. A series of recommendations have been drawn up by the research team for university senior management and European policy decision makers, including greater support for educators through training, agreements and grants for OIEs, which can be seen as a form of 'virtual mobility', the awarding of European credit transfer and accumulation system (ECTS) for student participation in OIE and some kind of formal recognition for educators' and institutions' involvement in OIE.

The INTENT team is also using the survey findings to support the rest of the project which involves the development of a set of tools, telecollaborative models and partner networks to overcome barriers and facilitate telecollaboration; publication of an online training manual and holding training workshops to train and inform the foreign language learning and teaching community about OIE and finally engaging decision makers at institutional, regional and national levels in a collaborative dialogue as to how telecollaboration can be effectively employed as a tool for the achievement of the Bologna process.

Acknowledgements. The survey report and the INTENT project have been funded with support from the European Commission. The study reported in this publication was developed principally by Francesca Helm, Sarah Guth and Robert O'Dowd in their role as the main researchers in this part of the INTENT project. However, we would like to acknowledge that all of the INTENT project team played a very active role in the development and dissemination of the survey and the report. More information about the INTENT project team and their activities can be found here: http://intent-project.eu.

References

Dooly, M. (Ed.). (2008). *Telecollaborative Language Learning: A guidebook to moderating intercultural collaboration online*. Bern: Peter Lang.

Guth, S., & Helm, F. (Eds.). (2010). *Telecollaboration 2.0 : language, literacies and intercultural learning in the 21st century*. Bern: Peter Lang.

Guth, S., Helm, F., & O'Dowd, R. (2012). *University language classes collaborating online. Report on the integration of telecollaborative networks in European universities*. Retrieved from http://intent-project.eu/sites/default/files/Telecollaboration_report_Final_Oct2012_0.pdf

O'Dowd, R. (Ed.). (2007). *Online intercultural exchange - an introduction for foreign language teachers*. Bristol: Multilingual Matters.

UNIVERSITY OF
GOTHENBURG

Longitudinal Study on Fluency Among Novice Learners of Japanese

Maki Hirotani[a]*, Kazumi Matsumoto[b], and Atsushi Fukada[c]

a. Rose-Hulman Institute of Technology, Terre Haute, IN, USA
b. Ball State University, W. University Ave. Muncie, IN, USA
c. Purdue University, West Lafayette, IN, USA

Abstract. The present study examined various aspects of the development of learners' fluency in Japanese using a large set of speech samples collected over a long period, using an online speaking practice/assessment system called *Speak Everywhere*. The purpose of the present study was to examine: (1) how the fluency related measures changed over time, and (2) which linguistic factors were correlated with each fluency measure. This study used oral production of English-speaking learners enrolled in the first year Japanese courses at a university in the U.S. The students submitted two types of speaking assignments using Speak Everywhere: (1) sentence-level oral reading and (2) short Q&A. The assignments were collected at the end of each chapter for two quarters. The study used speech rate and pause related fluency measures adapted from Ginther, Dimova, and Yang (2010). For the data analysis, we used Praat (Boersma & Weenink, 2011) for acoustic analysis and Mecab (Kudo, 2011) for morphological analysis. The results of one-way repeated measures ANOVA revealed that several measures of fluency deteriorated in both oral reading and Q&A tasks as expected from the previous research (Segalowitz & Freed, 2004). This study then examined what complexity factors affected these measures, using the mixed model approach. Overall, it was found that because various factors influence the development of fluency, temporal measures alone cannot explain fluency development.

Keywords: fluency, Japanese, Speak Everywhere, longitudinal study, objective measures.

1. Introduction

Previous research on fluency has shown that among temporal fluency measures, speech rate and total pause time significantly correlate with language proficiency (Iwashita, Brown, McNamara, & O'Hagan, 2008), but that fluency does not develop in a linear

---

* Contact author: hirotani@rose-hulman.edu

In L. Bradley & S. Thouësny (Eds.), *CALL: Using, Learning, Knowing, EUROCALL Conference, Gothenburg, Sweden, 22-25 August 2012, Proceedings* (pp. 129-133). © Research-publishing.net Dublin 2012

fashion (Ellis, 2009). Ellis (2009) suggested that there were trade-offs among fluency, accuracy, and complexity. This trade-off idea has yet to be substantiated. The purpose of the present study is to examine: (1) how the fluency-related measures change over time, and (2) which complexity factors (lexical and syntactic complexity) are correlated with each fluency measure.

2. Method

2.1. Participants
The participants were students enrolled in first-year Japanese courses at a university in the U.S. They were all native English speakers. The duration of the study was 20 weeks. Twenty students completed the two courses and oral data from these students were used for data analysis.

2.2. Materials
Two types of exercises were given as speaking homework in each chapter using an online oral practice/assessment platform called *Speak Everywhere*. At the beginning of each chapter, two to three exercises were assigned in which the students read sentences aloud following video cues. In this task, they repeated sentences after the instructor in the video. Each assignment included 12-13 items each of which consisted of one to four sentences containing new and old vocabulary words and structures. At the end of each chapter, the students worked on two types of review tasks: 1) oral reading of sentences without video cues and 2) short Q&A. In the oral reading task, 18 items, each of which consisted of one to four sentences, were given. In the Q&A task, one open-ended question was asked. The students' oral productions in these two review tasks were collected automatically by *Speak Everywhere* and used for data analysis.

2.3. Measures
The following speed-related and pause-related fluency measures were adapted from Ginther et al. (2010): speech time ratio, speech rate, articulation rate, running time, number of silent pauses, mean silent pause time, mean silent pause time within AS-units, mean silent pause time between AS-units, and silent pause ratio.

2.4. Data analysis
The audio data from Lessons 4, 7, and 11, which were collected at the beginning of the second term, at the end of the second term, and at the end of the third term, respectively, were used. All the fluency measures were calculated using Praat (Boersma & Weenink, 2011) and Mecab (Kudo, 2011), a Japanese morphological analyzer, and custom-written PHP scripts. They were then analyzed with one-way repeated measures ANOVA to answer research question 1. The within-subjects factor was lesson. To test sphericity assumption, Machly's test was used. For a post-hoc test, Fisher's Least Significant

Difference (LSD) was used. For question 2, the following complexity factors were examined using the mixed model approach: new structures, new words, katakana words (loanwords), the number of moras, and the number of moras within AS-units.

3. Results and discussion

3.1. Research question 1
Table 1 shows the means of the fluency measures.

Table 1. Means of fluency measures

	Lesson 4		Lesson 7		Lesson 11	
	oral reading	Q&A	oral reading	Q&A	oral reading	Q&A
Speech time ratio	.9367	0.7323	.7987	0.6139	.7614	0.6805
Speech rate	5.0058	3.9353	4.0954	3.1796	3.7687	3.6374
Articulation rate	5.3236	5.3723	5.1011	5.1784	4.9634	5.3381
Running time	13.3699	6.0134	8.5410	5.3708	8.1019	6.5704
Mean silent pause time	.1782	0.4384	.4607	0.7135	.4886	0.6084
Mean SPT within AS units	.1765	0.6482	.5627	0.9394	.5778	0.8037
Mean SPT b/w AS units	N/A	0.7931	.5824	1.2771	.6346	1.0649
Silent pause ratio	.0688	.2677	.2103	.3861	.2385	.3259

3.1.1. The oral reading task
Using one-way repeated measures ANOVA and t-test, the present study found the following. The students decreased their speaking speed over the course of learning. The utterance length between pauses became shorter in Lesson 7 and Lesson 11 than in Lesson 4 even though their learning experience increased. The pauses within AS units as well as between AS units significantly increased as the lessons moved on.

Although these results contradict some previous studies (Freed, 1995; Lennon, 1990; Towell, Hawkins, & Bazergui, 1996), they are consistent with Segalowitz and Freed (2004), who found no measurable improvement on fluency in a group of students who studied the target language in a formal foreign language classroom for one semester. Perhaps, 20 weeks is still too short to detect measurable gains in fluency.

3.1.2. The Q&A task
According to an ANOVA and a subsequent post hoc analysis, the speed-related measures showed a V-shaped pattern; i.e., they decreased between Lessons 4 and 7 and increased between Lessons 7 and 11. The pause-related measures, on the other hand, generally increased, meaning that pauses became longer over the course of learning.

There are two possible explanations for these results. First, for the deterioration of fluency observed between Lessons 4 and 7, trade-offs among fluency, accuracy, and complexity may have been a strong factor; some students may have struggled with difficult materials. Secondly, these results might indicate a delayed learning effect. As in the studies by Ellis (2009) and Lennon (1990), the students might have had difficulty in improving their fluency initially due to the trade-off effect, but in time they overcame it and developed their fluency towards the end of the study period.

3.2. Research question 2

The present study further analyzed the data with the mixed model approach in order to find out whether or not there were complexity factors affecting the students' fluency, and if so, which ones. The complexity factors we investigated were new structures, new words, katakana words (loanwords), the number of moras, and the number of moras within AS-units (see Table 2). The fixed effects were tasks, (oral reading or Q&A) and the repeat effects were lessons. Subjects were nested within sentences.

Table 2. Means of complexity factors in the oral reading and the Q&A tasks

Complexity factors	Oral reading	Q&A
Number of moras	42.66	78.53
Number of moras within AS units	22.70	18.91
New words	.85	.28
New structures	.43	.45
Katakana words	.44	.39

3.2.1. The oral reading task

It was found that the greater number of moras and new words had a negative effect on fluency, while Katakana and the number of moras within AS units had a positive effect. For the speed of utterances and pauses, the number of moras (i.e., sentence length) was the major disfluency factor. For the length of the utterances between pauses, new words and the number of moras shortened the utterances. For the total pauses, the number of moras and the number of moras within AS units were the factors to make the pauses longer. The pauses within AS units, however, became longer only when the number of moras increased.

3.2.2. The Q&A task

The Q&A task, on the other hand, had only one significant factor, new words, that affected fluency. When the students used new words, their utterances slowed down, the length between pauses became shorter, and the pauses became longer.

3.2.3. Discussion of the mixed model analysis

The significant factors in the oral reading task and those in the Q&A task were different, presumably corresponding to different production processes called for by the tasks. In the oral reading task, the students read aloud sentences created by the instructor focusing on the structures and vocabulary words introduced in each chapter, while in the Q&A task, they produced utterances on their own. Therefore, the tasks themselves also affect the fluency measures. For an illustration of this point, notice that in Table 1 the mean silent pause time is always longer in the Q&A task than in the oral reading task. This can be attributed to the assumption that students need longer preparation time in the Q&A task to first formulate what to say and to construct utterances to express it.

The number of moras per item in the oral reading task was much smaller than that in the Q&A task. However, fluency was affected only in the oral reading task by the number of moras. The reason may be that since the students chose the words and structures in the utterances, they were able to choose ones that they could use effortlessly. In the oral reading task, on the other hand, the students had no control over the sentences. Therefore, the number of moras (which translates into longer and perhaps more complex sentences) negatively affected the students' fluency.

4. Conclusions

This study found a generally declining trend in the fluency development of first-year learners of Japanese. Through the mixed model analysis, we were able to identify such complexity factors as new words putting pressure on fluency development. What is needed to overcome the pressure might be a greater amount of oral fluency building practice. Conducting a similar study at other levels (e.g., intermediate and advanced) might also be a fruitful avenue of research.

References

Boersma, P., & Weenink, D. (2011). *PRAAT*. Retrieved from http://www.praat.org

Ellis, R. (2009). The differential effects of three types of task planning on the fluency, complexity, and accuracy in L2 oral production. *Applied Linguistics, 30*(4), 474-509.

Freed, B. (1995). What makes us think that students who study abroad become fluent? In B. Freed (Ed.), *Second language acquisition in a study abroad context* (pp.123-148). Amsterdam: John Benjamins.

Ginther, A., Dimova, S., & Yang, R. (2010). Conceptual and empirical relationships between temporal measures of fluency and oral English proficiency with implications for automated scoring. *Language Testing, 27*(3), 379-399.

Iwashita, N., Brown, A., McNamara, T., & O'Hagan, S. (2008). Assessed levels of second language speaking proficiency: How distinct? *Applied Linguistics, 29*(1), 24-49. doi:10.1093/applin/amm017

Kudo, T. (2011). *MeCab: Yet another part-of-speech and morphological analyzer*. Retrieved from http://mecab.sourceforge.net (in Japanese)

Lennon, P. (1990). Investigating fluency in EFL: A quantitative approach. *Language Learning, 40*(3), 387-417. doi:10.1111/j.1467-1770.1990.tb00669.x

Segalowitz, N., & Freed, B. F. (2004). Context, contact, and cognition in oral fluency acquisition: Learning Spanish in at home and study abroad contexts. *Studies in Second Language Acquisition, 26*(2), 173-199. doi: 10.1017/S0272263104262027

Towell, R., Hawkins, R., & Bazergui, N. (1996). The development of fluency in advanced learners of French. *Applied Linguistics, 17*(1), 84-119. doi:10.1093/applin/17.1.84

UNIVERSITY OF
GOTHENBURG

How English Learners Manage Face Threats in MSN Conversations

Chi-yin Hong*

Department of Applied English, Kun Shan University, Tainan City, Taiwan

Abstract. This study explores how low- and intermediate-level English learners manage face threats in MSN conversations. The effects of the addressee's status are also studied. Forty English learners, who were further divided into beginner and intermediate groups according to their English proficiency, participated in this study. Based on six offensive situations, the subjects had two MSN chats with the instructor and four with their peers. The complainee's response needed to contain an upgrader, which intensified the offense. All of the subjects had the same topics for the two chats with the instructor, but in chats with the peers, each proficiency group was divided into two sub-groups, with one being the complainer, i.e., the group initiating the complaint, and the other being the complainee, i.e., the group being complained to. In the first two chats, one sub-group initiated the complaints and the other replied, and in the following two chats, the two sub-groups exchanged their roles. Nonetheless, only the complainers' strategy use was analyzed in this study. Results showed that the two learner groups used a similar range of complaint strategies, including hints, disapproval, requests for repair, explicit complaints, threats and warnings, and external moves which consisted of preparators, justifications, promises for future actions, expressions of politeness, and reconciliations, to express their unhappiness and react to the upgrader. The strategies and the moves most preferred by both groups were explicit complaints and providing justifications. Further analyses reveal that the two groups also tended to use requests for repair as a complaint strategy, but the intermediate group produced much more indirect requests than direct ones, whereas the beginner group tended to be balanced in the use of the two types. The addressee's status also influenced both groups' complaints in the strategy use. Although the two groups did not adjust strategy use well to fit the addressee's social status, the intermediate learners, who were likely to be more indirect when initiating complaints to the superiors than to the peers, appeared to be socially more appropriate than the beginners.

Keywords: face threats, complaints, MSN, status.

---

* Contact author: cathyhong0419@hotmail.com

In L. Bradley & S. Thouësny (Eds.), *CALL: Using, Learning, Knowing, EUROCALL Conference, Gothenburg, Sweden, 22-25 August 2012, Proceedings* (pp. 134-138). © Research-publishing.net Dublin 2012

1. Introduction

People often encounter face threats in daily life, which might make either the speaker or the addressee lose face, and these threats need to be carefully dealt with. Nowadays, computer-mediated communication (CMC) is widely used, particularly in cross-cultural interaction which may result in plenty of misunderstandings and communication breakdowns because of the reduced context in CMC. Thus, research into online speech behaviors of the users, including language learners, is needed, especially synchronous CMC which enables users to interact simultaneously. Some researchers have claimed that CMC conversations are more direct than natural talk because of the absence of the contextual cues (Smilowitz, Compton, & Flint, 1988) and the users' diminished regard for the normal conventions of politeness usually evident in face-to-face conversations (Simmons, 1994). Thus, the current study, with the focus on complaint strategies, examines how English learners manage face threats through MSN, a synchronous CMC. The research questions are:

- What are the complaint strategies used by beginners and intermediate learners to manage face threats in MSN conversations?
- Are there any differences in complaint strategies preferred by beginners and intermediate learners in MSN conversations?
- What are the differences in complaint strategies used towards superiors and peers by beginners and intermediate learners?

2. Method

2.1. Participants
Forty students participated in this study. The subjects were English learners in Taiwan. They were college students, further divided into two proficiency groups: beginner and intermediate groups. The subjects' proficiency was determined by their prior performances in proficiency tests. The beginners' proficiency equaled to CEF[*] A2 whereas the intermediate learners' proficiency was CEF B1.

2.2. Instrument
In this study, MSN Messenger was used as the instrument to collect speech data. The subjects had two MSN chats with the instructor and four with their peers. The instructor represented the higher-status addressee whereas the peers represented equals in status. All the subjects had chats with the instructor, but in chats with their peers, each proficiency group was divided into two sub-groups, with one group acting as the complainer and the other responding to the complaints. In the first two chats, one sub-group initiated the complaints and the other replied, and in the following two chats, the

---
[*] Common European Framework of Reference for Languages

two sub-groups exchanged their roles. All of the responses were required to contain an upgrader, which intensified the face threat and may have made the complainer even unhappier. The six topics were provided as follows.

- You just got your paper back from your teacher. When you see your grade, you are shocked because the grade is much lower than you expected. *Upgrader*: The teacher criticizes the assignment and says that you deserve the grade.
- You had an assignment due yesterday. You tried to turn in the late assignment today, but it was rejected. However, you heard that your teacher accepted your classmate's late assignment. *Upgrader*: The teacher says that you should not have missed the deadline and gives an excuse for your classmate.
- You are working on a project with your classmate, who doesn't do anything. Whenever you ask him/her to help, s/he always says that s/he has no time. *Upgrader*: Your classmate fights back by saying that you also always do the same thing.
- Your classmate is always at least half an hour late whenever you hang out with him/her, and you really don't like it. *Upgrader*: Your classmate says that you were also late for the last meeting, so it is fair for you to wait this time.
- Your classmate often borrows stuff from you, but s/he never returns your stuff unless you rush him/her to do so. *Upgrader*: Your classmate argues that you also haven't returned his/her iPod that you borrowed a long time ago.
- Your classmate never does his/her assignments and always asks you to lend yours for him/her to copy. *Upgrader*: Your classmate threatens to end the friendship if you don't let him/her copy.

2.3. Coding scheme and statistical analysis

This study examines the complaint strategies and external moves that learners used to manage face threats. Complaint strategies express the speakers' unhappiness to an offensive situation whereas external moves reduce the face-threatening effects of complaints. In this study, there were five types of complaint strategies: hints, disapprovals, requests for repair, explicit complaints, and threats, as well as five external moves: preparators, justifications, promises for future actions, expressions of politeness, and reconciliations. The strategies and moves produced by the two proficiency groups and the impacts of the status variability on their strategy preferences were processed by Chi-square analyses.

3. Discussion

In general, the two proficiency groups produced the same range of complaint strategies and external moves. Both groups utilized explicit complaints and justifications with the highest percentage among all the complaint strategies and external moves, and there was no significant inter-group difference in the use of either strategies or moves.

However, differences were found in the two groups' use of requests for repair as a complaint strategy. The intermediate group produced much more indirect requests (85%) than direct ones (15%), whereas the beginner group tended to be balanced in the use of two types of requests (indirect: 58%; direct: 41%). To sum up, the learners were straightforward in expressing their unhappiness. The findings support Sussman and Sproull's (1999) claim that CMC technology fosters more direct communication strategies than face-to-face communication because of its text-based nature and de-individuation. This could also be because of the relative easiness of direct expressions, which directly map the propositional meaning and the linguistic form.

The social status variable appeared to have some influences on the two groups' complaints. They were similar in their use of strategies and external moves towards superiors and peers and showed significant intra-group differences in their preference of complaint strategies. Although the two groups tended to use more explicit complaints towards both superiors and peers, differences were found in hints and disapprovals: they were likely to produce more disapprovals towards superiors and more hints towards peers. This appears to be similar to Trosborg (1995), who claimed that the learners had difficulty adjusting their performance sufficiently to the parameters of dominance. As hints avoid explicit mention of the offensive events or the speaker's unhappiness, their severity level should be lower than that of disapproval. The subjects used more disapprovals towards superiors than towards peers, who received more hints possibly because of the reduced effects of contextual cues, which connote social meaning in CMC, and the learners temporarily overlooked the etiquette that should have varied with the addressee's social identity.

Despite the similarities, further analyses of strategies used to initiate the complaints towards addressees of two status types exhibit the differences between the two groups. The frequency of each strategy that beginners used to initiate complaints towards superiors and equals was similar, and this is supported by Chi-square analyses, which revealed no significant differences. However, the intermediate learners were inclined to use more requests for repair as a complaint strategy to initiate their interaction with superiors, and this differentiates from their initiative strategy towards addressees of the two status types ($p < .05$), especially as most of the requests were polite, indirect requests (89%). As Blum-Kulka (1987) has claimed, hints and indirect requests can be equally polite, and indirect requests can reduce the hearer's processing burden because they stated the intended follow-up remedial action clearly but politely. From this angle, in addition to explicit complaints, which are a popular strategy towards addressees of either status type, the intermediate learners preferred indirect requests, with the attempt to reduce the face threats that might be caused. This reflects their consciousness of the effects of the addressee's status. In contrast, the beginners' initiative strategies did not reveal this tendency, indicating that the addressee's status might not be their concern in MSN conversations, or even if it was, the beginners failed to exhibit the differentiation in their management of face threats.

4. Conclusions

This study showed that the beginners and the intermediate learners were similarly straightforward, and the variable of social status also had similar effects on their management of face threats. However, compared with the beginners, the intermediate learners tended to be more indirect. Their directness brings the pedagogical attention to the relationship between using CMC and developing learners' pragmatic competence. As Sykes (2005) has pointed out, CMC users need to be cautious because all dissatisfactions are expressed by words, whereas face-to-face communication includes facial expressions and body language to modify the intensity of face threats. Instructors can guide learners to attend to net etiquette, the reduced context of CMC, and consequences of inappropriate speech behaviors, and then integrate polite linguistic forms and expressions into their lessons.

This study is constrained by two limitations which provide suggestions for future studies. As this study only included beginners and intermediate learners future research could recruit advanced learners or even native English and Chinese speakers for investigations of effects of proficiency, cultural backgrounds, and language transfer. Further comparisons of natural face-to-face conversations are also needed for a fuller picture of the speech behaviors of English learners in CMC.

Acknowledgements. I would like to thank the forty participants, who willingly accepted my invitation to participate in this study and offered valuable data for research analyses.

References

Blum-Kulka, S. (1987). Indirectness and politeness in requests: Same or different? *Journal of Pragmatics, 11*(2), 131-146. doi: 10.1016/0378-2166(87)90192-5

Simmons, T. (1994). *Politeness Theory in Computer-Mediated Communication: Face-Threatening Acts in a "Faceless" Medium*. Unpublished Master's thesis. Asthon University, Birmingham, England. (ERIC: ED381005)

Smilowitz, M., Compton, C., & Flint, L. (1988). The effects of computer mediated communication on an individual's judgment: A study based on the methods of Asch's social influence experiment. *Computer in Human Behavior, 4*(4), 311-321. doi: 10.1016/0747-5632(88)90003-9

Sussman, S., & Sproull, L. (1999). Straight talk: Delivering bad news through electronic communication. *Information Systems Research, 10*(2), 150-167.

Sykes, J. M. (2005). Synchronous CMC and pragmatic development: Effects of oral and written chat. *CALICO Journal, 22*(3), 399-431.

Trosborg, A. (1995). *Interlanguage pragmatics: Requests, complaints, and apologies*. Berlin: Walter de Gruyter & Co.

UNIVERSITY OF GOTHENBURG

Interactive Digital Kitchen: The impact on Language learning

Nor Fadzlinda Ishak* and Paul Seedhouse

Newcastle University, Newcastle upon Tyne, United Kingdom

Abstract. This study aims to investigate the usability of a newly developed technology – the Digital Kitchen – as compared to a normal everyday kitchen to teach English vocabulary. This interactive kitchen which was first developed to help people with dementia is equipped with sensors and different wireless communication technologies which allows it to give step-by-step cooking instructions and verbal feedbacks to the users. In this study, the task-based learning teaching (TBLT) approach was brought into the real world instead of the artificial real-world activities carried out in classrooms. Altogether, 54 intermediate level English learners took part in this study. They were divided into experimental and control group with one group using the Digital Kitchen and the other group in a normal kitchen setting. Working in pairs, they cooked 'Apple Crumble' (a traditional English recipe). After cooking, an immediate post-test was administered to find out whether vocabulary learning had taken place in the one hour cooking session. Feedback from the participants was also documented using open ended questionnaires. Additionally, a delayed post-test was carried out 10 days after the experiment to check whether the words learnt were retained. We will discuss the quantitative findings of this study to determine the impact of the technology on vocabulary learning.

Keywords: digital technology, instrumented kitchen, vocabulary, task-based.

1. Introduction

Over the past 30 years, many drastic changes have occurred in the field of education where technology is concerned. Advances in digital technologies are changing the profession of English language teaching and applied linguistics. In fact, it is predicted that in the next decade, as universities and colleges respond to global, social, political, technological, and learning research trends, the practices of teaching and learning will undergo a technology revolution (Siemens & Tittenberger, 2009).

---

* Contact author: n.f.ishak@newcastle.ac.uk

In L. Bradley & S. Thouësny (Eds.), *CALL: Using, Learning, Knowing, EUROCALL Conference, Gothenburg, Sweden, 22-25 August 2012, Proceedings* (pp. 139-143). © Research-publishing.net Dublin 2012

One new invention that has a high possibility to benefit language learners is the Ambient Kitchen* which was first developed to help people with dementia. As it is equipped with sensors and different wireless communication technologies, the kitchen can speak and provide helpful hints to its users. In order to be used as a learning tool, the kitchen was then equipped with more gadgets that could be utilised to meet pedagogical goals. For example, more accelerometers are attached to the utensils and the containers of the ingredients to allow the kitchen to monitor the activities of its users. The ubiquitous computing makes it possible for the kitchen to give step by step cooking instructions and at the same time allow the users to have control of the process through the interface displayed on a touch screen. They can either request for a repetition which would also give them the written text of the instruction, skip or go back to certain instructions.

Funded by the Engineering and Physical Sciences Research Council (EPSRC) Digital Economy Programme on "Research in the Wild: Getting research out there", the brand new Digital Kitchen was built for the French Kitchen Project** and is still undergoing some technical enhancements. Theoretically, the project aims to develop the next generation of technology applied to language teaching, namely the use of digital sensors together with a task-based learning approach.

Hypothetically, it is assumed that when the same task is carried out in a normal everyday kitchen, the outcomes may not be the same as when the tasks are carried out in the interactive Digital Kitchen. It can also be assumed that the Digital Kitchen, just like the other technological tools employed in teaching should be able to produce better learning outcomes. However, in reality, how much 'more' can the Digital Kitchen offer when compared to a normal everyday kitchen?

The research intends to evaluate and determine the impact of incorporating technology in tasks designed for vocabulary teaching. Therefore, the intent of this comparative experimental study is to test the usability of the Digital Kitchen as a tool in a task-based approach to facilitate vocabulary learning. Based on one cooking session, this study hopes to find out the difference in the learners' achievement when the same task is carried out in the interactive Digital Kitchen as compared to the real life setting (normal everyday kitchen).

2. Method

2.1. Participants

Participation was voluntary. 54 intermediate level English learners from the INTO Programme of Newcastle University who have been in the United Kingdom for not more than 6 months took part in this study. These students are academically

---

* The Ambient Kitchen project is available at http://culturelab.ncl.ac.uk/research/digital-interaction/ambient-kitchen-cels

** The French Digital Kitchen project is available at https://digitalinstitute.ncl.ac.uk/ilablearn/kitchen

qualified students who have already been accepted into a university undergraduate or postgraduate course. They were chosen for two main reasons: 1) They have limited English vocabulary, and 2) besides academic reasons, they are learning English to be able to communicate in everyday life tasks.

2.2. Procedure

The participants were divided into experimental and control groups with one group using the Digital Kitchen and the other group in a normal kitchen setting. When the project started, the participants came in pairs and were first asked to do a pre-test. Next, prior to cooking, the participants watched a video showing the food being prepared (highlighting the ingredients and utensils involved). Later, they cooked a traditional English recipe which was 'Apple Crumble'. The experimental group followed instructions from the system and the control group was given a printed recipe. A laptop was also provided for the learners to seek online help. After the cooking activity, they completed a set of vocabulary exercises as a post-task. Immediate post-test was then administered to find out whether vocabulary learning had taken place in the one hour cooking session. Feedback from the participants was also documented using open ended questionnaires. Also, a delayed post-test was carried out ten days after the experiment to check whether the words learnt could be retained.

2.3. Methodological framework

The task-based learning teaching approach was employed whereby TBLT was brought into the real world (Ellis, 2003) instead of the artificial real-world activities carried out in normal classrooms. In designing the vocabulary task, the involvement load hypothesis (Hulstijn & Laufer, 2001) was also being taken into account to ensure vocabulary learning opportunities.

2.4. Data analysis

In order to quantify our data, we used the SPSS software. Independent t-tests and sample paired t-tests were carried out to get the results of between group and within group performances in the pre-, post- and delayed tests.

2.4.1. The tests scores: comparison within group

Table 1 shows that the mean score of the experimental group pre-test and post-test were 7.39 and 17.6 respectively, with a level of significance value of 0.00 ($t = -24.02$, $df = 27$, $p < .05$). This confirmed that the difference in the students' performance after the intervention is highly significant. Meanwhile, the mean score of the control group pre-test was 7.27 and of the post-test was at 15.65. In fact, the difference between the two means was also statistically significant ($t = -16.58$, $df = 25$, $p < .05$). This depicts that the control group test scores also improved although they were not exposed to the Digital Kitchen.

Table 1. Significance of difference between mean scores of Experimental and Control group on pre-test, post-test and delayed test (raw data)

Group	Test	N	M	SD	t-test for equality of means			
					Mean difference	t value	df	p value
Experimental	Pretest	28	7.39	2.39	10.22	24.02	27	0.00
	Post-test	28	17.61	2.35				
Control	Pretest	26	7.27	2.65	8.38	16.58	25	0.00
	Post-test	26	15.65	3.62				
Experimental	Post-test	28	17.61	2.35	1.40	4.16	27	0.00
	Delayed	28	16.21	2.33				
Control	Post-test	26	15.65	3.62	1.84	4.59	25	0.00
	Delayed	26	13.81	3.76				

The paired sample t-test was then run on each group's post- and delayed test results to find out whether the same results found in the earlier test maintained the same. However, both the experimental and comparison group results show that the participants have lost some of the words that they have learnt. For the comparison group, it is significant ($t = 4.16$, $df = 25$, $p < .05$) with a post-test mean of 17.61 as compared to 16.21 for the delayed test. The experimental group had significant results ($t = 4.58$, $df = 27$, $p < .05$), with a post-test mean of 15.65 and 13.81 for the delayed test. These results demonstrate that both groups changed to a statistically significant extent.

2.4.2. The tests scores: comparison between groups

Table 2. Significance of difference between mean scores of experimental group and control group on the actual post-test scores (post- minus pre-test scores)

Group	N	M	SD	t-test for equality of means			
				MD	t value	df	p value
Experimental	28	10.21	2.41	1.83	2.78	52	0.007
Control	26	8.38	2.53				

Table 2 depicts that the mean score for the experimental group was higher than the control group ($t = 2.78$, $df = 52$, $p < .05$) with a mean difference of 1.83. This means that the difference in the test scores was significant and therefore, we can conclude that the experimental group performed better than the control group in the post-test.

Table 3. Significance of difference between mean scores of experimental group and control group on the actual delayed test scores (delayed minus pre-test scores)

Group	N	M	SD	t-test for equality of means			
				MD	t value	df	p value
Experimental	28	8.82	2.04	2.28	3.26	52	0.002
Control	26	6.54	3.04				

Table 3 reveals that the mean score of the experimental group was 6.54 and that of the control group was 8.82 on the actual delayed test scores. The mean difference was 2.28 with the p value .002 which shows that there was a statistically significant difference ($t = -3.26$, $df = 52$, $p > .05$) between the two groups. Hence, this confirmed that the learners in the experimental group had acquired more lexical items than those in the control group. The result above also shows the overall performance of both groups in the experiments. This indicates that the experimental group has performed significantly better throughout the experiment.

2.4.3. The open-ended questionnaire (experimental group)
100% of the students enjoyed the session. 82% said the task was easy. 14% claimed it was neither easy nor hard but one student (3.6%) thought that it was 'a bit difficult'. All of them claimed that they had learnt new words and five stated that they had learnt instruction patterns too. Only 53% of them reported that they had used the online dictionary/websites to look for meaning of words. 100% of them claimed that they could follow the instructions and believed that the activity could help them learn English. 64% of them turned to the interface, 21% on both interface and cooking partner, the rest on online dictionary/website and the interface when faced with difficulty.

3. Conclusion

The purpose of this study was to find out the impact of the Digital Kitchen to vocabulary learning. Based on the results of the tests scores, the Digital Kitchen does have an impact on the students' achievement. The overall performance of the experimental group was better than the control group throughout the experiment. However, as the statistical analysis is only data for the findings, we will need to look at the details of the students' feedback and also the video recording in order to understand why this happened. We need to get some insight into how the students interact among themselves and the digital system that would help them to learn more words than those who did not experience the technology.

Acknowledgement. The French Digital Kitchen project was funded by the Digital Economy Programme. The Digital Economy Programme is a Research Councils UK cross council initiative led by EPSRC and contributed to by AHRC, ESRC, and MRC.

References
Ellis, R. (2003). *Task-based language learning and teaching*. Oxford: Clarendon Press.
Hulstijn, J. H., & Laufer, B. (2001). Some Empirical Evidence for the Involvement Load Hypothesis in Vocabulary Acquisition. *Language Learning, 51*(3), 539-558. doi: 10.1111/0023-8333.00164
Siemens, G., & Tittenberger, P. (2009). *Handbook of Emerging Technologies for Learning*. University of Manitoba. Retrieved from http://www.scribd.com/doc/54496169/Handbook-of-Emerging-Technologies-for-Learning-Siemens-Tittenberger

UNIVERSITY OF
GOTHENBURG

Selected Can-Do Statements and Learning Materials for ATR CALL BRIX: Helping University Students in Japan Improve Their TOEIC Scores

Yasushige Ishikawa[a*], Mutsumi Kondo[b], Reiko Akahane-Yamada[c], Craig Smith[a], Hiroshi Hatakeda[d], and Norihisa Wada[e]

a. Kyoto Univeristy of Foreign Studies, Kyoto, Japan
b. Tezukayamagakuin University, Osakasayama-shi, Japan
c. ATR Intelligent Robotics and Communication Labs, Kyoto, Japan
d. Uchida Yoko Co., Ltd., Tokyo, Japan
e. IE Institute Co., Ltd., Tokyo, Japan

Abstract. This paper reports on the use of can-do statements (CDS) for the development of learning materials to prepare Japanese university students for the Test of English for International Communication (TOEIC). These learning materials have been made available on ATR CALL BRIX (http://www.atr-lt.jp/products/brix/index.html), a www-based courseware with a learning management system (LMS) which contains study logs, achievement rate reports on student-set goals, the identification of students' weak points, and advice on test-taking strategies. CDS, the specific behaviors that an examinee at a certain score level can be expected to be able to perform in English (Chauncey Group International, 2000) have been conventionally used as descriptors to explain test scores to educators and employers who use TOEIC scores to assess the English proficiency levels of students and prospective employees. Official CDS published for the TOEIC 600-score level, and the CDS, at comparable levels, for the Society for Testing English Proficiency test (STEP), and for the Common European Framework of Reference for Languages (CEFR) were used to compile this study's CDS set. The CDS were given to 592 students as a self-report inventory immediately after they took a TOEIC test. The CDS were then used to develop TOEIC learning materials which were trialed in a TOEIC skill-building course for 22 students. According to comparisons of pre- and post-course TOEIC scores, it was concluded that the use of CDS-based TOEIC learning tasks, which include advice on test-taking strategies, in a www-based course may help students improve their TOEIC scores.

Keywords: TOEIC, can-do statements, learning materials development, www-based courseware, test-wiseness.

---

* Contact author: yasuishikawa@hotmail.com

In L. Bradley & S. Thouësny (Eds.), *CALL: Using, Learning, Knowing, EUROCALL Conference, Gothenburg, Sweden, 22-25 August 2012, Proceedings* (pp. 144-150). © Research-publishing.net Dublin 2012

1. Introduction

In 2008, about 778,000 people in Japan took the TOEIC Listening and Reading Tests, administered for the creator of the test, Educational Testing Service, by a public-interest NPO, The Institute for International Business Communication (IIBC, 2011), at official test centers; and many more people took a special institutional version of the test at schools and companies (McCrostie, 2009). Because of its widespread use in the business community, today virtually every university student who hopes to get a job in which English proficiency is a requirement wishes to present evidence to company recruiters of a good TOEIC score. A 'good' TOEIC score has been defined by individual companies; and, certain levels of TOEIC scores are required for initial employment, promotions, and foreign assignments. It is believed, according to Terauchi, Koike, and Takada (n.d.), that people must have a score of more than 800 to be able to conduct international business negotiations in English; and thus, a TOEIC score of 800 is a common target for university students. However, the average TOEIC score of first-year university students in Japan is 419 (IIBC, 2011); and so, in order to prepare students for their careers, TOEIC test preparation courses and intensive seminars have become a standard part of the curriculum at many universities.

In order to help university students improve their TOEIC scores, the authors of this paper developed TOEIC learning materials based on can-do statements. In foreign language education, CDS have been defined as "descriptions of the competence of an individual language user" (Imig & O'Dwyer, 2010, p. 2) and used as a means of clarifying plans to improve general EFL teaching practices (e.g., Hiromori, 2009; Yamanishi & Hiromori, 2008). A new set of CDS was compiled by using CDS from three sources: TOEIC CDS at the 600-score level with a more or less balanced proficiency in the listening and reading sections of the test (Chauncey Group International, 2000), and the CDS, at comparable levels, for the Society for Testing English Proficiency test – STEP – (Society for Testing English Proficiency, 2006), and for the Common European Framework of Reference for Languages – CEFR – (Council of Europe, 2001).

The 600-score level was chosen because it was approximately mid-way between the average first-year university student's TOEIC score and the common fourth-year target of 800. A 600-score was seen as a reasonable target for most students after one or two years of EFL study. STEP and CEFR CDS were reviewed in the compilation process to make links with many students' past experiences with English-language proficiency testing through STEP tests which are commonly used in Japan from beginning to advanced levels of EFL study to measure progress and also with the CEFR standards used as benchmarks by international businesses in Japan. Experienced EFL teachers made the CDS selections intuitively based on their knowledge of students' learning needs.

The new set of CDS after confirmation of their recognition by EFL students as descriptors of TOEIC 600-level performance abilities were used to develop TOEIC learning materials. The materials have been published in ATR CALL BRIX, a www-based courseware in order to make the learning materials available to teachers for in-class coursework and outside-of-class assignments, and also to students to use independently of coursework through the use of computers with Internet access. To enhance independent learning, the courseware includes a learning management system which contains study logs, reports of achievement rates for student-set goals, identification of students' weak points, and advice on test-taking strategies.

The ATR CALL BRIX courseware was designed to create interoperability (Ishikawa, Kondo, & Smith, 2010) which is described in Figure 1. Interoperability, in this case, is the capacity of the ATR CALL BRIX courseware to create a single learning environment in which university students who are trying to improve their TOEIC scores and EFL teachers can collaborate in a learning enterprise. The learning environment is one of teachers and students in a partnership in which teachers can be said to be doing their work most effectively as the students gain independence and control over their own learning.

Figure 1. Design principles of ATR CALL BRIX

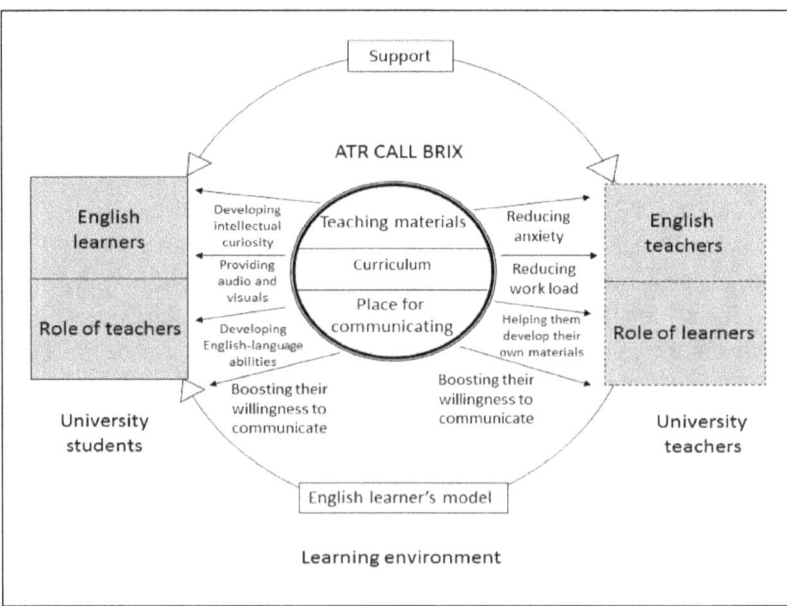

The TOEIC learning materials for this study consisted of 1,000 practice questions based on CDS, i.e., practice questions which could be supported by the teaching of English-language performance skills. If students completed the TOEIC learning tasks incorrectly, the LMS was activated and advice to overcome weaknesses in listening and reading abilities appeared on the display screen. Test-taking strategies for improving students' test-wiseness were also developed and included with the learning materials. Test-wiseness is defined as a capacity to utilize the characteristics and format of the test and the test-taking situation to achieve success (Millman, Bishop, & Ebel, 1965; Sarnacki, 1979). Test-wiseness training can be effective only under specific circumstances (Dolly & Williams, 1986), a learning environment which was created by the repeated use of ATR CALL BRIX system. Figure 2 shows a conceptual diagram of the relationship between the TOEIC learning materials and the LMS in the ATR CALL BRIX courseware.

Figure 2. TOEIC learning materials and the LMS in the ATR CALL BRIX courseware

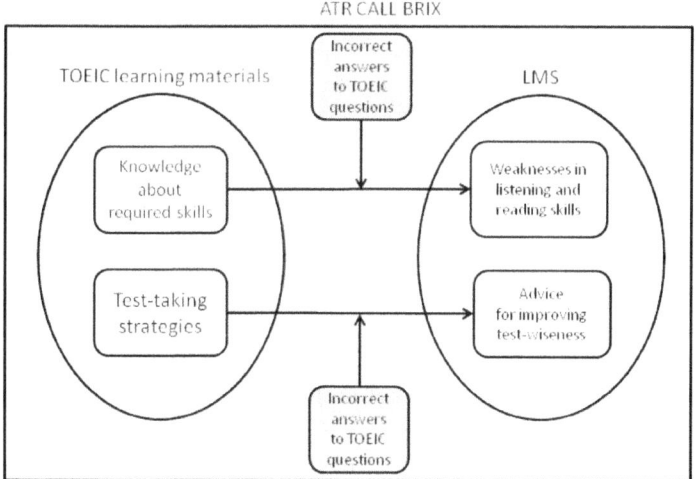

2. Research questions

This study investigated the following two research questions: 1) Would a new set of 600-score level CDS based on teachers' intuitions as to its potential for creating effective TOEIC learning materials correspond with the beliefs of students, who had received 600-level TOEIC scores, about their own English 'can-do' abilities? 2) Would there be improvements in the scores of students who used TOEIC learning materials developed from this study's CDS?

3. Investigation into research question No. 1

3.1. Participants

592 EFL students from first to third years at Kyoto University of Foreign Studies in Japan, who took the TOEIC test in January, participated in this study.

3.2. Method

In order to answer research question No. 1, the 592 students completed a self-report inventory of the items on the new CDS immediately after they had taken the TOEIC test. On a Likert scale of 1 to 5 the students indicated to what degree they had the English performance skills described by the CDS.

3.3. Results and discussion

Pearson's correlation analysis showed that there was a strong positive correlation between the CDS and students' TOEIC scores. Students who had scores of approximately 600 reported that they had the performance skills in English described by the study's CDS. Students who had lower scores reported that they were lacking in the CDS performance skills. Thus, the answer to research question 1 was that the new set of CDS corresponded to the beliefs students at the TOEIC 600-level had about their own English-language performance skills. It was concluded that because of the correspondence between the 600-score level students' beliefs about their performance skills, the lack of these skills as perceived by lower level students, and the EFL teachers views of a potential constructive relationship between the new CDS and learning materials, the new CDS set would be useful in the development of TOEIC learning materials for students who had lower scores but hoped to reach the 600-score level. Table 1 shows the correlation among the CDS and students' TOEIC scores.

Table 1. Correlation among the CDS and participants' TOEIC scores

4. Investigation into research question No. 2

Measure	Mean (SD)	TOEIC listening score	TOEIC reading score	Can-do listening task	Can-do reading task
TOEIC listening score	343.2 (71.95)	1.00	.69*	.45*	.38*
TOEIC reading score	267.00 (68.54)	.69*	1.00	.30*	.39*
Can-do listening task	47.84 (7.61)	.45*	.30*	1.00	.73*
Can-do reading task	60.97 (9.36)	.38*	.39*	.73*	1.00

$N = 592$, $*p < .001$

4.1. Participants

22 EFL students at Kyoto University of Foreign Studies in Japan who had TOEIC scores of below 600 participated in this study.

4.2. Method

In order to answer research question 2, TOEIC testing was conducted at the beginning of April before the semester started to select 22 students who had TOEIC scores below

600 for a TOEIC skill-building course. The participants used the TOEIC learning materials, which were developed based on this study's CDS set, both in class and outside of class. At the end of the course in July, the 22 students took the TOEIC test a second time.

4.3. Results and discussion

A two-tailed t-Test was used to measure the participants' listening and reading abilities at the end of the course. According to the results of the test, the participants' listening ability had improved significantly ($p < .01$, $r = .83$), and the participants' reading ability had also improved significantly ($p < .01$, $r = .53$). It was concluded that the participants' listening and reading abilities may have improved through the use of the TOEIC learning materials. Table 2 shows the results of the total scores of the TOEIC test, and the scores for both the listening and reading sections.

Table 2. Results of pre- and post-TOEIC testing

	N	Pre-TOEIC Test		Post-TOEIC Test		Gain	
		Mean	SD	Mean	SD	Mean	SD
Total	22	413.41	82.15	513.18	81.42	99.77	68.31
Listening	22	247.95	54.76	302.27	49.83	54.32	38.18
Reading	22	165.45	37.45	201.91	64.75	36.45	58.48

5. Conclusion

The study's two research questions were answered in the affirmative:
- The items on the CDS compiled for this study were confirmed by students at the TOEIC 600-score level to be English-language performance skills they believed they had;
- The TOEIC learning materials which were developed based on the study's CDS was useful in helping students improve their scores.

The next steps will be 1) to verify that the TOEIC learning materials in the ATR CALL BRIX courseware are effective in improving students' TOEIC scores by conducting a study with experimental and control groups, and 2) to identify which test-taking strategies in the TOEIC learning materials were used by students at various score levels in order to provide better advice in the LMS of the ATR CALL BRIX courseware.

Acknowledgements. This study was supported by Grant-in-Aid for Scientific Research #2324032 from the Japan Society for the Promotion of Science. The data presented, the statements made, and the views expressed are solely the responsibility of the authors.

References

Chauncey Group International. (2000). *TOEIC Can-do guide: Linking TOEIC scores to activities performed using English*. Retrieved from http://www.ets.org/Media/Research/pdf/TOEIC_CAN_DO.pdf

Council of Europe. (2001). *Common European framework of reference for languages: Learning, teaching, assessment*. Cambridge, UK: Cambridge University Press.

Dolly, J. P., & Williams, K. S. (1986). Using test-taking strategies to maximize multiple-choice test scores. *Educational and Psychological Measurement, 46*(3), 619-625. doi:10.1177/0013164486463014

Hiromori, T. (2009). The elaboration and validation of English language proficiency benchmarks (Can-do lists) for Ehime University. *ARELE: Annual Review of English Language Education in Japan, 20*, 281-290.

IIBC - Institute for International Business Communication. (2011). TOEIC® Test data & analysis 2010. Retrieved from http://www.toeic.or.jp/toeic/pdf/data/DAA2010.pdf

Imig, A., & O'Dwyer, F. (2010). A brief overview of the use of can do statements in language education, the CEFR and ELP. In M. G. Schmidt, N. Naganuma, F. O'Dwyer, A. Imig, & K. Sakai (Eds.), *Can do statements in language education in Japan and beyond: Applications of the CEFR* (pp. 2-8). Tokyo: Asahi Press.

Ishikawa, Y., Kondo, M., & Smith, C. (2010). Design and implementation issues of interoperable educational application: An ICT application for primary school English education in Japan. In F. Lazarinis, S. Green, & E. Pearson (Eds.), *Developing and utilizing e-learning applications* (pp. 100-124). Hershey, PA: Information Science Reference (an imprint of IGI Global).

McCrostie, J. (2009). TOEIC: Where does the money go? Nonprofit IIBC takes in 8-9 billion yen annually from English test fees. August 18, 2009. Japan Times Online.

Millman, J., Bishop, C. H., & Ebel, R. (1965). An analysis of test-wiseness. *Educational and Psychological Measurement, 25*(3), 707-726. doi:10.1177/001316446502500304

Sarnacki, R. E. (1979). An examination of test-wiseness in the cognitive test domain. *Review of Educational Research, 49*(2), 252-279. doi:10.3102/00346543049002252

Society for Testing English Proficiency. (2006). *Eiken can-do list* [STEP can-do list]. Retrieved from http://www.eiken.or.jp/about/cando/cando.html

Terauchi, H., Koike, I., & Takada, T. (n.d.). *Kigyo ga motomeru eigoryoku cyosa (Summary)* [A survey on English-language abilities that Japanese companies expect (Summary)]. Retrieved from http://www.toeic.or.jp/info/img/003/summary.pdf

Yamanishi, H., & Hiromori, T. (2008). Improving the general English education curriculum in Ehime University: The development and significance of English language proficiency benchmarks (Can-do lists). *ARELE: Annual Review of English Language Education in Japan, 19*, 263-272.

UNIVERSITY OF
GOTHENBURG

Impact of Native-Nonnative Speaker Interaction Through Video Communication and Second Life on Students' Intercultural Communicative Competence

Kristi Jauregi[*] and Silvia Canto

Utrecht University, Utrecht, The Netherlands

Abstract. One of the key concerns of educators is to come to know what works in language teaching and under which conditions (Intercultural) Communicative Competence can be furthered. This concern is even bigger among professionals experimenting or willing to experiment with new media. Following socio-constructivist theories of learning (Vygotsky, 1978) and interactionist theories within SLA (Mackey & Polio, 2009) that put interaction at the heart of the learning process, we present the results of a case study in which interaction patterns and cultural and language related episodes (Swain & Lapkin, 1995) conducive to intercultural language learning are analysed in three research conditions: (1) foreign language learners (FLLs) interacting with native speakers through video communication; (2) FLLs interacting with native speakers through Second Life; and (3) FLLs interacting with each other in the classroom setting. The study analyses the impact that (1) bringing native speakers into the foreign language course through new media and (2) the use of different voiced synchronous tools (video communication v. Second Life) have on interaction patterns conducive to rich learning contexts.

Keywords: SCMC, second life, videocommunication, intercultural communication, negotiation of meaning.

1. Introduction

For some years now and within the NIFLAR project[**] we have been designing and evaluating innovative e-learning tasks for synchronous interaction for their potential to create authentic contexts that make possible interactions with native speakers and

---

[*] Contact author: k.jauregi@uu.nl

[**] NIFLAR: Networked Interaction in Foreign Language Acquisition and Research
 (2009-2011, www.niflar.eu; www.niflar.ning.com)

that may support the development of intercultural communicative competence (Byram, 1997) in foreign language learning contexts.

The interaction tasks are carried out with native speakers (student teachers) in two different environments: *Second Life*, a well known 3D virtual world environment, and a video-web communication platform, Adobe-Connect.

This paper examines evidence from a case study that analyses the impact that (1) bringing native speakers into the foreign language course through new media and (2) the use of different voiced synchronous tools (video communication vs Second Life) have on interaction patterns conducive to rich learning contexts.

2. Method

In order to address these objectives we analyzed interaction sequences of three small groups during online task performance, focusing on negotiation sequences (Swain & Lapkin, 1995) during which meaning related episodes are overtly discussed and some information gap or non-understanding is dispelled during task completion.

We had two experimental triads composed each of two L1 Dutch students of Spanish from Utrecht University and one L1 Spanish student teacher from the University of Valencia, Spain. In the control group a group of four students carried out the same tasks face-to-face in the classroom with no presence of a native speaker.

The three groups carried out the same five tasks (see Table 1) at intervals of once a week but adapted to the specific context: (1) *Second Life* (SL), (2) the video communication (VC) platform Adobe-Connect and (3) the classroom setting.

The Spanish language course at B1 level for both VC and SL groups was blended learning, as each group met twice a week face to face with their teacher (the same one for all three groups) whereas the third meeting was computer-mediated with the native speaker.

Table 1. Description of tasks developed

Tasks	Description
Session 1: *Cool people*	Students: (1) visit an apartment they are meant to share (2) talk about themselves and exchange cultural information triggered by pictures & (3) choose an outing option (go to the cinema, to a museum or to walk in the city).
Session 2: *People & adventure*	Participants plan a holiday and reflect on past holiday experiences
Session 3: *Movie celebrity people*	Participants have to play different roles given the indications of a brief script
Session 4: *People with heart*	Participants impersonate different characters and experience the reactions caused on others
Session 5: *People & cultures*	Students participate in a cultural television-game style contest between a Dutch and a Spanish team.

3. Results

3.1. Negotiation of meaning

Most of the qualitative analysis of interactions across conditions come particularly from the second task, *People & adventure*. In the analysis of the recordings observed, we found instances of negotiation in all groups (see Table 2), although there was a substantial difference between the number of negotiations encountered when the task was performed by the experimental groups (VC: 23; SL: 27) as compared to the control group (C: 2).

Table 2. Number of negotiations per group – task 2

Group	Task duration	Negotiations
Second Life (SL)	01:15:01	27
video communication (VC)	01:20:04	23
control (C)	00:41:00	2

Analysis of the recordings reveals that lexical difficulties appear to be the principal triggers conducing to side-sequences of negotiations (see Table 3).

Table 3. Summary of negotiations with classification of triggers SL – Second Life group; VC – Video Communication group; C – Control group.

	SL	VC	C
Negotiations	27	23	2
Trigger (word)	27	23	2
• word recognition	16	17	
• misuse/misunderstanding	10	2	2
• pronunciation	1	1	

3.2. Negotiation of cultural misunderstanding

Further observation of the recordings of other tasks confirmed that negotiations occurred in all of them but that they were not always triggered at a word level. Task 5 (*People & cultures*) was seeded with overt triggers at a sociocultural level. Here there was again a higher level of negotiation in the VC and SL experimental groups than that registered in the control group (see Table 4).

Table 4. Number of negotiations per group – task 5

Group	Task duration	Negotiations
Second Life (SL)	01:46:08	26
video communication (VC)	01:05:33	24
control (C)	00:41:00	12

The task generated a high level of curiosity towards many aspects of the other culture and participants engaged in rich exchanges as can be observed in Table 5. This example had a photograph of a rucksack hanging from a flag as trigger, a well-known custom in The Netherlands meaning that the child living there has passed the state exams at secondary educational level. The Spanish team had to guess its meaning during the quiz. In the negotiation sequence the Dutch team provides the explanation.

Table 5.   Example – VC task 5*

NNS1: cuando has terminado el instituto/ ¿sí? hay una fiesta y ponemos nuestras mochilas fuera/ con la bandera de Holanda y / y es como una fiesta que todo el mundo sabe que has hmm terminado el instituto bien NS: ¡Ah! ¿y entonces se quedan ahi las mochilas? NNS1 : sí/ fuera/ por dos semanas o así (risas NS: ¡Ah! NNS1: porque es la idea que nunca tenemos que usar la mochila (risas) NS: ¡Ah! ¡qué originales!	NNS1: when you have finished your secondary educationcuando / yes? there is a party and we put our rucksacks outside/ with the Dutch flag and / and it is like a party that everybody knows that you have hmm finished your secondary education well NS: Ah! and then the rucksacks stay there? NNS1: yes/ outside/ for two weeks or so (laughter) NS: Ah! NNS1: because the idea is that we don't have to use the rucksack anymore (laughter) NS: Ah! how original!

This was possible not only due to the setting of the task, but also to the fact that the language learners' interlocutor was a native speaker (Jauregi, Canto, de Graaff, Koenraad, & Moonen, 2011).

In the control group the dynamics were different: there was no contrasting of opinions between the members of the team to reach an agreement over the correct answer and even when their answers were wrong not much curiosity was detected to find out more about the topic.

3.3. Differences according to the specific environment

As to the environments, *Second Life*, appeared to elicit a high degree of rich participation triggered by elements of the world. For example when the avatars were teleported to the pizzeria to discuss the holiday options they chatted about the movie posters hanging on the walls and whether they had seen or not the movies, and they even attempted to pay for the food; being able to drive a boat once they had reached their holiday destination prompted conversations about seatbelts and drivers' licences *("ponte el cinturón que vamos muy rápido - ¿tú tienes el carné de conducir?/ wear your seatbelt we're going very fast – do you have a driver's licence?")*; and visiting the hotel where they were meant to be staying during the holidays made possible the transaction of booking the room. The interactions from the VC group and control group were characterized by a more descriptive language limited by the photographs being used. In *Second Life* actions triggered conversations and there was more topic switching enabled by world elements.

---

*   NS: Native Speaker; NNS: Non-Native Speaker

4. Conclusions

The results of our qualitative analysis show that the opportunities offered for SCMC via VC and SL are much richer than those offered by the traditional educational setting, control group, where students have no opportunities to engage in group interactions with native peers.

The results indicate that this type of environment not only provides access to a wide range of interlocutors (including native speakers) but that it may also enhance cross-cultural understanding and knowledge of the target language; that the electronic medium seems to afford more opportunities for active participation, particularly SL, and that it also provides a forum where participants can engage in negotiation of meaning at their own pace.

References

Byram, M. (1997). *Teaching and Assessing Intercultural Communicative Competence*. Clevedon: Multilingual Matters.

Jauregi, K., Canto, S., de Graaff, R., Koenraad, T., & Moonen, M. (2011). Verbal interaction in Second Life: towards a pedagogic framework for task design. *Computer Assisted Language Learning Journal, 24*(1), 77-101. doi: 10.1080/09588221.2010.538699

Mackey, A., & Polio, C. (Eds.) (2009). *Multiple Perspectives on Interaction: Second Language Research in Honor of Susan M. Gass*. New York: Routledge.

Swain. M., & Lapkin, S. (1995). Problems in output and the cognitive processes they generate: A step towards second language learning. *Applied Linguistics, 16*(3), 371-91. doi:10.1093/applin/16.3.371

Vygotsky, L. S. (1978). *Mind & Society*. Cambridge, MA: Harvard University Press.

UNIVERSITY OF
GOTHENBURG

How Learners Use Automated Computer-Based Feedback to Produce Revised Drafts of Essays

Jonny Laing[a]*, Khaled El Ebyary[b], and Scott Windeatt[c]

a. INTO, Newcastle University, Newcastle upon Tyne, UK
b. Department of English, Alexandria University, Alexandria, Egypt
c. School of Education, Communication & Language Sciences, Newcastle University, Newcastle upon Tyne, UK

Abstract. Our previous results suggest that the use of *Criterion*, an automatic writing evaluation (AWE) system, is particularly successful in encouraging learners to produce amended drafts of their essays, and that those amended drafts generally represent an improvement on the original submission. Our analysis of the submitted essays and the feedback provided on the first drafts suggests, however, that the students use a variety of quite different strategies when using the automated computer-based feedback to produce amended drafts. These include simply accepting a suggested correction, interpreting a feedback comment to modify the text, and avoidance strategies such as leaving out text that was highlighted as incorrect or problematic. Our data suggest that the strategies the students use are at least partly influenced by the confidence they have in the feedback, and therefore in the system itself, but may also be influenced by their interpretation of how marks are awarded by the system. This presentation will discuss the findings of an in depth analysis of the changes made in second drafts submitted to the system, linking the changes to the automatic feedback provided on the first draft, and exploring the reasons for the changes made by the students. We will suggest ways in which teachers can explore the utility of various strategies with their learners.

Keywords: reflective practice, assessment and feedback, automatic writing evaluation.

1. Introduction

One of the more difficult tasks that learners face is developing proficiency in writing, and it is generally assumed that timely and appropriate feedback is important in developing such proficiency (Black & Wiliam, 1998a, 1998b; Hyland & Hyland, 2006). There is, however, less agreement on how feedback can be most effectively targeted (on grammar, lexis or organisation/structure), on whether feedback should be explicit or

---

* Contact author: jonathan.laing@ncl.ac.uk

In L. Bradley & S. Thouësny (Eds.), *CALL: Using, Learning, Knowing, EUROCALL Conference, Gothenburg, Sweden, 22-25 August 2012, Proceedings* (pp. 156-160). © Research-publishing.net Dublin 2012

implicit, and on whether feedback is best provided by tutors, or peers, or a combination of the two. Research does not provide a clear answer to these questions, and teachers have developed a variety of pragmatic solutions, usually involving provision of at least some feedback themselves. However, this is inevitably time-consuming, especially if they attempt to provide feedback which is individualised, content-related, and timely, and if they encourage the production of multiple drafts (Grimes & Warschauer, 2010; Lee, Wong, Cheung, & Lee, 2009).

Peer feedback is a widely used technique that can help to reduce the teacher's workload by shifting the focus in feedback from just the teachers' to both the teacher's and the learners' actions and opinions (e.g., Ferris, 2003). Research suggests, however, that learners see peer feedback as serving a different purpose from instructor feedback (Jacobs, Curtis, Brain, & Huang, 1998). Whatever approach is adopted, therefore, at least some teacher feedback is likely to be desirable and probably necessary, although this becomes increasingly difficult to provide as the number of students a teacher has to deal with increases. One possible solution is to exploit advances in technology such as computer applications which are claimed to be capable not only of assessing written work, but also of generating feedback for the learners – "intelligent CALL" which can interact with the material to be learned, including (providing) meaningful feedback and guidance (Warschauer & Healey, 1998).

There is published research on the use of such applications for assessing writing (e.g., Rudner & Liang, 2002), comparing human scoring to computer scoring (e.g., Wang & Brown, 2007), and validating computerised scoring systems (e.g., Powers, Burstein, Chodorow, Fowles, & Kukich, 2001), and it is claimed that such applications match the reliability of human raters in assessing writing (e.g., Dikli, 2006). However, there is still relatively little research that has investigated the value of computer-based feedback (CBF) on students' written work (e.g., Attali, 2004; Coniam, 2009), and much of it relates to L1, or English as an additional language (EAL) rather than English as a foreign language (EFL), writers of English. This paper reports the result of using one such automatic writing evaluation system – Criterion – with four different classes of EFL students in a variety of contexts over the last four years.

2. Method

2.1. Aims and participants

This paper is based on the results of four studies that were conducted in Alexandria University, Egypt ($N = 24$), Hail University, Saudi Arabia ($N = 23$), and Newcastle University, UK ($N = 11$ and $N = 15$) between 2008 and 2012. The participants were all university students studying academic English, though learning English in order to study a variety of different subjects (the Alexandria students were training to be English teachers, for example, while the Newcastle students were planning to study a variety of other subjects at postgraduate level).

Each study had its own particular focus, but aims that were common across the studies were to investigate learners' attitudes towards the computer-based feedback they were given, the nature of the feedback that Criterion provided, and what actions learners took as a result of the feedback. The aim of this paper is to use data from the four studies to investigate the ways in which AWE systems can be used, either on their own or together with teacher feedback, the actions of the learners once they received feedback, i.e., to study the changes made in second drafts submitted to the system, the content of the automatic feedback provided on the first draft which is linked to those changes, and, where possible, the reasons for the changes that learners made.

2.2. Results

There was a very high re-submission rate for the essays, i.e., almost all learners in the studies submitted a second revised draft for each title, using feedback provided by Criterion on what it categorises as *grammar, usage, mechanics, style and organisation*. The accuracy of the feedback in these categories varied in our studies with, for example, feedback on organisation and development tending to be rather unpredictable. Comments in this category which referred to missing "thesis statements", for example, sometimes accurately highlighted a problem but at other times simply failed to correctly identify that the essay did contain such a statement. Feedback in other categories sometimes correctly identified a problem, but not necessarily the cause (a missing auxiliary was sometimes the reason for Criterion highlighting a verb and labelling it as "ill-formed", for example). Criterion also had difficulty – not unexpectedly – in correctly identifying where the use of, or lack of, an article was a problem.

Nevertheless, according to Criterion's own marking system, the second draft submitted by a learner was almost always better, or at least at the same level as the first, and examination of some sample essays confirmed that this did indeed appear to be the case (in some of the studies there was some teacher correction of second drafts as well as computer feedback). One possible explanation for this is that Criterion managed to correctly identify sufficient surface-level errors that the learner was able to correct and produce a second draft that was at least better in terms of those features than the first draft. A second explanation is that the simple fact of receiving feedback on a first draft encouraged the learners to reflect not only on the highlighted problems, but on other aspects of their draft, before revising and resubmitting the essay. A third explanation is that even feedback that is ambiguous or inexplicit may, by encouraging reflection, lead a learner to find a correct, or more acceptable, alternative to a highlighted problem, suggesting that learners may be able to benefit from such feedback if they already have the required linguistic resources at their disposal. An example of the latter was a student who was observed reading a Criterion comment that referred to a "fragment, or a subject or verb missing". In fact the highlighted problem was a verb in the present simple, which should have been in the progressive. The learner was observed to consider the comment, and the highlighted problem, at some length, eventually correctly changing "begins" to "is beginning".

3. Discussion

Our preliminary analysis of the results suggests the following:
- Criterion proved useful in the variety of contexts in which it was tried, and especially in the situations where learners would normally be offered little, if any, teacher feedback;
- In classes with more proficient learners, where regular teacher feedback was expected, it was received positively, though with some reservations;
- It seemed to be most useful for learners at or below intermediate or upper-intermediate level;
- There was a high rate of submission of second drafts among all groups (for practical reasons learners were limited to submitting two drafts);
- Where teacher feedback was also available, learners found the process of receiving automatic feedback on drafts useful in helping them produce an improved final draft which they hoped would be well received by the teacher;
- The accuracy of the feedback provided by Criterion varied, as did its specificity, and its apparent value to the student. There is nevertheless evidence that the feedback encouraged the learners to reflect on their writing, to act on their reflections, and to produce improved drafts;
- There is also some evidence that reflection on even ambiguous feedback could result in successful correction, perhaps of "mistakes" rather than, in error analysis terminology, "errors".

4. Conclusions

There is still much to analyse in the data, but our tentative conclusion is that Criterion appears to be most suited to EFL learners at, or below, an intermediate or upper-intermediate level. It is especially effective at encouraging learners to reflect on their writing, and to produce second drafts. Given the nature of the feedback that Criterion provides, and the focus of the feedback, it is likely to be most useful when used in conjunction with teacher feedback. Work on the first two drafts can help learners eliminate some of the surface level errors, and encourage them to evaluate the structure and organisation of their writing, allowing the teacher more time to comment on content in subsequent drafts.

There are a range of strategies that remain to be explored for combining computer and teacher feedback, including the possibility of integrating computer- and teacher-feedback with peer-feedback. In addition, although our studies were carried out as an integral part of normal language courses, each lasted no more than a few weeks. We therefore have, as of yet, no data that would allow us to be confident that we have progressed beyond the possible influence of a novelty effect, and to investigate long term changes in attitudes towards computer-based feedback, and the long term effect on writing.

References

Attali, Y. (2004). *Exploring the feedback and revision features of Criterion.* Paper presented at the Paper presented at the National Council on Measurement in Education, San Diego, CA.

Black, P., & Wiliam, D. (1998a). Assessment and classroom learning. *Assessment in Education: Principles, Policy & Practice, 5*(1), 7-47.

Black, P., & Wiliam, D. (1998b). Inside the Black Box: Raising Standards through Classroom Assessment. *Phi Delta Kappan, 92(*1), 81-90.

Coniam, D. (2009). Experimenting with a computer essay-scoring program based on ESL student writing scripts. *ReCALL, 21*(2), 259-279. doi: 10.1017/S0958344009000147

Dikli, S. (2006). An Overview of Automated Scoring of Essays. *The Journal of Technology, Learning, and Assessment (J.T.L.A), 5*(1), 1-36.

Ferris, D. (2003). *Response to Student Writing: Implications for second language students.* Mahwah, New Jersey: Lawrence Erlbaum Associates.

Grimes, D., & Warschauer, M. (2010). Utility in a Fallible Tool: A Multi-Site Case Study of Automated Writing Evaluation. *JTLA, 8*(6), 1-43.

Hyland, K., & Hyland, F. (2006). Feedback on second language students' writing: State of the Art. *Language Teaching, 39*(2), 83-101.

Jacobs, G. M., Curtis, A., Brain, G., & Huang, S. (1998). Feedback on student writing: taking the middle path. *Journal of Second Language Writing, 7*(3), 307-317. doi: 10.1016/S1060-3743(98)90019-4

Lee, C., Wong, K., Cheung, W., & Lee, F. (2009). Web-based essay critiquing system and EFL students' writing: A quantitative and qualitative investigation. *Computer Assisted Language Learning, 22*(1), 57-72. doi: 10.1080/09588220802613807

Powers, D., Burstein, J., Chodorow, M., Fowles, M., & Kukich, K. (2001). *Stumping e-rater: Challenging the validity of automated essay scoring.* Princeton, NJ: Educational Testing Service. Retrieved from www.ets.org/Media/Research/pdf/RR-01-03-Powers.pdf

Rudner, L., & Liang, T. (2002). Automated Essay Scoring Using Bayes' Theorem. *The Journal of Technology, Learning, and Assessment (J.T.L.A), 1*(2), 1-22.

Wang, J., & Brown, M. (2007). Automated Essay Scoring Versus Human Scoring: A Comparative Study. *The Journal of Technology, Learning, and Assessment (J.T.L.A), 6*(2), 1-29.

Warschauer, M., & Healey, D. (1998). Computers and language learning: An overview. *Language Teaching, 31*(2), 57-71. doi: 10.1017/S0261444800012970

UNIVERSITY OF
GOTHENBURG

Students' Framing of Language Learning Practices in Social Networking Sites

Annika Lantz-Andersson*, Sylvi Vigmo, and Rhonwen Bowen

Department of Education, Communication and Learning, University of Gothenburg, Göteborg, Sweden

Abstract. The amount of time that people, especially young people, spend on communicative activities in social media is rapidly increasing. We are facing new arenas with great potential for learning in general and for language learning in particular, but their impact on learning is not yet acknowledged as such in educational practice (e.g., Conole, 2010; Lewis, Pea, & Rosen, 2010; Thorne, 2009). The aim of this case study is to scrutinize how social networking sites (SNSs) serve as new contexts for learning when implemented in school practices. The focus is mainly on how students frame (Goffman, 1974/1986) this activity to scrutinize the implications for their language learning and how they learn to communicate in culturally relevant and productive ways. By applying a socio-cultural-historical theoretical view of communication (Vygotsky, 1939/1978; Wertsch, 1998), this paper reports findings from ethnographic data of a Facebook group in formal English learning contexts with students aged between 13 - 16 years old comprising one school class in Colombia, Finland, Sweden and Taiwan, respectively. The results indicate that the students' communication was characterized by a) a communication in response to institutional requirements, b) their customary interaction in social media, or c) a juxtaposition of both.

Keywords: social media, English language learning, framing, practices.

1. Introduction

The amount of time that young people spend on communicative activities in social media is rapidly increasing. These media offer great potential for learning in general and for language learning in particular. However, national and international studies have pointed to the difficulties of making use of social media in school settings (e.g., Bonderup-Dohn, 2009; Thorne, 2009) and as yet, relatively little is known about the pedagogical implications of integrating social media in the context of language classrooms (Blattner & Lomica, 2012). Thus, on the one hand, we have societal

* Contact author: annika.lantz-andersson@ped.gu.se

In L. Bradley & S. Thouësny (Eds.), *CALL: Using, Learning, Knowing, EUROCALL Conference, Gothenburg, Sweden, 22-25 August 2012, Proceedings* (pp. 161-166). © Research-publishing.net Dublin 2012

knowledge of young people's considerable interaction and communication in social media using English and on the other hand, we have language education that does not make use of the language learning potentials on these new arenas. Sometimes they are even considered as conflicting with the aims of schooling as argued by Thorne (2009); "it is troublesome that new media literacies remain largely unacknowledged within instructed L2 contexts and curricula, or worse, are treated as stigmatized varieties that have no place in the classroom" (Thorne, 2009, p. 91).

This study aims at scrutinizing how social media cultures serve as a mediating resource in young people's language learning i.e., their potential impact on learning English in school contexts and how young people learn to communicate in culturally relevant and productive ways. The focus is on affordances of social media rather than the traditional language learning assignments.

1.1. English as a lingua mundi

The web and various social media applications, represent vast spaces and resources for using English as a lingua mundi, a world language, for communication. These conditions also have an impact on the roles of English. Globalisation through digital media has contributed to changing conditions, as most users of English today are non-natives who will interact with other non-natives. In addition, the presence of English in young people's daily life displays similarities with the use of a second language (L2), e.g., the language is met in unforeseen and unorganised and more complex contexts as opposed to more organised school settings.

This has implications for learners who today should be prepared to develop approaches to language learning, which are based on viewing *language as hybrid, as context transforming, as representational* – and that your mother tongue is considered as a resource for achieving metalinguistic awareness (Canagarajah, 2006). It is argued here that learning English is no longer easily framed in traditional terms and discrete competences. Using English in digital media contexts is characterised by more complex encounters and settings. Other linguistic repertoires or language use in digital media genres are examples of language in use, which however, are seldom acknowledged in schools.

1.2. Social media as part of the educational practices

Social media can be framed as involving social activities such as participation, interaction and collaboration using Web 2.0 technologies, and can be exemplified by Facebook, blogs, wikis, and Twitter. The focus is more on people's use and less on the technologies themselves, thereby indicating that technologies themselves do not bring about change, e.g., if the activity departs from traditionally framed educational practice (Bonderup-Dohn, 2009). Authorship, identity, agency, contribution and production are other concepts associated with acting and interacting in Web 2.0 modes (Warschauer & Grimes, 2007).

2. Method

The setting of the study is a closed Facebook group with students, 15-16 years old, of one invited class from Sweden, Taiwan, Finland and Colombia respectively. The Facebook group, which has been set up for this study, enables text, images, sound and video to be used for representing and expressing oneself, and all modes for language learning are explicitly encouraged already in the invitation. Initially, the students got assignments for their interaction but in the next phase they communicated with no instructions from the teachers.

The students' textual interaction has been logged and the screen has been recorded using Jing (a free Tech Smith software) to be able to study multimodal aspects, e.g., sound and videos that they used for representing and expressing themselves.

The research design involves following the language learners' interaction in social media, their contributions, their participation and collaboration. The analysis of the empirical material, i.e., the postings and comments in the Facebook group, focuses on interactions between students to explore how communication is managed using English as a lingua mundi. Goffman's (1974/1986) concepts of framing and an additional sensitivity to details in interactions, derived from Interaction Analysis (Jordan & Henderson, 1995) and some lines of reasoning within Conversation Analysis (e.g., Goodwin & Heritage, 1990; Macbeth, 2000; Sacks, Schegloff, & Jefferson, 1974) have been employed in the analysis of the empirical material.

In the works of Goffman (1974/1986), the concept of framing implies a 'definition of a situation' which the participants in the situation more or less share. Goffman argues that there are certain overall aspects that are part of every framing process that have a bearing on the possible ways of framing activities.

This also implies that framing in activities is constrained by social structures and social organisations, i.e., individuals are limited and not able to frame in situations entirely as they wishAccording to Goffman (1974/1986), in many cases, individuals do things "in relationship to cultural standards established for the doing and for the social role that is built up out of such doings" (p. 662). In line with this reasoning, Goffman argues that institutions often play important roles in the framing process.

Interaction Analysis is used to systematically analyse the students' reasoning, posting videos, commenting and engaging in discussions with other students and how the variety of communicative affordances in the social media environment are used (Jordan & Henderson, 1995). The analytical focus is on how the communications get their meaning in relation to the preceding and subsequent utterances and postings in the context, inspired by Conversation Analysis (e.g., Goodwin & Heritage, 1990; Macbeth, 2000; Sacks, Schegloff, & Jefferson, 1974) in order to find interaction patterns in culturally relevant and productive ways.

3. Discussion

The social practices of schooling have emerged through history, and include certain discursive procedures with many, both explicit and implicit, rules along with teaching practices (Edwards & Mercer, 1987). Students become used to 'doing school' through their own experiences, and through this extensive socialization. When a task is framed in educational learning environments, students often implicitly try to understand what is demanded. The reasoning and action performed by the students can be seen as a response to what Brousseau (1997) has called the *didactic contract*, that is, the rules of communication established in educational settings that participants learn to identify and use as resources. Expressed differently, students become used to 'doing school' through their own experiences, and through this extensive socialization they also learn how tasks are normally organized. On the other hand, young people's engagement in hybrid media practices in their spare time belongs to their 'self-directed practices' (Drotner, 2008), which are different from school practices in many ways. Tensions between school practices and young people's 'out-of-school world' in Web 2.0 could thus be seen as based on divergent goals and assumptions of what constitutes knowledge and learning (Bonderup-Dohn, 2009).

In our study, the students' communication is initially framed in relation to what counts as legitimate knowledge in a school context but as the communication continues these norms are negotiated and challenged.

4. Conclusion

In relation to this study, the 'didactical contract' (Brousseau, 1997), is an illustration of how the framing in educational situations operates and implies specific ways of framing in school activities, which include certain obligations. Goffman (1974/1986) argues that there are certain overall aspects that are part of every framing process with a bearing on the possible ways of framing situations. He assumes that "there is a main activity, a story line, and that an evidential boundary exists in regard to it" (Goffman, 1974/1986, p. 564). This means that defining the activity as 'doing school work' could function as superordinate in relation to defining the activity as e.g., 'interacting with friends'. This shows the dilemma that arises when trying to transfer personal motivation that is associated with a voluntary commitment in an 'out-of-school world' into a formal education context where the driving force may be in relation to a commitment, perhaps even more often motivated by other factors such as being assessed and getting good grades. The framings related to 'doing school work' could thus be visible in the interaction even though the social media environments also promote the relevance and inclusion of out of school experiences.

To conclude, our preliminary result indicates that these new social media arenas open up for great possibilities for learning to use English to communicate in culturally relevant and productive ways but the implementation has to be done with a sensitivity to the rules of the educational practice.

Acknowledgements. This work is funded by Marcus and Amalia Wallenberg Foundation and has been carried out at the Linnaeus Centre for Research on Learning, Interaction and Mediated Communication in Contemporary Society (LinCS), and within The University of Gothenburg Learning and Media Technology Studio (LETStudio).

References

Blattner, G., & Lomicka, L. (2012). Facebook-ing and the Social Generation: A New Era of Language Learning. *Alsic - Social media and language learning: (r)evolution? 15*(1). doi: 10.4000/alsic.2413

Bonderup-Dohn, N. (2009). Web 2.0: Inherent tensions and evident challenges for education. *Computer-Supported Collaborative Learning, 4*(3), 343-363.

Brousseau, G. (1997). *Theory of didactical situations in mathematics*. Edited and translated by N. Balacheff, M. Cooper, R. Sutherland, & V. Warfield. The Netherlands, Dordrecht: Kluwer Academic Publisher.

Canagarajah, S. (2006). An interview with Suresh Canagarajah. In R. Rubdy & M. Saraceni (Eds.), *English in the World: Global Rules, Global Roles* (pp. 200-212). London: Continuum.

Conole, G. (2010). A holistic approach to designing for learning: A vision for the future. *The Annual International CODE Symposium*, 18 February, 2010, Chiba, Japan.

Drotner, K. (2008). Leisure Is Hard Work: Digital Practices and Future Competencies. In D. Buckingham (Ed.), *The John D. and Catherine T. MacArthur Foundation Series on Digital Media and Learning* (pp. 167-184). Cambridge, MA: The MIT Press.

Edwards, D., & Mercer, N. (1987). *Common knowledge: The development of understanding in the classroom*. London: Routledge & Keagan Paul.

Goffman, E. (1974/1986). *Frame analysis: An essay on the organization of experience*. Boston, MA: Northeastern University Press.

Goodwin, C., & Heritage, J. (1990). Conversation analysis. *Annual Review of Anthropology, 19*, 283-307.

Jordan, B., & Henderson, A. (1995). Interaction Analysis: Foundations and Practice. *The Journal of the Learning Sciences, 4*(1), 39-103.

Lewis, S., Pea, R., & Rosen, J. (2010). Beyond participation to co-creation of meaning: mobile social media in generative learning communities. *Social Science Information, 49*(3), 1-19.

Macbeth, D. (2000). Classrooms as installations. In S. Hester & D. Francis (Eds.), *Local educational order: Ethnomethodological studies of knowledge in action* (pp. 21-69). Amsterdam: John Benjamins Publishing.

Sacks, H., Schegloff, E. A., & Jefferson, G. (1974). A simplest systematics for the organisation of turn-taking for conversation. *Language, 50*(4), 696-735.

Thorne, S. (2009). 'Community', semiotic flows, and mediated contribution to activity. *Language Teaching*, *42*(1), **81-94**.

Warschauer, M., & Grimes, D. (2007). Audience, authorship, and artifacts: The emergent semiotics of Web 2.0. *Annual Review of Applied Linguistics, (27)*, 1-23.

Wertsch, J. V. (1998). *Mind as action*. New York, NY: Oxford University Press.

Vygotsky, L. S. (1939/1978). *Mind in society: The development of higher psychological processes*. Cambridge, MA: Harvard University Press.

UNIVERSITY OF
GOTHENBURG

Learner Behaviour in a Collaborative Task-Based CALL Activity

Christine Leahy*

Nottingham Trent University, Arts & Humanities, Nottingham, United Kingdom

Abstract. This paper reports on the findings of a case study that set out to discover student behaviour in the computer room while the participants were engaged in a collaborative computer-assisted language learning (CALL) task in form of an electronic role-play which was designed for advanced learners of business German. The task mainly utilized information and communication technologies (ICTs). Data was collected using screen-capturing software that also recorded the oral interactions between students while they were completing the task. For the analysis two methods were applied: First, grounded theory methods facilitated capturing categories that can describe student behaviour. Second, a case study approach facilitated emerging vignettes to become visible which could be reported on separately. The study showed strategies students employed when dealing with problems, manifestations of collaboration, different working modes and steps in text production, as well as student focus on form. This project's findings contribute to the interest in study of student behaviour in computer-room learning tasks (Levy & Michael, 2011) as well as to the discussion about students' expression of their agency (Van Lier, 2008). Furthermore, they contribute to the discussion about useful methodologies and methods involving screen-capturing software.

Keywords: behaviour in the computer room, collaborative CALL task, task-based learning, electronic role-play, screen-capturing software, advanced L2 learners, grounded theory methods.

1. Introduction

CALL task design considers the medium's affordances and presumes that the learners make use of them when completing the given task. However, the number of detailed studies into student behaviour in the computer room which could support this assumption is still limited. Which computer tools are utilized in tasks, how students compose text, how much they focus on linguistic forms, is not always clear.

---

* Contact author: christine.leahy@ntu.ac.uk

In L. Bradley & S. Thouësny (Eds.), *CALL: Using, Learning, Knowing, EUROCALL Conference, Gothenburg, Sweden, 22-25 August 2012, Proceedings* (pp. 167-171). © Research-publishing.net Dublin 2012

The engagement with the computer's affordances is only in part a matter of skill and familiarity. In reference to Bakhtin, Lund (2003) referred to the appropriation of information and communication technologies (ICTs) as more than just the development towards mastering the technology, but to "relate to and interact with concepts, tools, and knowledge" (p. 1). Bakhtin (1981) saw appropriation of words as an act of "transformation into private property" and a form of "seizure" (p. 293). Following this argument, similarly, the student would size the technology's affordances, would make the technology their own to be used to express their volition. This project looks at the ways the participants in the study made use of technology in order to fulfill the CALL task.

The electronic role-play utilizes principles of task-based learning which, according to Motteram and Thomas (2010), is still an under-researched area within CALL. Besides task-based learning in CALL settings, collaborative approaches in class need to be understood in more detail (Hampel, 2009) in order to learn more about the general processes taking place while students are engaged in CALL tasks. However, one of the reasons why task-based learning and collaborative approaches are researched less, especially in the context of advanced learners and the use of multimedia, lies in the complexity of authentic settings with natural communication (Plass & Jones, 2005) which can create methodological problems.

This project addresses the research question of what students do when they are involved in a collaborative CALL task like the electronic role-play. It addresses a general interest in student behaviour and the resulting interactional patterns while engaged in such a task. The exploration of the computer room setting and its influence on the language learning process is of interest in order to inform future CALL task design. If the computer is used as a tool for and as a locus of language learning processes, it is helpful to explore the type of behaviour students engage in, how they make use of the computer's affordances. It is of interest whether and how the computer can support learning. Specific questions that emerge are:

- Do students take advantage of support tools, for example, electronic dictionaries?
- How do they use them?
- Do students just copy and paste information from the internet or do they alter, synthesise, and summarise text?
- How do they compose text?
- What kind of information do they seek out and how do they appropriate it for their purposes?
- How do they cope with problems they encounter?
- How do they communicate with their partners and between groups?

This project set out to find answers to these questions.

2. Method

2.1. Method of data collection

Data was collected using screen-capturing software (Camtasia). This software records all on-screen activities visually, not based on text or code. Playing back the recordings enables the viewer to follow the on-screen activities as if they were sitting next to the student, observing their actions. Camtasia also records sound in the vicinity of the computer. These recordings could then be transcribed and be used in conjunction with the on-screen activities. Therefore, the software offers different types of multimodal data, including visual and text-based, which can be viewed and listened to an infinite number of times.

The collected data was coded using grounded theory methods (Glaser & Strauss, 2006) that provide useful strategies to synthesize data and to make "analytical sense of them" (Charmaz, 2004, p. 496).

2.1.1. Method of data analysis

Grounded theory (GT) is a useful approach to complex data as was collected here with the aid of the recording software. GT can "help in structuring and organizing data [...] analysis" (Charmaz, 2004, p. 497). In particular, GT aids "creation of analytic codes and categories developed from the data, not from pre-conceived hypothesis, [...] the development of middle-range theories to explain behaviour and processes [... and] memo-making, i.e., writing analytic notes to explicate and fill out categories" (ibid.).

Through a process of data interrogation with questions like "What is going on? What is actually happening in the data? What is the main concern faced by the participants?", data could be organized. These questions facilitated open coding of the primary data which, in turn, generated initial categories. GT suggests two procedures for the generation process of categories: The first step generates categories through constant comparison of incident to incident and then incident to concept. In the second step, the same coding questions are applied to all incidents, namely "what category or property of a category does this incident indicate?" (Glaser, 1992, p. 39).

GT is fundamentally different from a hypothesis-based approach, it attempts to let the data speak for itself, requests from the researcher to empty their minds (as much as this may be possible) from pre-conceived ideas. GT as applied here is attempting to find meaning through the data without being guided by a specific hypothesis which could be verified or falsified.

3. Discussion

Through this study, student behaviour in the computer room became more visible, e.g., their strategies in dealing with encountered problems and other manifestations of their collaboration with each other and their working modes. Several categories emerged which can highlight the behaviour the subjects exhibited while they were engaged in the task. The electronic role-play took place during a period of 4 weeks, with 2 hour in-class activities per week in the computer room. The initial emerging categories were those of procedural discussions and how to deal with encountered problems in the target language (L2). Closely related was another category, that of the role of the 'expert'. The emerging role of the expert can be characterised by fluidity and could relate to different areas of expertise, e.g., an expert in the target language, technology or the subject-specific area. However, the spontaneously emerging role of experts is inherently problematic when some peers are elevated to it above others.

Students focused on form, often as a self-directed process but also with guidance from the tutor present. Common language-related areas students focused on included lexis, formal and informal way to address one another, and grammar, e.g., adjective endings and cases.

Different manifestations of collaboration emerged, forms of teamwork and the accompanying comfort and reassurance teamwork could provide for some. Off-task and private communication did not feature prominently.

Working modes varied and were in part directly influenced by the task requirements of each particular week. However, some noteworthy habits transpired, e.g., the way internet searches were conducted, the way online reading could be accompanied by cursor movements, the way some participants could multi-task and others were restricted by a single-tasking approach.

Other findings can be represented in mini-vignettes, e.g., forms of text production in technology-rich environments and navigation issues.

4. Conclusions

Applying screen-capturing software for data collection and accessing the recordings repeatedly during the period of data analysis made complex student behaviour visible during an in-class CALL task. Some unexpected expressions of student volition came to the fore.

This project reflects how research methodology and methods have an impact on research results in general and specific findings in particular. The research methods applied, in this case the involvement of technologies, shaped what was discovered.

References

Bakhtin, M. (1981). *The dialogic imagination. Four essays by M.M. Bakhtin*. Austin, TX: University of Texas Press.

Charmaz. (2004). Grounded theory. In S. Hesse-Biber & P. Leavy (Eds.), *Approaches to qualitative research: A reader on theory and practice* (pp. 496-521). New York / Oxford: Oxford University Press.

Glaser, B., & Strauss, A. (2006). *The discovery of grounded theory: strategies for qualitative research* [reprint of 1999 renewed version]. New Brunswick, USA, and London, U.K.: Aldine Transaction.

Glaser, B. G. (1992). *Emergence vs Forcing. Basics of Grounded Theory Analysis*. Mill Valley, CA: Sociology Press.

Hampel, R. (2009). Training teachers for the multimedia age: developing teacher expertise to enhance online learner interaction and collaboration. *Innovation in language learning and teaching*, *3*(1), 35-50.

Levy, M., & Michael. R. (2011). Analysing students' multimodal texts: The product and the process. In M. Thomas (Ed.), *Deconstructing Digital Natives*. New York: Routledge.

Lund, A. (2003). *The teacher as interface. Teachers of EFL in ICT-rich environments: beliefs, practices, appropriation.* (Doctoral dissertation). University of Oslo, Norway. Retrieved from http://www.uv.uio.no/ils/forskning/publikasjoner/rapporter-og-avhandlingen/AndreasLund-avhandling%5B1%5D.pdf

Motteram, G., & Thomas, M. (2010). Afterword: Future directions for technology-mediated tasks. *In*: M. Thomas, & H. Reinders (Eds.), *Task-based language learning and teaching with technology* (pp. 218-237). London, New York: Continuum.

Plass, J., & Jones, L. (2005). Multimedia Learning in Second Language Acquisition. In R. Mayer (Ed), *The Cambridge handbook of multimedia learning* (pp. 467-488). Cambridge: Cambridge University Press.

Van Lier, L. (2008). Agency in the classroom. In J. Lantolf, & M. Poehner (Eds.), *Sociocultural theory and the teaching of second languages* (pp. 163-186). London: Equinox.

UNIVERSITY OF GOTHENBURG

Effects of Multimedia Vocabulary Annotations on Vocabulary Learning and Text Comprehension in ESP Classrooms

Huifen Lin*

National Tsing Hua University, Hsinchu, Taiwan, Republic of China

Abstract. For the past few decades, instructional materials enriched with multimedia elements have enjoyed increasing popularity. Multimedia-based instruction incorporating stimulating visuals, authentic audios, and interactive animated graphs of different kinds all provide additional and valuable opportunities for students to learn beyond what conventional instruction relying mainly on print material can afford and achieve. Cognitive load theory, Sweller, Van Merrienboer, & Paas (1998) and Mayer's (2001) theory of multimedia learning, have suggested that replacing visual text with spoken text (i.e., modality effect) result in better learning outcomes and that less mental efforts would be required to learn the multimedia lessons. The aim of this study was to test the generalizability of the modality effect in animation-based multimedia instruction developed for learning English-for-specific purposes (ESP) in an EFL classroom. Specifically, the study investigated the effect of spoken (audio) annotation and text annotation embedded in a concurrent on-screen text accompanying computer-generated animations that depicts the process of blood flow in a human heart. The study also looked into the impact of language of the annotation (i.e., students' L1 vs. L2) and interactive effect of language proficiency and prior knowledge and above independent variables on the learning outcomes and cognitive load. Results indicated no significant differences between L1 and L2 glosses for all tests. Additionally, no significant differences were also found between audio and text annotations in all tests. However, L2 annotation significantly added more difficulties to the comprehension of the annotations than L1.

Keywords: multimedia annotation, ESP.

1. Introduction

The use of computers as well as technology-related applications have significantly affected every aspect of human life, including how we receive and deliver

---

* Contact author: huifen@mx.nthu.edu.tw

knowledge. Nowadays, people do not rely purely on print material as their major source of readings. Readings on the Internet, from PDAs or other electronic devices make a reading experience more enjoyable and move beyond a traditional linear fashion. Hypermedia links provided in selected nodes lead the readers to other nodes or links that provide extra information on the original nodes (Ariew & Ercetin, 2004). This "nodes and links" feature of hypertext provides potentials for designing more flexible and richer access to conventional linear reading material for which a predetermined fashion of viewing is adopted. Information accessed via nodes or links can be used as supplementary material to further understand a topic or could act as an aid to further explain a difficult concept.

With the advent of the technology information era, media of various types have been employed to assist learning of different kinds. However, several decades of research on multimedia facilitated or assisted learning have not been able to conclude that multimedia application is any better than conventional instruction without the aid of multimedia. Nevertheless, the technology era has arrived and deeply intertwined into every aspect of human living, it is not an issue to adopt or not to adopt certain technology but how to effectively adopt technology so that it would benefit human beings in every area.

Annotations have been used for several decades to assist reading comprehension. Annotations could occur as marginal notes or at the end of reading selection for readers to refer to when they experience difficulties in the reading process (Ariew & Ercetin, 2004; Hullen, 1989). Annotations could be developed in multiple forms such as text (verbal), audio or visual or a combination of these three. Also, in ESL/EFL texts, annotations could be provided in either students' target language or mother tongue.

Research on annotations in ESL/EFL for general English learning purposes has generally concluded that annotations of different types have promoted students' comprehension of the reading materials or at least are equally effective as when none are provided. Under what conditions, though, would annotations of different types promote English reading for specific purposes has rarely been discussed in the literature. Issues like when do multimedia material embedded with different forms of facilitation hinder learners' process of professional readings are not conclusively settled.

In addition, do learners with individual differences in their language ability or prior knowledge associated with the subject matter receive different types of multimedia annotations equally or differently? Do different forms of annotations induce cognitive load differently? The purpose of the study was to compare the effect of audio and textual annotations in the form of either L1 or L2 on EFL students' learning from professional reading and induced cognitive load. Additionally the study explored the effect of individual difference, i.e., language proficiency and prior knowledge of the subject matter on above dependent variables.

2. Method

2.1. Participants
The participants were 100 undergraduate students (78 females and 22 males) who were enrolled in a college of humanities at a teacher-development university in Taiwan. None of the students were native speakers of English and had received at least 7-10 years of formal English education. Students' ages were between 19 and 25. The students participated in the study voluntarily but were individually awarded a NT$400 book coupon after the study for their participation. Participants in this study were considered to be intermediate achievers and had passed an intermediate level of General English Proficiency Test (GEPT), an official general English ability test developed by The Language Training and Research Centre in Taiwan.

2.2. Materials and apparatus
The materials consisted of a multimedia animation program developed using Microsoft Flash. It presented a multimedia text illustrating general physiology knowledge on the functions of the human heart developed by Dwyer (1972). The reading text consisted of 2,000 words in English, presented in 20 pages. The 20 pages were further divided into 5 topics. Each topic consisted of approximately 200-300 words. The topic and page number were presented on the right side of the screen. Students were able to view their progress in the reading from the page numbers.

3. Discussion

Drawing on Mayer's (2001) split-attention effect, which is consistent with a dual-processing model of working memory, the study tested the hypothesis that annotations in the form of audio would be more effective than visual (textual) in enhancing vocabulary learning and reading comprehension of ESP material. Additionally, the study explored the amount of cognitive load experienced by learners when interacting with different types of annotations. Interactive effects of level of annotation language/medium and learners' language proficiency and background knowledge of the ESP material were also diagnosed to figure out if they were additional factors that might co-explain the effect of annotations on students' learning of ESP materials. The major findings can be summarized as following. First, students learned equally well from ESP material with annotations that used either their native or target language or delivered in the form of text or audio. Second, language proficiency was an important factor that would influence students' learning from ESP material supported by annotations. High language proficiency students performed consistently and significantly better than their counterparts both in vocabulary acquisition and reading comprehension. Third, although types of annotations did not differentiate effects on learning outcome, different types of annotations did result in various amounts of cognitive loads. Annotations developed using students' target language (i.e., English in this study) significantly added more difficulties to the comprehension of the annotations than annotations using students' native language. Fourth, annotations in audio form resulted in more cognitive load associated with the difficulties of the annotations than visual (textual) form. Fifth, low proficiency students experienced higher cognitive load associated with difficulties of the annotations than high proficiency students. Sixth, students consistently have a preference for annotations provided in their native language and in visual (textual) form, which they also found to be more useful.

4. Conclusions

The results of the study did not show any significant differences in vocabulary recall and text comprehension between the annotations developed using students' native language (Chinese) and their target language (English). This result is consistent with Yoshii's (2006) study, Jacobs, Dufon, and Hong's (1994) study, and Chen's (2002) study. However, previous studies conducted on whether glosses should be designed using L1 or L2 have produced mixed results. According to Bell and LeBlanc (2000) and Hayden (1997), students relied on L1 glosses more than L2 glosses because the former are more efficient in resolving their immediate lexical needs when reading a foreign text. When students are given the choice between L1 and L2 glosses, L2 glosses are seldom used (Bell & Leblanc, 2000; Davis & Lyman-Hager, 1997; Goyette, 1995; Hayden, 1997).

The self-reported data using a questionnaire in this study reconfirmed the finding that students like L1 glosses more than L2 and that L1 glosses are more useful than L2 in assisting with the comprehension, although the results in tests found no significant differences. Although annotations in the format of L1 did not add in more learning gains, annotations developed using L2 significantly added more difficulties to the comprehension than annotations using L1. This finding is not surprising because L2 annotation needs further interpretation and must become comprehensible to the learners before they can be used to assist vocabulary recall or text comprehension. The encoding process is actually conducive in potential extraneous cognitive load, but not germane load because it has not resulted in greater learning gains and performance of the learners. Extraneous cognitive load is the extra load resulting from poor instructional design. The level of extraneous cognitive load is determined by the format and manner in which the instructional material is presented and by the amount of capacity that working memory is used when learners engage in the instructional activities (Sha & Kaufman, 2005). It is suspicious that annotations in students' L2 have actually induced extraneous cognitive load by distracting students from performing irrelevant information coding or hypothesis-testing, i.e., meaning-making.

This suspicion was further supported by the finding that cognitive load associated with annotations did not correlate significantly with any level of learning in this study.

The finding of no significant differences between L1 and L2 annotations in facilitating vocabulary acquisition and reading comprehension has extended our understanding of equal or non-differential roles of language annotations played in conventional ESL/EFL reading to ESP reading. Furthermore, the same finding was further extended to annotations that developed to assist text comprehension which was contextually enriched through animation.

References

Ariew, R., & Ercetin, G. (2004). Exploring the potential of hypermedia annotations for second language reading, *Computer Assisted Language Learning, 17*(2), 237-259. doi: 10.1080/0958822042000334253

Bell, F., & LeBlanc, L. (2000). The language of glosses in L2 reading on computer: Learners' preferences. *Hispania, 83*(2), 274-285.

Chen, H. (2002). *Investigating the effects of L1 and L2 glosses on foreign language reading comprehension and vocabulary retention*. Paper presented at the annual meeting of the Computer-Assisted Language Instruction Consortium, Davis, CA.

Davis, J. N., & Lyman-Hager, M. A. (1997). Computers and L2 reading: Student performance, student attitudes. *Foreign Language Annals, 30*(1), 58-72. doi: 10.1111/j.1944-9720.1997.tb01317.x

Dwyer, F. M. (1972). *A guide for improving visualized instruction*. State College, PA: Learning Services, The Pennsylvania State University.

Goyette, E. S. (1995). *The effects of dictionary usage on text comprehension.* (Unpublished Doctoral Dissertation). University of McGill.

Hayden, S. (1997). *An investigation into the effect and patterns of usage of a computer mediated text in reading comprehension in French*. (Unpublished Doctoral Dissertation). University of Pennsylvania.

Hullen, W. (1989). In the beginning was the gloss: Remarks on the historical emergence of lexicographical paradigms. In G. James (Ed.), *Lexicographers and their works* (pp. 100-116). Exeter: University of Exeter.

Jacobs, G., Dufon, P., & Hong, F. (1994). L1 and L2 vocabulary glosses in L2 reading passages: Their effects for increasing comprehension and vocabulary knowledge. *Journal of Research in Reading, 17*(1), 19-28. doi: 10.1111/j.1467-9817.1994.tb00049.x

Mayer, R. E. (2001). *Multimedia learning*. New York: Cambridge University Press.

Sha, L. S., & Kaufman, D. M. (2005). *Managing cognitive load while playing computer games*. Paper presented at the 2005 American Educational Research Association (AERA) Annual Conference.

Sweller, J., Van Merrienboer, J. J. G., & Paas, F. G. W. C. (1998). Cognitive architecture and instructional design. *Educational Psychology Review, 10*(3), 251-296. doi: 10.1023/A:1022193728205

Yoshii, M. (2006). L1 and L2 glosses: Their effects on incidental vocabulary learning, *Language Learning & Technology, 10* (3), 85-101. Retrieved from http://llt.msu.edu/vol10num3/pdf/yoshii.pdf

UNIVERSITY OF
GOTHENBURG

The Effectiveness of Computer-Mediated Communication on SLA: A Meta-Analysis and Research Synthesis

Huifen Lin*

National Tsing Hua University, Hsinchu, Taiwan, Republic of China

Abstract. Over the past two decades, a large body of research has been conducted on the effectiveness of computer-mediated communication (CMC) employed as either stand-alone or instructional tools in SLA classrooms. Findings from this large body of work, however, are not conclusive, making it important to identify factors that would inform its successful implementations. This meta-analysis of empirical studies was conducted to examine the effects of CMC on language learning outcomes by calculating Cohen's *d* effect sizes (Cohen, 1988) for each study on different learning outcomes. Altogether 56 primary studies were retrieved as eligible studies between 2000-2011, including 27 journal articles, 12 dissertations, 12 theses and 5 conference papers. Each study went through a two-level coding, the first level being study-feature coding and the second level effect-size coding. Twelve substantive and methodological features were coded for each study in the first level, 6 of which were identified as potential moderator variables that would affect the effectiveness of CMC differently. Tentative findings of this meta-analysis include: (a) there was a small to medium effect for CMC compared to face-to-face communication, (b) the effect of CMC was not equal for all language skills, and (c) small group sizes produced the largest effect compared to no grouping at all or groups with more than 3 students.

Keywords: CMC, meta-analysis, SLA.

1. Introduction

Computer-mediated communication, defined as "multimodal, often (but not exclusively) Internet-mediated communication" (Thorne, 2008, p. 325), has been used extensively in second/foreign language classrooms since the late 1990s when the Internet became widely and immediately available for the general public, including educational sectors. CMC holds promise for language learning due to mounting evidence supported pedagogical benefits it brings to learning experiences. For example, the real-time nature

---

* Contact author: huifen@mx.nthu.edu.tw

of the synchronous mode of CMC, such as Internet Relay Chat (chat room), creates a communication environment that simulates face-to-face conversation without visual clues. Via networked connection, CMC also extends a traditional language classroom to one that includes global communication involving a diversity of cultures if possible. Access to target language users, which used to be a mission impossible, is now as easy as a click of the mouse via "the instrumentality of computers" (Herring, 1996, p. 1). Through the 1970s into the early 1990s, the primary CMC tools were text-based; among them, email, Internet Relay Chat (ICQ) and MOOs (text-based virtual environments), were most popularly adopted in the language classrooms. With the advance of second-generation web applications, such as blogs, wikis and podcasts, the shortcomings of text-based CMC have been greatly overcome via advanced technologies that could distribute sound, video and varieties of media (Thorne, 2008). Meta-analysis has been used to integrate and compare the result of several studies since it was first introduced by Glass (1976). With the advancement of statistical techniques and controversial issues being mostly dealt with, meta-analysis has now become a preferred way of synthesizing research findings in scientific disciplines (Aytug, Rothstein, Zhou, & Kern, 2012). Over the past two decades, research syntheses conducted to answer questions such as how effective are technologies in promoting language learning were abundant; yet, specific syntheses particularly focusing on CMC remain scarce.

1.1. Statement of the problem

The integration of CMC into a language classroom remains to be a trend, and as the amount of anecdotes and empirical studies on CMC in language field recently increased, there is an urgent need for a valid conclusion to confirm our instinct that CMC does help language educators achieve intended results for their students.

1.2. Research questions

To enable precise analyses and interpretations of primary research findings, the study adopted a quantitative meta-analysis approach to synthesizing findings from empirical studies published between 2000 and 2011. Two overarching questions guided this research synthesis:
- How effective is CMC in promoting second/foreign language skills (versus face-to-face communication or communication without computer/technology mediated devices)?
- What are potential factors that mediate the effectiveness of CMC in promoting the acquisition of language skills?

2. Methodology

Empirical studies reviewed in this paper should meet the following criteria:
- The study was published between 2000 and 2011;

- The study made use of some form of CMC (e.g., email, chat, conferencing, discussion forums, etc.) either exclusively or in conjunction with other instructional tools/methods;
- The study addressed either the nature of the language produced during CMC and/or the effect of CMC on L2 learning. (Both conditions required quantitative data);
- The study employed an experimental or quasi-experimental design;
- Studies recruited participants who were L2 or foreign language learners;
- Studies included should report adequate quantitative information for effect sizes to be calculated.
- For study reports across several sources, only one report was included in the meta-analysis.

2.1. Coding scheme

Each eligible study was coded at two levels: study level and effect size level. In the study level, coding, study characteristics, methodological characteristics and publication characteristics were coded (Lipsey & Wilson, 2001). Study level characteristics were further examined to decide whether they mediated the effectiveness of language learning outcomes. The entire coding consisted of three stages. In stage one, two coders independently coded each of the 56 primary studies in compliance with the coding sheet. In stage 2, half of the primary studies were selected randomly and codes were compared between the two coders. The initial inter-rater reliability was computed using the formula: number of agreed-upon codes over the total number of codes.

Table 1. Coding scheme

Characteristics	Description
Publication type	Journal article/Book or book chapter/ Dissertation/thesis/Technical report/Conference paper (proceedings)/Other
CMC Mode	Synchronous/Asynchronous/Both
CMC tool/platform	Email/Chat/Discussion forum/Instant Messenger/Blog/E-portfolio/Wiki/Other (specify)
CMC Tool	Voice/text
CMC activity conduction	In class/After class/Both
CMC option	Required activity/Optional activity/Other
Group size	1-5 people/6-10 people/11-15 people/More than 15 people/No grouping
Length of experiment	Short: Less than one month Average: between one month and four months (one semester) Long: more than one semester
Outcome measurement	Standardized achievement test (specify the title of the test) Teacher/Researcher developed achievement test Other (specify)
Sample's educational level:	Elementary school level and below/Middle school level/College level and above
Sample's L2	English/German/Japanese/Chinese/Spanish/Russian/Others
Sample's L1	English/German/Japanese/Chinese/Spanish/Russian/Others
Research design	Pretest/Posttest control group design/posttest only control group design/One group only pretest and posttest design/Non-equivalent comparison group design
Randomization	Yes/No
Reliability	Internal consistency, test-retest correlation, etc.

Low interference characteristics such as the total sample size of the study, research setting and participants' L2 were strived to reach the 100% inter-rater reliability. In stage 3, discrepancies in coding between the two coders for high-interference features such as the outcome measurement, treatment description, treatment duration, etc., were discussed and resolved. The final inter-rater reliability was 98%. Table 1 above provides the study-level coding scheme of major features in this meta-analysis.

2.2. Outcome measures

Treatment effects on four major language skills were measured and compared in this meta-analysis. Specifically, the outcomes included listening, speaking, reading and writing. Various competencies (e.g., grammatical, discourse, strategic, sociolinguistic competences, which make up specific language skills were classified into those specific skills. For example, studies that investigated grammatical or pragmatic competence were classified into the outcome category of writing. In the same vein, studies that investigated effect of CMC on pronunciation were classified into the outcome category of speaking.

2.3. Effect size calculation

The effectiveness of CMC on language skill acquisition was expressed by calculating effect sizes for each study on different learning outcomes. The effect sizes were calculated as the difference between the means of the treatment and the control groups divided by the pooled standard deviation of the sample, i.e., Cohens' d. The potential outliers were checked for their influence on the overall mean effect. The effect sizes were also weighted/corrected for small sample sizes (Bangert-Drowns, Hurley, & Wilkinson, 2004; Höffler & Leutner, 2007). If a study did not provide descriptive analysis data but F values, effect sizes were calculated using the procedure suggested by Glass (1976).

3. Results and conclusion

3.1. Overview of eligible studies in review

The final body of meta-analysis included 56 studies (data collection was completed by December 2011): 5 conference papers, 12 masters' theses, 12 doctoral dissertations and 27 journal articles. A total of 282 effect sizes were calculated from the 56 studies which contained a combined sample of about 3,713 participants. The sample size ranges from 12 to 354. 45 studies were published between 2006 and 2011; 11 studies were published between 2000 and 2005. Among the studies, 10 studies were carried out in middle schools, 2 in primary schools and the majority of studies were conducted in university/college settings ($N = 44$). In terms of research design, 49 studies included in the meta- analysis adopted a quasi-experimental design, using either a nonrandomized static-group posttest comparison design (5 studies), a nonrandomized one-group pretest-posttest design (16 studies), or a nonrandomized pretest-posttest control group design (28 studies). Only 7 studies adopted a true experimental design with participants randomly being assigned to treatment groups and a true control group. English (44 studies) is still the dominant target language of most CMC studies, followed by Spanish (9 studies), German (2 studies) and French (1 study).

3.2. The effectiveness of CMC on language learning outcomes

The results showed that of the 56 studies included, 79% (44 studies) of the study-weighted effect sizes were positive and favored CMC integration, while 21% (12 studies) of them were negative and favored face-to-face or communication without any computer-mediated devices. 19 studies (34%) reported large effect sizes, 11 studies (20%) reported medium effect sizes and 26 studies (46%) reported large effect sizes based on Cohen's (1988) interpretation guidelines of effect sizes. The overall effect size is .554, with 95% confidence interval between .482 and .626. Due to the limitation of space, moderator analysis results were not included in the paper; however, this meta-analysis found that task type, group size, participants' educational level, CMC mode, CMC tool and outcome measures were potential moderators that would affect the overall effectiveness of CMC intervention.

Reference

Aytug, Z. G., Rothstein, H. R., Zhou, W., & Kern, M. C. (2012). Revealed or concealed? Transparency of procedures, decisions, and judgment calls in Meta-Analyses. *Organizational Research Methods, 15*(1), 103-133.

Bangert-Drowns, R. L., Hurley, M. M., & Wilkinson, B. (2004). The effects of school-based writing-to-learn interventions on academic achievement: a meta-analysis. *Review of Educational Research, 74*(1), 29-58. doi: 10.3102/00346543074001029

Cohen, J. (1988). *Statistical power analysis for the behavioral sciences* (2nd ed.). New Jersey: Lawrence Erlbaum.

Glass, G. V. (1976). *Primary, secondary, and meta-analysis of research*. Presidential address to the Annual Meeting of the American Educational Research Association, San Francisco, April 21, 1976.

Herring, S. C. (1996). *Computer-mediated communication: Linguistic, social and cross-cultural perspectives*. Amsterdam: Benjamins.

Höffler, T. N., & Leutner, D. (2007). Instructional animation versus static pictures: A meta-analysis. *Learning and Instruction, 17*(6), 722-738. doi: 10.1016/j.learninstruc.2007.09.013

Lipsey, M. W., & Wilson, D. B. (2001). *Practical meta-analysis*. Thousand Oaks, CA: Sage.

Thorne, S. (2008). Computer-mediated communication. In N. Van Deusen-Scholl & N. H. Hornberger (Eds.), *Encyclopedia of language and education; Volume 4: Second and Foreign Language Education* (2nd ed.) (pp. 325-336). Springer Science+ Business media LLC.

UNIVERSITY OF
GOTHENBURG

Paradoxes of Social Networking in a Structured Web 2.0 Language Learning Community

Mathieu Loiseau[a]* and Katerina Zourou[b]

a. LIDILEM, Université Stendhal, Université Pierre-Mendès-France, Grenoble, France
b. Université du Luxembourg, FLSHASE/LCMI/DICA-lab, Walfer, Luxembourg

Abstract. This paper critically inquires into social networking as a set of mechanisms and associated practices developed in a structured Web 2.0 language learning community. This type of community can be roughly described as learning spaces featuring (more or less) structured language learning resources displaying at least some notions of language learning methodology. Taking Livemocha as an example, and especially the Culture space, social networking will be analyzed in terms of the extent to which it is used and taken up by language learners by means of social networking technologies comparable to those of a Social Networking Site (SNS). In addition, we critically examine the role of social networking architectures in sustaining peer language learning in highly networked spaces. We argue that social networking, both as a conceptual framework and as a technical incarnation, can be put in the service of collective activity and instrumented in a way that leads to effective language learning, beyond merely being a trendy or fun component of an SNS-like community.

Keywords: social networking, network effects, language learning, SNS, language interaction.

1. Social networking in language learning activities: context of research

The global socio-technical context sets the social Web as a point of interest of the CALL community. Various publications have analyzed the potential of Web 2.0 networked spaces in language learning activity. The study presented here builds on previous works in this direction. In Dixhoorn, van, Loiseau, Mangenot, Potolia, and Zourou (2010), we outlined a typology of Web 2.0 language learning communities that allowed us to broadly break them down into three types:

---

* Contact author: mathieu.loiseau@u-grenoble3.fr

- Language exchange sites, where users meet for language socializing purposes, without the help of learning material;
- Marketplaces, which allow users to hire language tutors and buy individual activities;
- Structured Web 2.0 language learning communities, which provide free (and possibly paid) distance language learning courses on a dedicated platform.

We focused on this last type in terms of the global approach to language learning in the context of these communities (Loiseau, Potolia, & Zourou, 2011) and then in terms of the quality of the language material and methodologies used on the platform (Potolia, Loiseau, & Zourou, 2011). Since structured Web 2.0 language learning communities are by definition spaces where networked collective activity happens in a self-motivated manner, they constitute exemplary spaces suitable for analysis of social networking and its implications for language education. The scope of our research is to provide elements contributing to conceptual and technical improvements with a view to facilitating peer language learning through social networking mechanisms and processes. Here we focus specifically on whether or not interaction in a highly social networking space can be instrumental for language learning.

2. Object of the analysis

We build our argument on an analysis of a specific section of Livemocha, possibly the most salient structured Web 2.0 language learning community, claiming 12 million registered users and resources for 38 languages. In February 2011, Livemocha designers launched a new section, aimed at allowing users to "discover what life is like around the world [and to] explore other members' cultural photos and stories or share [their] own with the community"*.

The section consists of discussion threads initiated by a user posting a picture associated with a short description or a story. Other users are invited to provide feedback by pressing a "like" button or commenting on the thread. In order to browse through the various threads users are offered two types of filter: countries – only the threads containing the selected country are displayed either by date or by popularity, and contribution – the user can access the threads they started, liked or commented on, sorted by date of the user's contribution.

Our study is twofold: we discuss the section as an artifact in terms of the possibilities offered to the user and as a host to the user's practices. These elements are presented (1) in comparison with mainstream SNS, including in terms of feature adoption by users, as a prerequisite to its effective use, and (2) with a language learning focus.

---

* http://www.livemocha.com/explore

3. Data collection and first results

To perform this analysis, we have used the fact that the threads are actually numbered, their url identifier being their actual rank in the chronology of the section, to select them randomly. Data collection took place around one year after the launch of the section, in February 2012 (more than 385,000 thread IDs). The rough dating principles at work in Livemocha made the distribution in time difficult but allowed us to establish that the timeline is broken down into 28-day periods.

We used both aspects to show that an average of approximately 16% of identifiers lead to broken links ($N = 248$) and to estimate that whereas during the first three periods an average of at least 1,235 threads per day were posted, during the three periods ending on June 28, 2012, at most 580 threads were posted daily*.

Considering the data available, this decrease cannot be attributed to any element in particular, especially since the intent behind the section is fuzzy and could concern the constitution of reusable resources as well as providing a space for interaction.

4. Analysis of the artifact

4.1. Data management mechanisms

Our study of the filtering and sorting mechanisms at hand compared with the mass of available data revealed that except in certain cases (the least represented countries), the data management infrastructure does not appear to allow access to older threads. A hypothesis which is consistent with the data, as at least 89% of the threads ($N = 105$) received comments spanning over less than one period (four weeks). Even though our indicator cannot be compared strictly with mainstream SNS available data, the use of the section is much more compliant with SNS type interactions than with the constitution of a pool of reusable resources for language learning.

This similarity prompted us to examine the functionalities by comparison with those available in mainstream SNS, including conditions for adoption. Burke, Marlow, and Lento (2009) provide factors influencing the adoption of new features in SNS. According to their study, newcomers tend to share more content if their contacts do so.

4.2. Social organization of data and notifications

We compared the use that is made of the social network of friends in mainstream SNS and the Livemocha culture section, which showed that while in SNS the network of friends, groups and interests act as a filter on the global amount of data. In the culture section, no such filter is available. The contributions of a user's network of friends are only available as such through each user's individual profile.

---

* 95% confidence interval.

Additionally, the onsite notifications of friends' activity shunt anything that happens in the culture section. On the other hand, offsite notifications (emails) include comments made on the user's threads, but have a different function, which does not favour interaction, considering the instantaneous nature of the activity. Interactions are also likely to be hindered by the lack of use of AJAX (Asynchronous JavaScript and XML) in the section.

5. Engagement with the culture section

Again, the data is consistent with the observations, as engagement with threads seems low (20% of threads without feedback, 90th percentile of the distribution of comments at 3 comments per thread). On a more qualitative basis, unanswered questions and lack of attention to previous comments are observed, even in threads displaying multiple comments; a fact that is underlined by a low number of explicit exchanges between users (47% of threads with comments, 15% of total threads, show at least one explicit exchange).

Engagement within the threads also seems lacking, as most comments constitute appreciative comments. Assessing linguistic complexity by counting words in comments shows that 62% of the comments are composed of 5 words or less.

These two observations are likely to be linked, as a correlation can be found between the mean length of comments in a thread and the length of the longest discussion in it. Moreover there is a significant difference between the number of words in comments, depending on whether they are part of an explicit exchange.

Despite showing a lack of engagement with and within the threads, the data underlines the well-founded nature of the use of social networking site features to trigger linguistic exchange, as social and linguistic engagement seem linked.

On a qualitative basis, our data contains some, though not many, examples of different types of activity likely to favor language learning:
- Rephrasing of the same idea in different ways by the same speaker;
- A learner reusing vocabulary used in a previous comment;
- Metalinguistic feedback;
- Explicit cultural explanation or debate.

It is worth noting that these examples essentially only occur in explicit exchanges between users.

6. Conclusion

This study is exploratory in the sense that more variables need to be taken into account, as well as the point of views of users and designers. All the same, it shows potential in the course chosen by Livemocha in its culture section. However, the community designers do not yet seem to have found an effective way to "harness collective intelligence through network effects" (Musser, O'Reilly, & the O'Reilly Radar Team, 2007, p. 101) towards language learning activity. The still numerous user contributions are nonetheless steadily decreasing in numbers. The social section displays lackluster functionalities, especially when it comes to social features.

We feel that two leads are worth exploring in respect of using these social features for language learning: improving the functionalities of the tools to enhance the possibilities of action left to users, and giving more guidance to learners' activities (possibly in a subset of the social networking tools).

These leads are not mutually exclusive as the first might provide the means for interactions to create didactically relevant activities. The second can provide users with more numerous use schemes to reuse and adapt when using the tools in an unconstrained context.

Acknowledgements. As part of the activities of the European network "Language learning and social media: 6 key dialogues" http://www.elearningeuropa.info/languagelearning, this article engages only its authors. We thank our project colleagues, the pole-emploi and the European Commission for their support.

References

Burke, M., Marlow, C., & Lento, T. (2009). Feed me: motivating newcomer contribution in social network site. *Proceedings of the 27th international conference on Human factors in computing system* (pp. 945-954). Boston, MA. Retrieved from http://www.thoughtcrumbs.com/publications/paper0778-burke.pdf

Dixhoorn, van, L., Loiseau, M., Mangenot, F., Potolia, A., & Zourou, K. (2010). *Language learning: resources and networks*. Language learning and social media. Retrieved from http://www.elearningeuropa.info/files/LS6/language learning resources and networks DEF.pdf

Loiseau, M., Potolia, A., & Zourou, K. (2011). Communautés web 2.0 d'apprenants de langue avec parcours d'apprentissage : rôles, pédagogie et rapports au contenu. *Actes de la conférence EIAH 2011* (pp. 111-123). Retrieved from http://hal.archives-ouvertes.fr/hal-00598762

Musser, J., O'Reilly, T., & the O'Reilly Radar Team. (2007). *Web 2.0 Principles and Best Practices.* Sebastopol, California: O'Reilly.

Potolia, A., Loiseau, M., & Zourou, K. (2011). Quelle(s) pédagogie(s) voi(en)t le jour dans les (grandes) communautés Web 2.0 d'apprenants de langue ?. *Actes de la conférence EPAL 2011* (pp. 19-22). Retrieved from http://w3.u-grenoble3.fr/epal/dossier/06_act/pdf/epal2011-potolia-et-al.pdf

UNIVERSITY OF
GOTHENBURG

Individualized Teaching and Autonomous Learning: Developing EFL Learners' CLA in a Web-Based Language Skills Training System

Zhihong Lu*, Fuan Wen, and Ping Li

Beijing University of Posts and Telecommunications, Beijing, P. R. China

Abstract. Teaching listening and speaking in English in China has been given top priority on the post-secondary level. This has lead to the question of how learners develop communicative language ability (CLA) effectively in computer-assisted language learning (CALL) environments. The authors demonstrate a self-developed language skill learning system with materials development and its application in a teaching process. It was proved from collected research data that the system had a positive effect on improving learners' CLA, especially their listening and speaking skills.

Keywords: communicative language ability (CLA), listening and speaking skills, EFL, system, CALL environments.

1. Introduction

It has been highly emphasized from *College English Curriculum Requirements* that college English teaching in China should adopt "the computer- and the classroom-based multimedia teaching model" (Department of Higher Education, 2007). Teaching objectives have been shifted from English reading skills to listening and speaking abilities, with much emphasis on communicative language ability and autonomous learning ability. However, large class sizes and instructors' academic preparation make it difficult to meet the requirements. Information and communication technology (ICT) could contribute to the solution of this problem in that it makes it possible to tailor the subject matter, assess the individual needs of students (Volman, 2005, p. 18) and "permit each student to proceed at his own rate" (Skinner, 1968, p. 30), so as to facilitate differentiation and individualization in education. In recent years, many CALL systems provide rich learning content for students by Web Browser (Bergasa-Suso, Sanders,

---

* Contact author: zhihonglu2002@yahoo.com.cn

& Tewkesbury, 2005; Wen, Zhang, & Tian, 2009). However, the interaction between students and the content in learning systems still needs further development.

2. A self-developed language skills learning system

2.1. To meet the needs in reality

According to Bachman (1990), language competence includes grammatical competence, textual competence, illocutionary competence, and sociolinguistic competence. A web-based language skills training system Rofall (Rainier Open Five Aspects Language Lab) has been designed and developed since 2008 and is based upon the implementation of more than ten top-notch national and city-level research projects hosted by the first two authors over the past five years. The system fits into a broad language teaching framework for the purpose of enhancing EFL learners' overall language competence, especially their listening and oral production skills, and integrates the Internet into college English classrooms. It allows the creation of a multi-media teaching environment, in which EFL learners can be highly motivated to learn and teachers are able to measure the improvement in their learning process.

2.2. Its role in EFL teaching and learning process

Rofall consists of three systems – Language Learning Smart Client (LLSC), Course and Teaching Management System (CTMS), and Resource Management System (RMS).

LLSC in Rofall is the key to keep the whole system reliable and stable and it enables EFL learners to conduct both in-class and out-of-class audio-video speaking activities, model tests, and questionnaires. Currently, it offers 18 different types of skill training task items which learners can choose from, combine, and sequence, and more items can be added if needed. The system contains over 10,000 items, including nearly 70 sets of national CET-4[*] and CET-6, 6,700 vocabulary items and 1,500 grammar training items. EFL learners' overall CLA can be improved step by step through instructors' guidance in the application of various task items and activities. LLSC enables 18 types of training items as illustrated in Table 1.

CTMS in Rofall allows EFL teachers to manage all aspects of teaching and learning. Teachers can arrange teaching content and activities to guide students in their learning process, collect data to construct or prescribe exercises, tests, and conduct surveys. It also enables instructors to comment directly on students' homework and tests separate from the automatically provided scores, and learners' feedback or comments can be collected. In a word, it helps EFL teachers to track learners' learning process.

---

[*] CET is the abbreviated form of "College English Test". The national College English Test Band Four (CET-4) in China aims to evaluate non-English majors' comprehensive language proficiency. Apart from CET-4, there is also CET-6, which is widely used to evaluate above-average students' language proficiency.

Table 1. Types of training items

No.	Types of task items	No.	Types of task items
1.	Short Answer Questions	2.	Multiple Choices
3.	True or False (1)	4.	True or False (2)
5.	Spot Dictation	6.	Compound Dictation
7.	Sentence Dictation	8.	Sentence Completion
9.	Constructing Questions (1)	10.	Summary Writing
11.	Essay Writing	12.	Sentence Repeat
13.	Intonation Practice	14.	Constructing Questions (2)
15.	Question-Answer Exercise	16.	Role Play
17.	Personal Statement	18.	Group Discussion

The last one in the Rofall system, RMS enables the course designers to prepare multimedia resources, such as learning material selection, task item developing, processing, and editing.

2.3. Features of the Rofall system
The system has the following features:
- Highly improved instruction and supervision in the language teaching and learning process through optimized sequencing in comparison to more general systems that are not optimized for language teaching and learning;
- Flexibility in changing teaching and learning activities. Easy updating of content and activities by various means like CD's, instructors' input, and network based general updates, etc.;
- Individualization: learners' portfolios are generated automatically, providing sophisticated scores of mastery for certain language components, as well as suggestions for further study through error analysis and feedback;
- High efficiency and validity – the system evaluates both objective and subjective items (apart from oral productive tasks) with a very high level of accuracy;
- Complete teaching and learning process: the system incorporates every single step of teaching and learning, including but not limited to information management, knowledge imparting, language teaching and learning activities, learning assessment, collaboration through exchange of learning experiences (learners' work display), and report management;
- Less dependence on stable Internet access – learning process will not be disrupted by Internet problems or low band-width connections, learners only need the Internet when downloading updates and uploading results;
- Different teaching techniques are used to make the teaching process more web-based and intelligent.

By using the system, classroom instructions are combined with online learning, allowing the instructor to select, combine, and sequence those tasks and activities for learners to hone their language skills, to thus create a more individualized teaching and autonomous learning process. This is so that "the computer- and classroom-based multimedia college English teaching model" requirements set by the government can be effectively supported, and teachers can not only manage every step in the language teaching and learning process, but also can motivate, supervise, and guide learners in real time through analysis of their performance, while learners can be empowered to have control over their own autonomous learning. Therefore, language teaching and learning processes become multimodal, individualized, measurable, and manageable in ways that were not possible in the past.

3. Applications of the system

The system was used in a five-week experimental teaching program in English grammar from November 24, 2008 to December 29, 2008. There were 286 students from 10 classes in total, of which 169 freshmen were from year 2008 and 117 sophomores from 2007. All of them were science and technology majors and were instructed by three different teachers. The result of using the system to develop students' ability to gain and refresh their English grammar knowledge shows to be very effective.

In 2009, the system was used again in a four-week program in grammar and vocabulary during the winter vacation. About 2800 freshmen and sophomores (they came from all areas of China) from 95 classes took part in the program. The test result was not valid since most students failed to do what they were told. There were two main reasons causing the problem, one was that a large number of the students had poor Internet connections at home, and the other was that the Chinese Spring Festival was on during the period so students were not highly motivated to accomplish such extra homework.

In October and December, 2009, a simulated test for CET-4 was conducted through the system. There were 100 sophomores from year 2008 and 50 freshmen from year 2009 who took part in the test and they were all non-English majors who were instructed by two different teachers. Performance of tests and grading were all done online.

From May 2010 till June 2010, the system was used for a four-week listening skill training program and pre- and post-simulated tests for CET-4. There were 2,358 students from 72 classes of year 2008 and they were all non-English majors instructed by 14 different teachers. The average score of the grade from the pre-simulated comprehension skills test was 54.9 while the average from the post-simulated test was 64.2, which implies that using the system to prepare students for taking the national CET-4 was very effective. Performance of tests and grading were all done online.

From 2009 to 2012, students taking the Audio-Video English Speaking Course (AVESC) all did their pre-test, mid-test, post-test, and a pre- and post-questionnaires through the system. Data about their learning and responses to the various activities were collected as well. It shows that this ICT-based course has greatly promoted students' CLA, proven by the data collected from over 2,000 students for four rounds of teaching sessions, including that from pre- and post-test scores, comprehension surveys, and follow-up interviews. It has also been established that the use of the Rofall system has played a very important role in students' learning processes.

The number of registered students has now reached 16,000, which includes 60 students from another university.

4. Conclusions

It has been demonstrated that the teaching materials and the interactive communicative activities designed and developed with the system have a positive effect on improving students' CLA, especially their listening and speaking skills, and the system further promotes the idea of individualized teaching and autonomous learning, therefore offering valid pedagogical suggestions and implications for other EFL instructors and designers in CALL environments.

Acknowledgements. This paper was made possible through the humanities and social sciences project – "Research on Multidimensional Assessment for a Web-based English Audio-video Speaking Course" (12YJA740052), supported by the Ministry of Education in China.

References

Bachman, L. F. (1990). *Fundamental considerations in language testing*. Oxford: Oxford University Press.

Bergasa-Suso, J., Sanders, D. A., & Tewkesbury, G. E. (2005). Intelligent browser-based systems to assist Internet users, *IEEE Transactions on Education, 48*, 580-585.

Department of Higher Education. (2007). *College English curriculum requirements*. Beijing: Foreign Language Teaching and Research Press.

Skinner, B. F. (1968). *The technology of teaching*. New York: Appleton-Century-Crofts.

Volman, M. (2005). A variety of roles for a new type of teacher educational technology and the teaching profession. *Teaching and Teacher Education, 21*(1), 15-31. doi: 10.1016/j.tate.2004.11.003

Wen, F. A., Zhang, J., & Tian, Y. F. (2009). Design and application of an E-learning platform for various learning groups. *International Conference on Network Infrastructure and Digital Content* (pp. 731-735). IEEE IC-NIDC2009.

UNIVERSITY OF GOTHENBURG

A Diagnostic Approach to Improving the Pedagogical Effectiveness of Tutorial CALL Materials

Paul A. Lyddon*

Kanda University of International Studies, Chiba, Japan

Abstract. Teachers and students alike would benefit from self-access materials to free up lesson time for activities requiring live face-to-face interaction, but such materials must first undergo thorough testing and evaluation of their pedagogical effectiveness. The present study is part of an ongoing project to develop a series of self-paced, interactive online modules on the use of grammatical voice. Previous acceptability judgment data showed these materials to be effective for improving performance on sentences with animate subjects but largely ineffective or even detrimental in cases with inanimate ones. Thus, 10 returning participants were individually recorded re-attempting the same acceptability judgments, this time stimulated by structured interview questions to probe decision-making processes and thereby permit step-by-step analysis of conceptual understanding. The findings included common failure to grasp the role of personification in permitting false agentive subjects in English, conflation of the use of inanimate subjects with passive voice, and unawareness of relationships between grammatical case-marking and thematic relations.

Keywords: pedagogy-driven design, language pedagogy, content-based instruction.

1. Introduction

Attainment of the advanced language proficiency necessary for academic and professional use generally requires many more hours of study than most programs can provide in the classroom (Lyddon, 2011). Exacerbating this problem are seemingly insurmountable difficulties such as the teaching of grammatical voice (Hinkel, 2002; Master, 1991; Owen, 1993). On this latter issue, Johnson and Lyddon (in preparation) have found promising signs of success with a concept-based approach to instruction, as advocated by Negueruela (2003). However, as the implementation of their face-to-face lessons takes three entire 90-minute class periods, Lyddon (2012a, 2012b) has experimented with an online alternative, only to find mixed results in learner outcomes,

---

* Contact author: palyddon@kanda.kuis.ac.jp

including inferior performance on acceptability judgments involving sentences with inanimate subjects and active verbs. Thus, the current study represents a post-use evaluation as part of a pedagogy-based approach to tutorial CALL development (Colpaert, 2006) in order to not only explain the previous findings but to inform the next iteration of the instructional design.

2. Method

2.1. Procedures

The data were collected in a two-hour, one-on-one session with each of 10 participants over a period of four weeks in the spring of 2012 at a computer science university in northern Japan. The 10 participants were a representative sample of the 31 who had participated in the immediately prior pilot study (Lyddon, 2012a).

Although each data collection session was conducted face to face, with the exception of paper-based mark sheets, all interactions between the participants and the researcher were mediated by a shared laptop computer and recorded using Camtasia Studio® screen capture software. Each session began with a self-paced, 10-frame Adobe® Director® movie giving a summary review of the three learning modules from the pilot study (i.e., on agency, animacy, and transitivity). Each participant then took a self-paced version of the otherwise identical pre-posttest acceptability judgment task (i.e., five randomized permutations of a single sentence for each of six regular verbs: analyze, damage, design, discuss, occur, and study). The researcher then revisited each item with the participant, asking whether the sentence appeared active or passive and recording the answer without comment.

Next, the researcher began a bilingual interview focused on a slide presentation featuring a systematic rearrangement of the same items as for the acceptability judgment task. First, the items were grouped alphabetically by verb, with the exception of 'occur', the only pure intransitive, which came last. Within each group, they were then ordered according to apparent conceptual difficulty: animate subjects with active transitive verbs (AAT), animate subjects with passive transitive verbs (APT), inanimate subjects with active intransitive verbs (IAI), inanimate subjects with passive verbs (IP), inanimate subjects with active transitive verbs (IAT).

The interview protocol proceeded with the researcher first showing the participant an isolated verb in its dictionary form and asking a short series of questions about its perceived properties. The participant was then shown the five permutations of the same sentence for the given verb in the order indicated above (i.e., AAT, APT, IAI, IP, IAT). For each sentence, a standard sequence of probe questions was used to elicit the participant's considerations in making an acceptability decision. Finally, the participant re-took the same self-paced version of the acceptability judgment task from the start of the session.

2.2. Results

With only 10 participants, this study was underpowered to find statistical significance for any but the largest of effect sizes. Nevertheless, paired-samples comparisons between the scores on the original pretest ($M = 23.1$, $SD = 3.04$) and those on the delayed posttest given just after the review ($M = 23.8$, $SD = 3.12$) were similar to those on the original posttest ($M = 24.2$, $SD = 2.90$), showing gains of .36 and .34 standard deviational units, respectively. In other words, the nominal decrease on the delayed posttest with respect to the original posttest was not important.

On revisiting each posttest item to identify it as either active or passive, 7 out of 10 participants named all 30 correctly. Of the items the other three participants missed, nearly 95% (17 out of 18) involved inanimate subjects with active verbs, two thirds of which were intransitive. Incorrect responses were observed for all verbs but 'analyze', with 'study' also posing no problem for the IAT sentences.

The probe later revealed not only confusion of the passive with the use of inanimate subjects but also initial conflation of passive voice with past tense. It also became clear that many students, although they correctly understood the terms for 'transitive' and 'intransitive' in Japanese, had them backwards in English.

Another finding was that most students seemed unaware of the general need for instrumental case marking in English, accepting sentences like 'Two main ways analyzed the results' until given a literal Japanese translation with the explicit nominative case marker '*ga*' on '*houhou*' ('ways'). Those who rejected such sentences focused exclusively on the literal capabilities of inanimate subjects. Consequently, no one correctly identified the acceptable use of the false agentive subject in 'A previous paper discussed the issue'.

Despite the limited number of participants, a paired-samples t-test at a .05 alpha level comparing the scores on the acceptability judgment task before ($M = 23.8$, $SD = 3.12$) and after ($M = 27.4$, $SD = 2.50$) the interview protocol showed a statistically significant increase and a large effect: $t(9) = 2.903$, $p = .02$, $d = .92$. Accounting for much of the difference was noticeable improvement on all sentence types for 'occur' (Table 1) and all verbs except 'damage' for IAT sentences (Table 2).

Table 1. Pre- and post-protocol acceptability judgments on the verb 'occur'

Sentence Type	Students Answering Correctly (%)	
	Pre	Post
AAT	20	90
APT	80	90
IAI	50	100
IP	60	90
IAT	30	90

Table 2. Pre- and post-protocol acceptability judgments on IAT sentences

Verb	Students Answering Correctly (%)	
	Pre	Post
analyze	50	80
damage	80	70
design	50	80
discuss	70	100
study	70	80

3. Discussion

Despite their re-randomized presentation order, the post-interview acceptability judgment items were the same as those used in the training. As such, although it is doubtful that the learners were able to make the correct judgments on so many seemingly similar sentences based simply on short-term memory, it is also unlikely that the magnitude of improvement would have been so great with a different set of verbs, for the probing procedure made the inadequacy of their lexical knowledge clearly evident. Nevertheless, such remarkable gains on even this small number of verbs suggest several insights from the interview protocol that might be fruitfully implemented in the next stage of the module development.

First, more attention needs to be given to vocabulary, starting with the essential terminology. While one might argue that the teaching of metalinguistic target language is premature or even unnecessary, most of the students who participated in this research, although they were monetarily compensated, chose to do so primarily for the opportunity to interact in English as much as possible. Thus, any initial use of the native language must serve the purpose of scaffold as well as explanatory tool. This part of the instruction will then need to include the difference between past and passive as well as transitive and intransitive and subject and agent. Of course, abstract explanations alone may be difficult to grasp, especially since they often contain additional unfamiliar words. As such, it may be necessary to use examples involving only animate entities (rare in computer science discourse) to illustrate phenomena such as the shifting position of the agent in the process of passivization (e.g., *The cat killed the mouse* vs. *The cat was killed by the mouse*).

Second, additional sensitization to grammatical form is needed. While learners might be excused for confusing the past tense with the past participle, it is clear that they were also ignoring the presence or absence of a preceding copula and the subsequent 'by' when deciding agent and patient roles. As it is easier to notice the presence of something rather than its absence, this training might be achieved through the juxtaposition of similar sentences, which might also serve to reinforce the differences between nominative and instrumental cases (e.g., *A computer simulation studied the effects* vs. *We studied the effects in a computer simulation*).

Finally, confirmation probes should be built into the instruction to guide the learners as they struggle to master the new concepts. For instance, often a participant would correctly identify a verb as transitive but then incorrectly accept a sentence using that verb without a direct object. After simply being asked again about transitivity, however, he or she usually not only quickly spotted the error but also explained it, thus reinforcing conceptual understanding.

4. Conclusions

The findings of the current investigation indicate that a number of factors, including confusion over linguistic terminology, inattention to grammatical forms, and insufficient knowledge of the target verbs, all may have contributed to the mixed results of the previous study. As the interview protocol employed to obtain these data led to unequivocally superior acceptability judgment performance thereafter, key elements from the probing procedure will be incorporated and evaluated in a future iteration of the pedagogical design.

Acknowledgements. I would like to thank the University of Aizu for funding this research and my 10 research participants for providing me with the necessary data.

References

Colpaert, J. (2006). Pedagogy-driven design for online language teaching and learning. *CALICO Journal, 23*(3), 477-497.

Hinkel, E. (2002). Why English passive is difficult to teach (and learn). In E. Hinkel & S. Fotos (Eds.), *New perspectives on grammar teaching in second language classrooms*. Hillsdale, NJ: Lawrence Erlbaum.

Johnson, N. H., & Lyddon, P. A. (In preparation). A concept-based approach to teaching grammatical voice in an English for computer science context.

Lyddon, P. A. (2011). Training Japanese university English learners for greater autonomy. In A. Stewart (Ed.), *JALT2010 Proceedings* (pp. 700-713). Tokyo: JALT. Retrieved from http://jalt-publications.org/proceedings/articles/1132-training-japanese-university-english-learners-greater-autonomy

Lyddon, P. A. (2012a). An evaluation of an automated approach to concept-based grammar instruction. *EUROCALL Review, 20*(1), 105-109. Retrieved from http://www.eurocall-languages.org/review/20/papers_20/24_lyddon.pdf

Lyddon, P. A. (2012b). An exploration of a technology-enhanced approach to teaching the concept of grammatical voice. *Procedia – Social and Behavioral Sciences, 34*, 137-141. Retrieved from http://www.sciencedirect.com/science/journal/18770428/34

Master, P. (1991). Active verbs with inanimate subjects in scientific prose. *English for Specific Purposes, 10*(1), 15-33. doi: 10.1016/0889-4906(91)90013-M

Negueruela, E. (2003). *A sociocultural approach to the teaching-learning of second languages: Systemic-theoretical instruction and L2 development.* Unpublished doctoral dissertation. The Pennsylvania State University. University Park, PA.

Owen, C. (1993). Corpus-based grammar and the Heineken effect: Lexico-grammatical description for language learners. *Applied Linguistics, 14*(2), 167-187. doi:10.1093/applin/14.2.167

UNIVERSITY OF GOTHENBURG

L2 Learners' Informal Online Interactions in Social Network Communities

Maria-Luisa Malerba*

Universitat Oberta de Catalunya, Internet Interdisciplinary Institute, Barcelona, Spain

Abstract. This paper reports on a study on the use of social network sites (SNSs) designed for L2 learning, such as *Livemocha* and *Busuu*, where learners autonomously seek opportunities for authentic interaction in spontaneous ways. The study consists in a longitudinal multiple case study approach to investigate learners' informal online interactions taking place in the SNSs. This paper will focus on the results related to the analysis of learners' interactions and to whether the construction of learning opportunities is fostered or impeded by the social dimension that is intrinsic in these communities. The objectives are to learn more about the dynamics and the behaviours enacted by learners with reference to the online interaction with peers, and to explore the role played by the social aspect and its relationship with the learning aspect. To attain these objectives, the paper analyses intercultural, open-ended, dyadic conversations occurring between learners and native speakers (NSs), and learners and non-native speakers (NNSs) in the semi-instructional context of these learning communities and in the absence of teachers and pedagogical tasks. Drawing on socio-cultural approaches, the paper also raises central issues that are related to the surrounding environment of online language learners, such as roles' definition, learners' identity, scaffolding and peer-assistance (macro-level). It then applies these issues to key-concepts in SLA, such as turn-taking, language selection, language alternation, repair strategies and noticing (micro-level). The data collection includes semi-structured interaction interviews and a wide and variegated corpus data consisting of textual private messages and emails, audio and video recordings and textual chats analysed respectively through virtual ethnography and Conversation Analysis (CA). The preliminary results provide insights on learners' ability or inability to manage both the social and the pedagogical trajectories simultaneously. These deliveries are expected to shed more light on their interaction patterns and to provide a better understanding of recent lifelong L2 learning practices in the naturalistic and out-of-class contexts of online communities.

Keywords: social network sites, online language learning, learner's autonomy, CALL.

---

* Contact author: mmalerba@uoc.edu

In L. Bradley & S. Thouësny (Eds.), *CALL: Using, Learning, Knowing, EUROCALL Conference, Gothenburg, Sweden, 22-25 August 2012, Proceedings* (pp. 198-203). © Research-publishing.net Dublin 2012

1. Introduction

Relevant studies have found that informal interaction of L2 learners with native speakers increase their self-confidence and willingness to use the L2, which has a positive effect on L2 learning (Archangeli, 1999; Stoller, Hodges, & Kimbrough, 1995; Yorozu, 2001). Tarone (1997, 2007), for example, argues that it is necessary to study L2 learning in natural settings for everyday communication and in the natural contexts of their social networks.

Some other studies (Haruhara, 1992; Kurata, 2004a, 2004b, 2011; Neustupný, 1995) have gone further and focused on the exploration of learners' interactions in their informal social networks looking at the characteristics and at the effects of these informal networks on L2 learning. Through the analysis of the interactive discourse that spontaneously occurred among learners in their social networks, they found that it is important for both learners and NSs to be provided with basic knowledge about how to interact with each other, when to offer assistance, how to take turns, and how to show difficulty in comprehending each other's utterances. These studies, in general, strengthen the idea of the positive features of informal social networks in terms of L2 learning.

With the spread of the Internet and social network sites in particular, the network concept has become an even more powerful analytical tool for better understanding of the dynamics of learners seeking opportunities to use the L2 outside of the classroom and in informal contexts. This study looks at the intercultural online chats among L2 learners in the dimension of online social networks designed specifically for language learning and will show how learners adopt specific strategies to offer or receive assistance in the target language (TL) and how they are engaged in both the social and the learning trajectory.

2. Method

2.1. The participants

The study employed a longitudinal ethnographic multiple case study to analyze learners' perceptions and behaviours within their experience of online social networks for L2 learning. The social networks selected for the study are *Livemocha* and *Busuu*. Some of the participants for the study were recruited by means of an online questionnaire sent to the members of the former of these online communities. The other participants were selected drawing on the researcher's personal acquaintances and contacts and by contacting people at random in both the online communities. The participants to this study are mainly NSs and NNSs of English, Spanish and Italian.

A wide range of qualitative methods have been adopted, including the online survey, the collection of samples of interactive discourse occurring in online social networks, and semi-structured interviews. In this way, the methodological triangulation allowed the cross-checking of the data collected, improving further internal validity.

2.2. Data collection

The data used in this study are of several kinds: audio-tape recording, excerpts from online chats, some diary entries by the interactants, semi-structured interviews and interaction interviews with the participants. Semi-structured interviews aimed to elicit information about if and how learners are able to take advantage of their learning experience in these social networks, and what their goals and motives are before and during their experience in the communities.

After this type of interview, interaction interviews followed. They consisted in very specific questions about speech events occurring in participants' interactions (Kurata, 2011; Neustupný, 2003). They were useful for understanding whether when interacting with both NSs and NNSs of their TL in the communities, learners are active and aware of their language use and of the assistance they autonomously provide and offer each other. While interviews were transcribed, codified and analyzed through *Atlas.ti*, the audio interaction data were transcribed according to CA conventions.

3. Discussion

Table 1 illustrates an online chat between Nastya, a NS of Russian, one of the interviewees, with her language partner, Tom, an American boy she met on *Livemocha*. In this excerpt the conversation between the two occurs only in English. As Nastya explained during the interview, no code-switching occurred since they agreed on using English to interact. This was due to the very basic level of Russian of Tom and to Nastya's strong intention of improving her language skills, having planned a stay in the US.

Table 1. Excerpt

1	N:	well it's funny but I also like hills))) *[heels]* even though I'm tall sometimes I wear it))))
2	T:	hahaha
3	T:	yes, heels are nice too))
4	N:	sorry
5	N:	heels)))
6	T:	LOL
7	T:	its ok
8	T:	i was confused at first (rofl)

The excerpt above illustrates a repair sequence where embedded correction occurs. Embedded correction is usually opposed to explicit correction and it consists in inexplicit indirect feedback (Gass, 1997; Tudini, 2010) not to interrupt the conversational flow. It permits interactants to correct with discretion and it is considered as the least likely to draw learners' attention to the formal aspects of a conversation (Tudini, 2010). As the excerpt will show, in this conversation the implicit correction allows the maintenance of the social trajectory.

In this chat session Nastya and Tom are engaged in an activity that is informal social interaction and are driven by the motive of intertwining their social relationship. On the other hand, as the interview further confirmed, there is another activity that Nastya is carrying out, language learning, driven by the motive of achieving a more proficient level of English. These motives shape the relationship between Nastya and Tom and the definition of their roles during their online interactions, being Nastya the novice and Tom the expert of the TL.

In line 1 the NNS produces the incorrect object [hills] and makes a spelling mistake. In line 2 the NS maintains the social trajectory replying the previous turn and does not interrupt the flow of the conversation. Moreover, he appears to be aware of the sensitivity of his interlocutor and, in order not to affect Nastya's identity and self-image as a proficient learner of the L2 (Kurata, 2011), in line 3 he makes the correction "on the fly". In other words, Tom produces the alternative [heels] without interrupting the conversational flow and by reincorporating the correct word in an interpersonal rather than pedagogical trajectory. In this way online participants keep their inter-subjectivity and both social and learning trajectories are maintained (Tudini, 2010).

The visual saliency (Tudini, 2010) typical of online interaction helps both of them and in particular the NNS in noticing her mistake, as the apologizing word in line 4 demonstrates. The apologizing sequence is followed by another sequence (line 5) where the NNS produces the alternative correct [heels]. The correct pushed output concludes the repair and starts a mitigation sequence in line 6 where the NS makes use of irony and of the chat acronym LOL (standing for "Laughing Out Loud"). Later, in line 7, Tom mitigates and softens the embedded correction, and in line 8 he provides a justification for his correction by completing the mitigation sequence with another ironic acronym, ROFL (standing for "Rolling On the Floor Laughing").

The abbreviations (LOL in turn 6 and ROFL in turn 8) display a playful attitude of proximity towards the learner's error and, at the same time, provide an adequate conclusion to this successful repair sequence. It is also worthy to underline that this excerpt shows a feature that is typical of online chats, that is, the presence of typographical, spelling and grammatical errors made by NSs, which are usually not corrected. In this case, "its" (line 7) should be spelled as "it's" or "it is" in order not to generate confusion between the neuter form of the English possessive personal pronoun and the conjugation of the neuter third-person singular of the verb "to be". These mistakes might create problems with less proficient NNS than the learner of this online chat.

4. Conclusions

As the excerpt discussed earlier shows, in the informal context of online social networks, conversational events like non-understanding, assistance-seeking and assistance-provision are authentic rather than pedagogically motivated. This study confirms what previous studies have already outlined (Pasfield-Neoufitou, 2007a, 2007b, 2009; Tudini, 2010): that online chat interactions have a potential for SLA. Moreover, the study reveals that learners display a high level of autonomy in the careful selection and creation of their own personal online network as well as in the management of their own learning, with pedagogical repair trajectories mainly coexisting with social ones.

A limitation of this study is the lack of a proper longitudinal approach to learners' online discourse. In other words, it would be useful to track whether learners show apperceived input and whether they are able to incorporate the correct utterance meaningfully in their interactions and employ it across several chat sessions. Nevertheless, it is very difficult to obtain online conversations at time distance from the same participants since their participation is totally voluntary.

Acknowledgements. Given that this paper is drawn from my PhD thesis, I would like to thank Christine Appel, my supervisor, for her valuable guidance during this process. My sincere gratitude also goes to the participants of this study, who enthusiastically collaborated with me and expressed me several times their interest and their confidence with this project.

References

Archangeli, M. (1999). Study abroad and experiential learning in Salzburg, Austria. *Foreign Language Annals, 32*(1), 115-124.

Gass, S. M. (1997). *Input, interaction and the second language learner*. Mahwah, NJ: Lawrence Erlbaum.

Haruhara, K. (1992). Nettowaakingu sutoratejii (Networking strategy). *Nihongogaku (Japanese Language Study), 11*, 17-26.

Kurata, N. (2004a). Communication networks of Japanese language learners in their home-country. *Journals of Asian Pacific Communication, 14*(1), 153-178.

Kurata, N. (2004b). Social networks of language learners and collaborative interaction with native speakers: A case study of two Australian learners of Japanese. *ASAA e-journal of Asian linguistics & language teaching, 7*, 1-22.

Kurata, N. (2011). *Foreign Language Learning and Use. Interaction in Informal Social Networks*. Continuum International Publishing Group.

Neustupný, J. V. (1995). *Atarashii nihongo kyooiku no tame ni (For new Japanese language education)*. Tokyo: Taishuukan Shoten.

Neustupný, J. V. (2003). Japanese students in Prague. Problems of communication and interaction. *International journal of the sociology of language, 162*, 125-143.

Pasfield-Neofitou, S. E. (2007a). Intercultural Internet chat and language learning: A sociocultural theory perspective. *Learning and Socio-cultural Theory: Exploring Modern Vygotskian Perspectives international workshop 2007, 1*(1), 146-162.

Pasfield-Neofitou, S. E. (2007b). Textual features of intercultural internet chat between learners of Japanese and English. *CALL-EJ Online, 9*(1), 1-18. Retrieved from http://callej.org/journal/9-1/pasfield-neofitou.html

Pasfield-Neofitou, S. E. (2009). Learners' participation in informal Japanese-English Internet chat. *New Voices, 3*, 43-63.

Stoller, F. L., Hodges, R., & Kimbrough, J. (1995). Examining the value of conversation partner programs. *Applied Language Learning, 6*(1 & 2), 1-12.

Tarone, E. (1997). Analysing IL in natural settings: A sociolinguistic perspective on second-language acquisition. *Communication and Cognition, 30*, 137-149.

Tarone, E. (2007). Sociolinguistic approaches to second language acquisition research – 1997-2007. *The Modern Language Journal, 91*(5), 837-848. doi: 10.1111/j.1540-4781.2007.00672.x

Tudini, V. (2010). *Online Second Language Acquisition. Conversation Analysis of Online Chat*. London: Continuum International Publishing Group.

Yorozu, M. (2001). Interaction with native speakers of Japanese: What learners say. *Japanese Studies, 21*(2), 199-213.

UNIVERSITY OF GOTHENBURG

Feedback: A Key Component in the Design, Development and Validation Stages of Online English/FL Materials

Antonio Martínez*, Ana Sevilla, Ana Gimeno, and José Macario de Siqueira

Universitat Politècnica de València, Dept. of Applied Linguistics, Valencia, Spain

Abstract. For the past few years, the authors have been working on the design and development of an online First Certificate in English (FCE) preparatory course and exam simulator in an attempt to provide a supplementary tool and resources for students aiming to achieve a B2 level of English. These materials have been designed in such a way that learners can follow and complete the activities either by being assessed by a remote tutor, or in a completely autonomous way. This makes the consideration, analysis and design of effective, efficient and constructive feedback an essential component in the whole design process. In this process, the concept of formative assessment needs to be taken into account from the initial stages of the design and development up to the last phase, and aims at validating the appropriateness of the contents and the resources which are part of the materials. This paper addresses feedback from a theoretical perspective while exploring its different roles from a practical point of view throughout these stages. The main objective is to present the pedagogical framework that has guided the whole design and development process, as well as to analyse the main parameters considered by the authors of these materials when designing and editing the feedback to be received by students after completing either automatically corrected or open input exercises and tasks. This entire process has been conductively aimed to offer learners the contents and all of the required additional tools, in particular corrective, personalised and formative feedback, in order to enrich the two main learning and assessment modalities: self-access and autonomous. Moreover, a description of the platform's main utilities, which allow material writers to edit, monitor and assess branched feedback in accordance with the students' performance, will be provided.

Keywords: feedback, online English/FL materials, design, development, validation.

---

* Contact author: anmarsae@gmail.com

1. Introduction

There is a need to explore students' errors and mistakes so that material developers can anticipate them to avoid and reduce them or to offer an adequate solution when they have been already made. Ferris (2012) states that "corrective feedback is more effective when it is selective or focused" and that the emphasis should be on "identifying patterns of error that students could work on rather than marking every single error in sight" (p. 9), an idea to bear in mind when developing tools and resources to be used in autonomous or distance learning contexts. This is the case of the *InGenio FCE Online Course & Tester*, courseware for learners of English as a Foreign Language (EFL) developed to provide students at the Universitat Politècnica de València (UPV) with a supplementary tool to achieve a B2 level of English. In many cases, material developers explore the multiple ways in which language learning occurs and the features related to the causes that could explain why some students fail while others are able to attain the target level in the language being learnt. This fact is especially interesting as students are neither always aware of their progress nor are they able to describe the process that led them to that particular level of expertise (Ellis, 1997).

2. Feedback

Levy and Stockwell (2006) have presented research approaches in the field of Computer-Assisted Language Learning (CALL) based on the "patterns of learner behaviour as learners engage with online tasks and tutoring programs" (p. 153). A study on how students respond and interpret automatic feedback and on how they are able to correct their first response or performance can lead to important improvements. Pujolà (2002), who dealt with the concept of "help facilities", studied how students respond to those additional tools alongside the learning strategies which take part in the process too. This author distinguishes between the categories of assistance and guidance. Travis and Joseph (2009) consider that all the resources and tools relating to e-learning have "the potential to enhance the learning process, by offering more flexible access to the curriculum and providing opportunities for support outside the classroom" (p. 314). Arnold and Ducate (2011) reflect on the idea of dynamic evaluation and on how the line between instruction/formation and evaluation could be erased.

Martínez Ruiz and Sauleda Parés (2001) present the concepts of formative evaluation versus summative evaluation. Formative evaluation would be aimed at understanding and improving the learning process by means of the effect of feedback when learners' behaviour and answers have been predicted beforehand. Lara Ros (2002) studies the need to individualise, personalise, adjust, and adapt the entire process to comply with students' particular requirements, an assumption related to the individualisation criteria aimed at responding to learning scenarios which are more and more focused on students' specific needs and less on group anonymity and standardisation.

3. Computer assisted feedback and the feedback utility in the *InGenio FCE Online Course & Tester*

An aspect which has been greatly agreed upon is the appropriateness of computer-aided evaluation, one of the most important reasons being the immediate reception of feedback by students (Lara Ros, 2002). Additionally, technology is often described as contributing very positively in every process, providing formative assessment as well as any other supplementary and supportive activity introduced to practice and improve specific contents. Lara Ros (2002) explores how the concept of evaluation, understood as help and orientation, is deeply related to the administration of constant feedback and reports, and refers to a study conducted by Stephens and Mascia (1996), for whom computer-assisted evaluation would enable students to know about their results at any point and detect problems, difficulties or drawbacks. These options would allow material developers and teachers alike to know which components are not working properly, as well as those general ideas or contents which are not being learned as predicted.

According to Arneil and Holmes (2003), innovation and sophistication criteria can be introduced progressively if students' production and performance are analysed in detail and compared with some possible correct answers. They consider that feedback could be immediate so that students could know whether their responses are correct immediately after completing the required tasks, enabling content and materials developers to introduce specific keys and hints as part of the activities and tasks implemented. Bangs (2003) concluded that feedback can be seen as one of the main components. Nevertheless, he alerts on the fact that an important part of the online materials, which are currently available, present some outstanding shortages, and sees the delivery of feedback as the factor which can lead to the conception of learning in an independent and individual way. Chapelle and Douglas (2006) also see feedback as an element to be taken into account when evaluating computer-assisted learning and assessment materials. Other authors such as Youngs, Ducate, and Arnold (2011) conceive interaction as a channel to provide students with very valuable feedback too. Hauck and Hurd (2005) present the important role played by tutorials, as many students need elements that could help them find similarities shared by CALL and face-to-face learning.

The *InGenio* online authoring tool and learning management platform includes a feedback editing system in all the templates used to develop and edit exercises (Figure 1) (Gimeno Sanz, 2006). Feedback is approached in an intrinsic and extrinsic way and in an immediate or asynchronous way (Bangs, 2003). The aim is to provide a consistent pedagogical and didactic framework, enabling material developers to offer materials closely linked to students' needs. Therefore, a student would not receive abrupt messages such as "wrong" or "wrong answer", but a constructive response that would contribute dynamically to their linguistic development (Figure 2).

Figure 1. *InGenio* template to edit specific feedback

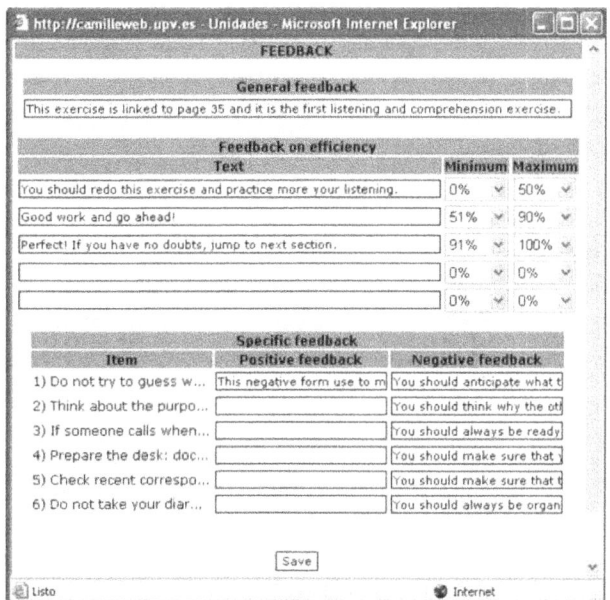

Figure 2. Feedback per item as seen by the user

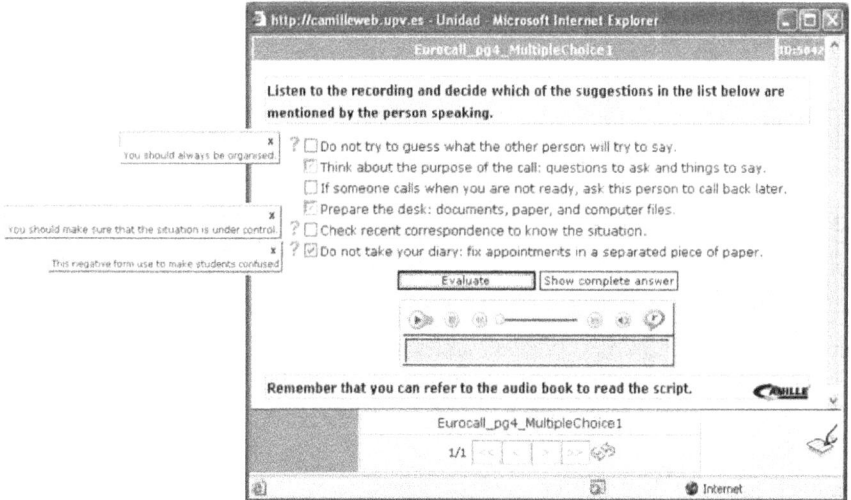

This is possible thanks to its branched feedback utility, which helps to provide feedback in accordance with the particular responses given. The provision of automatic feedback is possible across the different *Course & Tester* sections, with the only exception of the tasks which require the student to produce written texts or record oral performances. The correction and rating of these tasks would require a human tutor to interact with the platform and rate the exercise by using the *InGenio* tutor interface and the rating options. When automatic correction is not possible, a model answer or answer key is provided so that students can compare their production with a sample of what would be expected from them (Figure 3) (Gimeno Sanz, 2002).

Figure 3. Feedback in accordance with students' efficiency rate and sample automatic messages

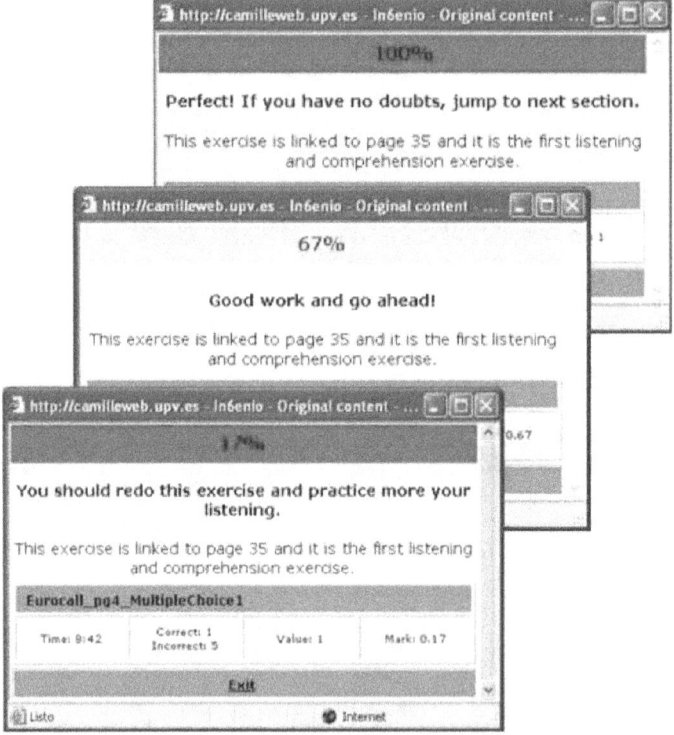

In September 2011 a group of 52 UPV students who had enrolled on a subject called Computer-Assisted English started working on the online B2 level courseware. The main component of this subject was the *FCE Online Course & Tester*, used as distance materials to be completed online, a learning modality to test the effectiveness of both the immediate and automatic feedback provided, as well as the asynchronous and personalised feedback offered to students. After the first semester, 27 students had completed the *Course & Tester*, and had responded to the final questionnaire designed to receive the students' impressions, opinions and suggestions. This questionnaire, a key component in the validation stage, included several questions which can shed light regarding the students' perceptions on the feedback utilities available in the *InGenio* system or offered by the materials and by the tutors who had been monitoring the process. According to their responses to the initial questionnaire, a very high percentage of the students were worried about making mistakes (Results: Strongly agree: 21%, agree: 58%, neither agree nor disagree: 21%, disagree: 0%, strongly disagree: 0%). However, they felt less anxious after using the online materials. In accordance with their responses to the final questionnaire, rating through a 1 (disagreement) to 7 (agreement) Likert scale, almost all of them considered that the materials encouraged autonomous and independent learning (Results: 1: 0%, 2: 0%, 3: 7%, 4: 7%, 5: 37%, 6: 41%, 7: 7%). Most of them reported that they enjoyed the fact of being able to self-assess their performance by accessing the progress reports (Results: 1: 0%, 2: 0%, 3: 4%, 4: 7%, 5: 37%, 6: 30%, 7: 22%), and perceived the feedback they received as being useful and relevant (Results: 1: 4%, 2: 0%, 3: 4%, 4: 15%, 5: 33%, 6: 26%, 7: 19%).

4. Conclusions

A representative number of studies have been conducted to observe and analyse students' errors and mistakes in order to introduce corrective feedback so as to help students overcome them. Despite the negative connotations of the words "mistake" and "error", their positive impact on language learning cannot be left aside. To study their origins or causes in depth could improve the learning process as well as offer feedback solutions to make it more effective and efficient. This idea has been taken into consideration during the design, development, implementation and validation stages of the *FCE Online Course & Tester*. The main goal has been to reinforce those resources as well as the learning and assessment modalities implemented. The idea of how important it is for students to receive materials suited to their own specific needs and demands has been addressed. Feedback has been approached from a theoretical perspective and a description of the utilities provided by *InGenio,* allowing material writers to edit, monitor and assess branched feedback in accordance with the students' performance, has been presented. The students who have already used these materials have rated the effects of the feedback received very positively.

Acknowledgements. Acknowledgements are due to the Valencian Regional Government (Generalitat Valenciana) for funding Antonio Martínez's and Ana Sevilla's FPI research grants.

References

Arneil, S., & Holmes, M. (2003). Servers, clients, testing and teaching. In U. Felix (Ed.), *Language learning online: Towards best practice* (pp. 59-80). Lisse: Swets & Zeitlinger.

Arnold, N., & Ducate, L. (2011). Technology, CALL and the Net generation: Where are we headed from here? In N. Arnold & L. Ducate (Eds.), *Present and future promises of CALL: From theory and research to new directions in language teaching* (1-22). San Marcos,TX: CALICO Monograph Series.

Bangs, P. (2003). Engaging the learner: How to author for best feedback. In U. Felix (Ed.), *Language learning online: Towards best practice* (pp. 81-96). Lisse: Swets & Zeitlinger.

Chapelle, C., & Douglas, D. (2006). *Assessing language through computer technology.* Cambridge: Cambridge University Press.

Ellis, R. (1997). *Second Language Acquisition.* Oxford: Oxford University Press.

Ferris, D. R. (2012). Technology and corrective feedback for L2 writers: Principles, practices, and problems. In G. Kessler, A. Oskoz, & I. Elola (Eds.), *Technology across writing contexts and tasks* (7-29). San Marcos,TX: CALICO Monograph Series.

Gimeno Sanz, A. (2002). *Aprendizaje de Lenguas Asistido por Ordenador: Herramientas de autor para el desarrollo de cursos a través de la web.* Valencia: Editorial UPV.

Gimeno Sanz, A. (2006). Proyecto InGenio: Gestor de recursos para el aprendizaje de idiomas. *Marco ELE: Revista de Didáctica Español como Lengua Extranjera.* Retrieved from http://marcoele.com/proyecto-ingenio-gestor-de-recursos-para-el-aprendizaje-de-idiomas/

Hauck, M., & Hurd, S. (2005). Exploring the link between language anxiety and learner self-management in open language learning contexts. *European Journal of Open, Distance and E-Learning II.* Retrieved from http://www.eurodl.org/materials/contrib/2005/Mirjam_Hauck.htm

Lara Ros, S. (2002). *La evaluación formativa en la universidad a través de Internet: Aplicaciones informáticas y experiencias prácticas.* Barañáin, Navarra: Ediciones Universidad de Navarra, S.A. (EUNSA).

Levy, M., & Stockwell, G. (2006). *CALL dimensions: Options and issues in Computer-Assisted Language Learning.* London: Lawrence Erlbaum Associates Publishers.

Martínez Ruiz, M. A., & Sauleda Parés, N. (2001). El tratamiento informático de las evaluaciones. In J. L. Rodríguez Diéguez & O. Sáenz Barrio (Eds.), *Tecnología educativa: Nuevas tecnologías aplicadas a la educación* (pp. 369-396). Alcoy, Alicante: Marfil.

Pujolà, J. T. (2002). CALLing for help: Research in language learning strategies using help facilities in a web-based multimedia program. *ReCALL, 14*(2), 235-262. doi: 10.1017/S0958344002000423

Stephens, D., & Mascia, J. (1996). The use of Computer Assisted Assessment in Biology in UK Higher Education: A survey. *Life Sciences: Educational Computing, 7*(2), 15-18.

Travis, P., & Joseph, F. (2009). Improving learners' speaking skills with Podcasts. In M. Thomas (Ed.), *Handbook of Research in Web 2.0 and Second Language Learning* (pp. 313-330). New York: Information Science Reference.

Youngs, B., Ducate, L., & Arnold, N. (2011). Linking Second Language Acquisition, CALL and language pedagogy. In N. Arnold & L. Ducate (Eds.), *Present and future promises of CALL: From theory and research to new directions in language teaching* (23-60). San Marcos,TX: CALICO Monograph Series.

UNIVERSITY OF
GOTHENBURG

Collaborative Strategic Reading on Multi-Touch and Multi-User Digital Tabletop Displays

Jaber Ali Maslamani[a]*, Scott Windeatt[a], Patrick Olivier[b], Phil Heslop[b], Ahmed Kharrufa[b], John Shearer[b], and Madeline Balaam[b]

a. School of Education, Communication & Language Sciences, Newcastle University, Newcastle upon Tyne, UK
b. Culture Lab, School of Computing Science, Newcastle University, Newcastle upon Tyne, UK

Abstract. This paper is part of a work-in-progress that reports on the design, development, and evaluation of a Digital Collaborative Strategic Reading (DCSR) application with regard to its effectiveness in improving English as a second language (ESL) reading comprehension. The DCSR application allows users to read collaboratively on multi-touch and multi-user digital tabletop displays that support both face-to-face and computer-based interaction. The application is designed to provide systematic instruction on tabletop computers using four main comprehension strategies that form the Collaborative Strategic Reading (CSR) instructional approach. The paper addresses one main research question: 'How does the use of the tabletop-based reading application (DCSR) affect learners' reading processes and outcomes?", and the following sub-questions: (1) What is the impact of the tabletop-based reading system on learners' reading scores with regard to the reading assessments? (2) How do learners collaboratively construct meaning on the tabletop? To answer these research questions, the subjects used the DCSR application on tabletop computers in groups of four, once a week for 5 weeks. Data were collected and analysed using both qualitative and quantitative methods. Each reading session was preceded by a cloze test and followed by two types of assessment: a written recall test and a cloze test; both tests were designed to reflect the students' comprehension of the reading passages. The paper will report on the design of the software and the administration of the study, but will focus on the analysis of the data from the different sources, and present insights into the nature of collaborative reading using the DCSR application on a tabletop computer.

Keywords: digital collaborative strategic reading, tabletop computing.

1. Introduction

The tabletop computer is an emerging technology which, with its large multi-touch surface that enables collocated synchronous collaboration, has clear potential for

---

* Contact author: jaber.maslamani@yahoo.com

application in learning contexts. This paper will investigate the effectiveness of a tabletop-based computer application (Digital Collaborative Strategic Reading – Digital CSR or DCSR) as a collaborative reading instructional tool for enhancing the reading comprehension of English as a second language students.

International ESL students at tertiary level institutions in the UK and elsewhere need to reach a level of proficiency in English which will allow them to cope linguistically with their studies. Proficiency in reading is especially important for such students, as is effective instruction of L2 reading (e.g., Anderson, 1999; Huckin & Bloch, 1993). They and other researchers argue that reading is probably the most important skill for L2 students in academic or learning contexts (Carrell, 1988; Fasheh, 1995; Hafiz & Tudor, 1989; Pretorius, 2000, p. 35; Saville-Troike, 1984).

One particular approach to teaching reading – Collaborative Strategic Reading – is based on the principles of reciprocal teaching (Palincsar & Brown, 1984), which include a number of clearly specified procedures such as collaborative group work and interactive dialogue (Kim et al., 2006). CSR has potential benefits for the teaching and learning of reading as it is designed to offer instruction of explicit specific strategies and 'clearly specified procedures' for reading comprehension, which are practised through collaboration at all stages of the reading activity. Instruction of this kind has been associated with positive results in enhancing reading comprehension and avoiding text comprehension failure (Bremer, Vaughn, Clapper, & Kim, 2002; Klingner & Vaughn, 1998, 1999, 2000; Klingner, Vaughn, & Schumm, 1998; Vaughn, Klingner, & Bryant, 2001).

Collaboration among learners usually takes place around a table, and the "traditional table" is a tool that is well known for its axiomatic and intuitive support for small group collaboration; a familiar picture in educational settings. These features, as well as the rich experience that learners carry as a result of daily contact with tables in classrooms have motivated technologists to introduce interfaces for digital tabletops that share a lot of the interaction and communication features that are associated with work around "traditional tables" (Kharrufa, 2010; Kharrufa & Olivier, 2010; Scott, Grant, & Mandryk, 2003). As a result, the current study is concerned with the development and evaluation of an integrated application for teaching and practising reading on a tabletop computer that combines the strengths of "traditional table" collaboration with the collaborative features offered by digital tabletop computers.

2. Method

This project started by looking at specific requirements for designing applications for collaborative learning around digital tabletops. Studies of interaction design recommend starting with observation of how people apply their knowledge of the physical world and their everyday experience when using collaborative learning tools (e.g., Preece, Rogers, & Sharp, 2002). In addition to design guidelines drawn from previous studies, most current tabletop-based systems are therefore based on "observational studies on the use of traditional tables" (Kharrufa, 2010, p. 7). Kharrufa and Olivier (2010), for example, developed design requirements based on a review of the relevant literature, and on their own observation of table-based collaboration, including the learners' use of gazing, body positions, and different tools while taking part in collaborative activities. Their observations confirmed the results of other similar studies regarding issues of territoriality on the tabletop surface, orientation of artefacts such as notes on the tabletop, use of gestures, and other aspects of collaboration.

The development of the DCSR application followed an iterative design approach that involved several stages, beginning with paper prototypes, followed by digital prototypes. The digital prototypes then underwent usability testing, with each digital prototype developed, evaluated in use, modified and re-evaluated. The design of the DCSR was based on the principles of the CSR approach, observation studies of paper CSR available in the literature and the most up-to-date studies on tabletop-assisted learning.

2.1. DCSR implementation

The paper addresses one main research question: 'How does the use of the tabletop-based reading application (DCSR) affect learners' reading processes and outcomes?", and the following sub-questions: (1) what is the impact of the tabletop-based reading system on learners' reading scores with regard to the reading assessments? and (2) how do learners collaboratively construct meaning on the tabletop computer? To answer these research questions, the subjects used the DCSR application on the tabletop computers in groups of four, once a week for 5 weeks. Five different reading texts of similar length and difficulty (intermediate level) were used; one reading text for every reading session. Each reading session started with previewing the whole text, followed by brainstorming then prediction of the content of the text. Then the learners read the text paragraph by paragraph to get the gist, dealing with unknown words, and then write down their understanding of each paragraph in digital notes. They conclude the task with a wrap-up stage in which they evaluate and monitor their understanding of the whole text by generating questions and answers. At the end of each of these stages they collaboratively organise their notes into groups based on similarities among the ideas. In order to assess reading comprehension, students take the same cloze test before and after the reading session and a written recall test after the session. Qualitative and quantitative methods are employed for both the data collection and the data analysis procedures.

2.2. Preliminary results and analysis

This work-in-progress is mainly qualitative, and the qualitative results form the core of the study. However, quantitative results can reflect a lot on students' achievement on the tabletop computer and about the impact of this technology on their performance.

Based on a preliminary analysis of qualitative data, the grouping feature, a tool for allowing the learners to organise ideas, questions or problems about the text into groups, was helpful in making students' thinking visible to their peers, thus leading to incidents of comprehension check, and encouraging requests for further explanation and elaboration as well as corrective feedback. Grouping also encouraged problem-solving and planning (e.g., by organising notes into groups), both of which require reasoning and decision making. The orientation of digital notes (i.e., who was able to read an individual learner's notes as a result of the way he or she chose to orientate them on the tabletop) and the multi-keyboard-based input facility (i.e., each learner had a keyboard they could use) acted as non-verbal prompts for feedback from other peers or for further explanation. Test results have shown an improvement in students' scores in the cloze test between the pre-test and the post-test. There is also a positive correlation between their scores in the cloze post-test and the written recall test as both variables move in tandem.

3. Discussion

Preliminary findings suggest that tabletop computers and the DCSR application have potential benefits in language learning and more specifically in collaborative reading. Findings suggest that the grouping tool used each of the main reading strategies to have been tried once (brainstorming, prediction, get the gist, and wrap-up) and that it supports the externalisation of the students' thinking. During the grouping activity, students engage in organising note-slips into groups. They have already summarised ideas and written them inside digital notes to share with others during grouping. Organising the notes that contain similar ideas into groups requires planning, making decisions, and reasoning about which notes belong to which group and engages students in problem-solving throughout the whole process. The grouping tool and digital notes can also encourage scaffolding, allowing high-achievers to see others' notes on the tabletop surface and pinpoint areas of confusion that low-achievers may have, and to offer appropriate help (Pressley, Hogan, Wharton-McDonald, Mistretta, & Ettenberger, 1996).

The orientation of objects on the tabletop was found to be a useful tool for comprehension as it allows for easier reading of the text, for communication with peers, and for coordination (see Kharrufa, 2010; Kharrufa & Olivier, 2010). Other elements of effective collaboration such as space, students' behaviour and actions also affected the design of the application and students' construction of meaning while reading on tabletop computers, though consideration of these is beyond the scope of this paper.

4. Conclusions

The current exploratory study of the use of a Digital Collaborative Strategic Reading application contributes to understanding how tabletop computers can support co-located synchronous face-to-face collaborative reading and to investigating the impact of the tabletop-based computer application, DCSR, on ESL students' reading comprehension. There is evidence from a preliminary analysis of the data that learners coped well with the technology. Also, features of the DCSR software such as orientation and grouping of notes are associated both with interaction and collaboration, and with an improvement in reading comprehension and reading scores.

References

Anderson, N. J. (1999). Improving reading speed: activities for the classroom. *English teaching forum, 37*, 2-5.

Bremer, C. D., Vaughn, S., Clapper, A. T., & Kim, A. (2002). Collaborative Strategic Reading (CSR): Improving secondary students' reading comprehension skills. *Research to Practice Brief, 1*(2). Retrieved from http://www.ncset.org/publications/viewdesc.asp?id=424

Carrell, P. L. (1988). SLA and classroom interaction: reading. *Annual review of applied linguistics, 9*, 223-242. doi: 10.1017/S026719050000091X

Fasheh, M. J. (1995). The reading campaign experience with Palestinian society: innovative strategies for learning and building community. *Hardvard educational review, 65*(1), 66-92.

Hafiz, F. M., & Tudor, I. (1989). Extensive reading and the development of language skills. *English language teaching journal, 43*(1), 4-13. doi: 10.1093/elt/43.1.4

Huckin, T., & Bloch, J. (1993). Strategies for inferring word meaning from context: A cognitive model: In T. Huckin, M. Haynes, & J. Coady (Eds.), *Second language reading and vocabulary learning* (pp.153-178). Norwood, NJ: Ablex Publishing.

Kharrufa, A. S. (2010). *Digital tabletops and collaborative learning.* (Unpublished doctoral dissertation). Newcastle University, UK.

Kharrufa, A. S., & Olivier, P. (2010). Exploring the requirements of tabletop interfaces for education. *International Journal Learning Technology, 5*(1), 42-62. doi: 10.1504/IJLT.2010.031615

Kim, A-H., Vaughn, S., Klingner, A., Woodruff, A. L., Reutebuch, C. K., & Kouzekanani, K. (2006). Improving the reading comprehension of middle school students with disabilities through computer-assisted collaborative reading. *Remedial and special education, 27*(4), 235-249.

Klingner, J. K., & Vaughn, S. (1998). *Using Collaborative Strategic Reading.* Retrieved from http://www.ldonline.org/article/103

Klingner, J. K., & Vaughn, S. (1999). Promoting reading comprehension, content learning, and English acquisition through collaborative strategic reading (CSR). *The Reading Teacher, 52*, 738-747.

Klingner, J. K., & Vaughn, S. (2000). The helping behaviors of fifth-graders while using collaborative strategic reading during ESL content classes. *TESOL Quarterly, 34*(1), 69-98. doi: 10.2307/3588097

Klingner, J. K., Vaughn, S., & Schumm, J. S. (1998). Collaborative strategic reading during social studies in heterogeneous fourth-grade classrooms. *The Elementary School Journal, 99*(1), 3-22.

Palincsar, A. S., & Brown, A. L. (1984). Reciprocal teaching of comprehension-fostering and comprehension-monitoring activities. *Cognition and Instruction, 1*(2), 117-175. doi: 10.1207/s1532690xci0102_1

Preece, J., Rogers, Y., Sharp, H. (2002). *Interaction Design, beyond human-computer interaction.* New York: John Wiley and Sons, Inc.

Pressley, M., Hogan, K., Wharton-McDonald, R., Mistretta, J., & Ettenberger, S. (1996). The challenges of instructional scaffolding: The challenges of instruction that supports student thinking. *Learning Disabilities Research and Practice, 11*, 138-146.

Pretorius, E. J. (2000). "What they can't read will heart them": reading and academic achievement. *Innovation, 21,* 33-41. Retrieved from http://www.innovation.ukzn.ac.za/InnovationPdfs/No21pp33-41Pretorius.pdf

Saville-Troike, M. (1984). What really matters in second language learning for academic achievement? *TESOL Quarterly, 18*(2), 199-219. doi: 10.2307/3586690

Scott, S. D., Grant, K. D., & Mandryk, R. L. (2003). System Guidelines for Co-located Collaborative Work on a Tabletop Display. Proceedings of ECSCW-3: *European Conference on Computer-Supported Cooperative Work* (pp. 159-178).

Vaughn, S., Klingner, J. K., & Bryant, D. P. (2001). Collaborative Strategic Reading as a Means to Enhance Peer-Mediated Instruction for Reading Comprehension and Content-Area Learning. *Remedial and Special Education, 22*(2), 66-74. doi: 10.1177/074193250102200201

UNIVERSITY OF GOTHENBURG

Visualizing Blogs:
The "to-do-or-not-to do dilemma" in EAP Writing Online

Terumi Miyazoe[a]* and Terry Anderson[b]

a. Tokyo Denki University, Senju-Asahi-Cho, Japan
b. Athabasca University, Athabasca, Canada

Abstract. This paper reports on a study examining the effects of visualizing online writing activities on student behaviors and learning outcomes. A design-based research approach was adopted to develop and integrate theory and practice in natural educational settings (Anderson & Shattuck, 2012). The study was conducted in an 18-week, semester-long undergraduate English for freshman engineering students course. The course was in a blended face-to-face/online format, using Moodle, and covering the four skills of listening, reading, speaking, and writing. A blog visualization tool, designed as a monitoring system visible to the instructor and all students, was implemented throughout the semester. Data from 28 students were analyzed, with the students' written consent. A mixed-method design was chosen for triangulation, using three data sources: pre-/post-course writing proficiency tests, an online post-course questionnaire, and online writings on Moodle. The research found that the self-regulatory mechanism supported a regular and high level of work performance of the entire class. The class average scores on writing tests showed gradual and steady progress. In addition, the phenomenon was observed in which students showed indecision about whether to work more or less relative to the performance of other students. Those students eventually deciding to work less showed certain regression in writing proficiency at the end, even if they started at a higher level than the class average. This situation, called the "to-do-or-not-to-do dilemma," is considered a potential negative effect of the monitoring system. A monitoring system for self and others can be a positive factor that improves the regular work performance of a learning community, leading to a higher outcome. However, the study suggests the need for appropriate counter-measures against possible demoralization in the individual and/or the entire class.

Keywords: information visualization, blog, forum, social dilemma, EAP writing, blended learning.

---

* Contact author: t.miyazoe@mail.dendai.ac.jp

In L. Bradley & S. Thouësny (Eds.), *CALL: Using, Learning, Knowing, EUROCALL Conference, Gothenburg, Sweden, 22-25 August 2012, Proceedings* (pp. 217-222). © Research-publishing.net Dublin 2012

1. Introduction

This paper reports on the final stage of a research study that examined the effects of visualizing students' online behaviors on their learning outcomes. The research was conducted in a basic English for Science Purposes (ESP) course for freshman engineering students.

A literature review of major CALL-focused international journals (CALICO, Computers and Composition, LL&T, ReCALL, Systems) over the past decade (2001-2011) reveals that similar research has not been reported examining the effects of visualizing learners' online writing on their learning outcomes in foreign language learning.

Prior to the current study, two pilot studies found correlations among the frequency of using a blog visualization tool, the amount of blog postings, and improvement in English writing ability (Miyazoe & Anderson, 2011). However, in a one-semester experiment, the observed progress in writing ability was small, and it was not clear if this positive effect occurred because of the novelty of implementing new technology. In its final stage, this research therefore sought to answer two questions: 1) Does an environment in which students can monitor their own and other class members' work performance produce net learning outcomes in terms of writing proficiency? and 2) Does this monitoring become a stable learning strategy for the students over a one-year longitudinal intervention?

2. Method

A total of 28 engineering students in a night program participated in the data collection and provided their written consent for analysis and possible publication of the results. The course included one year of spring and fall semesters, each lasting approximately 18 weeks with holidays and school events. Four-fifths of the students participated in both semesters; five students were new to the class in the fall.

The intervention included the use of a blog-viewing tool, regular blog writing, and pseudonym use, all developed and viewable on a Moodle course web space. Writing at least one blog post per week was recommended, without penalty for not posting. These conditions were the same throughout one year. As a natural part of the course design, to make it more challenging in the second semester, five optional essays (approximately one essay every two weeks) were required in the fall to allow the students to practice writing essays in addition to blogs. This assignment was accompanied by a one-time guidance session to introduce the academic writing structure before the due date for the second essay assignment.

For triangulation, a mixed-method approach of using both quantitative and qualitative approaches was chosen (Creswell & Plano Clark, 2007). Three data sources were consulted: 1) pre- and post-course writing proficiency tests, 2) an online survey, and 3) blog and forum essay postings that were stored on Moodle. Of the participants, 27 students completed the optional online survey.

The pre- and post-course English writing tests simulated the opinion essay writing section in the Test of English for International Communication (TOEIC). The tests were prepared and administered in a plain text format on Moodle with a 30-minute time limit. Different essay topics that used a compare/contrast structure with accessible topics were selectively chosen for pre-/post-test comparison. The digital TOEIC essays were copied onto paper scoring sheets, assigned randomized identification numbers, and evaluated by two experienced native English higher education teachers; for comparability of the results, the same raters were used for spring and fall.

To increase validity, the raters worked independently without being informed of the existence of the co-rater. The order of the essay topics (one was pre-test, and the other was post-test) was also not known by the raters. The same scoring rubrics used for scoring opinion writing in the Test of English as a Foreign Language (TOEFL) offered by the ETS (Trew, 2010, p. 157) were used. The rubrics provided scores ranging from 0 to 5 points, and the raters were asked to use 0.5-point intervals for accuracy of the results and interpretations.

A post-course online survey was administered in an anonymous format to ensure a high response rate. The survey contained a question regarding the frequency of use of the viewing tool to verify the possible correlation between tool usage and students' online behaviors.

The blogs and essay assignment posts on Moodle were copied from the system and used for quantitative analysis from various perspectives.

3. Results

Because of space limitations, only the critical findings are selectively reported. Overall, the students' participation in online writing was constant throughout the year. The average number of blog posts per student was 11.5 ($N = 28$, $SD = 6.95$) in the fall and 11.03 ($N = 31$, $SD = 4.24$) in the spring.

Figure 1 summarizes the total number of blog posts per week and essays per each assignment during the semester to depict the students' overall participatory behaviors. Blog and essay writing post frequencies are juxtaposed to highlight the possible interrelationships in terms of workload. The seven squares represent the total number of essays posted on each day of the week. The two squares in Week 2 and Week 18 correspond to the two TOEIC-type opinion essay tests, and the five squares in between represent the five essay assignments. The decline in Week 16 corresponded to winter break. In this research, the negative correlation between blog posts and essay posts is considered to reflect the students' strategy for balancing their workload between the two assignments.

Figure 1. Total number of posts per week during the semester*

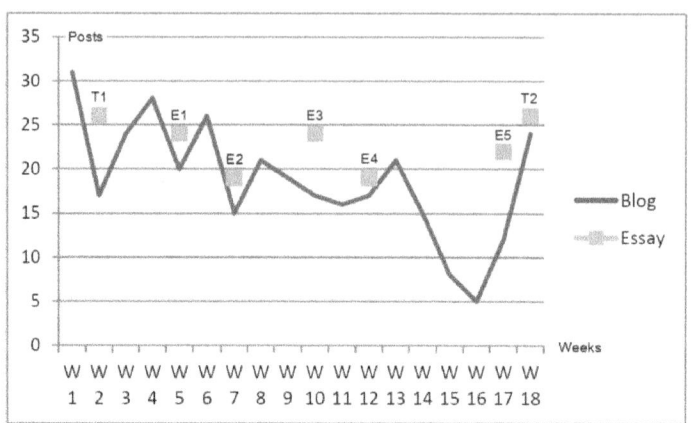

Figure 2 summarizes the average scores of the students who took both the pre and post TOEIC-type essay tests in both spring and fall semesters. The slight decrease from the spring post-test to the fall pre-test (2.05 to 2.03) can be explained by the inclusion of five new students in the fall as well as the two-month summer break between semesters. It is noteworthy that from the spring pre-test to the fall post-test, the average score for the entire class improved from 1.84 to 2.25 (an increase of 0.41 or 22.3%). Therefore, in this research, the writing proficiency of the students made continuous improvement over the course of the one-year experiment.

Figure 2. Change in English writing proficiency over the course of one year

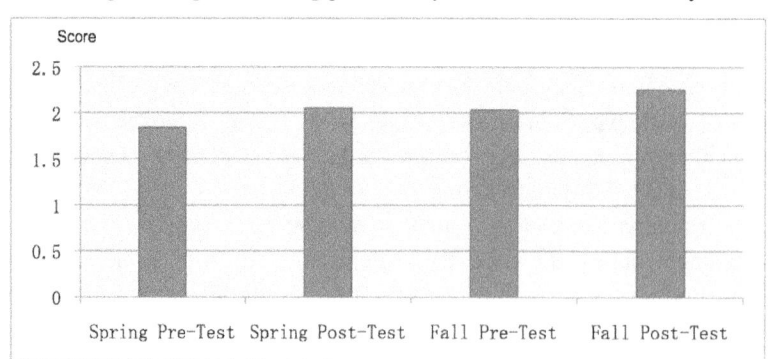

Figure 3 summarizes the changes in scores on the essay tests and the length of the Essay 2 assignment immediately after the essay structure guidance session (on the left)

---

* T: Test, E: Essay assignment

and the total length of blog and essay assignment posts in word count and the length of Essay 2 (on the right). All of the essay lengths were analyzed, and the length of Essay 2 proved particularly worthy of attention. The data of 25 students who completed both tests in the fall were included to find factors that produced the higher learning outcomes. Word count was used because in the tradition of research on writing, that statistic is considered an indicator of progress in writing ability (Wolfe-Quintero, Inagaki, & Kim, 1998). A high correlation was found between the change in test scores and the length of Essay 2 (Figure 2: left side, $r = .675$, $p < .01$). Moreover, a strong correlation between the post-test length and the total length of the blogs and opinion essays that each student produced (Figure 2: right side, $r = .672$, $p < .01$) is noted. This may suggest that among the five essay assignments, the length of Essay 2 was the most accurate predictor of the progress that the students would demonstrate toward the end of the course.

Figure 3. Post length and change in writing proficiency.

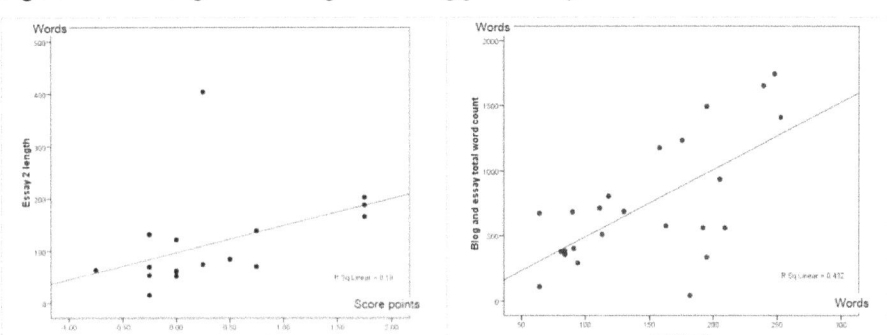

Finally, further analysis focusing on those students who made progress (improved group) and those who regressed (regressed group) over one year reveals that viewing the lower performance (in writing ability) of other members may have discouraged those with initial high scores from making efforts to improve. At the end of one year, the initial high scorers were overtaken by the initial low scorers.

4. Discussion

This research suggests that monitoring both one's own and others' work via the viewing tool appeals to the self-regulatory mechanism of a learning community supporting the regular and high levels of work performance of the entire class. The students in this study demonstrated adequate progress in writing ability over a one-year course period. However, the study also observed evidence of two diverging directions in class members who were motivated to work more and those who were motivated to work less, who eventually regressed in the targeted skill. The authors call this struggle of indecision whether to do more or less the "to-do-or-not-to-do dilemma," describing a situation in which a student hesitates about the degree of commitment to the workload of a learning community.

A monitoring system of work performance for self and others can be a positive factor that improves the regular work performance of a learning community, leading to a better outcome. However, the study suggests that this monitoring system should be accompanied by appropriate countermeasures against possible demoralization in the individual and/or the entire class.

Acknowledgments. We would like to thank Dr. Shinichi Sato for his kind support in maintaining his blog-viewing tool, PISION.

References

Anderson, T., & Shattuck, J. (2012). Design-based research: A decade of progress in education research? *Educational Researcher, 41*(1), 16-25.

Creswell, J. W., & Plano Clark, V. L. (2007). *Designing and conducting mixed methods research*. Thousand Oaks: SAGE Publications, Inc.

Miyazoe, T., & Anderson, T. (2011). *Viewing and participating: Blog visualization and its learning outcomes in blended learning*. IEEE International Professional Communication Conference: Communicating Sustainability, Cincinnati.

Trew, G. (2010). *Question 8: Write an opinion essay Scoring Guidelines. Tactics for TOEIC Speaking and Writing Tests*. New York: Oxford University Press.

Wolfe-Quintero, K., Inagaki, S., & Kim, H. (1998). *Second language development in writing: Measurements of fluency, accuracy & complexity*. Honolulu: University of Hawai'i Press.

UNIVERSITY OF GOTHENBURG

Improving the English Proficiency of Native Japanese Via Digital Storytelling, Blogs, and e-Mobile Technologies

Hiroyuki Obari* and Stephen Lambacher

Aoyama Gakuin University, Shibuya-ku, Shibuya,Tokyo, Japan

Abstract. This paper reports on the use of digital storytelling and blog activities to make CALL classes more dynamic and personalized for both instructors and learners alike. An empirical research study was carried out to determine if a blended-learning environment incorporating m-learning could help improve the English listening, presentation, and blogging skills of native Japanese undergraduate students at a private university in Tokyo, Japan. The blended-learning activities included three components: "iUniv" lectures, digital storytelling, and student blog activities. The goal of the study was to examine the effectiveness of the blended learning activities in improving the English language proficiency of native Japanese students, including their presentation skills through the use of blogs and PowerPoint. An assessment of pre-training and post-training computerized assessment system for English communication (CASEC) scores revealed that the students had adequately comprehended the iUniv lecture contents and their overall listening skills improved. A questionnaire administered to students after their exposure to the activities indicated they were satisfied with and motivated by their exposure to the blended learning environment incorporating m-learning.

Keywords: digital storytelling, blog writing, e-mobile technologies.

1. Introduction

Learning today takes place at any time and at any place due to of the swift development of mobile technologies. E-mobile learning technologies such as the iPhone, iPad, podcasting, video-casting, and others, are rapidly gaining popularity as an effective way to improve foreign language skills around the world. Mobile technologies have also transformed learning methodologies (Vinu, Sherimon, & Krishnan, 2011). One such type of methodology that has received great attention in recent years is blended learning (BL). BL combines traditional face-to-face classroom methods with computer-mediated activities, resulting in a more integrated approach for both

---

* Contact author: obari119@gmail.com

In L. Bradley & S. Thouësny (Eds.), *CALL: Using, Learning, Knowing, EUROCALL Conference, Gothenburg, Sweden, 22-25 August 2012, Proceedings* (pp. 223-227). © Research-publishing.net Dublin 2012

instructors and learners. BL can increase the options for greater quality and quantity of interaction in a learning environment (Wilson & Smilanich, 2005).

"Five years from now on the web for free you'll be able to find the best lectures in the world" (Gates, 2010). The above quote, uttered by Bill Gates at a conference in August 2010, was a bold prediction he made of the future state of "open" lectures, social media, and smartphones, which has helped to usher the world into "the next era" of the web. Social media and the smartphone have indeed brought about the "the next era" to the web, and have also created a new relationship between education/learning and society which current education or e-learning has not realized.

According to social constructionism (Burr, 1995, 2003), people can create new knowledge and learn most effectively through social interaction and exchanging information for the benefit of others. Constructionism holds that learning can happen most effectively when people are active in making tangible objects in the real world. In this sense, constructionism is connected with experiential learning and builds on some of the ideas of Jean Piaget (Bandura, 1977).

The present paper reports on the results of a year-long study to ascertain if a blended-learning environment incorporating m-learning can help improve the English listening, presentation, and blogging skills of native Japanese undergraduate students. We take advantage of the cyber community where 1) Learning Management Systems, 2) Blogs, 3) Digital Storytelling, and 4) Mobile Computing are all used to teach language and communication (Obari, Kojima, & Itahashi, 2010).

2. Methodology

2.1. Participants

The participants were 60 first year university students, all native speakers of Japanese, enrolled in an undergraduate course in English Writing and Communication. Each class met once per week for 90 minutes in a CALL laboratory during two consecutive 15-week semesters. The following explains the three-phased, blended-learning environment incorporating m-learning that the student participants were exposed to as a way of improving their English listening, presentation, and blogging skills.

2.2. iUniv lectures

During the first semester, the students were assigned to listen to at least six iUniv lectures on YouTube using their mobile devices. The students typically accessed the lectures out of the classroom using their mobile devices, and practiced listening to the lectures at their own pace. One of the more popular lectures the students downloaded was *Justice* by Harvard University's Michael Sandel. Students downloaded the iUniv lectures with scripts onto their mobile devices, listened to and summarized the lectures, and then broke up into small groups of four or five students to prepare

PowerPoint presentations based on their summaries. The presentations were delivered both individually and as a group in front of the class.

2.3. Digital storytelling

Digital storytelling includes the process of story creation with the impact of pictures and sounds, and it can be transferable, storable, and accessible in order to create communities where people can share goals, experiences, and teach each other what they have learned. Digital stories usually contain some mixture of computer-based images, text, recorded audio narration, video clips and/or music. During the second half of the first semester, after having summarized the iUniv lectures and given their PowerPoint presentations, the students created digital storytelling recordings of their summaries for the purpose of developing their speaking and pronunciation skills.

In addition, the students studied 15 lessons of the DVD series *World Adventures*. This DVD series enables students to learn about the main characteristics of 15 different countries by introducing famous UNESCO World Heritage Sites. Students broke up into small groups of four or five students and created a total of two PowerPoint presentations during the class meetings. Windows Movie Maker was used in the production of the two digital stories.

2.4. Blog activities

Next, the students worked on creating a social network of shared experiences through writing blogs, which took place during the second semester. The purpose of the blog writing was to help the students develop their own language skills by reflecting upon what they had learned during the first semester. Once again, the students broke up into small groups of four or five students and spent approximately 30 minutes of each classroom meeting to prepare for their blog presentations, as well as spending extra time outside of the classroom accessing the materials via their mobile devices. In total, it took the students approximately eight weeks to prepare their blog presentations before presenting them in front of the classroom. Finally, an evaluation sheet was uploaded on the bulletin board of a learning management system (LMS), which enabled the students to share and evaluate their blogs on the web and to assess their presentations later on for critical feedback and reflective learning.

3. Assessment

For the purpose of evaluating the effectiveness of the blended learning program using m-learning, we next present some empirical data that we collected before and after the students were exposed to the BL activities, including results from the CASEC test and a post-activity questionnaire that was administered to the students for the purpose of attaining their feedback on how they felt about their BL experience.

3.1. Computerized assessment system for English communication

CASEC evaluates English proficiency based on item response theory and consists of four sections: knowledge of vocabulary; knowledge of phrasal expressions and usage; listening ability – understanding of main ideas; and listening ability – understanding of specific information. All of the students were administered by the CASEC before and after their exposure to the blended learned activities. The results showed that the overall average score increased from 533 ($SD = 94$) in April 2011 to 588 ($SD = 84$) in January 2012. A series of t-tests revealed a significant difference between the pre-test and post-test CASEC scores ($p < .01$), indicating the blended learning program incorporating m-learning had a positive effect on the students' overall English proficiency. In addition, the pre-test (April 2011) and post-test (January 2012) data results indicated that the number of students who obtained a score of higher than 600 points (maximum score = 1000) substantially increased from 10 to 32 students out of a total of 60 students.

3.2. Student questionnaire

After their exposure to the blended learning activities, the students were administered by an on-line questionnaire to determine how motivating and beneficial they felt the activities were. The first question of the questionnaire dealt with student opinion of the usefulness of digital storytelling in learning English. Nearly 80% of the respondents felt that the digital storytelling was "useful" in learning English. The second question addressed whether the students considered the digital storytelling or the blog activities more useful in learning English. Overall, students felt that the blog activities (56%) were more "useful" than the digital storytelling (44%) in learning English. The third question asked whether the students thought the blog-making and presentations activities were useful in learning English, with 85% responding favourably. It is clear from the results of the questionnaire that many of the students felt the digital storytelling, presentation, and blog activities were all beneficial in learning English.

4. Discussion and conclusions

The results of CASEC revealed that a combination of blended learning activities with m-learning had a positive effect on improving the Japanese students' overall English language proficiency. The results of the questionnaire confirmed that the students considered the activities to be helpful in developing their English language skills. Also, the questionnaire feedback revealed the students were satisfied with and motivated by their exposure to the blended learning environment using m-learning. The students devoted a significant amount of time and energy in researching and discussing their topics, in learning how to create their blogs, and finally in planning, developing, and delivering their group and individual English presentations in front of the class. Through all of these processes the students could improve their English and acquire new knowledge about their topics and develop their ICT skills.

One of the main goals of our blended learning program incorporating m-learning was to try to motivate our students by offering them a more integrated approach to learning English, including individualized guidance and support during the learning process. Through the m-learning activities students were able to work both in and out of the classroom and to actively explore their learning environment to gain more experience in collaborating with their classmates, thus making their overall language learning experience much more fun and enjoyable.

Acknowledgement. A part of this research was supported by the Grant-in-Aid for Scientific Research (C) of MEXT of Japan under Grant No.23520698 and Aoyama Gakuin University, Information Science Centre Research Grant.

References

Bandura, A. (1977). *Social Learning Theory*. New Jersey: Prentice Hall.

Gates, B. (2010). *In Five Years The Best Education Will Come From The Web*. Retrieved from http://techcrunch.com/2010/08/06/bill-gates-education

Burr, V. (1995). *An Introduction to Social Constructionism*. London: Routledge.

Burr, V. (2003). *Social Constructionism* (2nd ed.). London: Routledge.

Obari, H., Kojima, H., & Itahashi, S. (2010). Empowering EFL learners to interact effectively in a blended learning environment. *Proc. World Conference on Educational Multimedia, Hypermedia and Telecommunications 2010* (pp. 3438-3447). Chesapeake, VA: AACE.

Vinu, P., Sherimon, P., & Krishnan, R. (2011). Towards pervasive mobile learning – the vision of 21st century, *3rd World Conference on Educational Sciences 2011*, Vol. 15, (pp. 3067-3073).

Wilson, D., & Smilanich, E. (2005). *The other blended learning*. San Francisco, CA: Pfeiffer Publishing.

UNIVERSITY OF GOTHENBURG

Development of an e-Learning Program for Extensive Reading

Hironobu Okazaki[a]*, Shinichi Hashimoto[b], Eri Fukuda[b], Haruhiko Nitta[c], and Kazuhiko Kido[d]

a. Akita Prefectural University,Tsuchiya, Yurihonjo-shi, Akita, Japan
b. Soka University, Hachioji-shi, Tokyo, Japan
c. Senshu University, Higashimita, Tama-ku, Kawasaki-shi, Kanagawa, Japan
d. International Pacific University, Setocho, Higashi-ku, Okayama-shi, Okayama, Japan

Abstract. As extensive reading becomes more commonplace in the EFL/ESL classroom, there is a rise in the number of instructors and administrators who are looking for cost-effective and space-saving methods to carry out extensive reading activities. Two extensive reading systems to respond to such concerns were developed with the support of a Grant-in-Aid for Scientific Research by the Japan Society for the Promotion of Science. PREMA (your Personal REading MAnager) and PREMA Beta, both allow online or offline texts to be used as extensive reading material, alleviating the need for libraries of graded readers. PREMA Beta is a web based program that allows for extensive and speed reading in English, and provides a management tool that both teachers and students can use to easily keep track of progress. The program runs in popular browsers such as Microsoft Internet Explorer, Mozilla Firefox and Google Chrome. PREMA is a browser-type software which works on a stand-alone PC. This software allows students to utilize texts (of any size) that they find online or offline, automatically tracks the total number of words read and students' reading speed, and rates the relative difficulty of a particular text based on vocabulary lists. In both systems, information from the Internet is used as a source for reading, as opposed to physical books, therefore, students have a vast endless supply of up-to-date reading material. Intrinsic motivation to read becomes higher, since there is no limit on the choice of topics, and students can progress freely at their own pace. For instructors, classroom management is made easy as this software can be used in or out of class, and individual student progress can be tracked instantaneously. From an administrative standpoint, the lack of need to continuously buy graded readers or find space to house them is an enticing prospect. In this paper, the philosophy of development will be explained, features of PREMA will be overviewed, and the future target for this program will be shared.

Keywords: extensive reading, speed-reading, web-based, original browser.

---

* Contact author: okazaki@akita-pu.ac.jp

In L. Bradley & S. Thouësny (Eds.), *CALL: Using, Learning, Knowing, EUROCALL Conference, Gothenburg, Sweden, 22-25 August 2012, Proceedings* (pp. 228-233). © Research-publishing.net Dublin 2012

1. Introduction

One of the biggest weaknesses of Japanese learners of English is their inability to correctly comprehend the simple daily conversations of native English speakers. Japanese learners rely heavily on a top-down approach to understanding the conversation, trying to piece together meaning from the few words they are able to discern and the overall direction of the content, and often give inappropriate responses because of miscomprehension. To minimize reliance on guessing, it is necessary to increase learners' ability to understand content bottom-up by building up their knowledge of English.

Our previous research project developed an effective e-learning system that personalizes tasks so that learners can intensively work on their weakest areas by increasing their percentage of using bottom-up approaches to understanding. This program clearly helped learners overcome problems of not being able to hear unstressed syllables and liaison sounds, and increased their ability to analyze phonemes (Okazaki & Nitta, 2005). The next challenge was to help learners process conversations at natural speed. This research project aims to develop a program to help increase learners' ability to process meaning by providing continuous and effective extensive and speed reading practice.

2. Development of the PREMAs

2.1. Background of the project

In an experiment examining the English reading speed of 193 Japanese undergraduate students in science and art programs at three different universities, the result showed that the average reading rate was 102.69 WPM (words per minute), and most respondents read 60 to 120 WPM (Figure 1). In comparison, the speech rate of the VOA Special English, a news broadcast for non-native English speakers, is approximately 100 WPM. Also, the speech rate of the VOA News, a news broadcast for native English speakers, is approximately 140 to 150 WPM, and that of CNN News, ABC News, and movies is approximately 180 to 200 WPM. Generally, reading at a faster rate than usual makes it difficult for the reader to comprehend the text. Likewise, the gap between speech rate and reading speed might indicate that listening to speech spoken at a faster rate than a listener's normal reading speed might hinder comprehension. In other words, average Japanese undergraduate students whose reading speed is 102.69 WPM may be able to process the stories in VOA Special English (100 WPM), but may have difficulty understanding VOA, CNN, ABC News, and movies (180-200 WPM). Consequently, the following hypothesis can be formulated: improving the speed to comprehend written text through reading is an effective approach to increase a language learner's ability to comprehend English speech at natural speed. Therefore, in the current research, systems for reading were developed to increase the learner's ability to process conversations.

This program enables instructors to provide sustainable and effective extensive reading and speed reading activities.

Figure 1. Reading speed of 193 Japanese college students

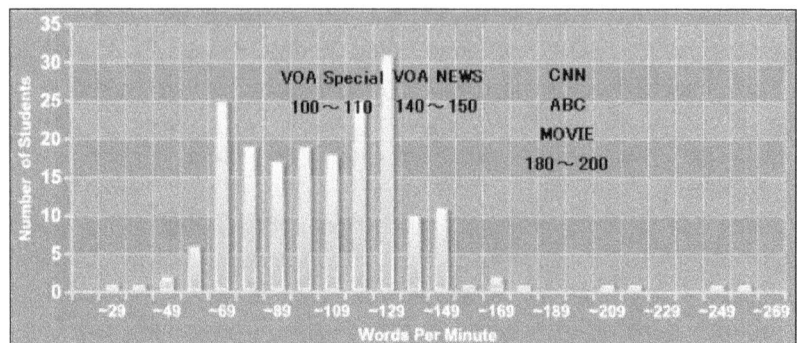

2.2. Development of PREMAβ (beta)

The list below shows the most basic things that might be required to carry out extensive reading in or out of class:
- A large number of graded readers;
- Stop watch;
- Score sheet, log sheet;
- Calculator.

However, it is very difficult to prepare all of these items in a regular English class, since a large investment of time, effort and money is required. For example, in a class of 30 students, a minimum of 30 books is needed. Obtaining enough books for a whole semester, not to mention additional sets for multiple classes, requires much money. In addition, physical storage space in the classroom or a carting system is also necessary.

In order to resolve the problems discussed above, our first stage of development involved making PREMAβ, a web-based program that allows for extensive and speed reading in English, and provides a management tool that both teachers and students can use to easily keep track of progress.

First, students choose an article from among the limitless amount of English texts available on the web, and copy it into PREMAβ. Then the students give this pasted article a title, and hit the save button. This action changes the screen to the Training Page screen. The Training Page displays the word count, and the date and title of the article are logged. After the student finishes reading, they hit the Finish reading button, and the time taken to read the article is recorded and the Result Indicator appears.

The Result Indicator shows title, word count, reading time, and reading speed (words per minute). This information can be viewed by both students and teachers on a daily or monthly basis. Teachers can also use the Scoring Manager to see students' progress at a glance.

2.3. Development of PREMA

PREMAβ was developed to allow for automatic logging and retrieval of data concerning students' reading practice. However, one serious issue, the issue of determining the appropriateness of the level of the learners and the process of manually copying and pasting text, was yet to be resolved. The newly developed part of PREMA is a browser which has the following features:

- Highlighting target text, and with a click, be able to obtain word count, reading time, and reading speed;
- Estimate and display the level of difficulty of the target text, so that learners can judge for themselves what is very difficult, a little difficult, appropriate level, a little easy, or very easy (Okazaki, 2008);
- Provide a list of reading materials of appropriate vocabulary level for each learner based on Krashen's (1982) i+1 theory;
- Automatically log students' practice time.

Figure 2 below shows a screenshot of the PREMA Reading Browser. It looks and works just like a usual web browser, and students can search for an article they want to read by inputting keywords or the URL into the address bar, so manipulation of the program is very intuitive. In addition, there are some added functions to help analyze the readability and the vocabulary levels of the stories shown on the web pages, and is also equipped with a Time Keeper for measuring reading speed.

Figure 2. PREMA Reading Browser

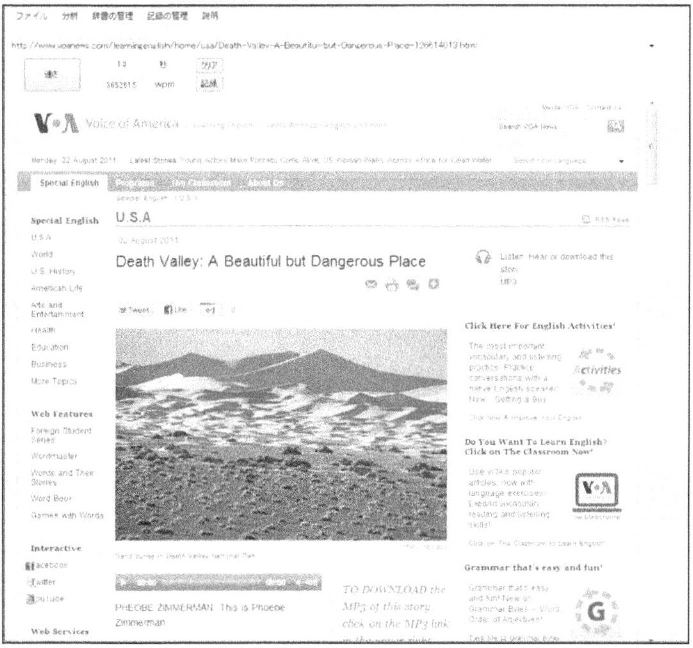

First, the user highlights the passage they want to read, and hits "Ctrl + c" to copy the passage. Next, instead of having to paste the text somewhere, the user just clicks the "Analysis2" button on the browser. A new window pops up which displays the number of characters, number of words, number of sentences in the passage, the Flesch Reading Ease and Flesh-Kincaid Grade Level score of readability, and the vocabulary difficulty index which is based on a word list.

Students can start reading practice with stories appropriate to their own English ability, with reading time and reading speed recorded automatically with the click of a button as shown below.

In addition to the attractive features stated above, we have developed an option to customize the word list system in order to allow for customization for English for Specific Purposes (ESP) uses. This Switchable Word List System enables users to change the word list from the default list to their own ESP one, for example, medical or engineering. On top of that, users can do this with basic computer skills – copying and pasting by clicking. Especially in the case of this kind of new software, it is important for the interface to be intuitive for any user (Figure 3).

Figure 3. Interface of Switchable Word List System

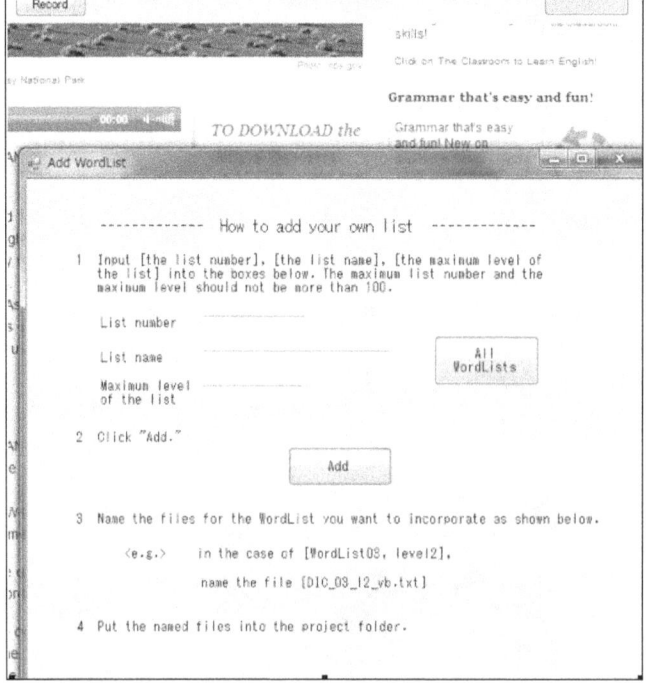

Now, students can start reading practice with stories appropriate to their own English ability, with reading time and reading speed recorded automatically with the click of a button as shown above. The records related to their practice, reading time, reading speed, date and the title of the article (if they type it) will be recorded as a CSV file.

3. Next target and conclusions

In the present study, the researchers have developed two computer systems. PREMAβ has already been employed in language classrooms in multiple universities, and its utility has been refined. Also, a project called "100,000-word extensive reading and speed reading challenge" was held for students who were interested during summer vacation. In this project, the researchers observed whether or not it is possible to speed up learners' semantic processing through reading. Eighteen volunteers participated in this project, but only five students were able to read the target word count. Although the data cannot be analyzed statistically because the number of words read and the reading materials varied, the reading speed of the participants who put effort into the task apparently ameliorated. The possibility for boosting reading speed through the use of the current program was observed, but the data does not indicate that the preliminary hypothesis, "improving the speed to comprehend a written text through reading is an effective approach to increase a language learner's ability to comprehend English speech at natural speed," is valid, according to the results of a listening test taken by the respondents. For future research, the number of the participants should be increased, and further attempts should be made to enhance their reading speed by providing sustainable and effective extensive reading and speed reading approaches.

References

Krashen, S. (1982). *Principles and practice in second language acquisition.* Oxford: Pergamon Press.

Okazaki, H., & Nitta, H. (2005). Internet-based Personal Listening Program: a program for Japanese EFL learners to overcome individual weaknesses. *FLEAT5 Proceedings,* 92-99.

Okazaki, H. (2008). An attempt to index reading materials using e-learning. *Studies in English Language & Literature, 48,* 73-87.

UNIVERSITY OF
GOTHENBURG

Corrective Feedback and Noticing in Text-Based Second Language Interaction

Therese Örnberg Berglund[*]

Linköping University, Department of Culture and Communication, Linköping, Sweden

Abstract. This paper discusses the concept of 'noticing' (Schmidt, 1990; cf. Smith, 2010) in relation to text-based second language interaction (instant messaging). Data has been collected at an upper secondary school, where students of English as a foreign language interact with the researcher, providing feedback on language and content. In addition to chat logs and screen recordings, data from keystroke logging and eye tracking have also been collected, enabling analysis of both verbalized and non-verbalized signs of noticing (cf. O'Rourke, 2008; Smith, 2010). The focus of this paper is on how signs of noticing can be defined in this context, and preliminary results concerning the relationship between noticing and different types of corrective feedback are presented.

Keywords: SCMC, noticing, eye tracking, keystroke logging, corrective feedback, repair.

1. Introduction

In some theories of language learning, it is argued that learners need to notice the difference between one's linguistic production and the patterns of the target language (Schmidt, 1990). Such *noticing* has primarily been addressed and discussed in psycholinguistic accounts of SLA, but has also received attention in interactional research, with a focus on how certain features are brought to the students' attention and how the students then verbally account for their noticing of particular phenomena (Markee, 2000; Seedhouse, 2004).

The current study is part of a larger project aiming to merge psycholinguistic and interactional approaches on language learning by investigating text-based interaction. Text-based interaction provides particular affordances for language learning, and it also provides opportunities for the researcher to get a more detailed view of language learning processes than in face-to-face interaction, for instance through the employment of keystroke logging and eye-tracking equipment (cf. O'Rourke, 2008).

---

[*] Contact author: therese.ornberg.berglund@liu.se

In L. Bradley & S. Thouësny (Eds.), *CALL: Using, Learning, Knowing, EUROCALL Conference, Gothenburg, Sweden, 22-25 August 2012, Proceedings* (pp. 234-239). © Research-publishing.net Dublin 2012

The study presented here builds on a study by Bryan Smith (2010), which is one of the few examples of eye-tracking technology being employed to investigate language learning in text-based synchronous computer-mediated communication (SCMC) (cf. also O'Rourke, 2008). While Smith (2010) focused on fixations of recasts, the current study aims to empirically explore patterns indicative of noticing both in relation to recasts and to metalinguistic feedback. As a first step in identifying relevant gaze patterns, the focus is on cases where noticing is also verbalized.

2. Method

The setup of the current study is adapted from Smith (2010). Participants ($N = 8$) were students of English at a Swedish upper secondary school, who were given the option to participate in a chat task with a teacher (the researcher). The participants were shown a short animated video clip (no verbal content), and were then asked to retell the story in the text chat with the researcher, located in the other room, providing feedback on content and language. The researcher restricted herself to providing two types of feedback: recasts and metalinguistic feedback. The students were then asked to retell the story once more in a word document, and this post-chat writing task was used for triangulation. Throughout the session, the gaze of the participants was tracked (using a SMI remote eyetracker with a 60Hz sampling rate), and their keystrokes were logged (using Inputlog). The chat sessions lasted about 10-15 minutes each.

The verbal data in the chat logs were coded for errors and feedback (of different types), and the chat logs together with the post-chat writing task were coded for uptake/repair and continuous errors. Only the errors in the chat log that received feedback and that resulted in uptake/repair or in continuous errors were included for further analysis. These sequences of errors and feedback were then analyzed in more detail, and in this process, data from both eye tracking and keystroke logging were considered. Due to lack of space, the current paper will focus on exemplifying gaze patterns potentially indicative of noticing, as identified through the coding of relevant Areas of Interest (AOIs) in the analysis software BeGaze.

3. Signs of noticing in gaze patterns

While exploratively and empirically identifying gaze patterns of relevance, certain expectations have guided the analysis. When the correct form is given, through a recast, it is hypothesized that extra long gaze fixations on the recast should be indicative of noticing. This is in line with Smith (2010), who defines noticing as a fixation on the correct form for more than 500 ms. It is further hypothesized that another sign of noticing in relation to recasts would be if participants were to compare the correct form with the incorrect form in the chat log visible (cf. the *noticing the gap hypothesis*,

Schmidt, 1990). When no correct form has been given, but metalinguistic feedback has been provided instead, being able to re-identify the error is hypothesized to be a sign of noticing (and of understanding, cf. Schmidt, 1990).

Preliminary results indicate that these predictions do seem relevant when distinguishing signs of noticing, and in the current paper, I will exemplify patterns of noticing through a qualitative excerpt, involving repair/uptake in relation to both metalinguistic feedback and a recast.

The following chat log excerpt (Table 1) shows interaction between a student and the researcher. Only errors that receive feedback have been highlighted, as well as the feedback itself and later correct usage.

Table 1. Exemplifying verbalized noticing of recast and metalinguistic feedback in SCMC

Time	Nr.	From	Message
04:17:050	M8	Student	It was a apple to, who fell down from a tree. Then a giraff was in it too! have I missed something?
04:55:530	M9	Teacher	Please note the form of the indefinite article there.
05:18:430	M10	Teacher	A giraffe and a penguin, I believe.
06:02:480	M11	Student	indefintite article? whats that?
06:12:720	M12	Teacher	Good question!
06:37:800	M13	Teacher	It is the word that comes before "apple" in the previous sentence.
06:56:960	M14	Teacher	So you say you didn't understand the message, but what was the male turtle trying to do?
08:27:410	M15	Student	should it be an apple maybe? hmm, I don't now actually, I don't remember. I'm sorry
08:49:200	M16	Teacher	Yes, that is correct, an apple.
09:00:921	M17	Teacher	Can you tell me about the episode with the boat?
10:13:321	M18	Student	Yeah, that I remember for sure! The giraffe was driving the boat and he didn't watch up, so they hit a stone in the water, and some animals fell in the sea.

3.1. Noticing in relation to recast: extra long fixations and comparison between incorrect and correct forms

The first fixation on the recast "giraffe" in M10 is only 298 ms long. However, before attempting to write it again in M18, the recast is revisited ten times, and one of these revisits is over 500 ms long. According to Smith's (2010) threshold, this would be a sign that the recast has been noticed. Furthermore, when attempting to type it again, the participant is clearly scanning for the recast. This we can see in Table 2, where it is shown that less time is spent on irrelevant messages during scanning, and more time on the relevant messages (M8 and M10), including the crucial words, with a special focus on the correct form in the recast (this is in line with eye tracking measures used to investigate global text processing, cf. Hyönä, Lorch, & Rinck, 2003).

Table 2. Glance duration, glances count and fixation count in "giraffe" retyping sequence (00:09:05:680 – 00:10:13:321)

AOI	Glance duration total (ms)	Glances count	Fixations count
M8	1551.5	1	8
Error	636.4	3	4
M9	1093.9	3	4
M10	2844.5	2	7
Recast	2108.6	3	4
M11	258.6	1	1
M12	556.9	2	3
M13	298.4	1	1
M14	238.6	2	2
M15	218.7	1	1
M16	0	0	0
M17	616.5	1	2

The most crucial part of the same sequence can be illustrated through a visualization from the BeGaze software provided by SMI (Figure 1).

Figure 1. Scan path visualization from BeGaze: re-identifying previous erroneous spelling and recast in "giraffe" retyping sequence

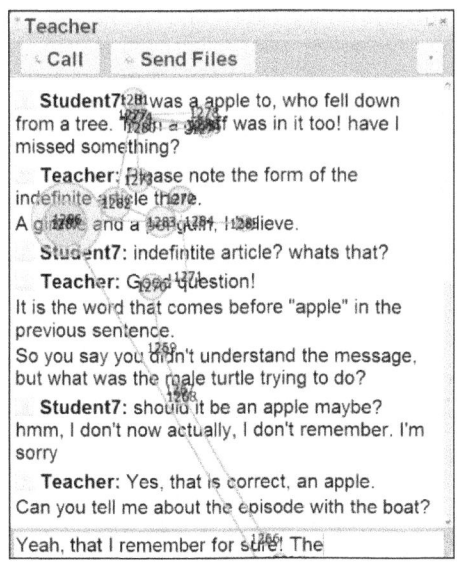

- Visualization of fixations at 00:09:29:081
- Trailer: 7 seconds
- Raindrop fixations: 80px = 500 ms

The numbers within the circles here illustrate the order of the fixations. Furthermore, the larger the circles, the longer the fixation. A drawback with this type of visualization is that it can only be made as long as the background stays stable. Furthermore, it can be difficult to distinguish the details due to the many layers. If we compare this visualization with details concerning the individual fixations in the analysis software, we can see that 14 subsequent fixations move from the crucial M8 (8 fixations, of which 3 are on the crucial word) via M9 (1 fixation) to M10 (5 fixations, of which the two final, long ones are on the crucial word). This illustrates that the two spellings of the word are, in fact, compared.

3.2. Noticing in relation to metalinguistic feedback: re-identifying the error

As for the metalinguistic feedback, Table 3 below shows that the metalinguistic feedback (M9) is not successful when first delivered, since the participant is not able to re-identify the error, but instead fixates the metalinguistic feedback itself. After the clarification (M13), the student is able to re-identify the error. This example also illustrates the importance of clarification requests.

Table 3. Glance duration, glances count and fixation count for metalinguistic feedback and related error (03:36:120 -10:13:320)

AOI	Glance duration total [ms]	Glances count	Fixation count
a apple (in M8)			
After metalinguistic feedback (M10)	0	0	0
After clarification (M13)	2605.8	3	4
Metalinguistic feedback (M10)			
Before clarification (M13)	31487.7	31	87
After clarification (M13)	3958.3	6	11

4. Conclusions

The preliminary results of the current study suggest that certain gaze patterns are indicative of noticing in text-based interaction, and such patterns have been qualitatively described in the current paper. Through a more systematic comparison of patterns which result in correct usage (uptake/repair), to those that result in incorrect usage, future publications will contribute to confirming these suggested non-verbalized signs of noticing in SLA.

Acknowledgements. I would like to thank the students who participated in the project, as well as my research assistants, Marjan Adibi Dahaj and Setareh Hassanzadeh Nezami, in particular for their help when gathering the material.

References

Hyönä, J., Lorch, R. F., & Rinck, M. (2003). Eye Movement Measures to Study Global Text Processing. In R. Radach, J. Hyönä, & H. Deubel (Eds.), *The Mind's Eye. Cognitive and Applied Aspects of Eye Movement Research* (pp. 313-334). Amsterdam: Elsevier.

Markee, N. (2000). *Conversation Analysis.* Mahwah, NJ: Erlbaum.

O'Rourke, B. (2008). The Other C in CMC: What Alternative Data Sources Can Tell Us About Text-Based Synchronous Computer Mediated Communication and Language Learning. *Computer Assisted Language Learning, 21*(3), 227-251.

Schmidt, R. (1990). The Role of Consciousness in Second Language Learning. *Applied Linguistics, 11*(2), 129-158. doi: 10.1093/applin/11.2.129

Seedhouse, P. (2004). *The Interactional Architecture of the Language Classroom: A Conversation Analysis Perspective.* Malden, MA & Oxford: Blackwell.

Smith, B. (2010). Employing Eye-Tracking Technology in Researching the Effectiveness of Recasts in CMC. In F. M. Hult (Ed.), *Directions and Prospects for Educational Linguistics* (pp. 79-97). New York: Springer.

UNIVERSITY OF
GOTHENBURG

Mobile Technologies Put Language Learning into Young Second Language Learners' Hands

Martine Pellerin*

Campus St. Jean, Universiy of Albert, Edmonton, AB, Canada

Abstract. This paper examines the use of mobile technologies such as iPods and tablets in promoting the development of oral competencies and literacy skills in early French immersion classrooms in Canada. The paper is based on a two-year collaborative action research project involving 16 teachers in two schools. Data collection involved digital ethnographic observation in the classroom, students' artifacts (examples of the use of iPods and tablets by students), teacher interviews, and student interviews. The findings demonstrate that the young language learners use these mobile devices as tools to practice not only their oral skills in the target language through individual and group activities, but also their literacy skills (reading and writing). In addition, by providing more authentic and frequent experiences in using the target language, the use of the iPods and tablets has positive outcomes on the development of oral language skills. The young learners also demonstrate an increase in their motivation to use the target language following the use of the mobile devices. The results indicate the potential of the use of oral language and iPods/tablets in promoting the development of early literacy skills (reading and writing). The iPods/tablets also provide a kind of scaffolding to the writing process by linking the oral language with the written form. Finally, the use of the oral language with the support of mobile technologies promotes new forms of assessment tools for the teachers; it also promotes self-assessment by the learners, as well as peer assessment.

Keywords: mobile technologies, young learners, oral language, second language, literacy skills, assessment.

1. Introduction

Research in the field of second language learning in the last few decades has provided ample evidence of the positive impact of the use of technologies in assisting students' language learning. However, most of the studies have been mainly concerned with the language learning processes of high school students and

---

* Contact author: pellerin@csj.ualberta

mature learners. The emergence of mobile technologies such as iPods and tablets into the classrooms, particularly in settings that involve young learners, is bringing new possibilities to assist language learning and early literacy development. Educators are also starting to contemplate the potential of these emergent technologies to support authentic language experiences and literacy development, as well as new forms of assessment. The present study investigated the use of mobile technologies such as iPods and tablets in promoting the development of oral competencies and literacy development in early French immersion classrooms in the Canadian context.

2. Method

The study used a qualitative, interpretative research methodology that made use of *collaborative action research* (CAR). The CAR approach calls for direct participation from the teachers in the inquiry process, which then impacts upon the teachers' beliefs, attitudes, knowledge, and skills; such changes in turn contribute to changes in their pedagogical practices (Kemmis & McTaggart, 2005; Nolen & Vander Putten, 2007). The study involved 16 teachers and their students from two elementary schools that hosted early French immersion programs, in a rural school district in a western Canadian province. The distribution of the French immersion teachers was as follows: four Grade 1 teachers, three Grade 2 teachers, one multilevel teacher (Grades 1 and 2), three Grade 3 teachers, two Grade 4 teachers, and two resource teachers.

The CAR model used for the study was based on the model developed by Pellerin (2011), which focuses on a university – school partnership in order to implement an alternative model for professional development. The teachers in their respective classrooms collected the initial data on an ongoing basis. Teachers gathered digital documentation (audio and video recordings) achieved by the students themselves using mobile devices such as iPods and tablets. The university researcher was also engaged in data collection through classroom observation, and digital ethnography about how students were documenting their own language learning process with the use of these mobile technologies.

Further data were gathered at the end of the first and second years of the project through semi-guided interviews with the teachers, which allowed the teachers to share their experiences with the use of the new and emergent technologies in their classrooms. The triangulation of these data from multiple sources allowed for interpretation (Denzin & Lincoln, 2008), and continual data analysis was achieved by means of "thick description" or layers of interpretation (Geertz, 1973). The data analysis was achieved with the use of a coding process aligned with qualitative research approaches (Miles & Huberman, 1994).

3. Findings and discussion

Several key themes that emerged from this inquiry have contributed to the co-construction of new knowledge and understanding about how the use of mobile technologies such as iPods and tablets contribute to the development of oral competencies and literacy skills in young language learners. First, the findings show that the use of iPods and tablets have positive outcomes on the development of oral language skills by providing more authentic and frequent experiences in using French, the target language. The young learners in the study were able to engage in different activities that called on the use of the oral language with the support of the iPods and tablets. For example, students were making audio and video recordings of puppet shows, storytelling and retelling, dramatic play, creation of songs, show and tell about personal experiences, sharing of their background knowledge and thinking process, describing authentic and meaningful tasks such as "how to make a bubble with gum" or "how to eat an Oreo cookie". Through listening to and viewing their own audio/video recordings of their use of the second language, students were able to reflect on their work and to judge what was good about it and what needed to be improved. The young learners also demonstrated an increase in their motivation toward using the target language following the use of the mobile devices, by making several recordings of the same activities with the intent to improve each time.

The results also indicate the potential of the use of the iPods/tablets in promoting the development of early literacy skills (reading and writing). Students used the iPods/tablets to record their voices while reading, as well as to video record their reading process. The digital documentation (digital audio and video recording) made by the students provided the teachers with tangible evidence of their students' reading process. Teachers had access to evidence of how their students were trying to decode, the types of strategies they were using, and the mistakes they were making. The students' nonverbal language and their actions (for example, coming back to the beginning of the line to reread a word) were also captured through the video recording. Together, the teachers and the students were able to engage in dialogue and interpretation about the students' abilities to read, and the strategies that needed to be developed in order to increase reading fluency. During the period dedicated to literacy centers in the Grade 1 and Grade 2 classrooms, iPods were also used to listen to audio-recorded books based on students' own reading abilities and interests. Therefore, the use of these technological tools allowed for more reading aloud experiences that model good use of the second language. It also enabled students to hear vocabulary being used in context.

The iPods/tablets also provided a kind of scaffolding to the writing process by linking the oral language with the written form. Teachers from Grades 1 to 4 encouraged their students to use the iPods and tablets to document their planning process for their writing project. For some students, the act of putting ideas on paper represents a true challenge, especially in the context of second language learning. Therefore, students were encouraged to use the technological tools to first record their ideas orally. Then they could go back and revisit the recording to guide their writing process. For many students, this documentation and self-assessment became part of their writing process. They would first dictate their ideas on the iPod in French, and then they would listen to the digital recording to help them transfer their ideas onto paper. Later, the same students would read aloud what they had written and record it once again on the iPod. They would revisit the latest digital documentation and would orally add new ideas or changes that they felt could contribute to improving their story.

Finally, the findings demonstrate that the use of iPods and tablets contributed to gathering digital documentation about the students' learning and thinking process in the second language. Moreover, it enabled both teachers and learners to revisit the digital documentation, allowing for a deepening of the learning process. The revisiting process also promoted a process of reflection on learning by the teachers, thus acting as a form of formative assessment. The revisiting of the documentation between teacher and student also provided scaffolding for self-assessment and peer assessment. By engaging students in revisiting the content of their audio/video recordings, the teacher modeled the process of reflection and self-assessment necessary for the students to become aware of their own language learning process and progress.

4. Conclusions

This study demonstrated that the use of mobile technologies such as iPods and tablets holds great potential for promoting the development of oral competencies and early literacy skills in the second language context. Moreover, the use of these new and emergent technologies by young language learners contributes greatly to our understanding of early literacy development in the second language context. In particular, the use of such technologies can provide valuable information about the learning processes of students with specific needs and/or students who are experiencing difficulties with literacy skills or showing delays in second language development. The use of mobile technologies also allows teachers and researchers to explore how digital video and audio recordings can be used as assessment tools to inform teachers' instructional practice. It also contributes in guiding the learner in his or her own learning process. Finally, and perhaps more importantly, the use of mobile technologies such as iPods and tablets allows young learners to become ethnographers of their own second language learning and literacy development.

References

Denzin, N. K., & Lincoln, Y. S. (2008). *Collecting and interpreting qualitative materials* (3rd ed.). London, England: Sage.

Geertz, C. (1973). Thick description: Toward an interpretive theory of culture. In *The interpretation of cultures* (pp. 3-30). New York, NY: Basic Books.

Kemmis, S., & McTaggart, R. (2005). Participatory action research. In N. Denzin & Y. Lincoln (Eds.), *The Sage handbook of qualitative research* (3rd ed., pp. 559-604). Thousand Oaks, CA: Sage.

Miles, M. B., & Huberman, A. M. (1994). *Qualitative data analysis* (2nd ed.). Thousand Oaks, CA: Sage.

Nolen, A. L., & Vander Putten, J. (2007). Action research in education: Addressing gaps in ethical principles and practices. *Educational Researcher, 36*(7), 401-407. doi: 10.3102/0013189X07309629

Pellerin, M. (2011). University–school collaborative action research as an alternative model for professional development through AISI. *AISI Journal, 1*(1). Retrieved from http://www.uleth.ca/education/research/research-centers/aisi/aisi-journal/new-issue/vol1-no1-2011

UNIVERSITY OF GOTHENBURG

From Research to Development on Virtual Language, Content and Intercultural Learning Across European Schools

Maria Dolores Ramírez-Verdugo*

Universidad Autónoma de Madrid, Spain - City University of New York, US

Abstract. This paper presents an overview of the research conducted within a funded Comenius project which aims at developing a virtual European CLIL Resource Centre for Web 2.0 Education**. E-CLIL focuses on Content and Language Integrated Learning (CLIL), creativity and multiculturalism through digital resources. In this sense, our prior research on CLIL programmes across Europe revealed the need to equip teachers with relevant methodological strategies and appropriate materials. We also detected the need of specific guidelines for implementation together with specific resources which should guarantee excellence in language learning (Ramírez-Verdugo, 2010). To reduce the identified shortcomings, an interdisciplinary group of scholars have developed a resource centre for Web 2.0 Education which aims at increasing children's exposure to European languages and to improve the quality of teaching and learning through the implementation of CLIL. E-CLIL has a three-folded objective. First, it intends to provide support to current and future CLIL educative programmes all over Europe and beyond. Accordingly, E-CLIL is currently disseminating high quality and proven materials and resources for content and language learning. Second, E-CLIL material design and the guideline for teachers are founded on sound language and content learning principles. Third, E-CLIL attempts to enrich teachers' and children's knowledge of other European cultures. The paper shows the results from the pilot study and initial experiences at E-CLIL school network across Europe.

Keywords: virtual learning, European languages, CLIL, intercultural perspectives.

1. Introduction

In a global world where English has the status of the international language for communication, it is not always easy to preserve the current European linguistic

---

* Contact author: dolores.ramirez@uam.es

** E-CLIL, 504671-2009-LLP-ES-COMENIUS-CMP

diversity. For obvious reasons, learners will need to have a high command of English as a second or foreign language to attain success in their education and professional careers. Yet, this reasonable target could clash against the European policy of maintaining children's first language and promoting at least two foreign or second languages. This philosophy demands a well-designed syllabus across Europe to allow children time to learn specific contents and acquire fundamental competences, skills, strategies and languages to become citizens of the continent and of the world in the next few years and beyond.

An important attempt to achieve this aim has taken place in the last decades across Europe with an approach known as *Content and Language Integrated Learning* (*CLIL*, cf. Marsh, 2002). CLIL has already been established as a valuable methodology to both teaching foreign languages and specific subjects since it creates a meaningful context for learning. More specifically, CLIL pedagogical project involves using one or more foreign languages as the vehicle to teach certain subjects within the curriculum (cf. Marsh & Wolff, 2007). In a global CLIL model "both language and content are conceptualised on a continuum without an implied preference for either" (Coyle, 2007, p. 543). In Europe, core elements common to all CLIL practice coexist with diverse varieties in implementation depending on national, regional and local characteristics (cf. Ramírez-Verdugo, 2010).

Nevertheless, in spite of all the attention devoted to CLIL during the last few years, recent research reveals that even though this approach is gaining popularity across Europe, further work is still necessary on relevant methodological strategies and available materials (Ioannou-Georgiou & Pavlou, 2010). Therefore, it seems there is an important need for specific materials, resources and implementation guidelines to guarantee excellence in language and content learning. Our proposal, then, is to maximize the gains CLIL is achieving by the use of a technological enhanced learning environment. Our purpose is to create motivational resources that will raise engagement and confidence in language and content learning. This is one of the main goals within the project called *European CLIL Resource Centre for Web 2.0 Education**, funded with support from the European Commission. One of the main objectives of E-CLIL is to increase children's exposure to European languages and to improve the quality of teaching through the implementation of CLIL within the European demand for acquiring a mother tongue plus two foreign languages (MT+2, Eurydice, 2006, p. 8). E-CLIL falls within the European philosophy of long life learning programme. It focuses on language learning, learning strategies, multilingualism and multiculturalism. The approach used within E-CLIL involves CLIL and ICT as recommended pedagogical procedures and resources, respectively. Within this background, multilingual interactive resources for the use of CLIL teachers and learners have already been designed and developed, as explained below.

---

* E-CLIL, 504671-LLP-1-2009-1-ES-COMENIUS-CMP

2. Research design

Within the framework of this three year investigation, an initial piloting of the resources created was conducted June 2011 in Madrid (Spain). The feedback provided by teachers and learners was taken into account to specify the enhancement still required both in terms of content, language and technology development. Once that improvement was complete, the research was extended to a new pilot study in Belgium, Bulgaria, Turkey, Austria and Spain. When this pilot phase concludes, we intend to make the project resources available worldwide so that a large community of children and teachers can benefit from E-CLIL.

In the present paper I report on the findings obtained from the second piloting phase in Madrid from February to April 2012. This study investigates the worth interactive digital resources may bring to a Primary education context. In this sense, a central digital story and related CLIL Internet-based games, all originally created for this project, entail three main learning objectives which involve exposing young learners to European languages, children's literature and science content. Our main hypothesis at this stage of the study was to prove whether these interactive digital resources may enhance 8 to 10 year-old students' learning involvement and CLIL achievement. In this piloting phase of the study, these digital materials were presented to over three hundred students enrolled in six different CLIL schools in the region of Madrid. Six experienced English teachers participated in the study and followed the guidelines provided by the project researchers. In order to gather objective data that may prove our hypothesis, both learners and teachers completed specific pre- and post-questionnaires which were then statistically analysed. The data gathered through questionnaires, interviews and field observation has been used to extend the piloting progressively to other European countries participating in the project. This larger study will hopefully provide information on cross-cultural similarities or differences regarding the results already obtained here. The initial findings indicate this approach adds a very positive value to a CLIL learning context at linguistic, content, literary, cognitive, social and cultural levels. This outcome is very much in line with the ideas expressed earlier by scholars such as Johnstone, Kubanek-German, and Taeschner (1998), Marsh, Maljers, and Hartiala (2001), Marsh (2002), or Mehisto, Frigols, and Marsh (2008).

3. A digital story and interactive games in a CLIL context

Draco's Band is an original digital story written specifically for this project. It aims at stimulating a positive response towards the storyline, and increasing learners' motivation towards learning. It is interactive and includes sounds and visual elements. The use of the digital resources also promotes learners' autonomy. They can choose to listen or read the story at their own pace or they can listen and read the story as a whole group in a choral activity.

Another important motivation for writing this story refers to the need of providing coherence to the different content topics covered at schools within a CLIL approach. Science topics are integrated within a storyline which favours a feeling of achievement and development. The initial chapter presents the characters, the main situation and some hints for following chapters which take place in different settings. Each of those chapters implies a new adventure and challenge that needs to be accomplished. The *fantastic worlds* where the characters travel to correspond to the curriculum areas covered in Primary Education across Europe. The digital games designed are based on sound learning principles and are integrated within the storyline plot and development.

4. The European dimension

These resources have been translated into the project languages to promote multilingualism among European learners. The use of blogs and videos enables partners to show the most remarkable festivals and traditions in their countries. This visual, oral and written information is intended to encourage children to learn about the cultural richness and diversity within Europe in a meaningful way. These multicultural resources should also, hopefully, enhance mutual understanding and respect.

5. Results

A qualitative analysis of the pre- and post-questionnaires provides an interesting picture of teachers' and learners' expectations toward ICT resources for language learning. These kinds of resources are mainly expected to increase their motivation and provide amusement. However, in the post questionnaires, the teachers participating in this project's piloting phase consider that the storyline helps children grasp the story's global meaning and identify specific information, both oral and written. These teachers believe the digital resources help children read, chorally and individually, and understand varied and simple content relating to their communicative competence and science topics. They also agree when they state that both the story and the related games help learners perceive and use common L2 forms and structures. They valued very positively the fact that *Draco's Band* exposes learners to the L2 sound, melody, rhythm and intonation within meaningful communicative contexts.

Learners participate actively in the proposed games, riddles and puzzles. These resources help children to activate their prior knowledge on the content and language, anticipating, guessing, deducing, receiving appraisal, etc. Their responses to the questionnaires were very positive and indicated they had enjoyed this way of learning.

Teachers considered the fact that these materials could be accessed in different languages important. This multilingual dimension raised their learners' awareness towards people from other countries, cultures and languages and their curiosity to learn more.

6. Conclusion

The positive feedback and outcome obtained so far commit us to advance in the current areas of research involved in E-CLIL, mainly, bilingual and multi-language learning; CLIL implementation and outcome; the impact of technology enhanced environment on language learning, content and culture; and the important correlation between cognition and bilingualism. Elements that are all present in a digital context when resources are thoughtful and well designed.

Finally, the initial development of this project has focused on science topics at a Primary Education level. However, in line with the project philosophy, future work will progressively include both early and advanced levels of education. We believe the findings presented here address the objectives and priorities stated by European Commission with regards to the quality and relevance which should be involved in language learning: To promote language learning & literacy skills; to support innovative ICT programme and to promote cultural and linguistic diversity.

References

Coyle, D. (2007). Content and language integrated learning: towards a connected research agenda for CLIL pedagogies. *International Journal of Bilingual Education, 10*(5), 543-562.

Eurydice Report. (2006). *Content and Language Integrated Learning (CLIL) at School in Europe*. Brussels: Eurydice, the information Network of Education in Europe.

Ioannou-Georgiou, S., & Pavlou, P. (Eds.) (2010). *Guidelines for CLIL Implementation in Primary and Pre-primary Education*. Cyprus: Cyprus Pedagogical Institute.

Johnstone, R., Kubanek-German, A., & Taeschner, T. (1998). *Foreign Languages in Primary and Pre-School Education: A Review of Recent Research within the European Union*. Report for DG 22, European Commission.

Marsh, D. (2002). *Content and Language Integrated Learning: The European Dimension - Actions, Trends and Foresight Potential*. DG Education & Culture, European Commission. Retrieved from http://ec.europa.eu/languages/documents/doc491_en.pdf

Marsh, D., & Wolff, D. (Eds.). (2007). *Diverse Contexts - Converging Goals: CLIL in Europe*. Frankfurt: Peter Lang.

Marsh, D., Maljers, A., & Hartiala, A.-K. (2001). *Profiling European CLIL Classrooms – Languages Open Doors*. Jyväskylä: University of Jyväskylä.

Mehisto, P., Frigols, M. J., & Marsh, D. (2008). *Uncovering CLIL: Content and Language Integrated Learning in Bilingual and Multilingual Education*. Oxford: Macmillan Education.

Ramírez-Verdugo, M. D. (2010). CLIL varieties across Europe. In S. Ioannou-Georgiou, & P. Pavlou (Eds.), *Guidelines for CLIL Implementation in Primary and Pre-primary Education*. Cyprus: Cyprus Pedagogical Institute.

UNIVERSITY OF
GOTHENBURG

Get Networked and Spy Your Languages

Mercedes Rico*, Paula Ferreira,
Eva M. Domínguez, and Julian Coppens

University of Extremdaura, Santa Teresa de Jornet, Mérida, Spain

Abstract. Our proposal describes ISPY, a multilateral European K2 language project based on the development of an Online Networking Platform for Language Learning (http://www.ispy-project.com/). Supported by the Lifelong Learning European Programme, the platform aims to help young adults across Europe, secondary and vocational school programs, learn a new language and gain insights into the cultural knowledge implicit to those languages. Conducted by the University of Wolverhampton in collaboration with five other countries in Europe (Spain, Poland, Netherlands, Germany and Romania), the project will promote interaction between learners from different countries who will partly work together to learn a new language via a set of spy missions promoting problem-solving challenges, deductive tasks and collaboration through extension activities in the Moodle platform. The ISPY platform can be used to support face to face in class teaching or outside instruction to enhance language acquisition. It is designed in short scenes in flash movies and comprises a set of ten espionage missions. Available in each of the target languages, all of these multimedia pills consist of a range of activities including photo stories, video presentations, Webquests, quizzes, listening and extended tasks that call for collaboration through a moderated forum. Each country will also have the option to add extra activities in a Moodle application created purposely for the project, additional tasks which, in essence, are new spy missions for those who have already been awarded as 'Qualified' spies.

Keywords: interaction, language learning platform, Moodle, spy missions, training.

1. Introduction

Considering the changes in mobility experienced during the last decades and bearing in mind the growing need to learn languages for academic, professional, and occupational purposes, or simply for personal interests, language learning has become one of main aims of our society (Fisher & Baird, 2007; Frohberg, Goth, & Schwabe, 2009). For

---

* Contact author: mricogar@unex.es

In L. Bradley & S. Thouësny (Eds.), *CALL: Using, Learning, Knowing, EUROCALL Conference, Gothenburg, Sweden, 22-25 August 2012, Proceedings* (pp. 250-253). © Research-publishing.net Dublin 2012

the sake of this growing dynamism, and if second language acquisition relies on a far broader scope than a number of hours of instruction in class – learning is not confined to the four walls of your classroom. Should teaching be bounded by these physical limits?

In this context, the main European policy initiatives, established in the Council of Lisbon (2001), emphasize the development of ICTs in education. With the purpose of breaking down physical barriers and easing teaching and acquisition, ICTs enhance the creation of alternative language-networked environments and promote intercultural understanding to open new opportunities and perspectives for language learning.

Our proposal describes ISPY, a multilateral European K2 language project based on the development of an Online Networking Platform for Language Learning, a platform which aims to help young adults across Europe, secondary and vocational school programs, learn a new language and gain insights into the cultural knowledge implicit to those languages.

2. Method

2.1. Methodology and phases

Conducted by the University of Wolverhampton in collaboration with five other countries in Europe (Spain, Poland, Netherlands, Germany and Romania), the project will promote interaction between learners from different countries who will partly work together to learn a new language via a set of spy missions. The application is also devised to work on problem-solving challenges, deductive tasks and collaboration through extension activities in the Moodle platform.

Regarding the project's development and methodology, we can distinguish four main phases. The contextualization stage has involved each partner carrying out a detailed research covering a range of general education and specific language information concerning their home country. After this phase, we moved on by setting the chosen environments and writing scripts and activities. Thirdly, according to activities and content design, the project will consist of two parts: an interactive game created in short scenes in flash movies where users are given inputs for developing their skills by using motivating material and learning scenarios, and; a Moodle application where they study thoroughly the topics learnt during the game and interact with other students. The last stage will be evaluating the project (June-October 2012). Students from general and pre-vocational education and training will trial the new platform alongside teachers and trainers.

2.2. Course description

Designed in short scenes in flash movies and comprising a set of ten espionage missions, the ISPY platform can be used to support face to face in class teaching or outside instruction to enhance language acquisition. Available in each of the target languages, all of these multimedia pills consist of a range of activities including photo stories, video presentations, WebQuests, quizzes, listening and extended tasks that call for collaboration through a moderated forum.

During the missions users will need to learn key language skills such as booking hotel rooms, using money, telling the time, ordering food, arranging meetings, purchasing travel tickets and reading documents in order to complete the modules. Once a learner has completed all 10 modules s/he will be recognized as a "trained spy". Each country will also have the option to add extra activities in a Moodle platform created purposely for the project, additional tasks which, in essence, are new spy missions for those who have already been awarded as 'Qualified' spies.

3. Discussion

The proliferation of ICTs has generated the creation of alternative language-networked environments promoting intercultural understanding and opening new opportunities and perspectives for language learning. Lessening barriers, the ubiquity of technology has allowed people to interact on a global scale, setting new instruction grounds for the effective fusion of those elements (language acquisition, cultural understanding and ICTs). In our case the outcome of the project will be an encouraging spy games-based language proposal. Although we cannot provide final discussion at this stage, we will continue working on the final completion of the project to ensure the creation of a network platform for language learning.

4. Conclusions

The interest of this project focuses on the development of an interactive platform which fits the needs and preferences of young adults and trainers, especially by setting new instruction and learning grounds for an effective fusion of language acquisition, cultural understanding and ICTs. The goal-based language missions in which the platform is based facilitates the learning process, makes users aware of their progress and become more deeply involved in their learning. Likewise, teachers will be better-equipped with a wide range of material and tools, improving consequently the quality and effectiveness of education and training outside the four walls of the traditional classroom.

Acknowledgements. This project has been funded with support from the European Commission. This publication reflects the views only of the author, and the Commission cannot be held responsible for any use which may be made of the information contained therein. ISPY: Online Networking Platform for Language Learning (KA2 Languages) Project N°. 511558-LLP-1-2010-1-UK-KA2-Ka2MP.

References

European Parliament and the Council. (2001). *Recommendation of the European Parliament and of the Council on European cooperation in quality evaluation in school education (2001/166/EC).* Official Journal of the European Communities, 1.3.2001. L 60/51. II.

Frohberg, D., Göth, C., & Schwabe, G. (2009). Mobile Learning Projects – A Critical Analysis of the State of the Art. *Journal of Computer Assisted Learning, 25*(4), 307-331. doi: 10.1111/j.1365-2729.2009.00315.x

Fisher, M., & Baird, D. E. (2007). Making Learning Work: Utilizing Mobile Technology for Active Exploration, Collaboration, Assessment, and Reflection in Higher Education. *Journal of Educational Technology Systems, 35*(1), 3-30.

UNIVERSITY OF GOTHENBURG

KungFu Writing, a New Cloud-Based Feedback Tool

Jan-Mikael Rybicki[a]* and Juhana Nieminen[a,b]

a. Aalto University Language Centre, Aalto, Finland
b. KungFu Writing, Ilmalankuja, Helsinki, Finland

Abstract. As a part of language learning at schools and universities, students write a variety of texts, such as essays, short compositions and reports, which are then read by teachers who typically comment on the content and grammar of these texts to help the students improve their skills as writers. Although teachers can simply use pen and paper, or a text processor, to provide written feedback, the traditional annotation methods do not usually allow easy and systematic re-use of self-explanatory comments for helping the students to revise their writing. For these reasons, we have developed a new online-based commenting/annotation tool, KungFu Writing, which was designed for giving more elaborate feedback on written assignments. As the system is accessible online through a web browser, the tool also allows new opportunities for teachers to collaborate in teaching writing skills at all levels of education. This paper describes the main features and typical uses of this new feedback tool.

Keywords: writing, feedback, online, commenting tool, collaboration, blended learning.

1. Introduction

At many levels of education, students are expected to make a variety of written assignments, such as essays and reports, as a part of their learning process. Similarly, teachers are expected to read and grade these assignments as well as comment on the texts. The content and extent of written comments and feedback, of course, may greatly vary from teacher to teacher and subject domain. Nevertheless, particularly in teaching writing skills, a teacher can offer a valuable contribution to the learning process by giving feedback on a student's written assignments.

Language teachers frequently read and comment on texts written by students in order to help them become better writers or simply to improve their language skills. Depending on the teacher's pedagogical approach, the students may simply read

---

* Contact author: jan-mikael.rybicki@aalto.fi

In L. Bradley & S. Thouësny (Eds.), *CALL: Using, Learning, Knowing, EUROCALL Conference, Gothenburg, Sweden, 22-25 August 2012, Proceedings* (pp. 254-258). © Research-publishing.net Dublin 2012

through the written feedback they have received on their writing or revise their texts based on the written teacher feedback.

However, it is very time consuming to provide clear explanations and examples for frequently appearing writing problems. Some teachers spend a considerable amount of time manually re-writing or typing feedback and explanations on student papers. Due to lack of time and limited commenting options available in regular text processing tools, teachers may be able to give less feedback on student work than they would desire. In addition, using these traditional methods, teachers cannot easily collect and analyse statistics of typical language problems in student texts and to study the impact of teacher feedback on learning.

To address these challenges in teaching writing, we designed and created a tool for annotating and commenting on texts, known as KungFu Writing, which allows teachers to give flexible feedback on almost any type of written text. Although some feedback tools already exist on the market, they often lack functions that we felt would improve user-friendliness of the feedback process as well as would allow easier sharing of knowledge and teaching materials among teachers. This paper briefly describes important features of KungFu Writing and gives an overview of main approaches to giving feedback on student writing.

2. Approaches to written feedback on writing

There has been considerable debate over the effectiveness of different approaches to giving written feedback on second language (L2) writing. One such approach, grammar correction, is to some degree regarded as an ineffective form of feedback (Ferris, 2004, 2006; Truscott, 1996), particularly when the teacher only corrects the grammatical errors on behalf of the student. As opposed to grammar correction, so-called non-corrective approaches seem to promote learning more effectively, by letting students independently find solutions, for example, to grammatical problems in their text (Ferris, 2004; Milton, 2006). These non-corrective approaches are expected to result in deeper learning and understanding because the students spend more time actively thinking and analysing their own writing.

It is not always self-evident how specific or detailed the feedback should be for the students to revise their own text. In some cases, it is enough to add simple marks, symbols or short comments on the students' text, after which the students are able to understand the feedback properly and improve their writing (Ferris, 2006; Hyland & Hyland, 2006). When possible, the written feedback can also be supplemented with face-to-face feedback where the teacher can further explain any unclear segments of the written feedback.

In our writing courses at the Aalto University Language Centre, students have often said that they want to see concrete examples that illustrate and explain grammatical rules or stylistic recommendations. In such cases, a simple comment may not suffice as an explanation, and extended written feedback is needed. For some stylistic principles and grammar rules, the Internet can provide useful learning materials, and the teacher can include links to written feedback, especially for those students who need detailed explanation.

3. Feedback process

Although text processing programs, such as MS Word and OpenOffice Writer, include simple tools for adding comments to texts, the process of extensive commenting with these programs is somewhat laborious since these programs are primarily designed for text editing and not for text commenting.

However, giving unique comments is not usually very practical for teaching purposes, particularly in courses with specific learning goals and a large number of students. When giving feedback on writing in a course setting, it is usually the case that many students share similar problems in their writing, and in these situations, using a text annotation tool saves time, as standard comments with explanations and examples can be reused simply by highlighting the error and adding a comment by clicking a button. Naturally, KungFu Writing also includes the same possibility to adding unique, freeform comments as text processing programs do, but often it is enough to quickly modify an existing feedback item to a new situation. Figure 1 illustrates the teacher interface of KungFu Writing feedback tool with a simple reusable feedback item.

Figure 1. KungFu Writing teacher interface

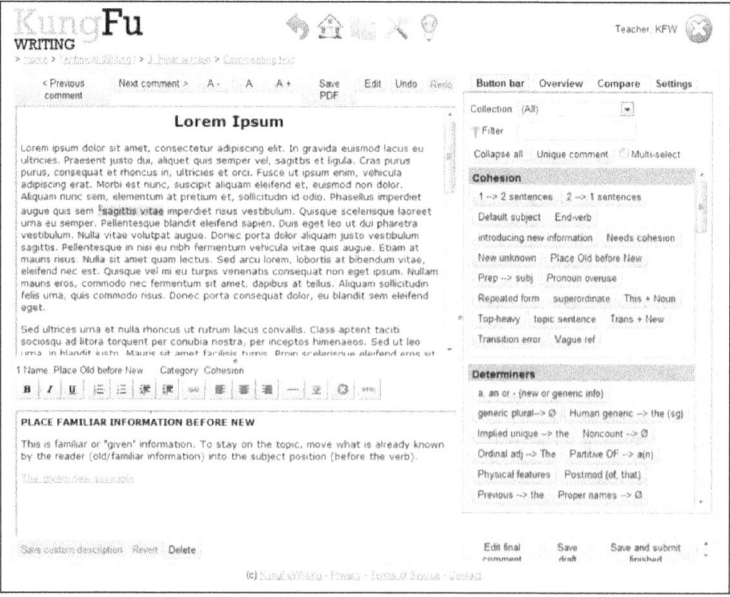

4. Giving feedback using KungFu Writing

The most basic approach for implementing the KungFu Writing tool in a writing course entails three phases. In the first phase, a student writes a text on a given course task and submits the text to the teacher. Second, the teacher reads through the student text and gives feedback, after which the teacher submits the text back to the student. Finally, the student reads through the feedback and revises the text accordingly and re-submits the text to the teacher who then reviews the revised version of the text. Depending on the learning goals or in order to deepen the student learning, the teacher can add more phases to the writing process, such as peer feedback, face-to-face consultations or extra revision tasks.

KungFu Writing allows the teacher to compare changes made between the different versions of the student text, as the tool automatically highlights the changes in the text. In this way, the teacher can quickly see how well a student has understood and responded to the written teacher feedback. KungFu Writing can compile statistics of given feedback on, for example, an individual student or an entire group. This is particularly useful when planning in-class teaching because this information can help the teacher to decide which areas of grammar or style should be reviewed or emphasized in the class lesson.

5. Benefits of an online feedback system

Most of the existing feedback tools require that the users install the program on their work or home computer, which sometimes causes compatibility problems with different versions of operating systems. In addition, many students as well as teachers are not particularly keen on spending extra time and effort on installing and configuring computer programs. With ever-faster network connections, the problems related to stand alone programs can be avoided with an online feedback tool. Therefore, KungFu Writing is designed to be used via a web browser, such as Mozilla Firefox, thus making the tool platform independent. A cloud-based system also eliminates the need for transferring the student texts as well as standard feedback templates between computers. Overall, this cloud-based tool offers a number of benefits by allowing:

- Easy reusability of pre-written comments or feedback;
- Ability to link online instructional material to the feedback;
- New possibilities for educators to share pedagogical knowledge and expertise;
- A platform for teacher/instructor collaboration in content creation;
- Consistent quality of feedback through standardization.

The new ability to share pre-written comments can also help new instructors to learn from experienced instructors who typically have tacit knowledge that may not otherwise be easily shared. An alternative approach to using a text commenting tool would be to use it either in the review or grading process. In this way, each grader or reviewer can rely on the standard evaluation criteria, thus enhancing the transparency and consistency of assessment.

6. Future Developments

Since autumn 2011, over twenty teachers of writing from different universities and upper-secondary schools in Finland have participated in piloting the KungFu Writing tool. With the help of the teacher feedback, we are working on adding new features to the system that would extend its usability. Such planned features include Shibboleth and/or OpenId authentication; features that would expand ways of collaboration between colleagues; increased flexibility in assignment submission and commenting processes (e.g., email); and offline support.

Acknowledgements. We would like to extend special thanks to Team Partaveikot (especially Henri & Timo) who have managed to make sense of our ideas and create an excellent piece of software. Furthermore, we would like to extend our sincere thanks to Aalto University Language Centre for allowing us the time needed for developing and piloting the tool. Last, but not least, we are grateful to all the teachers (>20) and students (>1000) involved in piloting the tool and giving us all the constructive feedback over the last academic year.

References

Ferris, D. (2004). The "Grammar Correction" Debate in L2 Writing: Where are we, and where do we go from here? (and what do we do in the meantime . . .?). *Journal of Second Language Writing, 13*(1), 49-62. doi:10.1016/j.jslw.2004.04.005

Ferris, D. (2006). Does error feedback help student writers? New evidence on the short- and long-term effects of written error correction. In K. Hyland & F. Hyland (Eds.), *Feedback in Second Language Writing. Contexts and Issues* (pp. 81-102). Cambridge: Cambridge University Press.

Hyland, K., & Hyland, F. (2006). Feedback on second language students' writing. *Language Teaching 39*(2), 83-101. doi:10.1017/S0261444806003399

Milton, J. (2006). Resource-rich Web-based feedback: Helping learners become independent writers. In K. Hyland & F. Hyland (Eds.), *Feedback in Second Language Writing. Contexts and Issues* (pp. 123-139). Cambridge: Cambridge University Press.

Truscott, J. (1996). The case against grammar correction in L2 writing classes. *Language Learning, 46*(2), 327-369. doi: 10.1111/j.1467-1770.1996.tb01238.x

UNIVERSITY OF
GOTHENBURG

The Effect of Computer-Assisted Language Learning on Reading Comprehension in an Iranian EFL Context

Mahnaz Saeidi* and Mahsa Yusefi

Department of English Language, Tabriz Branch, Islamic Azad University, Tabriz, Iran

Abstract. This study is an attempt to examine the effect of computer-assisted language learning (CALL) on reading comprehension in an Iranian English as a foreign language (EFL) context. It was hypothesized that CALL has an effect on reading comprehension. Forty female learners of English at intermediate level after administering a proficiency test were randomly selected as the participants of this study and assigned into two groups of experimental and control. The experimental group received treatment using three types of software. The control group had the same materials as on the printed texts. T-test was employed to compare students' reading comprehension post-tests. The results of t-test supported our research hypothesis that there is a significant difference between experimental and control groups in terms of reading comprehension. The findings of this study carry important implications for foreign language syllabus designers, curriculum planners, and language instructors.

Keywords: CALL, reading comprehension, EFL, software, multimedia.

1. Introduction

Recently, computers have become so widespread in schools and homes and their uses have expanded so dramatically that the majority of language teachers must now begin to think about the implications of computers for language learning (Warschauer, 1996). CALL is a term used by teachers and students to describe the use of computers as part of a language course (Hardisty & Windeatt, 1989). It is traditionally described as a means of 'presenting, reinforcing and testing' particular language items.

Initially, there were some innovative uses of software which contained drills, practices and exercises. As the technology advanced, we began to see more interactive uses of CALL as well as an increase in the integration of various media into the computer system (Pusack & Otto, 1990). Kulik and Kulik (1991) reviewed more than 500 studies which compared learners who received computer-assisted instruction with

---

* Contact author: mnsaeidi@yahoo.ca

In L. Bradley & S. Thouësny (Eds.), *CALL: Using, Learning, Knowing, EUROCALL Conference, Gothenburg, Sweden, 22-25 August 2012, Proceedings* (pp. 259-263). © Research-publishing.net Dublin 2012

the learners who received traditional instruction. They found that learners tend to learn more and in less time with computer-assisted learning.

Reading is an active skill that involves the reader, the text, and the interaction between the two. The acquisition of reading skills is a very important aspect of first language, as well as second or foreign language (FL) literacy. Reading in an L2 or FL is a dynamic and interactive process during which learners make use of a variety of skills and strategies, combined with background knowledge, L1-related knowledge and real-world knowledge to arrive at an understanding of written material (Aebersold & Field, 1997).

A review of the reading comprehension literature has shown that specially designed software, computer-assisted language learning program, online lessons, animated texts, use of multimedia contexts, interactive multi-modal materials, online dictionaries, e-books and a hypertext/hypermedia environment have been used to teach L2 reading comprehension. The different learning modes, skills and activities used in reading comprehension instruction in CALL environments are reported below.

Sawaki (2001) listed the studies carried out on computer-based and paper-based reading comprehension. The studies done by Heppner, Anderson, Farstrup, and Weiderman (1985) showed that students outperform in the computer-based version of the reading tests, whereas some studies showed that they are equal.

The present study examined the effect of computer-assisted language learning on reading comprehension in the Iranian EFL context. The research question is as follows: Does computer-assisted language learning have any effect on reading comprehension?

2. Method

2.1. Participants and instruments

A total of 53 EFL learners initially participated in this experiment but after selection they were reduced to 40. The participants were Iranian female intermediate EFL learners with an age range of 18 to 25. The participation was voluntary and they had already enrolled in the English Language Institute. They shared the same linguistic and cultural background. The first language of the students was Azari. For the purpose of the study and to investigate the hypotheses, several instruments were utilized. The Reading section of the Cambridge ESOL Preliminary English Test (PET) was used for homogenizing the participants regarding their reading comprehension. For the post-test standard, a reading comprehension test was used. The allotted time for each test was 30 minutes.

Three types of software were used in the experimental group. The first software which was used was Rosetta Stone, which is a software for learning more than 30 different languages. It covers four language skills. This software is based on multimedia which presents picture and sound. The reading part of this software contains texts with pictures. One of the features of this software is immediate feedback. The second software was VOA (Voice of America) Special English. It has 40 texts in different subjects for reading comprehension. This software reads the text for learners, so there is an opportunity for learners to learn correct pronunciation as well. One of the features of this software is a dictionary, Babylon which can present the meaning of words in more than 50 different languages. Learners can get the meaning of the word which is in the text just by one left click. The third software used was Learn to Speak English; it covers four language skills. This software is based on multimedia and presents picture, sound, practice and drills. In the reading part, this software presents the text with motion pictures which can affect comprehension positively. The control group had the same materials as on the printed texts.

2.2. Design and procedure

The design of the study was quasi-experimental. Two intact groups, after administering the proficiency test, were assigned randomly into two groups of experimental and control groups.

First, the Reading section of the proficiency test, PET, was administered as a pre-test to determine students' homogeneity regarding reading comprehension. The students in the control group read texts from the printed pages during ten sessions in a conventional classroom, while the experimental group read the same texts from the computer screen using three different types of software. The two groups followed the same aim and scope of the course and they were taught by the same teacher. Finally, both groups took the post-test. In order to make students familiar with the software, the second session was devoted to training. The treatment started from the third session for 10 sessions.

3. Results

In order to make sure that the participants in both control and experimental groups were at the same proficiency level, a 20-item test in reading comprehension was used. As shown in Table 1, there was no significant difference in scores for the experimental group ($M = 12.45$, $SD = .2.76$) and control group ($M = 12.20$, $SD = .2.19$), $t(38) = -.317$, $p = .753 > .5$. This suggests that students in the two groups were fairly homogeneous in the reading comprehension knowledge at the beginning of the study.

Table 1. Independent t-test based on pre-test for experimental and control groups

	Group	N	Mean	Std. Deviation	Levene's Test for Equality of Variances		t-test for Equality of Means		
					F	Sig.	t	df	Sig. (2-tailed)
pre-test	Control	20	12.20	2.19	1.349	.253	-.317	38	.753
	Experimental	20	12.45	2.76					

As shown in Table 2, there was a significant difference in post-test scores for the experimental group ($M = 16.10$, $SD = 1.17$) and control group ($M = 13.80$, $SD = 1.36$), $t(38) = -5.741$, $p = .0001 > .5$. This suggests that there was a significant difference between post-test scores of the experimental and control groups in terms of reading comprehension ability.

Table 2. Independent t-test based on post-test for experimental and control groups

	Group	N	Mean	Std. Deviation	Levene's Test for Equality of Variances		t-test for Equality of Means		
					F	Sig.	t	df	Sig. (2-tailed)
post-test	Control	20	13.80	1.36	.563	.458	-5.741	38	.000
	Experimental	20	16.10	1.17					

According to the results of this study, CALL can enhance and improve the reading comprehension of EFL learners; in other words, the students who were taught using CALL performed better than students who were taught by the traditional printed text.

4. Discussion

The purpose of the present study was to investigate the effects of computer-assisted reading support on the comprehension of EFL learners. To reach this goal, two modes of teaching reading were compared with regard to their effectiveness for foreign language reading comprehension: the computer-assisted reading and the traditional print mode. The results of the data analysis indicate that comprehension scores increase when readers read computerized texts that provide reading support. According to this research, this increase in comprehension is the function of the computer that permits deeper and more interactive information between the reader and the text.

Researchers using CALL in the area of reading have frequently reported beneficial effects of such instruction. In these studies, researchers reported improvement in pre- and post-test measures of comprehension and reading proficiency (Sawaki, 2001). The findings of the present study are in line with the aforementioned studies.

5. Conclusion

The superior performance of the learners in the experimental group might be contributed to the interactive nature of CALL, which, in turn, can make language learning more interesting. Moreover, using the interactive computer software in the class may have encouraged the readers to process the meaning of the text more deeply and more actively.

This interpretation suggests that the computer might provide unique opportunities for managing readers' interaction with the text during the independent reading.

The result of this study provides insight into the effect of interactive computer software on students' reading comprehension and supports the conclusion that computer-assisted language learning can enhance the reading comprehension of EFL learners.

Acknowledgements. We would like to thank the participants of the study.

References

Aebersold, J. A., & Field, M. L. (1997). *From reading to reading teacher: Issues and strategies for second language classroom.* Cambridge: Cambridge University Press.

Heppner, F. H., Anderson, J., Farstrup, A. E., & Weiderman, N. H. (1985). Reading performance on a standardized test is better from print than from computer display. *Journal of Reading, 28*(4), 321-325.

Hardisty, D., & Windeatt, S. (1989). *CALL*. Oxford: Oxford University Press.

Kulik, C. L., & Kulik, J. A. (1991). Effectiveness of computer-assisted instruction: An updated analysis. *Computers in Human Behavior, 7*(1-2), 75-94. doi: 10.1016/0747-5632(91)90030-5

Pusack, J. P., & Otto, S. K. (1990). Priority instruction: Applying instructional technologies. *Foreign Language Annals, 23*(5), 409-417. doi: 10.1111/j.1944-9720.1990.tb00396.x

Sawaki, Y. (2001). Comparability of conventional and computerized tests of reading in a second language. *Language learning & technology, 5*(2), 38-59. Retrieved from http://llt.msu.edu/vol5num2/sawaki/default.html

Warschauer, M. (1996). Computer-assisted language learning: An introduction. In S. Fotos (Ed.), *Multimedia language teaching* (pp. 3-20). Tokyo: Logos International.

UNIVERSITY OF
GOTHENBURG

From a Gloss to a Learning Tool: Does Visual Aids Enhance Better Sentence Comprehension?

Takeshi Sato[a]* and Akio Suzuki[b]

a. Tokyo University of Agricultural & Technology, Tokyo, Japan
b. Toyo University, Tokyo, Japan

Abstract. The aim of this study is to optimize CALL environments as a learning tool rather than a gloss, focusing on the learning of polysemous words which refer to spatial relationship between objects. A lot of research has already been conducted to examine the efficacy of visual glosses while reading L2 texts and has reported that visual glosses can be effective for incidental vocabulary learning. This study, however, discusses the efficacy of visual aids on vocabulary learning, from the following three different standpoints. The first point is that previous studies have not covered the meaning of these words and have concluded the aids become effective regardless of the part of speech of these words. That is, some words are easy to learn, but the others are difficult depending on the part of speech. Paying more attention to the meaning structures is necessary. The second is that previous studies have focused on visual aids in vocabulary learning using CALL in terms of a gloss while reading texts. As CALL environments have been developed, however, glosses are now used not merely as a reference tool, but as a learning tool. Finally, a lot of research on vocabulary learning with multimedia has been conducted in reading activities, although visual aids can be effective in other activities such as listening activities, in which deeper discourse comprehension is required. Taking these standpoints into consideration, we hypothesize that the intentional learning of those words with multimedia-oriented visual aids could enhance not only comprehension of vocabulary meanings but also better comprehension of a script that includes those words. To examine our hypothesis, we will conduct an experimental study with computer-mediated learning material for English prepositions which we developed for this study. The findings of this study can contribute to the better CALL environments, leading to more effective web or mobile-based learning tools.

Keywords: L2 vocabulary, prepositions, image schema, sentence comprehension, intentional learning.

---

* Contact author: tsato@cc.tuat.ac.jp

In L. Bradley & S. Thouësny (Eds.), *CALL: Using, Learning, Knowing, EUROCALL Conference, Gothenburg, Sweden, 22-25 August 2012, Proceedings* (pp. 264-268). © Research-publishing.net Dublin 2012

1. Introduction

The efficacy of pictures or images as visual glosses has been discussed in L2 vocabulary learning and CALL. Most of the studies related to this issue focus on the efficacy for the long retention through incidental learning such as reading (for example, Al-Seghayer, 2001; Chun & Plass, 1996; Lomicka, 1998; Yoshii & Fraitz, 2002). With the development of CALL with multimodality, however, an electronic dictionary as a collective of glosses has been used not only for reference tools but also for learning tools (Pachler, 2001) to intentionally obtain certain vocabulary items, for example. In that sense, it would be better to reexamine the conditions of better use of glosses in intentional L2 vocabulary learning, leading, we believe, to the development of CALL materials. We therefore would like to address this issue by comparing planar still images and animated stereo ones, which depicted conceptual schemes of L2 spatial prepositions.

2. Background

As mentioned above, many studies concerning L2 vocabulary learning with visual glosses have been conducted and then recognized for their positive impact on L2 vocabulary learning. However, we have concerns about the fact that the previous studies focus less on the following points (Sato & Suzuki, 2010, 2011); the first is that they may examine L2 vocabulary learning as incidental learning. As a result, less discussion has not been made about the relationship between certain type of glosses and vocabulary. In addition, they may regard longer retention of words as the goal of successful learning.

In this study, on the other hand, L2 vocabulary should be learned intentionally because we know some types of words which are easier to learn and also harder to learn in terms of meanings. Given our claim that comprehension of the meanings is regarded as successful L2 vocabulary learning, we revalidate the effectiveness of pictures or images as visual glosses.

3. Our study

Therefore, our study focuses on prepositions, schematic image as a visual gloss, and pictorial image and live-action image. The reason we focus on English spatial prepositions is owing to the fact that learning English prepositions is regarded as important but difficult. This is because prepositions appear very frequently in any discourse, but learners do not always understand their meanings (Lindstromberg, 1996). They might learn prepositions as idioms or chunks, but they cannot use them according to context only by memorization (Lindstromberg, 2001). In addition, L2 translation of a sense of the word may confuse us because the connection among the senses becomes unclear (Tanaka, 1990). These problems L2 learners have encountered in learning L2 prepositions show that more focus on meanings is needed than on the retention of the vocabulary.

Then we focus on image schema as a visual gloss to learn English prepositions. Johnson (1987) defines "image schemata [as] abstract patterns in our experience and understanding that are not propositional" (p. 2), which can be served as a mediator to connect the senses of the word. The image schema can reflect the prototypical sense of the word, but it can be extended into other examples. As a result, the image can cover all the senses. This means that if L2 learners understand image schema as a medium of each sense of the word, they could differentiate senses of other prepositions.

Finally, we compare planar still images with animated stereo images. This is because both images are theoretically supported by different frameworks: CALL and Cognitive Linguistics. CALL research supports the effectiveness of animation as we see Al-Seghayer's (2001) research. On the other hand, in the field of cognitive linguistics, from which the image schema was derived, schematic images have flexibility and changeability such as their foregrounding, rotation and focusing (Langacker, 1987), which implies that simple image is better while live-motion images might prevent learners from modifying the images due to their fixed configuration.

Therefore, our research question is whether planar still images or animated stereo ones can serve a better facilitator to learn the meanings of English prepositions. We will explain the detail of our experimental research in the next chapter.

4. Research

4.1. Procedures
Fifty-two Japanese university students from freshmen to postgraduates joined our research. They are from the university the first author works at and are not majoring in English language. They were randomly divided into two groups: a control group and an experimental group. First of all, both participants were asked to answer multiple questions about the sense of eight spatial prepositions: above, across. along, below, in, into, on and over. The test consists of forty-five questions and no feedback was given after the test. Then they learned the sense of prepositions using the two kinds of dictionaries we gave them respectively for ten minutes. They were then asked to answer the post vocabulary test which consists of the same questions as the pre-test, but they are randomized. The data we have got are analysed through ANOVA with between and within subject variables.

4.2. Findings
The result we have got from the analysis shows that in both groups participants could get higher scores in post-test than those in pre-test. As a result of ANOVA, in terms of

image, a big difference was found (Images: $F(1,50) = .018$, $p > .05$; Tests: $F(1,50) = 112.5$, $p < .05$). The results tell us that there is no statistical significance between the two groups. However, significant difference is found between pre-test and post-test after the treatments, while no interaction between the two factors is found (Figure 1). These results may indicate visual glosses can facilitate intentional learning of senses of English prepositions even if they are planar still images or animated stereo ones, which is different from the results many studies relating to L2 vocabulary learning with visual glosses.

Figure 1. The result of ANOVA analysis

```
A = Image
B = Test
------------------------------------------------
S.V      SS          df      MS        F
------------------------------------------------
A        0.4712      1       0.4712    0.02 ns
subj     1343.2500   50      26.8650
------------------------------------------------
B        706.1635    1       706.1635  112.49 **
AxB      0.4712      1       0.4712    0.08 ns
sxB      313.8654    50      6.2773
------------------------------------------------
Total    2364.2212   103     +p<.10 *p<.05 **p<.01
```

5. Discussion and conclusion

In conclusion, our experimental research shows that the images as visual glosses can be a good facilitator of learning L2 prepositions regardless of their configurations. We have to admit, however, more analysis must be conducted like a delayed test, but our previous studies also show the same result. In terms of L2 vocabulary learning in this setting, technologically advanced visual glosses do not always bring about a better result. Of course, this result does not mean using technology or multimedia functions has no meaning, all we want to say is optimization of the glosses according to the target should be required. We have to think about the condition to make learning successful. Either way, further research is needed.

References

Al-Seghayer, K. (2001). The effect of multimedia annotation modes on L2 vocabulary acquisition: a comparative study. *Language Learning and Technology*, 5(1), 202-232.
Chun, D. L., & Plass, J. L. (1996). Effects of multimedia annotations on vocabulary acquisition. *Modern Language Journal*, 80(2), 183-198.
Johnson, M. (1987). *Body in the Mind*. Chicago: Chicago University Press.

Langacker, R. W. (1987). *Foundations of Cognitive Grammar, Volume I, Theoretical Prerequisites*. Stanford, California: Stanford University Press.

Lindstromberg, S. (1996). *English Prepositions Explained*. Amsterdam/Philadelphia: Benjamins.

Lindstromberg, S. (2001). Preposition Entries in UK Monolingual Learner's Dictionaries: Problems and Possible Solutions. *Applied Linguistics*, 2(1), 79-103.

Lomicka, L. L. (1998). "To Gloss or Not To Gloss": An Investigation of Reading Comprehension Online. *Language Learning & Technology*, 1(2), 41-50. Retrieved from http://llt.msu.edu/vol1num2/pdf/article2.pdf

Pachler, N. (2001). Electronic reference tools for foreign language learners, Teachers and users: Offline vocabulary look-up programs. *The Language Learning Journal*, 24(1), 24-29. doi: 10.1080/09571730185200181

Tanaka, S. (1990). *Ninchi Imiron* [Cognitive Semantics]. Tokyo: Sanyusha.

Sato, T., & Suzuki, A. (2010). Do multimedia-oriented visual glosses really facilitate EFL vocabulary learning? : A comparison of planar images with three-dimensional images. *Asian EFL Journal*, 12(4), 160-172.

Sato, T., & Suzuki A. (2011). Verifying Multimedia Gloss: Image Schema and Polysemous Vocabulary in English. *Proceedings of the annual conference of the European Association for Computer-Assisted Language Learning*, 285-293.

Yoshii, M., & Fraitz, J. (2002). Second Language Incidental Vocabulary Retention: The Effect of Text and Picture Annotation Types. *CALICO Journal*, 20(1), 33-58.

UNIVERSITY OF
GOTHENBURG

Online Scientific Language Teaching and Web 2.0

Flora Sisti*

University of Urbino "Carlo Bo", Urbino, Italy

Abstract. This presentation examines the application of Web 2.0 to an online scientific language course. The online Computer Science English Course (CSEC), funded by a national PRIN project and targeted to students enrolled in the undergraduate course in Applied Computer Science (ACS) at the University of Urbino – Italy, aims to promote the acquisition of applied computer science micro-language. The CSEC aspired to a CEFR B1/B1+ level of competency in reading, writing, grammar and vocabulary skills. The innovative element was its foundation on a blog, posted regularly by a senior bilingual student attending the university ACS course while in the US for an internship. Tested during the experimental phase of the project (2007-08), the course has been recently augmented in order to develop the oral skills which were not sufficiently practised and to create more personal teacher-student and peer relationships. Web 2.0 tools have been used to enhance learners' English professional oral language skills in an engaging learning environment. The decision to implement Web 2.0 was also influenced by the targeted students' interests in information and communication technology (ICT). Student motivation therefore played an important role in the design and implementation of the new activities aimed to encourage an autonomous active learning of the foreign language (FL). The implemented version of the course will be offered to the first year students of the 2012/13 academic year enrolled in the distance-learning degree programme in ACS. New interaction modes will be fostered to cater for collaborative learning and knowledge building by means of web 2.0 social spaces (Bates, 2011) and through constant tandem learning organized with other ACS English speaking students

Keywords: distance and collaborative learning, EFL teaching, scientific English.

1. Introduction

The online computer science English course, funded by a national PRIN project and targeted to students enrolled in the undergraduate course in applied computer science at the University of Urbino - Italy, aims to promote the acquisition of applied computer science micro-language.

---

* Contact author: flora.sisti@uniurb.it

In L. Bradley & S. Thouësny (Eds.), *CALL: Using, Learning, Knowing, EUROCALL Conference, Gothenburg, Sweden, 22-25 August 2012, Proceedings* (pp. 269-273). © Research-publishing.net Dublin 2012

The course is part of a broader research project which combines the CLIL approach (Content and Language Integrated Learning) and Computer-Mediated Learning within the context of university instruction. The above-mentioned degree course is offered in two versions: via classroom instruction in the students' mother-tongue language, and online in the English language (http://e-learning.sti.uniurb.it/).

To provide the online instruction group with adequate support, the existing didactic materials were revised and adapted to the CLIL approach and an English course was created to foster active use of scientific micro-language in the field of ACS. The online CSEC mainly focused on building reading, writing, grammar and vocabulary skills related to the specific needs of ACS students and it was founded on a blog which was regularly posted by a senior, bilingual ACS student, Bob, doing his internship in the United States. The blog-inspired content was highly motivating for our students and the activities suggested met their needs and interests but it also required constant revision. Therefore, three years later, the syllabus has been re-elaborated, adapting its content to develop the oral skills which were not sufficiently practised and to create more personal teacher-student and peer relationships. The new version of the online CSEC is enriched with additional activities based on Web 2.0 tools and new interaction modes included collaborative learning and knowledge building (Harasim, 2011).

2. Method

2.1. Course structure

The CSEC aspires to a CEFR B1/B1+ level of competency in the written skills. Each of the 20 units consists of four activity areas, namely: *Warm up; Application; Language notes; My contribution*. The first two areas, including listening and reading materials with relative exercises, introduce the topic of the unit and offer the opportunity to develop it by adding details. The third area consists of grammar and vocabulary notes completed with activities referred to standard English supplemented with Computer Science micro-language; while in the last section (*My contribution*) students are invited to produce short written texts (e-mail messages, comments, CVs) to be submitted for individual correction.

The topics, directly connected to cultural aspects of English-speaking countries or sector-specific issues, are frequently inspired by Bob's posts.

2.2. Implementation

Tested during the experimental phase (Sisti, 2009), the course has been recently augmented to develop oral skills more efficiently and foster stronger teacher-student and peer relationships. This implementation was carried out using selected free software and web 2.0 tools.

Since the ACS degree course is in English, the *de facto* lingua franca of new technologies, students are strongly motivated to increase their competence in a language that is indispensable for their professional advancement. Moreover, they are very interested in computer software and ICT as a vocation. To enhance collaborative knowledge construction and practise oral interactive skills, students will be asked to use the following free web-based tools.

- **Mailvu**: a free video-authoring tool which enables to record short videos and to store them. Video clips may also be shared within a community through a short link that may be posted on Facebook, LinkedIn, Twitter, or in a text message to fellow students and/or the instructor;
- **Natural Reader**: free text-to-speech software which converts written material into audio format (MP3 or WAV files). The reading voice is very natural and offers a choice between British and US English accents. The software highlights each word as it is read and offers the option of slowing the reading speed down, allowing learners to improve their spelling and pronunciation;
- **SoundCloud**: audio recording tool able to capture the student's voice and transform it into a visual format (a waveform);
- **Glogster**: an interactive visual platform allowing learners to create their multimedia posters or web pages in groups;
- **FolioSpaces**: a free ePortfolio service used to create a personal space (private or shareable) to write and store media related to learning activities;
- **Skype**: well-known software allowing students to talk to their classmates and international partners about topics related to their professional sector. Moreover, the instant messaging feature, which allows users to clarify questions in writing in real-time, avoids misunderstandings due to poor competence in the FL and helps effective tandem learning.

3. Discussion

Two learning objects involving CLIL methodology and English for Specific Purposes were created to promote greater awareness of the language-teaching context. They consisted in Power Point presentations of slides with written and audio comments that students were asked to read, listen to and then discuss with their classmates and instructors in online synchronous seminars and written chat sessions. These two learning objects were transformed, thanks to *Mailvu*, into video clips so as to allow learners to actually see their instructors while commenting the slides. Moreover, the video-authoring tool will also be used by students who will be invited to create their virtual presentations in a video format. By doing so at the beginning of the course, they can get to know one another by sharing information about their personal and professional lives but, starting from next year, also associating names with faces. In addition, their video clips can be sent to their international partners so as to help them socialize and build closer cross-cultural online communities.

As mentioned, all teaching units propose readings, chosen from various Internet sources, accompanied by notes and completed with comprehension exercises. Students will be asked not only to read but also to listen to these original materials using *Natural Reader* to get ready for synchronous Skype conferences where special emphasis will be placed on their ability to articulate sounds correctly. Students should become aware of English intonation and of the difference between the graphic and phonologic systems by choosing the speech speed adequate for their needs and working autonomously on the synchronized highlighting of sentences.

The *My contribution* writing exercises will be recorded by students using *SoundCloud*. The course instructors, after reviewing the short texts will send them back to the authors in a final version ready to be transformed into an audio file. This will encourage learners to practise pronunciation and allow teachers to focus on relevant prosodic features (weak syllable deletion, intonation etc.). Students will be able to see their waveform audio track pinpointed with teacher's comments while listening to it.

Various topics dealt with in the online CSEC units are particularly relevant to Computer Science studies while others are more related to intercultural issues given the fact that students attending the online course might be native speakers of any language. In units such as: Techie Jargon, Multiculturalism at the Table, Meeting and Eating, Travel, and others, *Glogster* will be used to create web posters. Learners will be asked to work in groups on this multimedia platform to carry out a project related to the topic of the unit through a creative use of multi-media relevant Internet resources. A virtual classroom will be constituted where each student can use diverse formats – according to his/her cognitive style – to provide his/her personal contribution to the topic of the unit; at the end, the best multimedia poster will be voted and rewarded. These projects, as others, will be stored, managed and displayed in student university e-Portfolios created with *FolioSpaces*.

Individual audio-video presentations, audio recordings of *My contribution* short texts, and group *glogs* may be embedded in a personal, virtual portfolio hosted in *FolioSpaces*. The instructor can provide feedback which is visualized by the student while the archive is constantly updated. This repository of diverse artifacts is also very useful for tandem activities where learners are expected to work with foreign students attending the same degree course.

Indeed, thanks to *Skype,* our undergraduates will be able to discuss professional and cultural issues with their Erasmus partners using autonomous, cooperative learning methods. In doing so they will improve their linguistic competence and Computer Science knowledge. Language learning in tandem via the Internet is generally considered an effective way to learn a partner's language while teaching one's own, in this case English is used as a *lingua franca* to work together across great distances.

4. Conclusions

The improved version of the course will be offered to first year students of the 2012/13 academic year with the aim of promoting greater practice in oral skills through authentic social interactions. Indeed, in computer-mediated FL courses, the lack of face-to-face interaction, which plays a key role in promoting the acquisition of socio-pragmatic conversational skills, seems to be a serious drawback. Learners taking online courses usually study and carry out activities in isolation, and this may hinder effective interaction in a FL in real-life communicative situations. To counteract this tendency, students will be encouraged to speak and listen to their partners much more, working in groups in virtual social communities.

By means of Web 2.0 tools they will be urged to express independent and creative thought and to become confident problem solvers in a challenging and motivating learning environment where collaborative learning and knowledge building are promoted.

References

Bates, T. (2011). Understanding Web 2.0 and its Implications for E-learning. In M. J. W. Lee & C. McLoughlin (Eds.), *Web 2.0-Based E-Learning: Applying Social Informatics for Tertiary Teaching* (pp. 21-42). New York: Information Science Reference.

Harasim, L. (2011). *Learning Theory and Online Technologies*. Abingdon, Oxon: Routledge.

Sisti, F. (Ed.). (2009). *CLIL Methodology in University Instruction: Online and in the Classroom. An Emerging framework (Part I)*. Perugia: Guerra Edizioni.

UNIVERSITY OF GOTHENBURG

Text and Language Practices in One-to-one Environments in a Swedish Primary School

Sylvana Sofkova Hashemi[*] and Leona Johansson Bunting[**]

Dept. of Social and Behavioural Studies, University West, Trollhättan, Sweden

Abstract. Recent investments in schools in Sweden focus on increased availability of technology and ways to incorporate digital media in the classroom. Via the computer screen, students are involved in a new type of writing and communication culture that allows for new approaches in literacy instruction and learning (Lorentzen & Smidt, 2010). The purpose of the present study was to investigate how the availability and every day access to technology in a one-to-one laptop programme in primary school impact on text and language practices. The objective was to explore what text genres the students meet and what artefacts they use to facilitate their work, the modalities they engage in and if they work on their own or in collaboration. Also, what new demands are put on the instruction. The empirical results are based on classroom observations of a sample of lectures in two classes in year three and two classes in year five where the students had been using computers for about 2.5 years. In both year three and five the students expressed great enthusiasm for the work on computers. Narrative and expository strategies were prominent in the development of text and language competencies. New practices facilitating multimodal and digital expression occurred more on the students' own initiative. The activities in year three provided opportunities for both individual and collaborative work, whereas year five mainly did individual work. The assignments in both years were mostly designed to result in products of the same type and were published on their computers for a restricted audience. We interpret these practices as being mainly teacher-controlled and for the benefit of the teacher and fellow classmates. This stands in contrast to previous analyses on changes in literacy processes in laptop classes that report on more student autonomous and public uses (e.g., Warschauer, 2008).

Keywords: one-to-one classroom, primary school, text competencies, language practices, multimodal analysis.

---

[*] Contact author: sylvana.sofkova-hashemi@hv.se

[**] Contact author: leona.johansson-bunting@hv.se

In L. Bradley & S. Thouësny (Eds.), *CALL: Using, Learning, Knowing, EUROCALL Conference, Gothenburg, Sweden, 22-25 August 2012, Proceedings* (pp. 274-279). © Research-publishing.net Dublin 2012

1. Introduction

Investments in laptop computers in schools are increasing, despite the high costs, raising questions about the best ways to incorporate technology into the curriculum (Devaney, 2009). The largest and earliest initiatives have been reported from the U.S., where whole states were equipped with laptop computers (Silvernail, 2004). The research results are generally positive and several studies report on significant gains in student engagement and motivation for learning, writing competency, and critical thinking (Suhr, Hernandez, Grimes, & Warschauer, 2010). An increased use of technology in the classroom and in the home has also been reported (Keengwe, Schnellert, & Mills, 2012; Zucker & McGhee, 2005). Students participate in more authentic and diverse literacy activities with increased opportunities for scaffolding and feedback (Penuel et al., 2001; Warschauer, 2008). Some of the holdbacks are the preparation time for learning new technology, poor administrative support and perceiving computers as a competitive or disruptive distraction (Dunleavy, Dexter, & Heinecke, 2007; Zucker & McGhee, 2005). In Sweden, similar results have been reported regarding motivation for schoolwork and changes towards thematic, subject-integrated and more learner-centered instruction (Tallvid, 2010). Initial results from the ongoing study *Unosuno* of several laptop programmes in Sweden show evidence of more individualized work and also a focus on presentation rather than content (Grönlund et al., 2011). There is also an on-going discussion on the relationship between the knowledge required for standardized tests and what is taught in laptop-enhanced instruction (OECD, 2010; Pedró, 2007; Warschauer, 2008).

Our study complements this research investigating *long-term* impact (i.e., not implementation) of a one-to-one laptop programme on text and language practices for *primary level students*. At the time of our study, the two classes in year three and two classes in year five had been using the computers for about 2.5 years. The objective of the study was to explore and map the text genres the students meet, the modalities they engage in and the artefacts (digital or not) they use. The instructional approaches and collaborative impacts are also reported upon.

In the following, the method will be presented and then followed by analyses of teaching design, text genre and modes, resources and artefacts and collaborative impact.

2. Method

The empirical results are based on a sample of 11 classroom observations (10 hours) in year 3 and on 10 occasions (13 hours) in year 5 during a term. For year 3, the sample includes lessons on Writers Workshop, ancient times, dinosaurs, formal training of spelling, reading comprehension, note-taking in a school diary and free work. The sample from year 5 concerns lessons on activities related to The Famous Person Project, textbook work and World Spelling Day.

The analyses of text and language practices are based on theories of school genres (Knapp & Watkins, 1994; Liberg, af Geijerstam, & Wiksten Folkeryd, 2011) and a multimodal analysis in a socio-cultural context (Jewitt, 2008; Purcell-Gates, Perry, & Briseño, 2008). The variables include *text genre* defined as the purpose of the text, *text form* as how the text is realized, *resources* used and *collaborative impact*. The instructional design is also reflected upon based on the observations.

3. Text and language practices in year 3 and 5

3.1. Teaching design

In year 3, lessons were in general organized according to a model of *mini-lessons* based on *Units of Study for Teaching Writing* (Calkins, 1994). A mini-lesson began by explaining the aim of the lesson and how to proceed to fulfill that aim. The students were then encouraged to try themselves or together with their "writing partner". Then the students were sent off to work on their own or in pairs to be reassembled at the end for feedback and further planning.

The lessons in year 5 usually began with a teacher-led warm-up activity. The agenda of the lesson was then explained and instructions written on the board. The teacher would move around in the classroom and the other areas where the students were seated in order to help them. At the end of the lesson, the teacher would typically reassemble the students, sometimes providing them with feedback on their work.

3.2. Text genres and modes

The students in year 3 wrote narrative texts in descriptions and introductions to their text. These activities concerned the writing and revising of a text and reading out loud. Students compared the number of words in their texts, fonts and backgrounds, added links to webpages and sent their texts to the teacher. They also met narratives during reading and in reading comprehension exercises. Expository texts appeared in a variety of text forms. Students collected facts and images in textbooks and on webpages. They organized facts on post-it notes and in mind maps on the computer and reported facts in several formats: as a slideshow presentation, a manuscript and an animation. They also watched a film about dinosaurs.

Furthermore, they produced lists of words for spelling practice, of facts and contacts for their account on the learning platform. They sent instant messages to each other in the classroom, uploaded pictures of themselves and communicated via Skype. During their free work, many students enjoyed taking pictures of themselves for slideshows and desktop backgrounds. Others composed posters, wrote narratives formed as presentations, created musical pieces, edited previously created films and slideshows or played games on-line.

The students in year 5 encountered narrative texts both in their textbooks and on the computer. They also read and listened to narrative texts in easy to read novels. They did exercises both on paper and digitally, e.g., reading comprehension and dictation, based on narrative texts. Some also wrote narrative texts on their computers and those who did carefully chose fonts and size for their text. Upon finishing, they sent the texts to the teacher.

Some of the texts in the students' textbooks were expository. They worked with them in a similar manner as explained above. When working on the Famous Person Project they read expository texts on the Internet and wrote their chosen facts down in a word processing program. Then they composed an expository text of their own to be presented in a slideshow. To accompany their text they also recorded their own voices reading the text. One student filmed herself while talking, thus providing her slideshow with a visual narrator.

When working on the Famous Person Project, the students also worked with pictures. They watched Youtube clips when gathering information and they collected images from the Internet to paste in their slideshows. Many students spent as much, or more, time on editing pictures as gathering data and writing. Many students also listened to music on Spotify while working.

3.3. Resources and artefacts

Concerning digital and non-digital activities, the 3rd graders read, did spelling exercises, took notes and collected facts without the use of a computer. Activities that occurred with the help of computers concerned writing down facts from textbooks, making a faircopy from a handwritten draft and reading text projected on the screen. On the Internet, the students collected facts and images, wrote instant messages, watched films, played games and communicated via Skype. On the computer they mostly wrote in a word editor, created presentations and mind maps.

The students in year 5 did not use their computers when working with the non-digital workbook, reading dialogues or novels. The remaining work observed during lessons was however done with the aid of a computer. This involved collecting facts and pictures from the Internet for a slideshow, and doing exercises in their digital workbook.

3.4. Collaborative impact

While the activities in year 3 were both individual and collaborative, the activities in year 5 were mainly individual. However, assignments involving computer work tended to be individual in both years.

4. Discussion and conclusions

The study demonstrates that the narrative and expository texts dominated in both years with the latter including more diverse text formats and modes. In year 3, lists and instant messaging also occurred. Genres and modes varied more on the students' initiative in both years. The activities in year 3 provided opportunities for both individual and collaborative work supported both by digital and non-digital resources. The activities in year 5 were mainly individual, especially concerning digital work. Concerning the instructional approach, explicit modelling was the main objective in the development of text and language competencies while in year 3 and in year 5 it was more project-based.

In conclusion, the traditional genres were in these classes accompanied by some new practices facilitating multimodal and digital expression with more individualized work for the older students in year 5. Assignments in both years were mostly designed to result in products of the same type and published on computers for a restricted audience. We interpret these practices as being mainly teacher-controlled and for the benefit of the teacher and fellow classmates. This is in contrast to previous analysis on changes in literacy processes in laptop classes that report on more student autonomous and public uses (e.g., Warschauer, 2008).

Acknowledgements. We would like to thank the students and teachers who participated in this study and University West for funding it.

References

Calkins, L. (1994). *The Art of Teaching Writing*. Portsmouth: Heinemann.

Devaney, L. (2009). Study: *Ed tech leads to significant gains. Benton Foundation. eSchool News*. Retrieved from http://www.eschoolnews.com/2009/04/22/study-ed-tech-leads-to-significant-gains

Dunleavy, M., Dexter, S., & Heinecke, W. F. (2007). What added value does a 1:1 student laptop ratio bring to technology supported teaching and learning? *Journal of Computer Assisted Learning, 23(*5), 440–452. doi: 10.1111/j.1365-2729.2007.00227.x

Grönlund, H., Englund, T., Andersson, A., Wiklund, M., Norén, I., & Hatakka, M. (2011). Årsrapport Unosuno 2011 vuxenutbildning [Annual report Unosuno 2011]. Örebro university. Retrieved from http://www.hyperfinder.se/wp-content/uploads/2012/05/arsrapport_unosuno_2011.pdf

Jewitt, C. (2008). Multimodality and Literacy in School Classrooms. *Review of Research in Education, 32*(1), 241-267. doi:10.3102/0091732X07310586

Keengwe, J., Schnellert, G., & Mills, C. (2012). Laptop initiative: Impact on instructional technology integration and student learning. *Education and Information Technologies, 17*(2), 137-146. doi:10.1007/s10639-010-9150-8

Knapp, P., & Watkins, M. (1994). *Context, text, grammar: Teaching the genres of grammar of social writing in infants and primary classrooms*. Sydney: Text Productions.

Liberg, C., af Geijerstam, Å., & Wiksten Folkeryd, J. (2011). *Utmana, utforska, utveckla! Om läs- och skrivprocessen i skolan*. Studentlitteratur, Lund.

Lorentzen, R. T., & Smidt, J. (2010). *Det nödvändiga skrivandet: om att skriva i förskolan och skolans alla ämnen*. [Necessary writing: writing in pre-school and all subjects in school.] Liber.

OECD (2010). Are the New Millennium Learners Making the Grade? Technology Use and Educational Performance in PISA 2006. *Educational Research and Innovation*, OECD Publishing.

Pedró, F. (2007). The New Millennium Learners: Challenging our Views on Digital Technologies and Learning. *Nordic Journal of Digital Literacy, 2*(4), 244-264.

Penuel, W. R., Kim, D. Y., Michalchik, V., Lewis, S., Means, B., Murphy, B., Korbak, Ch., Whaley, A., & Allen, J. E. (2001). *Using technology to enhance connections between home and school: A research synthesis.* Menlo Park, CA: SRI International.

Purcell-Gates, V., Perry, K. H., & Briseño, A. (2008). *Analyzing Literacy Practice: Grounded Theory to Model. National Reading Conference*, Orlando, Fl, Dec. 3, 2008.

Silvernail, L. (2004). *The Impact of Maine's One-to-One Laptop Program on Middle School Teachers and Students.* Maine Education Policy Research Institute, University of Southern Maine Office.

Suhr, K. A., Hernandez, D. A., Grimes, D., & Warschauer, M. (2010). Laptops and fourth-grade literacy: assisting the jump over the fourth-grade slump. *Journal of Technology, Learning and Assessment, 9*(5), 5-45.

Tallvid, M. (2010). *En-till-En Falkenbergs väg till Framtiden? Utvärdering av projektet En-till-En i två grundskolor i Falkenberg kommun.* Delrapport 3. [One-to-one. Falkenberg's way to the future? Evaluation of the project One-to-one in two comprehensive schools in Falkenberg municipality. Partial report 3]. University of Gothenburg. Falkenberg municipality.

Warschauer, M. (2008). Laptops and Literacy: A Multi-Site Case Study. *Pedagogies: An International Journal, 3*(1), 52-67.

Zucker, A., & McGhee, R. (Eds.). (2005). *A study of one-to-one computer use in mathematics and science instruction at the secondary level in Henrico county public schools.* SRI International.

UNIVERSITY OF GOTHENBURG

Computer-Assisted L2 English Language-Related Activities Among Swedish 10-Year-Olds

Pia Sundqvist[a]* and Liss Kerstin Sylvén[b]

a. Karlstad University, Faculty of Arts and Education, Karlstad, Sweden
b. University of Gothenburg, Department of Education and Special Education, Gothenburg, Sweden

Abstract. This paper presents findings from a study investigating young Swedish learners' extramural (out-of-school) contact with English. In contemporary Sweden, the influx of English is great and research has shown that extramural contact with English correlates positively with students' proficiency in English (Olsson, 2011; Sundqvist, 2009; Sylvén, 2004). While Sylvén (2004) investigates type and amount of involvement in extramural English activities among upper secondary students and Sundqvist (2009) as well as Olsson (2011) among 9th graders, little on the same topic is known about younger learners. However, in a nationwide survey, more than half of Swedish 5th-graders indicate that they have learned English as much or more outside of school than in school (Skolverket, 2004), but empirical studies on the topic remain scarce. Based on data collected from young learners ($N = 112$; grade 4; age 10), this paper presents results regarding their type and amount of extramural language activities in English as well as in Swedish and other languages. Previous research has shown that digital gaming may contribute to L2 English learning, in particular with regard to vocabulary (Cobb & Horst, 2011; Miller & Hegelheimer, 2006; Ranalli, 2008; Sundqvist & Sylvén, 2012). Therefore, the first focus of our presentation is on these young learners' L2 English language-related use of computers, for instance in playing digital games. A comparison is made between digital gaming habits in English and Swedish. The second focus is on analyses of playing digital games from the perspectives of gender and the learners' first languages. The final focus is on learner motivation and self-assessed L2 English proficiency.

Keywords: young learners, computer-assisted language learning, digital games, motivation, extramural English, informal learning, second language acquisition.

1. Introduction

In contemporary Sweden, the influx of English is great. Unlike many other European countries, Sweden broadcasts English-speaking films and TV-productions in the

---

* Contact author: pia.sundqvist@kau.se

original language with Swedish subtitles. In France and Germany, for instance, English-speaking productions are instead dubbed. Other sources of English are music, the Internet, and digital games. Thus, it is possible for people of all ages to come into contact with authentic English on a daily basis. Furthermore, English is the first foreign language (FL) encountered in school, where it is an obligatory subject introduced at the latest in grade 4 (Malmberg, 2000). It is fair to say, then, that English has a particular status in Swedish society and in recent years there has even been a debate on whether English should be regarded as a second language (L2) rather than as a FL (see, e.g., Hyltenstam, 2002; Viberg, 2000). Empirical studies among secondary and upper secondary learners have shown that extramural English (EE) correlates positively with proficiency (Olsson, 2011; Sundqvist, 2009; Sylvén, 2004), but studies on primary school learners remain scarce. However, in a nationwide survey, more than half of Swedish 5th-graders indicate that they have learned English as much or more outside of school than in school (Skolverket, 2004). In sum, L2 English among young learners and out-of-school factors that might affect learning is a topic that calls for more research, not only nationally, but also internationally.

2. Method

2.1. Participants and data

The present study is based on data collected from young Swedish learners ($N = 112$; grade 4; age 10). A questionnaire that mapped their EE activities as well as provided information about other variables (e.g., experiences of traveling abroad, L1, motivation, and self-assessed English ability) were filled out at school. Then, a language diary was introduced which was to be filled in at home during one week with the purpose of yielding information about both type and amount of extramural activities (reading, watching TV or films, playing digital games, etc.). Similar information was filled in for Swedish and any other language(s) that the learners might come into contact with. The teachers used this diary as "English homework" that particular week. For the learners who forgot to fill it in, the teachers arranged time daily to do so in school.

2.2. Results: extramural activities in English, Swedish, and other languages

Based on data from the language diary, Table 1 shows the order of popularity of the extramural activities in English and Swedish. Watching TV is the most popular activity both for English and Swedish, whereas least time is spent on reading newspapers and/or magazines and 'other'. As for EE, digital game play is popular, and more time is spent on gaming in English as compared to doing so in Swedish. Independent samples t-test for gender revealed statistically significant differences for the total time spent on extramural English (boys: 11.5 hrs/w; girls: 5.1 hrs/w; $p < .01$), for playing digital games (boys: 3.4 hrs/w; girls: .4 hrs/w; $p < .01$), and for watching films (boys: 1.8 hrs/w; girls: .6 hrs/w; $p < .01$). With regard to extramural Swedish, there were statistically significant differences between the boys and the girls for the total time (boys: 8.0 hrs/w; girls: 11.5 hrs/w; $p < .05$) and for using the Internet (boys: .5 hrs/w; girls: 2.4 hrs/w; $p < .05$). As for extramural activities in other languages, the reports were so few that they come across as negligible.

Table 1. Extramural English and Swedish activities in order of popularity and in total

Order	Extramural English		Extramural Swedish	
	Activity	Hours/week	Activity	Hours/week
1	TV	2.3	TV	4.3
2	Digital games**	1.4	Internet*	1.8
3	Music	1.4	Books	1.1
4	Films**	1.0	Films	1.0
5	Internet	1.0	Digital games	.8
6	Books	.1	Music	.7
7	Newspapers/magazines	.1	Newspapers/magazines	.4
8	Other	.1	Other	.2
	Total**	7.2	Total*	10.3

*Significant gender-related difference at the .05 level.
**Significant gender-related difference at the .01 level.

2.3. Three digital game groups

Since previous research has shown that digital gaming may influence L2 English proficiency (see, e.g., Cobb & Horst, 2011; Kuppens, 2010; Sundqvist, 2011; Sylvén & Sundqvist, 2012), we divided our sample into three digital game groups based on how much time the learners had recorded for game play in their language diaries, see Table 2. Digital game group 1 (non-gamers) did not report any time at all for playing digital games. Digital game group 2 (moderate gamers) played some but less than four hours per week. Finally, in digital game group 3 we find the frequent gamers, here defined as those who reported playing digital games in English for four hours or more.

The distribution of boys and girls in the groups is shown in Table 3. We will discuss gender further in the section that follows, where we also address L1, motivation, and the learners' self-assessed level of English proficiency.

Table 2. Three digital game groups

Digital game group	N	Time interval (hours/week)		Mean (hours/week)	SD
		From	To		
1 (non-gamers)	31	0	0	0	0
2 (moderate gamers)	27	> 0	< 4	1.5	1.1
3 (frequent gamers)	8	≥ 4	≤ 14	6.6	3.2
Total	66	≥ 0	≤ 14	1.4	2.4

Table 3. Gender distribution in the digital game groups

Digital game group	Total		Boys		Girls	
	N	%	N	%	N	%
1 (non-gamers)	31	47	4	13	27	87
2 (moderate gamers)	27	41	11	41	16	59
3 (frequent gamers)	8	12	7	88	1	12
Total	66	100	22	33	44	67

3. Discussion

First, the gender distribution in the digital game groups (see Table 3) is such that in the non-gamers group the vast majority are girls, in the moderate gamers group the division between boys and girls is fairly equal, and among the frequent gamers all are boys but one. As has been shown elsewhere (Sundqvist & Sylvén, 2012; Sylvén & Sundqvist, 2012), gender differences are not only apparent regarding amount of gaming but also regarding preferred game types/genres. Girls seem to prefer single-player games, whereas boys primarily engage in the more interactive types of game referred to as massively multiplayer online role-playing games (MMORPG).

Second, in our sample, the majority of the learners have Swedish as their L1. However, eight learners (12%) have another L1. When we examined the distribution of students according to L1 in the digital game groups, the ratio of students who had another L1 than Swedish was 10% in the non-gamers group, 7% in the moderate gamers group, and 38% in the frequent gamers group. Thus, when the three groups are compared with regard to L1, learners with another L1 than Swedish are clearly overrepresented in the frequent gamers group.

Third, motivation is important for all learning, not least language learning (Dörnyei, 2001). In one of the items in the questionnaire, the informants were asked to rate the extent to which they agreed with the statement 'English is interesting', which we view as an indicator of motivation. The results revealed that all the learners in the frequent gamers group 'agreed' or 'agreed strongly'. Although a large proportion of the learners in the non-gamer and moderate gamer groups also thought English was interesting, the proportion was not as large as for the frequent gamers. In fact, the proportion of learners who 'disagreed' or 'disagreed strongly' was largest among the non-gamers, indicating that they were the least motivated ones.

Finally, the learners were asked to rate how good they thought they are at English. Results showed that, overall, the learners self-assess their L2 English proficiency as rather high. At least half of the learners in each digital game group consider themselves to be 'good' or 'very good' at English. The non-gamers include the largest proportion of positive assessments, but on the other hand there are also learners in this group who responded that they are 'very bad' at English. In comparison, none of the frequent gamers rated themselves as 'very bad'.

4. Conclusions

The present study focuses on 10-year-old learners in primary school and the results indicate that already at this early age, children are exposed to and engage in EE activities extensively. The findings reported here corroborate previous studies on secondary and upper secondary school learners (Olsson, 2011; Sundqvist, 2009; Sylvén, 2004) in that the boys engage in more digital gaming in English whereas the girls opt for social interaction on the computer in Swedish. We have also shown that the students in the frequent gamers group seem to be more motivated to learn English than those in the other two digital game groups. With regard to self-assessed L2 English proficiency, the majority of the young learners seem confident. Thus, the pattern unveiled for older learners indicating a clear relationship between digital gaming, gender, and self-assessed English proficiency (cf. Sundqvist, 2009; Sylvén & Sundqvist, 2012) seems to hold also for this sample of 10-year-olds.

Acknowledgements. We would like to thank the Erik Wellander Foundation and the Center for Language and Literature in Education (CSL), Karlstad University, for funding our study.

References

Cobb, T., & Horst, M. (2011). Does Word Coach coach words? *CALICO Journal, 28*(3), 639-661.
Dörnyei, Z. (2001). *Teaching and researching motivation.* Harlow: Longman.
Hyltenstam, K. (2002). Engelskundervisning i Sverige. *Mål i mun - Förslag till handlingsprogram för svenska språket. SOU 2002:27. Bilagor* (pp. 45-72). Stockholm: Regeringskansliet.
Kuppens, A. H. (2010). Incidental foreign language acquisition from media exposure. *Learning, Media and Technology, 35*(1), 65-85. doi: 10.1080/17439880903561876
Malmberg, P. (2000). De moderna språken i grundskolan och gymnasieskolan från 1960. *Språk Gy2000:18. Grundskola och gymnasieskola. Kursplaner, betygskriterier och kommentarer* (pp. 7-26). Stockholm: Skolverket.
Miller, M., & Hegelheimer, V. (2006). The SIMs meet ESL. Incorporating authentic computer simulation games into the language classroom. *Interactive Technology & Smart Edcuation, 3*(4), 311-328.
Olsson, E. (2011). *"Everything I read on the Internet is in English" - On the impact of extramural English on Swedish 16-year-old pupils' writing proficiency.* (Licentiate thesis). University of Gothenburg, Gothenburg.
Ranalli, J. (2008). Learning English with *The Sims*: exploiting authentic computer simulation games for L2 learning. *Computer Assisted Language Learning, 21*(5), 441-455. doi: 10.1080/09588220802447859
Skolverket. (2004). Nationella utvärderingen av grundskolan 2003: huvudrapport - svenska/svenska som andra språk, engelska, matematik och undersökningen i årskurs 5. *Skolverkets rapport 251.* Stockholm: Skolverket.

Sundqvist, P. (2009). *Extramural English matters: Out-of-school English and its impact on Swedish ninth graders' oral proficiency and vocabulary.* (Doctoral dissertation). Karlstad University, Karlstad.

Sundqvist, P. (2011). A possible path to progress: Out-of-school English language learners in Sweden. In P. Benson, & H. Reinders (Eds.), *Beyond the language classroom* (pp. 106-118). Basingstoke: Palgrave Macmillan.

Sundqvist, P., & Sylvén, L. K. (2012). World of VocCraft: Computer games and Swedish learners' L2 vocabulary. In H. Reinders (Ed.), *Computer games in language learning and teaching* (pp. 189-208). Basingstoke: Palgrave Macmillan.

Sylvén, L. K. (2004). *Teaching in English or English teaching? On the effects of content and language integrated learning on Swedish learners' incidental vocabulary acquisition.* (Doctoral dissertation). University of Gothenburg, Gothenburg.

Sylvén, L. K., & Sundqvist, P. (2012). Gaming as extramural English L2 learning and L2 proficiency among young learners. *ReCALL, 24*(3), 302-321. doi: 10.1017/s095834401200016x

Viberg, Å. (2000). Tvåspråkighet och inlärning av språk i och utanför skolan. *Språk 2000:18. Kursplaner, betygskriterier och kommentarer* (pp. 27-41). Stockholm: Skolverket.

UNIVERSITY OF
GOTHENBURG

Scoring Rubrics and Google Scripts: A Means to Smoothly Provide Language Learners with Fast Corrective Feedback and Grades

Sylvie Thouësny*

Independent Researcher, Dublin, Ireland

Abstract. Language teachers, as one might expect, are often confronted with the task of assessing and grading students' assignments, which should ideally be addressed with respect to not only reliability and validity, but also functionality. Based on Knoch's (2011) taxonomy features with regards to design and development of writing assessments, an analytic approach was devised to assign scores to a certain amount of independent aspects of language learners' performance through the means of specific rubrics. The rubrics, elaborated with the graders and students in mind, describe the rating of the various tasks intermediate learners of French had to undertake. Following a brief description of one assignment, this short paper highlights the significance of following the scoring grids to maintain a relatively constant grading style across students and teachers alike. Additionally, it illustrates how Google documents and forms, used in conjunction with simple and undemanding scripts, assisted in the process of correcting and providing students with timely feedback.

Keywords: scoring rubrics, Google scripts, corrective feedback, language learning.

1. Introduction

Responding to Yancey's (1999) call for a "fourth wave" of writing assessment (p. 500), i.e., a call for assessment that moves beyond multiple-choice questions, scored essay tests, and portfolio assessments, Wardle and Roozen (2012) propose an ecological model of writing assessment that considers both the vertical and horizontal dimensions of students' development. In short, they emphasise the idea that "the breadth of students' [...] literate experiences – in *and* out of school – impacts their ability to 'do' academic literacy tasks" (Wardle & Roozen, 2012, p. 107, emphasis in original). While the authors' reflection seems appropriate and full of common sense, adapting their model

---

* Contact author: sylvie.thouesny@icall-research.net

In L. Bradley & S. Thouësny (Eds.), *CALL: Using, Learning, Knowing, EUROCALL Conference, Gothenburg, Sweden, 22-25 August 2012, Proceedings* (pp. 286-291). © Research-publishing.net Dublin 2012

of writing assessment would be a rather complicated endeavour as it implies including data from different modules and other non-canonical texts from outside the academic structures.

Assessing learners' writing is a challenging task for teachers, as it involves serious considerations on how to evaluate the learners' ability to write. As Behizadeh and Engelhard (2011) reported, "[i]t was much easier to objectively score multiple-choice tests, as compared to complex writing samples" (p. 202). Whichever approach is used, one aim of assessing and evaluating written language is to diagnose learners' weaknesses and strengths, in other words, to "identify those areas in which a student needs further help" (Alderson, Clapham, & Wall, 1995, p. 12). Knoch (2011) further points out that "integral to diagnostic writing assessment is the rating scale" (p. 81).

Weigle (2002) discusses factors that should be considered when designing rating scales and scoring rubrics, such as who is going to use them and how the scores will be reported (pp. 122-124). Rubrics are generally defined as "systematic scoring guidelines to evaluate students' performance [...] through the use of a detailed description of performance standards" (Zimmaro, 2007, p. 1). Knoch (2011) observes that "no currently available theory can serve by itself as a basis for the design of a rating scale for writing for diagnostic assessment" (p. 90). To remedy, she proposes a taxonomy of features – accuracy, fluency, complexity, mechanics, cohesion, coherence, reader/writer interaction, and content – that could be used as a basis for the design of a rating scale (Knoch, 2011, p. 91).

Based on Zimmaro's (2007) practical steps in designing rubrics to grade a student's performance, and Knoch's (2011) taxonomy features, this short paper illustrates how rubrics combined with Google scripts help provide language learners with fast corrective feedback and grades.

2. Educational setting and assignment

Students were enrolled at university level in various Bachelor degrees in which the French language was either an obligatory or a facultative component of their formation. As part of their assignment, they had to experience French autonomously and were asked to write an account of their activities as well as to reflect on their learning outcomes. A minimum of 800 words with at least eight different entries was imposed on students.

3. Elaboration of the scoring rubrics

Learners' written documents were assessed according to five criteria carrying equal weight: (1) content, (2) vocabulary, (3) conjugation, (4) syntax, and (5) reflection. The first category identified whether the texts provided were adapted to the task and whether the instructions were respected. The second criterion of assessment acknowledged the lexical diversity, whether the vocabulary was sufficient for explaining the chosen activities. The third criterion identified whether the verbs were correctly conjugated with an appropriate tense. The fourth criterion evaluated the syntax of the sentences, whether the structures were simple or complex. Finally, the last criterion examined the breadth of the learners' reflection and whether it was thoughtfully considered.

All criteria were rated on a 5-point rating scale in accordance with the university's regulations[*], i.e., Fail (<40%), H3 (40-49%), H2.2 (50-59%), H2.1 (60-69%), and H1 (>=70%), as illustrated below with the "reflection" criterion (Table 1). Note that the original rubrics were in French, but were translated into English for the purpose of this publication.

Table 1. Scoring rubrics

	Fail (<40%)	H3 (40-49%)	H2.2 (50-59%)	H2.1 (60-69%)	H1 (>=70%)
Reflection	No reflection on the language learning is present. Newfound skills cannot be identified.	Reflection on language learning is inept. Newfound skills can be identified.	Reflection on language learning is still inept, but newfound skills are clearly identifiable.	Good reflection on language learning and newfound skills are clearly identifiable.	Excellent reflection on language learning and newfound skills are clearly identifiable.

4. Template, form and script to report grades

Google documents, forms, and scripts were used to assess the learners' written account of their learning experience, as well as to provide them with their respective scores. The template, as illustrated below in Figure 1, was created with the same word-processing tool. The shaped document served as a starting point for each student, and variables – preceded with the @ sign – were automatically filled in depending on the teacher's scoring.

Figure 1. Template

---

[*] Marks and Standards. (2012). Retrieved from: http://www4.dcu.ie/sites/default/files/registry/pdfs/M-S_version-2012.1.0.pdf

The Google form (Figure 2) enabled the assessment of the written texts in accordance with the scoring grades. Once the data was entered into the form, and that the form was saved, the data was sent to the spreadsheet that was automatically generated by the system.

Figure 2. Form

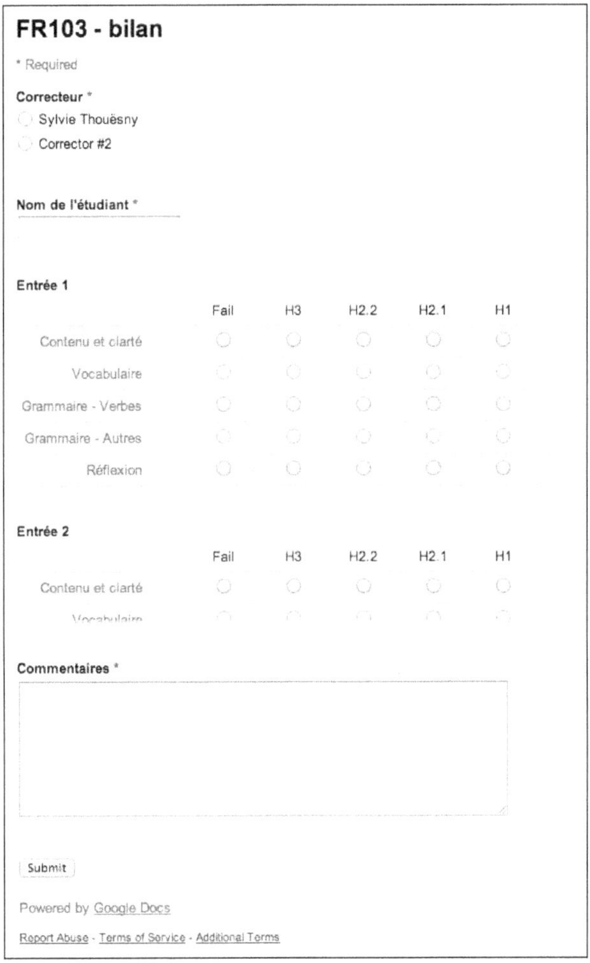

```
FR103 - bilan
* Required
Correcteur *
  ○ Sylvie Thouèsny
  ○ Corrector #2

Nom de l'étudiant *
_____

Entrée 1
                        Fail    H3    H2.2    H2.1    H1
Contenu et clarté        ○      ○      ○       ○      ○
Vocabulaire              ○      ○      ○       ○      ○
Grammaire - Verbes       ○      ○      ○       ○      ○
Grammaire - Autres       ○      ○      ○       ○      ○
Réflexion                ○      ○      ○       ○      ○

Entrée 2
                        Fail    H3    H2.2    H2.1    H1
Contenu et clarté        ○      ○      ○       ○      ○
Vocabulaire              ○      ○      ○       ○      ○

Commentaires *
[                                              ]

[Submit]

Powered by Google Docs
Report Abuse - Terms of Service - Additional Terms
```

The aim of the script was then to get the last data entered in the active spreadsheet so as to fill the information into the template. Each variable in the template was replaced with its corresponding data, as illustrated in Figure 3 below[*].

---

[*] A more detailed account on the script can be found on my website: http://blog.icall-research. net/2011/10/23/template-and-script-to-report-grades-of-learners-of-french

Figure 3. Script

```
37    //insert information into template from spreadsheet
38    copy_body.replaceText("@comments", comments);
39    copy_body.replaceText("@corrector", corrector);
40    copy_body.replaceText("@student", student);
41
42    //retrieve results per question
43    var sum = 0;//to compute average
44    var count = 0;//to compute average
45    var question_number = 1;
46    for (var i = 0; i <= index_comment; i++) {
47      if (data[0][i] in levels || data[0][i] == ""){
48        var index = 0;
49        for (var j = 1; j <= amount_of_controls; j++) {
50          //replace text in template by result e.g. "Q11" => "H2.2" or 0 if question not answered
51          if(data[0][i+index] == "" && question_number<=entries_required){
52            copy_body.replaceText("@q"+question_number+j, 0);
53            count++;
54          }
55          else if(data[0][i+index] == "" && question_number>entries_required) {
56            copy_body.replaceText("@q"+question_number+j, "-");
57          }
58          else {
59            copy_body.replaceText("@q"+question_number+j, data[0][i+index]);
60            sum = sum + levels[data[0][i+index]];
61            count++;
62          }
63          index++;
64        }
65        question_number++;
66        i=i+index-1;
67      }
68    }
```

The result was as follows (Figure 4):

Figure 4. Result

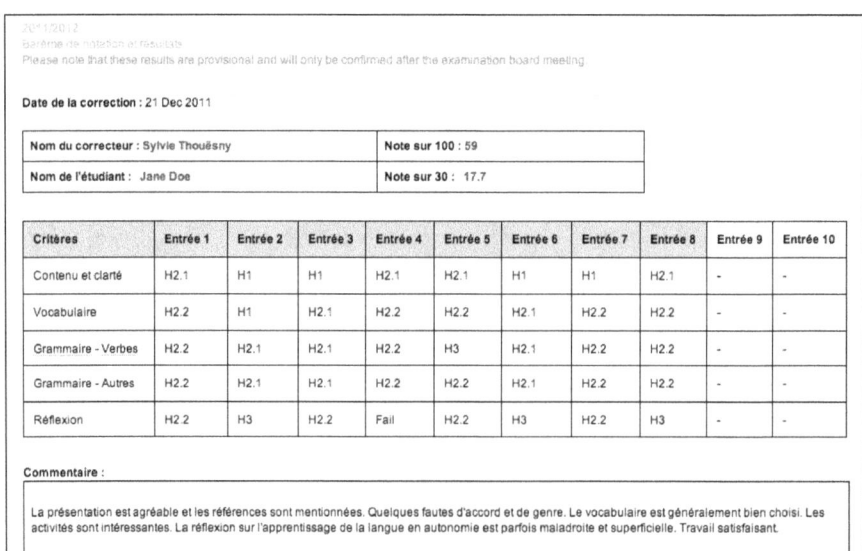

Each score sheet was accompanied with the score grids so that students knew exactly what the rating on each section implied. This sheet could then have been shared with the student through Google Drive (formerly Google Docs) or sent via email.

5. Discussion and conclusion

This short paper illustrated how scoring grids combined with the use of Google documents, forms, and scripts would assist in assessing and scoring texts written by learners as a response to an open task. Although Kulhavy (1977) reported that "delaying the presentation of feedback for a day or more leads to significant increases in what students remember on a retention test" (p. 214), more recent research has highlighted the significance of timely feedback (e.g., Denton, Madden, Roberts, & Rowe, 2008). By following a scoring grid and using a script that automatically fills in a template, it is manageable to have a rapid and constant grading across students and tasks, which means that variations due to tiredness or subjectivity can be easily avoided. It is nevertheless always pertinent to perform a second rating by another rater, which will indicate fairness to students (see Penny and Johnson (2011) for a classification of resolution procedures in scoring writing assessment).

References

Alderson, J. C., Clapham, C., & Wall, D. (1995). *Language test construction and evaluation.* Cambridge: Cambridge University Press.

Behizadeh, N., & Engelhard, J. G. (2011). Historical view of the influences of measurement and writing theories on the practice of writing assessment in the United States. A*ssessing Writing, 16*(3), 189-211. doi:10.1016/j.asw.2011.03.001

Denton, P., Madden, J., Roberts, M., & Rowe, P. (2008). Students' response to traditional and computer-assisted formative feedback: A comparative case study. *British Journal of Educational Technology, 39*(3), 486-500. doi:10.1111/j.1467-8535.2007.00745.x

Knoch, U. (2011). Rating scales for diagnostic assessment of writing: what should they look like and where should the criteria come from? *Assessing Writing, 16*(2), 81-96. doi:10.1016/j.asw.2011.02.003

Kulhavy, R. W. (1977). Feedback in written instruction. *Review of Educational Research, 47*(2), 211-232. Retrieved from http://www.jstor.org/stable/1170128

Penny, J. A., & Johnson, R. L. (2011). The accuracy of performance task scores after resolution of rater disagreement: a Monte Carlo study. *Assessing Writing, 16*(4), 221-236. doi:10.1016/j.asw.2011.06.001

Wardle, E., & Roozen, K. (2012). Addressing the complexity of writing development: toward an ecological model of assessment. *Assessing Writing, 17*(2), 106-119. doi:10.1016/j.asw.2012.01.001

Weigle, S. C. (2002). *Assessing writing.* Cambridge: Cambridge University Press.

Yancey, K. B. (1999). Looking back as we look forward: historicizing writing assessment. *College Composition and Communication, 50*(3), 483-503. Retrieved from http://www.jstor.org/stable/358862

Zimmaro, D. M. (2007). *Using rubrics to grade student performance.* Austin: University of Texas at Austin, Centre for teaching and learning. Retrieved from http://ctl.utexas.edu/assets/Evaluation--Assessment/Using-Rubrics-to-Grade-Student-Performance-10-15-07.pdf

UNIVERSITY OF
GOTHENBURG

What's Wrong with Welsh Adjectives?

Cornelia Tschichold*

Department of English Language and Literature, Swansea University, Swansea, Great Britain

Abstract. Why are some words harder to learn than others? In a long-term CASLR (computer-assisted second language research) study, a vocabulary flashcard program that employs spaced repetition for explicit vocabulary training was used in order to arrive at data on the difficulty of individual words. The vocabulary content of a beginner's Welsh course was periodically entered into the program as one learner progressed through the course and studied vocabulary with the help of the electronic flashcards. The Welsh words were trained both receptively and productively, and in a few cases also as part of a short phrase or sentence. The program automatically collects statistical information for each individual electronic card, including the number of times each card had been seen. Data was collected for an initial period of two years of non-intensive learning, and the resulting statistics for the individual flashcards allow an interesting insight into the very highly variable number of repetitions needed for each word.

Keywords: CASLR, vocabulary, electronic flashcard programs, spaced repetition.

1. Background

Vocabulary flashcard programs have the crucial advantage of providing immediate feedback to the learner (Nagata, 1993). This is more effective than delayed feedback, and is especially suitable for procedural and conceptual knowledge building, including verbal tasks. Immediate feedback is also better for low-achieving learners and for beginners (Shute, 2008). Learners are normally aware of the need to study vocabulary, so there is a natural market for software that promises to help them do just this. However, many commercially available applications are poorly designed and contain poor quality content. The multimedia advantage of CALL and MALL (mobile-assisted language learning) is rarely used well, as any critical look at some of these applications will show. Poor illustrations abound, and mistakes are easily found. Of course it is quite easy to add a good illustration for a noun such as *sheep*,

---

* Contact author: c.tschichold@swansea.ac.uk

but a preposition such as *by* is considerably harder to illustrate well. For this reason, the experiment described here does not contain any pictorial material at all, despite the fact that the software used allows the addition of both picture and sound files. The software used is VTrain (www.vtrain.net), a flexible system based on the Leitner learning principle of spaced repetition.

2. Learning Welsh vocabulary

A long-term, single-subject study on learning Welsh vocabulary was started in 2009. The learner was a complete beginner at the start of the course and had very little contact with Welsh outside of class, despite living in Wales. Welsh is natively spoken by a minority of the population in Wales, and while many road signs are bilingual, English clearly dominates most Welsh inhabitants' lives in almost all respects. The learner entered all the vocabulary contained in the Welsh language course into the VTrain database as the classroom-based course progressed. The taught element of the course was a non-intensive beginners' class of one hour a week (30 weeks per academic year). The course material ("Cymraeg i oedolion" – Welsh for adults) consisted of the course book and CD-ROMs containing audio files of much of the material in the course book. The course material takes a broadly communicative approach to teaching. One lesson in the book typically contains between 20 and 30 items of new vocabulary and was covered in two classroom lessons. In addition to this, the learner normally spent a few short (15-20 minutes) sessions every week working on the vocabulary that had been entered into the VTrain database, with longer breaks over the summer.

The software was set up with 10 'boxes' for the word cards, with a one-day interval from the first to the second box, and roughly doubling the interval length for every subsequent box. These intervals provided the guideline for revision. With the increase in the number of cards in the database, the number of word cards due for revision increased as well, and in the latter half of the training period, there were always cards due or overdue for revision. The boxes were set up to alternate between Welsh to English and English to Welsh questions.

Word cards progress through the system if the user types in the correct answer, or return to the first box if the learner's answer is not correct. Answers are evaluated by simple string matching, thus only recognized to be correct if they are spelled exactly right. If the question is "What is the Welsh for: *some time*?", the correct answer is "rhywbryd". The following forms are not recognized "rywbryd", "rhwybryd", "rhywbrud" and cause the word card to be returned to the first box. In the direction of L1, the difficulties for the learner are somewhat different. To the question "What is the English for: *dechrau*?", only the string "to start" is accepted as correct; the variants "start", "begin", or "to begin" are not recognized as correct and also cause the word to be returned to the first box.

3. Data collection and analysis

After two years, the learner had covered the first 30 lessons of the Welsh course and the VTrain database contained over 900 cards. At this point, the statistical information that is compiled by the system was retrieved. For every flashcard, VTrain records the total number of repetitions, the total numbers of correct and of incorrect answers, and the highest 'box' the flashcard reached. For the present study, all double entries, phrases, and items that were entered in order to practice grammatical aspects were deleted, so for example, the data for *go* was kept, but the card data for *I went* was deleted. This resulted in data from a total of 549 word cards. The averages of the statistics for all cards are given in Table 1.

Table 1. Average number of repetitions across all word classes

Average total number of repetitions	29.13
Average number of correct answers	17.50
Average number of incorrect answers	11.71
Average of highest 'box' reached	7.26

It should be kept in mind that as the system was set up with ten 'boxes', every word that ends up in the last box will have accumulated a minimum of ten repetitions. On the other hand, few cards had actually reached the last box at this point. The 549 single words were then sorted into word classes, with the distribution shown in Table 2.

Table 2. Number of words in each word class

verbs	72
nouns	278
adjectives	89
adverbs	33
numerals	20
other (prep, conj, dem, etc.)	67
TOTAL	549

The number of repetitions was then broken down by word class, resulting in the averages seen in Table 3.

Table 3. Average number of repetitions for individual word classes

	NOUN	VERB	ADJ	ADV	FUNCTION	ALL WORDS
Average total	12.37	39.64	40.30	31.70	39.60	29.13
Average correct	9.34	20.43	20.87	17.91	24.26	17.50
Average wrong	3.08	19.21	19.44	14.09	16.23	11.71
Average highest	6.99	7.66	6.98	6.94	7.39	7.26

This analysis showed that nouns were the easiest word class to learn, with adjectives the hardest. Adjectives are often taught in semantic groups, e.g., colours or in pairs of antonyms, a presentation mode that is not conducive to learning (Tinkham, 1997). The next step involved a closer look at those words that had particularly high numbers of repetitions, as these clearly presented more difficulties to the learner. Analysis of words with 50 or more repetitions showed that certain spelling patterns correlate with increased difficulty as measured by the number of repetitions needed by the learner. Because completely accurate spelling is critical for the program to recognize the learner's answer as correct, it could of course be argued that exact spelling is given far too much weight in this context, and that the learner would ideally be given partial credits for otherwise correct answers.

4. Concluding remarks

One interesting finding is that the spelling of Welsh words seems to present a major obstacle to the beginning learner despite the fact that Welsh is said to have a shallow orthography, which should therefore be relatively unproblematic to acquire. Another conclusion this long-term study suggests is that learners need considerably more repetitions than the figures of five to twelve typically found in the literature on vocabulary acquisition (cf. Nation, 2001). Despite the obvious shortcomings on the part of the software used, the analysis sheds some new light on the complexities of the long-term process of incremental vocabulary learning.

References

Nagata, N. (1993). Intelligent Computer Feedback for Second Language Instruction. *Modern Language Journal, 77*(3), 330-338. doi: 10.1111/j.1540-4781.1993.tb01980.x

Nation, I. S. P. (2001). *Learning Vocabulary in Another Language*. Cambridge: Cambridge University Press.

Shute, V. J. (2008). Focus on Formative Feedback. *Review of Educational Research, 78*(1), 153-189. doi: 10.3102/0034654307313795

Tinkham, T. (1997). The effects of semantic and thematic clustering on the learning of second language vocabulary. *Second Language Research, 13*(2), 138-163. doi: 10.1191/026765897672376469

UNIVERSITY OF GOTHENBURG

Mobile Learning in Foreign Language Learning: Podcasts and Lexicon Acquisition in the Elementary Instruction of Italian

Eva Maria Unterrainer[*]

University of Innsbruck, Innsbruck, Austria

Abstract. This paper illustrates the research design (including the pilot study) of a work-in-progress study aimed at examining the potential of bilingual podcasts for the vocabulary acquisition in Italian as an L3 in the Austrian school context for beginning learners. The longitudinal study tries to link findings of the Lexical Approach (Lewis, 1993, 1997) and the Mental Lexicon (Aitchison, 2005) by taking into account lexical learning and the importance of spoken language for acquisition and by connecting them to the opportunities offered by podcasts as a means of mobile (micro) learning (cf. Hug, 2007a, 2007b, 2010a, 2010b; Hug & Friesen, 2007). In order to investigate the effects of podcasts on the lexical acquisition of Italian as an L3 two groups of participants will be analysed: (a) an experimental group (students use self-made, bilingual podcasts – German-Italian – to learn the lexical items), and (b) a control group (students are presented with lexical input without using podcasts). During the study, classroom teaching of the two groups will be observed in order to conduct a third-party-observation (cf. Bortz & Döring, 2009) of the participants and to compare and contrast their lexical input. A pre- and a post-test of lexical acquisition will be carried out at the beginning and the end of the observation period. As the use of podcasts as a tool of mobile learning might considerably change the vocabulary learning strategies of the participants in the experimental group, a questionnaire at the beginning and the end of the study will be applied in addition. It is assumed that, due to the Lexical Approach and the Mental Lexicon and enhanced by the mobile nature of the podcasts, the experimental group will achieve a higher increase of Italian lexicon than the control group. However, the executed pilot study has revealed weaknesses in the research design, which have to be adapted for the final case study.

Keywords: lexicon, mobile learning, Italian.

---

[*] Contact author: eva.unterrainer@uibk.ac.at

1. Introduction

Digital media play an increasingly important part in our lives; the property and accordingly the use of digital media increase constantly. This case study aims at trying to take advantage of the students' use of media such as mobile phones and iPod/MP3 players in their leisure time for the learning of languages. Specifically, students will learn the lexicon in their first year of learning Italian as a foreign language at school by using self-created audio podcasts; as Lewis (1993) has already suggested with his "lexical approach", the focus lies on listening: "[…] a well-balanced learning programme will, in the early stages, place great emphasis on receptive skills, in particular, listening" (p. 8). Previous research has tended to focus on reading (cf. Read, 2000, p. 47) and there is little research and knowledge of how vocabulary is learned from listening (cf. Schmitt, 2010, p. 38). Furthermore, "[o]ne of the main shortcomings of …[some vocabulary research] is that it has focused attention on the acquisition of vocabulary divorced from use […]. Many of the subjects tested in the methodological comparisons were not real language learners, the time-scale studied was short […], and the vocabularies learned were actually quite small […]." (Meara, 1999, p. 565, cited in Schmitt, 2010, p. 43). Therefore, this case study aims at bridging this research gap and in addition at including the concept of mobile learning.

2. Mobile (micro) learning in the language classroom

The term "microlearning" as such is relatively young; Hug and Friesen (2007) state that the term has been in use for only about ten years, even though the underlying concept partially goes back far into the past (p. 16). Microlearning contains various forms of learning: informal learning activities in the context of social software applications, incidental learning with digital media, etc. (cf. Hug, 2010a, p. 202; Hug, 2010b, p. 200), but it is not simply equated with informal and lifelong learning (cf. Hug & Friesen, 2007, p. 18). Microlearning in the broadest sense can be viewed rather as "learning with micro-content" (ibid.), that is, learning with small individual units; in summary, microlearning can be understood as "special moments or episodes of learning while dealing with specific tasks or content, but engaging in small but conscious steps. These moments, episodes and processes may vary depending on the pedagogies and media involved, but the measures of scale of the amount of time and content involved can be made fairly constant" (Hug & Friesen, 2007, p. 18).

This leads us to a possible combination of microlearning and mobile learning. The term "'mobile learning' is frequently used to refer to the use of handheld technologies enabling the learner to be 'on the move', providing anytime, anywhere access for learning" (Price, 2007, p. 33). Hug (2010a) calls this a narrow sense of mobile learning, in which mobile devices and software applications are at the centre. More broadly, mobile learning is not only about the transfer of content using mobile devices, it rather means "die Befähigung zur Aneignung und Entwicklung jenes Wissens, das für erfolgreiches Handeln in veränderlichen Lagen und Kontexten […] erforderlich ist"[*] (ibid., p. 200). Therefore, mobile microlearning can emphasise vocabulary learning instead of teaching; the latter is too focused nowadays (cf. Nation, 2011).

3. Research design

The present paper is intended to investigate the effect of the use of podcasts on the lexical acquisition of Italian as an L3. The following two groups of test subjects will participate in the case study:
- Experimental group: students who learn the vocabulary with the help of self-made (German – Italian) audio podcasts;
- Control group: students who learn the vocabulary without audio podcasts.

The case study tries to answer the following question: What differences in a) vocabulary and b) used vocabulary learning strategies arise between students who learn the Italian vocabulary with audio files, and those who learn these without audio files?

To answer this question – as part of the 4-month-pilot study[**] – written surveys on vocabulary learning strategies and a vocabulary test have been used, as will be presented in the following.

3.1. Written survey on vocabulary learning strategies
As an instrument of written survey the questionnaire was chosen (cf. Bortz & Döring, 2009, p. 236) to investigate the applied vocabulary learning strategies of the students. It mostly follows the questionnaire designed by Neveling (2004) as part of her dissertation. However, the questionnaire was adapted for this study and the scale was changed from a dichotomous to an ordinal scale. At the beginning of the school year a detailed version was used, at the end of the first semester the questionnaire was reduced and new aspects were included.

3.2. Vocabulary test
To state differences in terms of vocabulary between the experimental and control group the "Vocabulary Knowledge Scale" (VKS) by Paribakht and Wesche (1997) was chosen. Students can thereby assess a word presented in written form on a scale from I to V, where I stands for full unfamiliarity of the given word, and V for the ability to correctly use the word grammatically and semantically in a sentence. For the analysis, this means that students are given a point for ticking Category I. If a semantically

---

[*] Translation: "the ability to acquire and develop the knowledge which is necessary for successful behavior in varying situations and contexts, and in changing learning spaces".

[**] The real case study will be carried out in the following school year (September 2012 – July 2013).

appropriate and grammatically correct sentence was offered for the tested word, the maximum of five points would be given. For the present study with 30 Italian words, this means that students can achieve a minimum of 30 points and a maximum of 150 points.

Basically the VKS assesses the development of vocabulary in the context of experiments and seems to be a reliable and valid "measure of incidental vocabulary acquisition [...]" (Read, 2000, p. 135). The following chapters provide insights into the pilot study and draw first conclusions for the "real" case study.

4. Insights into the pilot study

The pilot study involved a total of 36 students, but only 30 students were present at the time of the two data collections and therefore only their data was used.

Regarding the learning strategies, some differences, which have been proven by SPSS using the Mann-Whitney U-test[*], will be presented (cf. Unterrainer, 2012). At the beginning of the school year the following differences between the two groups were found:
- Speaking out loudly helps the experimental group significantly more ($p = .029$) to learn collocations (e.g., *lavarsi i denti*);
- The students of the experimental group significantly more often call ($p = .011$) the corresponding Italian words to mind when they observe their environment;
- The control group speaks significantly ($p = .018$) more often with Italian-speaking people on vacation.

At the end of the pilot study the following differences emerged:
- The students of the experimental group write two-column lists more frequently ($p = .015$) than those of the control group;
- The students in the experimental group write significantly more often ($p = .019$) a sample sentence with the word;
- The copying of Italian words from the textbook is significantly more common ($p = .041$) in the control group than in the experimental group.

According to the reliability analysis with SPSS 18.0, the used VKS shows $\alpha = .96$ and is therefore located at the upper end of the scale, since in language tests values ranging from .70 to .90 are accepted as reliable (cf. McNamara, 2008, p. 58). Before the study[**], the control group reached an average of 92.63 points, whereas the experimental group

---

[*] The Mann-Whitney U Test can – in analogy to the T-test – be used to elicit differences between two groups. Unlike the T-test this is a non-parametric test that can be used from ordinal scale up and in the absence of a normal distribution (cf. Raab-Steiner & Benesch, 2008, pp. 122-124), as it is the case with the small sample size of the study.

[**] In early October 2011.

scored 60.77. The control group performed significantly ($p = .001$) better than the experimental group. After the pilot study*, the control group has still a higher average value (111.63), however, the gap between the two groups has reduced from an average of 31.86 to 21.45.

5. Discussion and conclusion

First it has to be said that the majority of the students of the experimental group did not create the audio podcasts. The reasons therefore are manifold, but mainly lie in the lack of time of the students and the subjectively low liability because the students received no grade for the project. Hence the results of the VKS have to be considered critically. Furthermore, due to the difficulty of finding teachers of Italian who are willing to participate together in this project with their pupils, the study could not be carried out as planned. Therefore, two teachers took part, which meant that different teaching styles and schools came into play. These are additional intervening variables that could not be prevented. Another weakness of the study is the difference between the groups when it comes to vocabulary. As already mentioned, the students of the control group achieved better results in the VKS at the beginning of the semester, but at the end of the semester the experimental group was able to compensate because the results of the two groups were closer together; however, the reasons for this could be manifold. For the full study to be carried out another vocabulary test will be used as well as more tests each time (cf. Nation & Webb, 2011) and different types of podcasts (e.g., videopodcasts). Furthermore, the subjective learning progress of the students will be focused using qualitative research methods.

Acknowledgements. I would like to thank the students participating in the study as well as their teachers.

References

Aitchison, J. (2005). *Words in the Mind. An Introduction to the Mental Lexicon* (3rd ed.). Malden: Blackwell.

Bortz, J., & Döring, N. (2009). *Forschungsmethoden und Evaluation für Human- und Sozialwissenschaftler. Mit 156 Abbildungen und 87 Tabellen* (4th ed.). Heidelberg: Springer.

Hug, T. (Ed.). (2007a). *Didactics of Microlearning. Concepts, Discourses and Examples.* Münster: Waxmann.

Hug, T. (2007b). Didactics of Microlearning – Introductory Note. In T. Hug (Ed.), *Didactics of Microlearning. Concepts, Discourses and Examples* (pp. 10-14). Münster: Waxmann.

---

* At the end of January 2012.

Hug, T. (2010a). Mobiles Lernen. In K.-U. Hugger, & M. Walber (Eds.), *Digitale Lernwelten* (pp. 171-190). Wiesbaden: VS Verlag für Sozialwissenschaften.

Hug, T. (2010b). Mikrolernen und bricolierende Bildung. Theoretisch motivierte Erwägungen und Praxisbeispiele. In B. Bachmair (Ed.), *Medienbildung in neuen Kulturräumen. Die deutschsprachige und britische Diskussion* (pp. 197-212). Wiesbaden: VS Verlag für Sozialwissenschaften.

Hug, T., & Friesen, N. (2007). Outline of a Microlearning Agenda. In T. Hug (Ed.), *Didactics of Microlearning. Concepts, Discourses and Examples* (pp. 15-31). Münster: Waxmann.

Lewis, M. (1993). *The Lexical Approach. The State of ELT and a Way Forward*. London: Heinle.

Lewis, M. (1997). *Implementing the Lexical Approach. Putting Theory into Practice*. Andover: Heinle.

McNamara, T. (2008). *Language Testing.* (reprint). Oxford: Oxford University Press.

Meara, P. (1999). Lexis: Acquisition. In B. Spolsky (Ed.), *Concise Encyclopedia of Educational Linguistics* (pp. 565-567). Amsterdam: Elsevier.

Nation, I. S. P. (2011). Research into Practice: Vocabulary. *Language Teaching, 44*(4), 529-539.

Nation, I. S. P., & Webb, S. (2011). *Researching and Analyzing Vocabulary*. Boston: Heinle.

Neveling, C. (2004). *Wörterlernen mit Wörternetzen. Eine Untersuchung zu Wörternetzen als Lernstrategie und als Forschungsverfahren*. Tübingen: Narr.

Paribakht, T. S., & Wesche, M. (1997). Vocabulary Enhancement Activities and Reading for Meaning in Second Language Vocabulary Acquisition. In J. Coady, & T. N. Huckin (Eds.), *Second Language Vocabulary Acquisition. A Rationale for Pedagogy* (pp. 174-200). Cambridge: Cambridge University Press.

Price, S. (2007). Ubiquitous Computing: Digital Augmentation and Learning. In N. Pachler (Ed.), *Mobile Learning: Towards a Research Agenda* (pp. 33-54). London: WLE Centre. Retrieved from http://www.wlecentre.ac.uk/cms/files/occasionalpapers/mobilelearning_pachler_2007.pdf

Raab-Steiner, E., & Benesch, M. (2008). *Der Fragebogen: Von der Forschungsidee zur SPSS-Auswertung*. Wien: Facultas.wuv.

Read, J. (2000). *Assessing Vocabulary*. Cambridge: Cambridge University Press.

Schmitt, N. (2010). *Researching Vocabulary. A Vocabulary Research Manual*. Basingstoke: Palgrave Macmillan.

Unterrainer, E. M. (2012). *Mobile Learning im Fremdsprachenunterricht. Eine empirische Fallstudie zum Wortschatzerwerb mit Hilfe digitaler Medien*. (Unpublished Master Thesis). University of Innsbruck.

UNIVERSITY OF
GOTHENBURG

Mobile Learning and High-Profiling Language Education

Jane Vinther*

University of Southern Denmark, Campusvej, Denmark

Abstract. The number of students learning a second or foreign language and participating in instruction in languages other than English has been in decline for some time. This seems to be a general tendency across nations albeit for a variety of reasons idiosyncratic to the particular national conditions. This paper gives an account of a diversified national project designed to infuse foreign language learning classes in upper secondary schools in Denmark with renewed enthusiasm through systematically experimenting with the new media by taking advantage of the social aspect in their application. The aim has been to make language classes attractive and relevant and to highlight the attractiveness and fun in learning through web 2.0 and mobile units. The umbrella project was supported by the Danish ministry of education as well as the individual participating upper secondary schools. The individual projects were selected through an application process and assessed before being allocated funds. The overall project as well as individual minor projects were monitored and assisted by a select group of researchers, who helped guide and support the participating secondary school teachers through seminars and individual consultations. The collaborative efforts and reciprocal benefits enhanced the outcome of the project, and this paper will discuss some of the advantages and disadvantages of such action research collaboration. The focus of the paper will be on results concerning motivation and the reported perception of the status of foreign language learning ensuing from the participation in the experimental classes. The participating students have been surveyed on-line and individually to assess the effect of the projects on student motivation and autonomy. The investigation throws light on personal experiences as well as the generally perceived image and status of foreign language learning in upper secondary schools. The overall results show an encouraging student belief in the power of the new media to improve interest in language learning. They perceive the new methods and approaches as a way to lift the image of language learning in general. It is clear that the potential imbued in mobile learning and social media has given rise to a strengthening of student participation and engagement. The projects have had the side effect of invoking an interest in new ways of teaching and learning also among the teaching staff not directly involved in the project.

Keywords: mobile learning, digital media, social media, motivation, action research.

---

* Contact author: jvinther@language.sdu.dk

In L. Bradley & S. Thouësny (Eds.), *CALL: Using, Learning, Knowing, EUROCALL Conference, Gothenburg, Sweden, 22-25 August 2012, Proceedings* (pp. 302-306). © Research-publishing.net Dublin 2012

1. Introduction

The dominance of English permeates all spheres of education in the wake of globalization in general and internationalisation of education in particular. The on-going project reported on in this paper reflects the desire to strengthen language education at the national level and to encourage upper secondary schools to adopt foreign language education at a high level in a variety of languages in addition to English while encouraging students to select language options in their choice of specialisations. The project came about as a result of a determined effort to modernise language education and to give language education a new profile through digitally based teaching methods while sharing knowledge and experiences with local and national colleagues through project seminars. Autonomy and motivation are key concepts in this project which has allowed ideas and initiatives to develop in local projects while supported through national as well as local funding.

The individual projects were partly funded out of the budgets of the participating upper secondary schools and partly by supplementary funds from the Danish ministry of education. The overall project as well as individual minor projects were monitored and assisted by a select group of researchers who through seminars and individual consultations helped guide the participating secondary school teachers. The primary aim has been to make language classes attractive and relevant and to highlight the attractiveness and fun in learning through web 2.0 and mobile units through systematically experimenting with the new media by taking advantage of the social appeal in their application (Liaw & Huang, 2011). The hope was to infuse foreign language learning classes in upper secondary schools in Denmark with renewed enthusiasm in both students and teachers.

The study reported in this paper was the one common study embracing all the participating individual projects. One common feature for all individual projects was the digital approach to language teaching and learning, and this study was created to gauge the effect on motivation and the perception among the participating students of the incorporation of the digital media and ensuing change in teaching methods. The students were all upper secondary students attending language classes at one of the participating fourteen schools. At each participating school project, teams worked together to plan and implement the activities in the various languages. A total of fifty-eight language teachers and their students participated in the project comprising seven languages other than Danish.

2. This study

2.1. Aim

The national project aimed to improve and sharpen the profile and to bring the interactive aspect of foreign language learning to the forefront. Each participating project had individual aims for their school's project, but in addition it was important to investigate the effect of the new media on the perception of the general language learning environment as well as the attitude of individuals towards language teaching and learning through new methods. The affective and motivational aspects, which were a common influence on the success of all the projects, became a priority area of investigation.

2.2. Data collection

The method employed to collect information of the attitude towards new ways of learning a foreign language was an on-line questionnaire which each participating student could access and return anonymously. It was important to get as many respondents to fill in and return the questionnaire and to this end the assistant of the participating language teachers were enlisted. In practice it meant that the language teachers took time out from their teaching to ask the students to go online and answer the questions in the questionnaire. Respondents were anonymous but tracked through IP-addresses and the system was set up so that each respondent could only return one questionnaire. The respondents filled in the questionnaire after having been involved in the experimental language classes for two-thirds of the school year.

2.3. Participants

The online questionnaire was filled in by 431 students enrolled in foreign language classes across the nation and receiving experimental instruction in English (202), German (230), French (79), Spanish (105), and other languages (11). However, only 369 respondents completed the questionnaire.

2.4. The questionnaire

The items in the questionnaire can be grouped in three categories: a) respondent details, b) instructional details, and c) affective and motivational details. The questionnaire items in b) and c) sections were based on a six-point Likert-type scale (Dörnyei, 2010) ranging from *Strongly agree* to *Strongly disagree*. All in all there were seventeen main items, but the items comprising sections b) and c) each had a number of discrete sub-items pinpointing information completing the overall knowledge of the respondents' attitudes and perceptions.

2.5. Research questions

Particularly interesting for the evaluation of the project were questions about which digital tools had been applied, how the students received them and the accompanying changes in teaching methods. The most pertinent issues were:

- What methods and applications did the students prefer to work with?
- What were the students' perceptions of the digital learning environment?

- How did the digital learning environment influence the students' motivation for learning the L2?
- How did the students perceive the influence of the digital learning environment on their autonomy?

The answer to these research questions are clearly based on a qualitative and subjective assessment of the personal experience of the respondents which is always a depiction of a momentary situation. However, the method of data collection with the high number of respondents and the guaranteed anonymity underwrite the reliability of the results.

2.6. Results

The range of tools and applications that students interacted with was very varied, reflecting the various instructional approaches and pedagogical principles applied by the individual teachers to fit the language, level of proficiency, and the particular language skill to be developed. The reported results are made brief and only the results of the pertinent issues are reported here.

The issue of digital methods in contrast to traditional language classes has a very clear majority for digital learning methods in that 73% prefer this to 27% of respondents who prefer the traditional methods. Out of the digital tools, the preference is to use PC or Mac (94% positive vs. 6% negative) rather than mobile applications (29% positive vs. 71% negative). This needs further investigation. In fact, 74% of respondents have access to a smartphone of one version or another, and they are appreciative of the possibilities of mobile learning of the respondents. 61% say they like mobile learning because they can download apps and because there are many possibilities for mobile learning. However, only 35% agree that they have good language learning apps. Of the possible modalities there is a clear preference for using YouTube (61% positive vs. 39% negative), for other modalities the respondent attitudes are more negative than positive. It is also quite clear that when asked specifically the respondents prefer a combination of digital and traditional methods (91% positive vs. 9% negative).

The digital learning environments were evaluated with regard to the effect on the active participation of the students in learning activities. The majority agreed that digital learning made them more active in class (67%) and agreed that 47% of their classmates became more active. In other words, a respondent perceived herself/himself as being more active but only 47% could detect that heightened level of activity. This illustrates the qualitative method and inherent subjectivity of attitudinal research. The same situation – level of activity – is evaluated differently depending on the perspective of the respondent.

The influence of digital learning on motivation (Stockwell, 2010) was investigated through a number of sub-items approaching the issue from different angles. When it comes to assessing their own learning outcome, the majority of respondents evaluate their own learning as better with digital learning (54%), but the difference between those who say they benefit more from digital learning is not great since 46% do not agree.

In order to evaluate the perceived influence on autonomy, the respondents were given statements which related to their self-determination as well as their own perception of autonomy (Ushioda, 2011). The respondents overwhelmingly reported an increased ability to take responsibility for their own work (86% positive vs. 14% negative). The majority of respondents were positive in the evaluation of their own autonomy (75% positive vs. 25% negative), and 83% said that they were free to work in a different way (Vinther, 2005), reporting that they have the possibility of being creative (80%) in their work with and in the foreign language.

3. Conclusion

The results warrant the conclusion that the experimental classes have achieved positive outcomes with regard to active participation, motivation and autonomy. The respondents report that they become more independent, more creative, and happier in their language learning activities. It is also evident that multimodal approaches to teaching and learning find favour with these Danish upper secondary school students.

The study answers many questions, but it also opens new trajectories for research of a more detailed kind as the need for more depth becomes apparent in relation to some of these issues. One case in point is the application of smartphones. Here the appreciation of possibilities is high among the learners, but the actual assessment of the application is low.

References

Dörnyei, Z. (2010). *Questionnaires in Second Language Research*. London and New York: Routledge.

Liaw, S.-S., & Huang, H.-M. (2011). Exploring Learners' Acceptance toward Mobile Learning. In T. Teo (Ed.), *Technology Acceptance in Education: Research and Issues* (pp. 147-157). Rotterdam: Sense Publishers.

Stockwell, G. (2010). Using mobile phones for vocabulary activities: Examining the effect of the platform. *Language Learning & Technology*, *14*(2), 95-110. Retrieved from http://llt.msu.edu/vol14num2/stockwell.pdf

Ushioda, E. (2011). Why autonomy? Insights from motivation theory and research. *Innovation in Language Learning and Teaching*, *5*(2), 221-232. doi:10.1080/17501229.2011.577536

Vinther, J. (2005). Cognitive processes at work in CALL. *Computer Assisted Language Learning*, *18*(4), 251-271. doi:10.1080/09588220500280388

Developing an Open-Source Web-Based Exercise Generator for Swedish

Elena Volodina* and Lars Borin

*Språkbanken (Swedish Language Bank), Department of Swedish,
University of Gothenburg, Gothenburg, Sweden*

Abstract. This paper reports on the ongoing international project *System architecture for ICALL* and the progress made by the Swedish partner. The Swedish team is developing a web-based exercise generator reusing available annotated corpora and lexical resources. Apart from the technical issues like implementation of the user interface and the underlying processing machinery, a number of interesting pedagogical questions need to be solved, e.g., adapting learner-oriented exercises to proficiency levels; selecting authentic examples of an appropriate difficulty level; automatically ranking corpus examples by their quality; providing feedback to the learner; and selecting vocabulary for training domain-specific, academic or general-purpose vocabulary. In this paper we describe what has been done so far, mention the exercise types that can be generated at the moment as well as describe the tasks left for the future.

Keywords: intelligent computer-assisted language learning, ICALL, natural language processing, NLP, language technology, corpora, exercise generator, interoperability.

1. Introduction

Learning languages with the assistance of a computer – computer-assisted language learning (CALL) – has become widespread since the early 1980s. Traditional CALL applications are inflexible; they provide limited exercise types or number of items, along with limited ability to provide feedback, because the exercises are static, i.e., pre-programmed, and the answers pre-stored. In an attempt to remedy this, researchers have turned to the field of Natural Language Processing (NLP). As a result, the interdisciplinary field of Intelligent CALL (ICALL) has emerged over the past 20 years or so.

At present, there are many mature NLP resources and tools potentially available for re-use in ICALL applications for some languages, but this opportunity has so far

---

* Contact author: elena.volodina@svenska.gu.se

remained relatively underdeveloped. In the project *System Architecture for ICALL** funded by NordPlus Sprog we are trying to address this issue. The main task in this project is to design and implement an open-source system architecture for ICALL that would:
- Allow the re-use of NLP tools and resources for language learning tasks;
- Allow the addition of new modules on a plug-and-play basis;
- Be language independent and therefore easily adapted to different languages.

Our system architecture design is such that relevant previous theoretical and applied research results may be added to the system on a plug-and-play basis benefiting language learning and teaching. This calls for cooperation between several fields making ICALL a truly interdisciplinary endeavor. In this project researchers from NLP, linguistics, pedagogy and human-computer interaction (HCI) are working together.

2. An emerging ICALL architecture for Swedish

2.1. Lärka's architecture in a nutshell

A minimal prerequisite for our architecture is an existing infrastructure of interoperable tools and resources, Språkbanken's web-service based infrastructure components for language-resource access.

Figure 1. Lärka's architecture

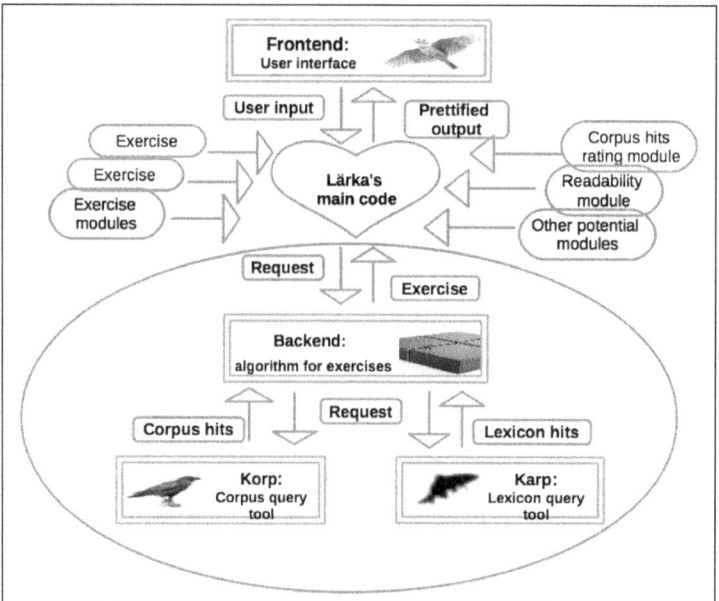

---

* Participating partners: Reykjavik University, University of Iceland, University of Gothenburg
http://spraakbanken.gu.se/swe/forskning/system-architecture-icall

The application developed to test the architecture is web-based and is called Lärka – "LÄR språket via KorpusAnalys" ('learn language via corpus analysis'; in English *Lark* – "Language Acquisition Reusing Korp"). The four main components of Lärka's architecture are presented in Figure 1:

- *Korp* is Språkbanken's existing web-service based infrastructure for maintaining and searching a constantly growing corpus collection at the moment amounting to about one billion words of Swedish text (Borin, Forsberg, & Roxendal, 2012). The corpora available through Korp contain multiple annotations: lemmatization, compound analysis, part-of-speech (POS) tagging, and syntactic dependency trees;
- *Karp* is the corresponding infrastructure for Språkbanken's collection of lexical resources (Borin, Forsberg, Olsson, & Uppström, 2012);
- The Lärka *backend* is a collection of web services for creating language exercises and selecting distractors. For copyright reasons, the unit used in exercise generation is the sentence. The backend can be used for other applications, for example mobile apps;
- The *frontend* (Figure 2) is the graphical user interface that collects user input and sends requests to Lärka's backend. The design has been inherited from Korp and Karp, so that, for instance, exercise configurations (exercise type, training mode, corpus, level, etc.) can be referenced directly as URLs, saving the user the hassle of always going through the menus on the main webpage.

Each exercise is added as a separate module to the architecture with minimal additions to the user interface code.

Figure 2. Lärka user interface, exercise generator view, self-study mode.
POS exercise with reference support window to the right.

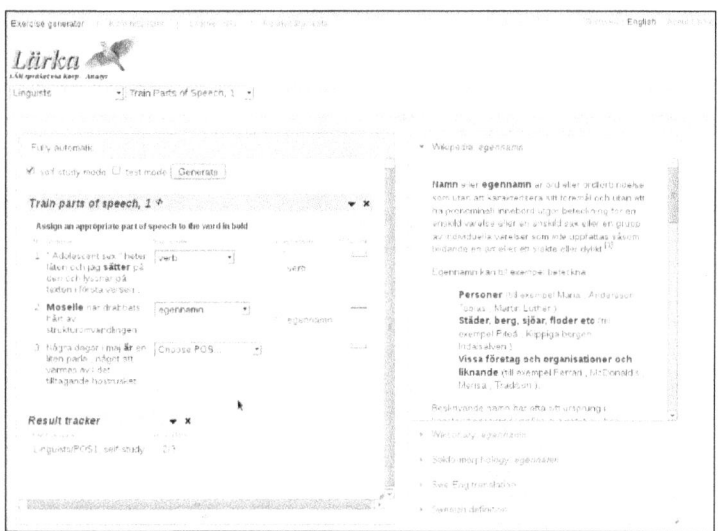

309

2.2. Annotated corpora as a basis for exercises

The exercises are generated using authentic sentences retrieved from two Swedish corpora that have been manually processed, thus ensuring the annotation quality.

SUC is a one-million word corpus of texts from the 1990s, carefully selected to comprise a representative, balanced sample of general-purpose published language, and annotated with lemmas and POS tags (Källgren, Gustafson-Capková, & Hartmann, 2006). The texts have been assigned readability levels using several indices (Volodina, 2010) and the levels are used by Lärka for selection of appropriate sentences for learners of different language proficiency levels.

Talbanken is a manually constructed treebank from the 1970s, containing both written and spoken parts (Einarsson, 1976; Nivre, Nilsson, & Hall, 2006; Teleman, 1974). Currently, the professional prose part of the corpus is used for the exercise generation (about 86,000 words).

2.3. Learning "modes" and feedback

Two exercise modes are available: *self-study* and *test* activities. The s*elf-study mode* offers the learner an opportunity to consider different answers, come back to the previously (incorrectly) answered item and change the answer; the correct answer is not revealed until the user selects it. Every time the user makes some choice, relevant reference material (e.g., Wikipedia articles and dictionary entries) is available to support the learning process (Figure 2 and Figure 3).

In *test mode* the user can answer each item only once. Reference material is not shown to avoid revealing the clues. Eventually one more test mode variant will be added: a timed test when the item should be answered in an assigned period of time (defined by the user). No reference material will be provided in this mode.

A *result tracker* keeps record of correct/incorrect answers.

2.4. Exercise types

Currently three exercise types are offered: (1) *POS*; (2) *syntactic relations*; and (3) *multiple-choice vocabulary exercises*.

The *POS* exercises are designed primarily for linguistics students (Figure 2). Here, a random sentence containing a relevant POS is selected from SUC. The target word is presented to the user in bold in its sentence context, and a menu with five potential answers. The distractors are generated dynamically so that two of the distractors are close to the target POS (e.g., *subjunction* or *preposition* for the target POS *conjunction*) and the other two less close (e.g., *determiner* and *pronoun* in the case of *conjunction*). Once the item has been answered a new one is automatically generated.

The *syntactic relation* exercises are also aimed at linguistics students (Figure 3). The design is similar to the POS exercises, but sentences are retrieved from the Talbanken treebank. The distractors are always the same since only seven of the (clause-level) syntactic categories in the corpus are currently used.

Figure 3. Exercise Train syntactic relations with reference support window to the right.

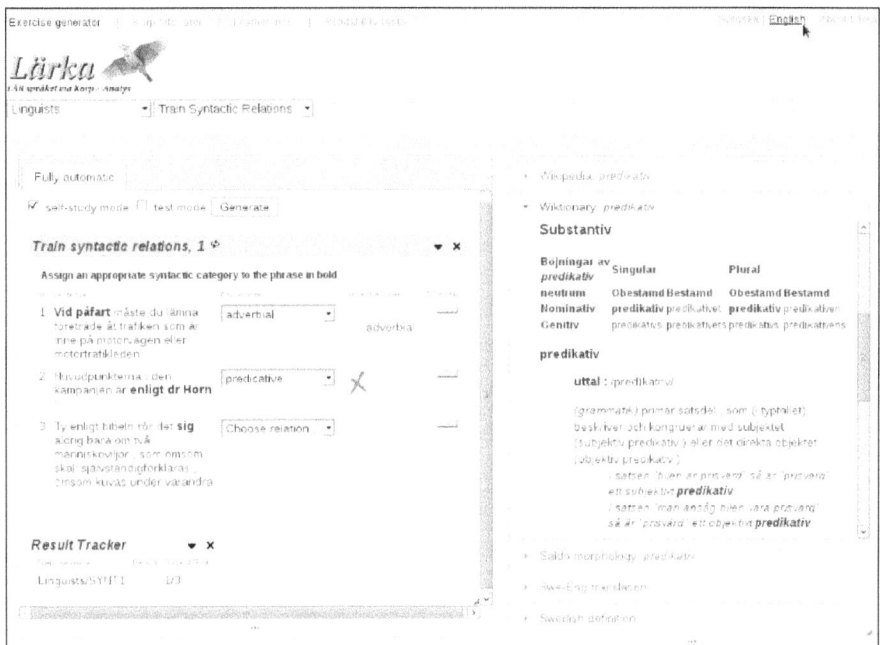

The *multiple-choice vocabulary* exercises (Figure 4) target learners of Swedish and take into consideration sentence difficulty and the desired vocabulary for training. Sentence difficulty level is determined using the LexLIX readability index (Volodina, 2010). The target vocabulary characteristics are chosen by the users, e.g., restricted as to POS, domain, or proficiency level. For this purpose precompiled vocabulary lists are needed, e.g.,:
- Frequency-based word lists with assigned proficiency levels. We are currently using the Swedish Kelly-list (Volodina & Johansson Kokkinakis, 2012) and the Base Vocabulary list (Forsbom, 2006);
- Domain-specific vocabulary lists. At the moment we can use: the academic wordlist (Jansson, Johansson Kokkinakis, Ribeck, & Sköldberg, 2012) and topic vocabulary lists from the Lexin picture series (Lexin, 2006).

Distractors are chosen according to proficiency level or frequency band, and morphosyntactic form. There is, however, an idea to test a more refined approach for the lower proficiency levels where distractors are graded by difficulty level, for example, two of them come from a different part of speech.

Figure 4. Multiple-choice exercise with POS constraints set on the target vocabulary

3. Future plans

During the development of Lärka we have formed a clearer picture of both system requirements and the pedagogical activities we would like to realize. In the near future we plan to add a number of vocabulary training exercises, namely gap cloze and wordbox exercises as well as a diagnostic test for evaluating the learner's vocabulary knowledge level. Additionally, we plan to add a syntactic tree to every sentence; hyperlink all words in a sentence to relevant encyclopedia and lexicon entries; and provide a possibility to save generated items in a number of formats (e.g., QTI (Question and Test Interoperability); IMS (2006)). Further down the road we are planning to add:
- An option of modifying automatically generated exercises by providing user-defined word lists or texts or by providing user-selected distractors;
- A module for ranking corpus hits according to different linguistic features and parameter settings;
- The possibility to test texts for readability using several readability indices;
- The possibility to select and save sub-lists from learner lists of domain or general vocabulary;

- Several new exercise types, e.g., for grammar, word-building, morphology, etc.

Another important issue which we plan to focus on in the future is formal evaluation of Lärka's architecture as well as of the learner activities offered by Lärka.

4. Conclusion

In designing an open-source system architecture for ICALL we want to promote reuse of available mature NLP resources and tools in language learning and teaching. Of course, many aspects of teaching and learning cannot be successfully handled by computers. However, some of the more mechanical aspects of language learning can be successfully implemented – e.g., (some) test item production(s), selection of appropriate corpus examples, analysis of text complexity by proficiency level, feedback generation, etc. – leaving more scope for teachers to develop the more creative aspects of language teaching.

References

Borin, L., Forsberg, M., & Roxendal, J. (2012). Korp – the corpus infrastructure of Språkbanken. *Proceedings of LREC 2012* (pp. 474-478). Istanbul: ELRA.

Borin, L., Forsberg, M, Olsson, L.-J., & Uppström, J. (2012). The open lexical infrastructure of Språkbanken. *Proceedings of LREC 2012* (pp. 3598-3602). Istanbul, Turkey: ELRA.

Einarsson, J. (1976). Talbanken: Talbankens skriftspråkskonkordans/Talbankens talspråkskonkordans. Lund University.

Forsbom, E. (2006). Deriving a Base Vocabulary Pool from the Stockholm Umeå Corpus. Retrieved from http://stp.lingfil.uu.se/~evafo/resources/baseformmodels/

IMS. (2006). IMS Question and Test Interoperability Overview. Version 2.1 Public Draft (revision 2) Specification. IMS Global Learning Consortium. Retrieved from http://www.imsglobal.org/question/qtiv2p1pd2/imsqti_oviewv2p1pd2.html

Jansson, H., Johansson Kokkinakis, S., Ribeck, J., & Sköldberg, E. (2012). A Swedish Academic Word List: Methods and Data. Forthcoming in *Proceedings of the XV Euralex International Congress*. Oslo: EURALEX.

Lexin. (2006). *Svenska ord med uttal och förklaringar*. Språkrådet.

Källgren, G., Gustafson-Capková, S., & Hartmann, B. (2006). *Manual of the Stockholm Umeå Corpus version 2.0*. Department of Linguistics, Stockholm University.

Nivre, J., Nilsson, J., & Hall, J. (2006). Talbanken05: A Swedish Treebank with Phrase Structure and Dependency Annotation. In *Proceedings of the fifth international conference on Language Resources and Evaluation (LREC2006)* (pp. 1392-1395). Genoa: ELRA.

Teleman, U. (1974). *Manual för grammatisk beskrivning av talad och skriven svenska*. Lund.

Volodina, E. (2010). *Corpora in Language Classroom: Reusing Stockholm Umeå Corpus in a vocabulary exercise generator*. Saarbrücken: Lambert Academic Publishing.

Volodina, E., & Johansson Kokkinakis, S. (2012). Introducing Swedish Kelly-list, a new lexical e-resource for Swedish. *Proceedings of LREC 2012* (pp. 1040–1046). Istanbul: ELRA.

UNIVERSITY OF
GOTHENBURG

Designing and Delivering an e-Presessional Course in EAP for the 21st First Century International Student

Julie Watson* and Steven White

Modern Languages, University of Southampton, Highfield, Southampton, UK

Abstract. Summer pre-sessional courses in English for academic purposes (EAP), which prepare growing numbers of international students for degree programmes at UK universities, are facing greater challenges in how to provide the physical space and human resources for their effective and efficient delivery. The affordances of the internet now make other options available and this paper will present a possible solution: an e-presessional for the 21st century learner. At the University of Southampton, building on prior experience in the delivery of online distance learning (ODL), the repurposing of face-to-face courses and in designing courseware in the form of interactive learning objects, a tutored online pre-sessional course was developed and delivered to 60 international students holding confirmed offers of places on MSc and MBA programmes in the School of Management. Adopting a new practice in pre-sessional provision, the students undertook a five week pre-sessional preparatory online course whilst still in their home countries before arriving at the University to complete the remaining ten weeks on the face-to-face pre-sessional programme. Tutored by UK-based EAP tutors, they produced assignments and received online feedback at the same time as developing their academic writing and reading, study skills, vocabulary and grammar. The paper will present and reflect on the design and delivery of the e-presessional course, aiming to show how the adoption of a hybrid approach to pre-sessional provision can have a number of benefits. It will highlight from the student evaluation how the approach may also help develop confidence, independent learning, and prepare students for UK academic culture prior to their arrival.

Keywords: e-presessional, online distance learning, online tutoring, courseware creation, online course design, learning objects, EAP.

1. Introduction

Online distance learning is entering a new phase in the twenty first century as increasing numbers of substantive programmes of study are being developed for online delivery,

---

* Contact author: j.watson@soton.ac.uk

In L. Bradley & S. Thouësny (Eds.), *CALL: Using, Learning, Knowing, EUROCALL Conference, Gothenburg, Sweden, 22-25 August 2012, Proceedings* (pp. 314-319). © Research-publishing.net Dublin 2012

taking advantage of the affordances of the internet and more innovative approaches to design for online learning. Online courses which include e-tutoring and assessed elements require particularly careful design. At many UK universities, summer pre-sessional courses in English for academic purposes have to deal with growing numbers of international students in a conveyor belt fashion and often in a short time span in order to prepare them as well as possible for the demands of UK higher education.

This paper will present one recent foray into designing for ODL in the form of an e-presessional course. Experimenting with a hybrid approach; five weeks online from their home countries followed by ten weeks face-to-face (f2f) in the UK, two groups of thirty students undertook an extended pre-sessional course in the summer of 2011. This paper will firstly introduce the design and development of the e-presessional. Then, it will discuss content delivery and the mediating role of the online tutor. Finally, an overview of the students' course evaluation will be given.

2. Course learning design

2.1. Background

The impetus for the development of an e-presessional came from teaching colleagues in the School of Management at the authors' institution. The school has a large intake of international students on its MSc and MBA programmes and there is a recognised need to improve the level of academic preparedness of international students starting such programmes. In 2011, the school introduced a requirement for students with 5.5 international English language testing system (IELTS) to do an extended pre-sessional course in EAP (15 weeks instead of 10) to better prepare for the demands of masters degree programmes. When they start face-to-face pre-sessional courses, students with a lower IELTS level may present with significant gaps in key areas of reading and writing, as well as displaying weaknesses in grammar control and vocabulary range. They often also lack the necessary study skills needed for transition to UK academic culture. To extend their preparation time a blended approach was chosen, offering students the first 5 weeks of their pre-sessional course online whilst still in the familiar environment of their home countries and without the adverse effect of culture shock. The focus of the online component or e-presessional was on academic writing and reading, study skills, and vocabulary and grammar development in the context of discipline-specific course content.

2.1.1. Pedagogic approach

The development of the e-presessional builds on a successful model for online course design, which has recently included the repurposing of a full masters degree programme for online delivery (Baker & Watson, 2012). A key element of the online course design is the use of an activity-based framework based on a dialogic learning approach which aims to retain the interactive features of f2f learning. The dialogic perspective on e-learning draws on recognition of the crucial role of the e-tutor (Salmon, 2011) and also on the iterative aspect of the 'conversational framework' within which learner and teacher interaction takes place (Laurillard, 2002, 2012). This perspective highlights the need for learning to be 'scaffolded' both in terms of content and also in relation to the e-learning environment. In our approach to online course design, scaffolding of learning is offered through the role of the e-tutor and through the design of the core content itself (activity-based learning objects). For these, an explicit pedagogic design is adopted, which includes the sequencing of activities, scaffolded with optional help and feedback – answers and further explanation (Watson, 2010). Students engage in the activities which are designed to challenge and encourage reflection. Through this interaction the teaching point (e.g., how to write a paraphrase) is 'unpacked' and the included feedback allows evaluation of student's answer, review and development of their understanding through additional explanation. Moreover, the online tutor has a role in scaffolding students' understanding of content through online discussion and feedback on course assignments, checking, clarifying and consolidating, students' learning (see Section 3). A model of the course learning design can be seen in Figure 1.

Figure 1. Model of course learning design

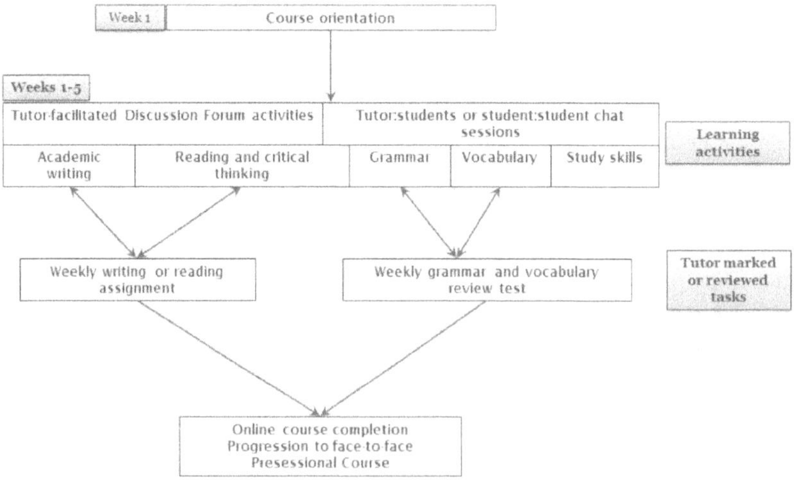

3. Course delivery and online tutoring

The e-presessional course was delivered through Moodle (v.1.9) over a five week period in May/June 2011 to two student cohorts, each with their own online tutor. Tutors had three main areas of responsibility:

- Guiding students through the course and demonstrating the workspace;
- Bridging between themes of learning resources, assessment tasks, and overall course aims;
- Facilitating and monitoring student learning activity, recording students' progress and providing personalised feedback.

Initially, there was a need to provide course orientation for students, explain workspace functions, and highlight key aspects of course structure. Each week was structured to provide learning objects (LOs) linked with thematic forum discussions and live chat sessions, leading to an assessed reading of writing task (with personalised tutor feedback), and a formative grammar/vocabulary review test with automatic feedback (see Figure 1).

LOs relating to specific skills and topics were chosen and sequenced each week to develop students' understanding of key academic skills and in relation to the weekly assessed task. Tutors helped facilitate students' learning through forum discussions on themes and points arising from LOs, and through direct interaction with students during synchronous chat sessions. Questions which were too complex to be dealt with through live chat were addressed through a forum discussion, which allowed for greater visibility and could continue to be developed.

Students were also encouraged to interact directly with each other to share ideas and develop their understanding collaboratively, with the tutor only adding detail/clarification as necessary. Weekly assignments led towards a final writing task which demanded use of all skills covered on the course, along with a requisite level of language development in terms of accuracy and appropriateness of use.

Tutors engaged in practical tasks such as monitoring to ensure all students were participating fully in the course by checking use of LOs, contributions to chats/forum discussions, and punctual online submission of assignments. General announcements were made regularly to inform/remind students of the weekly subject/skill focus, upcoming assignment deadlines, and expectations in terms of their participation.

Tutors also marked assignments and sent personalised feedback, kept records, and produced final reports on each student. These reports contained grades, comments on performance/progress, and noted areas for further work. Students and teaching staff on the f2f pre-sessional course received copies.

4. Student evaluation

At the end of the e-presessional, students were asked to complete an online course evaluation form anonymously. 61 students responded. Questions investigated satisfaction levels with aspects of the course using a 5 point Likert scale (see Table 1) and invited further comments.

Table 1. Summary of student satisfaction levels of aspects of course

Aspect of e-presessional course	% of students rating highly
Course learning materials	Excellent or very good (**88.5%**)
Course overall	Excellent or very good (79%)
Weekly assignments, grammar and review tests	Excellent or very good (70.5%)
Tutoring and tutor feedback	Excellent or very good (**92%**)
Moodle learning environment	Excellent or very good (61%)
Info received before the course	Excellent or very good (57%)
Progress you have made	Very pleased (38%); satisfied (57%); dissatisfied (5%)

Students mentioned benefits regarding course learning outcomes (reading, writing, grammar and vocabulary development), expressing particular appreciation of the formative grammar and vocabulary weekly review tests and tutor help and feedback on assignments. Their comments also highlighted some interesting perceived gains in important areas such as metacognitive skills; confidence building; time management and independent study skills:

- *The course showed me a lot of basic knowledge of the language, and **taught me the study skills to improve my learning ability.***
- *I think (an) online course is a good way to prepare the international students before arrival in the UK.* ***This course made me confident to communicate with many people and I made friends.***
- *I think this online course **can help me to manage my time overall, it's really helpful for us to manage our time to study.***
- *This course helped me improve in English language and also **guides me in self learning.***

A few felt unable to participate as much as they would have liked in the course due to work commitments and other factors. This may have impacted on perceptions of their own progress (see Table 1).

5. Conclusion

Overall, the model adopted was felt to have been successful both in terms of building these students' key skills and in bolstering their confidence for the face-to-face pre-sessional. Interestingly, an analysis of the final pre-sessional grades (beyond the scope of the current paper) suggested that students who had taken the e-presessional may have progressed further overall, compared with those who only took the face-to-face pre-sessional course but who had higher IELTS entry grades at start. Following refreshment and enhancement, the e-presessional course is being delivered again in 2012 and it is expected that more online courses will be developed based on this model.

References

Baker, W., & Watson, J. (forthcoming). Mastering the online Master's: developing and delivering an online MA in English language teaching through a dialogic based framework.

Laurillard, D. (2002). *Rethinking University Education: A conversational framework for the effective use of learning technologies* (2nd ed.). London: Routledge Falmer.

Laurillard, D. (2012). *Teaching as a Design Science: Building Pedagogical Patterns for Learning and Technology*. London: Routledge.

Salmon, G. (2011). *E-moderating: The Key to Teaching and Learning Online* (3rd ed.). London: Routledge Falmer.

Watson, J. (2010). A Case Study: Developing Learning Objects with an Explicit Learning Design. *Electronic Journal of e-Learning, 8*(1), 41-50. Retrieved from http://www.ejel.org/issue/download.html?idArticle=159

UNIVERSITY OF GOTHENBURG

Perceptions of the IWB for Second Language Teaching and Learning: the iTILT Project

Shona Whyte[a*], Gary Beauchamp[b], and Emily Hillier[b]

a. University of Nice-Sophia Antipolis, UFR LASH, Nice, France
b. Cardiff Metropolitan University, Cardiff, United Kingdom

Abstract. Recent emphasis on target language interaction in task-based, technology-mediated language classrooms makes the interactive whiteboard (IWB) an attractive tool: it constitutes a "digital hub" particularly suited to younger learners who require greater visual support and active learning. However, recent research in UK and French primary classes suggests that teachers do not always use the IWB to promote interactivity and may provide only limited opportunities for synergistic interactivity (Beauchamp & Kennewell, 2010) or unplanned interaction (Whyte, 2011), and this lack of room for participation can lower learners' motivation (Hall & Higgins, 2005). Ineffective exploitation of IWB affordances may be related to teachers' beliefs about language acquisition and pedagogy (Borg, 2006) as well as their views of technology (Orlando, 2009). This research suggests a need for greater investigation of teachers' views on language learning with technology and more longitudinal research and training. This study focuses on an EU-funded project iTILT (interactive Technologies In Language Teaching) on IWBs for communicative language teaching, involving 42 teachers of different languages and proficiency levels from primary school to higher education contexts in seven countries. The paper examines eight teachers in five French and Welsh primary schools in the context of this wider data set: data include pre-training questionnaires on teachers' perceived confidence and competence with the IWB and information and communication technology (ICT) in general; 27 video clips of classroom interaction selected by the teachers for the project website; and teacher and learner interview data. Results provide an overview of the teachers' use of IWB features and tools for particular language learning objectives with specific teaching methods, as well as insights into the perceptions of both primary teachers and learners of how the features of the IWB both facilitate and support effective communicative language teaching and learning in primary foreign language (FL) classes.

Keywords: IWB, interactivity, young learners, teacher education, classroom instruction, EFL, Welsh.

---

* Contact author: whyte@unice.fr

In L. Bradley & S. Thouësny (Eds.), *CALL: Using, Learning, Knowing*, EUROCALL Conference, Gothenburg, Sweden, 22-25 August 2012, Proceedings (pp. 320-326). © Research-publishing.net Dublin 2012

1. Introduction

The interactive whiteboard often seems an attractive classroom teaching tool since it represents a "digital hub" for multimedia resources and multi-sensory support (Cutrim Schmid & van Hazebrouck, 2010) and facilitates pedagogical interactivity to promote active learning (Kennewell & Beauchamp, 2007). However, teachers do not always fully exploit opportunities for interactive learning with the IWB (Beauchamp & Kennewell, 2010), perhaps particularly in the second language classroom (Cutrim Schmid & Whyte, 2012; Whyte, 2011). The reasons for this include technical difficulties but also teachers' beliefs about learning, technology and pedagogy, suggesting a need for more investigation of teachers' perceptions of these issues.

2. Background

The IWB is basically a computer projected onto a large screen and controlled with the touch-sensitive surface of the board using a pen or fingers. This enables high quality projection of images or text, making the IWB particularly effective for whole class teaching (Gillen, Staarman, Littleton, Mercer, & Twiner, 2007). Although the use of the IWB began with an "exponential increase" in their numbers in UK schools (Mercer, Hennessy, & Warwick, 2010), its use in other countries is also growing (Higgins, Beauchamp, & Miller, 2007).

The IWB provides good quality presentation and motivates learners (Miller & Glover, 2007) in a range of subjects, including languages (Mathews-Aydinli & Elaziz, 2010). This alone, however, would not merit widespread IWB use in education and Higgins, Beauchamp and Miller (2007) note that the IWB can also capture and maintain pupils' attention; increase the pace of lessons; model conceptual ideas in novel ways; and make it easier to integrate and use a range of multimedia resources in lessons. Others (Jewitt, Moss, & Cardini, 2007; Maher, 2011; Twiner, Coffin, Littleton, & Whitelock, 2010) have noted that the IWB also facilitates a multimodal approach to teaching and learning. These benefits apply to learners of all ages but there is evidence that learners in primary school, who form the focus for this study, feel that the IWB can impact positively on their learning (Hall & Higgins, 2005; Şad & Özhan, 2012).

To take full advantage of the IWB, teachers and pupils proceed through developmental phases as they master a range of technical and pedagogical skills (Beauchamp, 2004; Jones & Vincent, 2010; Lewin, Somekh, & Steadman, 2008; Miller & Glover, 2007; Somekh & Haldane, 2005). As teachers gain confidence with the IWB and allow pupils to use it as well, the IWB can be used effectively to orchestrate classroom dialogue (Mercer et al., 2010). Nevertheless, evidence suggests such attainment gains are mainly related to the length of IWB use, with technology becoming embedded in the teacher's pedagogy over time (Somekh et al., 2007).

3. Method

This paper presents preliminary findings from the EU-funded project iTILT on the IWB for communicative language teaching (CLT), whose main outcome is a website featuring classroom video clips supported by teacher and learner commentary, as well as additional teaching resources. Data for the present study concern a subset of 8 primary teachers in France and Wales from a pool of 42 teachers of different languages, proficiency levels and teaching contexts in 7 countries followed in the iTILT project, and include pre-training questionnaires on teachers' IWB use and general ICT competence/confidence; class video clips (27 clips selected by teachers for the project website), and teacher and learner interview data (8 post-session learner focus group interviews and 8 video-stimulated teacher interviews). The research questions are:
- How confident are teachers a) in using the IWB and b) in their general ICT skills?
- How do teachers use the IWB for language teaching in terms of a) methods, b) tools and features, and c) language learning objectives?
- How do teachers and learners perceive IWB use in the language classroom?

The following section addresses each of the three research questions in turn.

4. Analysis and discussion

4.1. Teachers' confidence in IWB and ICT skills

In a questionnaire administered prior to project training, teachers expressed their degree of agreement with 40 statements on a 5-point Likert scale ranging from 1 (strongly agree) to 5 (strongly disagree or no knowledge of IWB feature in question). These were analysed by using the mean (average) response of the sample with 1.0 being the most positive response, 3.0 representing a neutral response and 5.0 representing the highest level of disagreement with the statements. The questions covered general information, IWB use, and general ICT skills. The group comprised 4 French and 4 Welsh primary teachers, 7 female, and one male (Welsh), all with constant access to an IWB in their classrooms and all currently teaching a foreign language to their own pupils. The teachers from the two countries showed broadly similar general characteristics: 50% of the group were aged 31-40, and had less than 10 years' teaching experience. They differed only in their IWB experience: the French teachers had less than their Welsh counterparts: one was a beginner while the rest had 2-3 years' experience, while one Welsh teacher had 2-3 years' experience but the others more than 6 or 8.

4.1.1. IWB features
Table 1 below shows that teachers in both countries had varying levels of confidence using different tools or features (highlighted in grey in the table, and based on at least six of the eight teachers responding). The most negative response in both countries

concerned the use of additional IWB devices, with only four teachers responding to this statement.

Table 1.

		pen tool	eraser tool	hand recognition tool	split screen tool	highlighter tool	shading tool	underlining tool	spotlight tool
WALES	Mean	1.25	1.25	3.5	4	2	2	1.67	3
	N	4	4	2	2	4	4	3	2
FRANCE	Mean	1.75	1.75	3.67	4.33	1.67	4	1.67	4
	N	4	4	3	3	3	3	3	1

		hide & reveal tool	drag & drop text/ images	playing audio files on IWB	playing video clips	insert images	save students' work	print students' work	additional IWB devices
WALES	Mean	3	3	3	3	2.75	2.75	3.5	4
	N	2	3	4	4	4	4	4	2
FRANCE	Mean	2.5	1.67	2.5	2.75	2.75	2.25	3	4.5
	N	2	3	4	4	4	4	4	2

4.1.2. IWB access and use
Results in this section were more positive and remarkably similar in both countries. Table 2 shows that teachers had access to the IWB at all times and generally used the IWB for whole class and group teaching, rather than for individual work.

Table 2.

	IWB access at all times, as often as needed	IWB for whole class teaching in L2 lessons	IWB for small group work in L2 lessons	IWB for individual work in L2 lessons	use IWB for every L2 lesson	use IWB every lesson for other subjects
WALES	1.00	1.75	2.75	3.50	2.50	2.25
FRANCE	1.00	2.00	2.75	3.67	2.50	2.75

4.1.3. General ICT skills
All teachers in both countries were confident in general ICT skills as shown in Table 3 below.

Table 3.

	confident using Internet for own purposes	confident using systems to track relevant web pages	confident using e-mail for own use	confident using social networking sites for own use	confident using Microsoft Office or Open Office for own use
WALES	1.5	1.75	1.5	1.75	1.75
FRANCE	1.25	1.5	1	2.5	1.5

4.2. IWB use in classroom practice

The video clips of IWB use in language teaching were coded in terms of IWB-supported teaching method or type of classroom activity, IWB features used, and language area in focus. The latter category focused specifically on learners' use of a second language, including the traditional four skills (reading, writing, speaking, listening) plus pronunciation, vocabulary, grammar and spelling.

4.2.1. IWB teaching methods

The teachers generally selected activities where learners, rather than teachers, were using the IWB: in the 27 clips from the 8 teachers three quarters of the episodes (20 out of 27, or 74%) showed learners at the IWB, mainly individual learners (41%). The French teachers selected slightly more examples of teacher-fronted activities than the Welsh.

4.2.2. IWB tools and features

Embedding images in IWB software pages was the most popular feature for both groups of teachers: 85% of the clips involved photos or clipart. The most common activity type used the drag and drop feature of the IWB (41%), followed by hide and reveal, interactive objects and embedded sound (30% each).

4.2.3. Language areas

Parallel to the high use of images in the IWB materials, the clips showed a strong focus on vocabulary (70%), since the images were generally used to support word meaning in lexical sets (e.g., animals, weather). The second most common language area was reading (41%), with a bias towards the Welsh teachers (9 out of 11 clips). The third most popular language area was listening (26%), where again the Welsh teachers selected more listening activities than the French, corresponding to their greater use of embedded audio in their teaching materials, while the French focused more on pronunciation activities (5 out of 7 examples).

4.3. Teacher and learner perceptions of IWB use

A number of common themes emerged from the analysis of transcripts of teacher and learner interviews. Seven of the eight teachers felt the IWB increased learner motivation (being "fun", "enjoyable", or "appealing"); two said this meant more drilling or repetition was possible. The next more common comment (by 5 teachers) concerned interaction, active learning, and tactile/multisensory features; three teachers added that more learner collaboration allowed the teacher to take a less directive role. Teachers also thought the board allowed more effective teaching ("correct", "clear" input) and greater efficiency (demonstrating activities, saving time). The learners all claimed to enjoy games at the IWB and cited different tools and features which they appreciated.

Some learners also thought the board helped them to learn, or remember what they had forgotten, and made things easier.

5. Conclusion

This preliminary report provides insights into teaching practices in primary schools in two different European contexts. First, teachers are not particularly comfortable using the different tools and features of the board, irrespective of length of experience with the IWB, and in spite of confidence in general ICT skills. Second, it shows a somewhat conservative or cautious approach to IWB use for language teaching, with teachers focusing on a limited repertoire of basic functions such as dragging and dropping images to fulfil relatively circumscribed language learning objectives (vocabulary, pronunciation, receptive skills), often with a teaching method involving an individual learner working at the IWB before the class.

Acknowledgements. We would like to thank Dimitri Voilmy and Julie Alexander for assistance with data collection and transcription.

References

Beauchamp, G. (2004). Teacher Use of the Interactive Whiteboard in Primary Schools: towards an effective transition framework. *Technology, Pedagogy and Education, 13*(3), 327-348.

Beauchamp, G., & Kennewell, S. (2010). Interactivity in the classroom and its impact on learning. *Computers & Education 54*, 759-766.

Borg, S. (2006). *Teacher cognition and language education: Research and practice.* London: Continuum.

Cutrim Schmid, E., & van Hazebrouck, S. (2010). The interactive whiteboard as a digital hub. *Praxis Fremdsprachenunterricht, 4,* 12-15.

Cutrim Schmid, E., & Whyte, S. (2012). Interactive Whiteboards in school settings: Teacher responses to socio-constructivist Hegemonies. *Language Learning and Technology, 16*(2), 65-86.

Gillen, J., Staarman, J.K., Littleton, K., Mercer, N., & Twiner, A. (2007). A learning revolution? Investigating pedagogic practice around interactive whiteboards in British primary classrooms. *Learning, Media and Technology, 32*(3), 243-256.

Hall, I., & Higgins, S. (2005). Primary school students' perceptions of interactive whiteboards. *Journal of Computer Assisted Learning, 21*(2), 102-117. doi: 10.1111/j.1365-2729.2005.00118.x

Higgins, S., Beauchamp, G., & Miller, D. (2007). Reviewing the literature on interactive whiteboards. *Learning, Media and Technology, 32*(3), 213-225.

Jewitt, C., Moss, G., & Cardini, A. (2007). Pace, interactivity and multimodality in teachers' design of texts for interactive whiteboards in the secondary school classroom. *Learning, Media and Technology, 32*(3), 303-317.

Jones, A., & Vincent, J. (2010). Collegial mentoring for effective whole school professional development in the use of IWB technologies. *Australasian Journal of Educational Technology, 26*(4), 477-493.

Kennewell, S., & Beauchamp, G. (2007). The features of interactive whiteboards and their influence on learning. *Learning, Media and Technology, 32*(3), 227-241.

Lewin, C., Somekh, B., & Steadman, S. (2008). Embedding interactive whiteboards in teaching and learning: The process of change in pedagogic practice. *Education and Information Technologies, 13*(4), 291-303.

Maher, D. (2011). Using the multimodal affordances of the interactive whiteboard to support students' understanding of texts. *Learning, Media and Technology, 36*(3), 235-250.

Mathews-Aydinli, J., & Elaziz, F. (2010). Turkish students' and teachers' attitudes toward the use of interactive whiteboards in EFL classrooms. *Computer Assisted Language Learning, 23*(3), 235-252.

Mercer, N., Hennessy, S., & Warwick, P. (2010). Using interactive whiteboards to orchestrate classroom dialogue. *Technology, Pedagogy and Education, 19*(2), 195-209.

Miller, D., & Glover, D. (2007). Into the unknown: the professional development induction experience of secondary mathematics teachers using interactive whiteboard technology. *Learning, Media and Technology, 32*(3), 319-331.

Orlando, J. (2009). Understanding changes in teachers' ICT practices: a longitudinal perspective. *Technology, Pedagogy and Education, 18*(1), 33-44.

Şad, S. N., & Özhan, U. (2012). Honeymoon with IWBs: A qualitative insight in primary students' views on instruction with interactive whiteboard. *Computers & Education, 59*(4), 1184-1191. doi: 10.1016/j.compedu.2012.05.010

Somekh, B., & Haldane, M. (2005). *A typology of interactive whiteboard pedagogies*. Paper presented at BERA Conference, University of Glamorgan, Wales, September.

Somekh, B., Haldane, M., Jones, K., Lewin, C., Steadman, S., Scrimshaw, P., & Woodrow, D. (2007). Evaluation of the Primary Schools Whiteboard Expansion Project - summary report. P. a. L. Centre for ICT, Trans.: Manchester Metropolitan University.

Twiner, A., Coffin, C., Littleton, K., & Whitelock, D. (2010). Multimodality, orchestration and participation in the context of classroom use of the interactive whiteboard: a discussion. *Technology, Pedagogy and Education, 19*(2), 211-23.

Whyte, S. (2011). Learning to teach with videoconferencing in primary foreign language classrooms. *ReCALL, 23*(3), 271-293.

Author Index

Absalom, Matthew 1
Agudo, J. Enrique 59
Akahane-Yamada, Reiko 144
Allen, Christopher 5
Alshahrani, Ali 10
Anderson, Terry 217
Appel, Christine 15

Balaam, Madeline 211
Beauchamp, Gary 320
Berns, Anke 20
Borin, Lars 307
Borthwick, Kate 26
Bowen, Rhonwen 161
Brooks, David L. 32

Camacho Fernández, David 20
Canto, Silvia 151
Carloni, Giovanna 37
Chang, Mei-Mei 43
Charalabopoulou, Frieda 49
Codreanu, Tatiana 54
Combe Celik, Christelle 54
Coppens, Julian 59, 250
Correia Martins, Maria de Lurdes 64

De Marco, Anna 70
Dickens, Alison 26
Domínguez, Eva M. 250

Ebyary, Khaled El 156

Fauville, Géraldine 76
Ferreira, Paula 250
Fouz González, Jonás 81
Fredriksson, Christine 88
Fukada, Atsushi 129
Fukuda, Eri 93, 228

Author Index

Garnier, Marie 99
Gavrilidou, Maria 49
Gimeno, Ana 204
Guth, Sarah 124

Hamada, Mayumi 104
Handley, Zöe 111
Hartwell, Laura M. 117
Hashimoto, Shinichi 93, 228
Hatakeda, Hiroshi 144
Helm, Francesca 124
Heslop, Phil 211
Hillier, Emily 320
Hirotani, Maki 129
Hong, Chi-yin 134

Ishak, Nor Fadzlinda 139
Ishikawa, Yasushige 144

Jacques, Marie-Paule 117
Jauregi, Kristi 151
Johansson Bunting, Leona 274
Johansson Kokkinakis, Sofie 49

Kerstin Sylvén, Liss 280
Kharrufa, Ahmed 211
Kido, Kazuhiko 228
Kondo, Mutsumi 144

Laing, Jonny 156
Lambacher, Stephen 223
Lantz-Andersson, Annika 76, 161
Leahy, Christine 167
Leone, Paola 70
Lin, Huifen 172, 177
Lin, Mei-Chen 43
Li, Ping 187
Loiseau, Mathieu 182
Lu, Zhihong 187
Lyddon, Paul A. 192

Macario de Siqueira, José 204
Malerba, Maria-Luisa 198
Martínez, Antonio 204
Maslamani, Jaber Ali 211
Matsumoto, Kazumi 129
Miyazoe, Terumi 217
Moreira, António 64
Moreira, Gillian 64
Moré, Joaquim 15
Mullen, Tony 15

Nieminen, Juhana 254
Nitta, Haruhiko 228

Obari, Hiroyuki 223
O'Dowd, Robert 124
Okazaki, Hironobu 93, 228
Olivier, Patrick 211
Örnberg Berglund, Therese 234

Palomo-Duarte, Manuel 20
Pellerin, Martine 240

Ramírez-Verdugo, Maria Dolores 245
Richardson, David 5
Rico, Mercedes 59, 250
Robbins, Jackie 15
Rybicki, Jan-Mikael 254

Saeidi, Mahnaz 259
Säljö, Roger 76
Sato, Takeshi 264
Seedhouse, Paul 139
Sevilla, Ana 204
Shearer, John 211
Sisti, Flora 269
Smith, Craig 144
Sofkova Hashemi, Sylvana 274
Sundqvist, Pia 280
Suzuki, Akio 264

Thouësny, Sylvie 286
Tschichold, Cornelia 292

Unterrainer, Eva Maria 296

Vigmo, Sylvi 161
Vinther, Jane 302
Volodina, Elena 49, 307

Wada, Norihisa 144
Watson, Julie 314
Wen, Fuan 187
White, Steven 314
Whyte, Shona 320
Windeatt, Scott 10, 156, 211

Yusefi, Mahsa 259

Zourou, Katerina 182